EUROPE IN ZIGZAGS

HINDENBURG AS SEEN BY CABROL

EUROPE
IN ZIGZAGS

By SISLEY HUDDLESTON

AUTHOR OF "PARIS SALONS, CAFÉS, STUDIOS"

SOCIAL, ARTISTIC, LITERARY
AND POLITICAL AFFAIRS ON
THE CONTINENT

WITH 36 ILLUSTRATIONS

PHILADELPHIA & LONDON
J. B. LIPPINCOTT COMPANY
MCMXXIX

DEDICATORY LETTER
TO GENERAL K. READER, J. G. F.

Dear General Reader,

We have been close friends for more years than I care to count; and your sympathy and interest have never failed me. This is the first time that I have specifically dedicated a book to you, but there is a sense in which all my books and all my scattered and ephemeral writings have been dedicated to you. There are subjects on which I flatter myself I have some special knowledge, but it is not my ambition to present it in what is usually regarded as the expert's manner. A critic once wrote some such phrases as these: "I know all this. A few of my associates know all this. For whom then is this re-hash intended?" He was of course an exceptional critic, a superior critic; fortunately most critics are kindly, well-informed persons, who realise the need of books which shall be not only informative, but shall be, as far as their author can make them, entertaining.

I do not pretend to teach anything new, though I think I clarify many vague ideas; nor do I attempt to be comprehensive. Concerning each of the countries I have visited there are numerous and bulky volumes. And there are more countries in Europe than in a French pack of cards, to say nothing of contiguous countries in the East, and on the Southern shores of the Mediterranean, which greatly affect the life of Europe. Nevertheless these glimpses of Germany, of Austria, of Spain, of Italy, of Czecho-Slovakia, and its neighbours along the Danube, will, I trust, be sufficient to indicate the complexity and to suggest the prospects of a large part of Europe.

It will not trouble you overmuch whether these commentaries are classified under the head of topography and travel, politics and sociology, literature and art, reminiscences and gossip, or any other watertight compartment constructed for the convenience of the professionals and traders in books. I confess that I forgot about categories; but then you too have confided to me your indifference to labels. Let us say that this book is a hotchpotch of personal experiences and impressions, of political speculations and social studies, of travel pictures and portraits of men whom I have for the most part known, in greater or lesser degree, privately or publicly; but let us also say that these ingredients are not mixed without purpose. I have blended them, as I hope, with at least as much art as the culinary chef who seeks to please your palate.

So, if I speak of Karel Capek and Mazaryk, of Stresemann and

v

Thomas Mann, of Pirandello and Mussolini, of the Pope and d'Annunzio, of Miguel de Unamuno and Primo de Rivera, of Seipel and Einstein, my arrangement is less casual and arbitrary than may be apparent. You have been good enough to ask me questions about reparations, about security, about dictatorship and democracy, about Fascism, about Germany's intentions, about Austria's future, about the Vatican's place in politics, about minorities, about the diplomacy of pacts, about the Youth Movement, about the prospects of another war, and so forth, and though these are questions which cannot be answered dogmatically, I have tried to throw a little light on the problems of Europe. And perhaps in the sequel I shall extend my excursions and observations to other fields. In the meantime, my dear General Reader, please accept these European Zigzags as a token of our long-tried affection for each other.

SISLEY HUDDLESTON

Saint-Pierre d'Autils (Eure)
June 28, 1929
Tenth Anniversary of the
Signing of the Versailles Treaty

CONTENTS

ILLUSTRATIONS

All the above photographs are by
The Wide World Company to which
acknowledgment is herewith made

PART I
INTRODUCTORY

I. TRAVEL IN EUROPE

WHAT is your favourite reading?" a European diplomatist was recently asked in one of those newspaper inquiries which are so popular in France.

"Time-tables," he replied.

They are indeed interesting—and if they are, like dictionaries, slightly disconnected, there is a good deal of fun in finding the connections. I too have studied European time-tables, and I believe them to be as important, for an understanding of the relations of the many peoples of the Continent, as diplomatic documents. A Blue Train may explain more than a Blue Book.

The expresses which link together European capitals do more than minister to our pleasure and our convenience. "I don't like the English," said a young Frenchwoman, "but I like the English whom I know." The Golden Arrow enables many French men and women to know English men and women; and for me there is pure magic in the words Simplon-Orient-Express—an Open Sesame to Paris, Lausanne, Milan, Trieste, Bucharest, Belgrade, Sofia, and Stamboul. Blessings on the Sud-Express which took me to Spain! I cannot think of the Nord-Express without having a vision of Brussels, Cologne, and Berlin. Rome and Vienna and Prague and Warsaw are expressed for me in terms of trains. . . .

The literature of travel is immense. I have no doubt that it constitutes the backbone of the publishing business. The profits of authorship are not what a vain reading public supposes. A French *éditeur* once asked me to guess the greatest success of the year. I tried again and again, mentioning this famous author and that "best-selling" book; but I was hopelessly wrong. It appeared that the most remarkable triumph was that of a saintly biography. Its author figures in no "Who's Who"; it is not to be found in library lists; its name is never mentioned in cultured circles; yet it has been read by far more people than read the works of the world's six recognised most popular writers.

An Englishman confessed to me that for many years he had enjoyed a steady income from his Treatise on Fencing; an

3

American publisher told me that the book on which his house was built was a school arithmetic.

Similarly, I suppose that guide-books must be exceedingly lucrative. For tourism has become one of the leading trades of several European countries. Unquestionable estimates are hard to obtain, but according to certain calculations American visitors to Europe alone spend well over five hundred million dollars. To this huge sum must be added the amounts spent by European travellers in Europe. It does not seem to be an exaggeration to suggest that the equivalent of two British budgets is expended annually by travellers on the Continent.

With this relatively new factor in international affairs (for the old Grand Tour which formed part of a liberal education was enjoyed by a relatively few persons) it becomes practically impossible to ascertain whether a particular country has a sound commercial balance in its favour or not. According to the statistics, it may well be that imports exceed exports; but according to the facts, it may well be that exports exceed imports.

Tariff walls may be erected to keep out foreign goods; but each returning traveller brings back with him a quantity of foreign goods. And he has, besides, consumed a quantity of foreign goods in the countries where he has stayed.

It would be difficult to estimate with any degree of accuracy the annual average expenditure of English tourists; but an attempt has been made to ascertain the amount spent by different categories of Americans who arrive at European ports. Students, and others from the Universities, are placed in the category of those who take five hundred dollars with them on their trip to the Old World—and leave it behind them. What are called "ordinary" travellers run up bills to the tune of one thousand eight hundred dollars. "Wealthy" travellers spend five thousand dollars. The average, it appears, works out at about 1,254 dollars a head.

This means that the hundreds of thousands of travellers who leave American docks carry out of the country hundreds of thousands of dollars which do not appear in the commercial balance of the United States. Nor do these amounts appear in the commercial balance of the countries to which they go; but they nevertheless are a real portion of the income of such countries. There is, every year, an increase in these amounts. In 1919 fifty million dollars were thus taken from the United States—

though not all, of course, to Europe—and in the following year a hundred and fifty million dollars. Then the amount leaped to two hundred millions, and in 1923 it was as high as four hundred millions. Thence it climbed to five hundred and sixty millions in 1925. In 1926 it was over seven hundred millions. In 1927 it neared the eight hundred million mark. It shows no sign of diminishing. Such sums are much higher than the total investments abroad of Americans only a few years ago.

Here is one reason—were there no other—which sufficiently indicates the stupidity of various schemes of taxation which would discourage the tourist were he not so determined to wander about the world. There are luxury taxes, and *taxes de séjour,* and other taxes which would obstruct rather than encourage travel. There are a few countries which cling to the visa, which is not only a nuisance but is expensive. At the same time these countries seek to advertise themselves and to attract the tourist. They complain that the tourist traffic is being deflected by nations which have had the good sense to abolish the visa. They seem to be unable to see the inconsistency of their conduct. They seem to be unable to see where their own interest lies.

One government department uses publicity to bring visitors. Another government department does its best to keep them out. Passports and visas are relics of the war. They are ineffective in every sense. They do not prevent undesirables from entering—for the undesirables take special steps to provide themselves with papers. It is the desirable traveller who suffers hardships.

Then there are questionnaires in the hotels, and identity cards, and all kinds of formalities which are more irritating than serious. One European country, which has been the principal centre of travel since the war, is now complaining that, having acquired the reputation of annoying visitors, it is being abandoned in favour of its neighbours. The remedy is simple. . . .

That there should be freedom of travel is surely obvious. The world belongs to us all, and though it is proper for each community to have regulations for its self-preservation, it has no right to molest or hinder the harmless tourist who, while primarily travelling for pleasure, profit, or instruction, may well add to the wealth of the countries he enters, and may above all be a missionary in the cause of good international relations.

II. FOR TO ADMIRE . . .

THAT we are still, in spite of immensely improved methods of locomotion, extraordinarily ignorant of each other, is shown by a little joke that was played by my friend M. Alain Mellet. On his note-paper he had printed the heading: "Committee for the Defence of Poldavia." On this note-paper he addressed to a number of deputies a stirring appeal in favour of the people of Poldavia, who were, according to his text, still oppressed.

By return of post he received a large number of responses. His correspondents offered to speak, to write, to vote in defence of the unfortunate Poldavians.

There is, of course, no such country in Europe as Poldavia. Perhaps the pleasantry was unnecessarily cruel; but it demonstrates that Europeans themselves are not familiar with Europe. How then can they expect far-off nations to have a clear conception of a Continent in which there are over thirty countries and an inextricable criss-cross of races?

How many of us indeed could recite the names of the capitals of the Baltic States? How many of us could even enumerate the Balkanic capitals? During the peace-making at Paris it was considered disgraceful that one of the leading statesmen should ask where and what was Teschen. In view of his position he ought not to have confessed his ignorance; yet probably the majority of those who laughed at him could not have answered his question.

There once called on me in Paris a well-known candidate for one of the highest offices in the world, who informed me that he had been making investigations and had discovered that when the plebiscite was held in Alsace there would be an overwhelming vote in favour of Germany. When I suggested that he was probably thinking of the Saar, where a plebiscite is indeed, if the Versailles Treaty is fulfilled, to be held, and not of Alsace, which was restored unreservedly to France, he assured me that I was mistaken. I insisted, but he became rather warm.

"Have it your own way, Governor," was all that I could say. I found it regrettable that public men are sometimes so ill-informed.

I am told that in Argentina a newspaper announced that "our famous compatriot, Francesco di Paulo Blanco Escalada, who has been touring in Europe, is now on his way home." For three months the arrival of this imaginary personage was prepared by a press campaign. Finally the celebrated Escalada landed, and was received with the greatest honours. Not until four years later was the "mystification" revealed.

Gutenberg is, in part, the culprit. We take it for granted that whatever is printed, whether on letter-headings or in newspapers, is necessarily true. The responsibility of the printing presses—of journalists and of authors—is considerable and is not always sufficiently realised. Nevertheless it behoves us, as members of the public, to make ourselves better acquainted with a world that is brought immeasurably nearer to us by the cinema and by the radio, by the aeroplane and by the motor-car, by the train and by the steamer. Even when we sit at home, time and space are annihilated for us. But it is better still to travel. It is better to see for ourselves, as far as our opportunities serve, the diversity and the unity of this wonderful world.

It is there for us to enjoy—its different cultures, its variegated scenery, its architecture, its painting, its sculpture of all the ages, its music which expresses the universal genius of mankind. There is no education which can compare with the study of history in the places where history was made, and of particular customs in other lands. National habits teach us that our differences are largely conventional, and that fundamentally humanity is the same everywhere.

Especially during the war and the first few years which followed the war we were persuaded that there were utterly bad and entirely good nations. A little travelling convinces us that every nation has excellent qualities though doubtless it has also less desirable qualities.

It is quite impossible for the cultured man who has seen many peoples to paint them as either black or white. During the war we were bidden to regard Germany as black, and Russia as white. But when the Bolsheviks overthrew the Tsarist régime, Russia suddenly became black. Germany, on the other hand, is in process of becoming white. France has been alternately white or black, according to the propagandists— white when we agree with its policy, and black when we disagree. So it is with Bulgaria; I remember how we praised

Bulgaria as the virile nation of the Balkans when we expected that country to come in on our side, but when Bulgaria joined the Germans it became peopled overnight with the Huns of Eastern Europe. I have interested myself in public affairs long enough to have seen mass opinion turned both for and against nearly every European nation.

Roland Dorgelès, an indefatigable traveller, who makes his record of things seen as interesting as a romance, believes that one should read nothing in advance about the places one visits; one should be free of prejudices and see with one's own eyes. But although the method has been successfully adopted by him, he is surely wrong in recommending it to others. A certain documentation does not prevent one from observing; on the contrary, it may wisely direct one's observations. Yet it is true that travelling should never be undertaken as a formal duty. If one is not interested in museums at home, there is no good reason why one should force oneself to be interested abroad. If in Czecho-Slovakia, for example, one prefers the immense Skoda works to the Prague palace, then by all means visit the Skoda works. Nothing is more useless than enforced admiration; and I am always sorry for personally conducted parties which are obliged to keep strictly to an imposed itinerary— though this kind of travel too has its advantages. There is nothing to be ashamed of in having failed to see the Sixtine Chapel at Rome or Notre Dame at Paris. But something one should see, and on the whole it is better to see those things of which the cities themselves are most proud. For they are usually the most characteristic, and help to explain the citizens.

The truth is, however, that travelling is for every taste. We should not permit ourselves to enter on a dreary round of sightseeing that is not to our taste, when there is so much that is to our taste. A French author, Henry de Montherlant, declares that of all pleasures travelling is the saddest, precisely because we feel compelled to make a desperate effort to interest ourselves in matters that are outside our own domain. But nothing really compels us to interest ourselves in matters outside our own domain. We are at liberty to avoid them. Yet, since we have more leisure as a rule when we are travelling, it may well be that we shall discover an interest in matters which are normally indifferent to us. In any case, every new town, every new village, has something to show in which we can take delight.

A Sky-Scraper in Stuttgart

> "For to admire and for to see,
> For to be'old—the world so wide,
> It never done no good to me,
> But I can't drop it if I tried." . . .

Obviously, the singer was wrong: it is good in itself, and must do good, to admire and to see. . . .

Whether systematic or discursive sightseeing is the better can be determined only by the individual temperament. It is like reading; there are those who find their nourishment in systematic reading, and others in discursive reading. But it is certain that nobody can go abroad without being mentally enriched. One learns to appreciate one's own country in other countries, for, as Kipling sings:

"What do they know of England who only England know?" —and for England one can read France, Germany, Italy, or the United States of America.

Above all, travelling enlarges our horizon; we learn a broader tolerance, we acquire a more sympathetic understanding; and in our day, when it has become essential to the human race that there should be no more wars, and that peace should be established as a positive institution, and not merely as a negative interlude between wars, it is good that there should be more and more intelligent travellers who will help to dissipate the darkness of ignorance, that still, in spite of steamers, trains, motor-cars, and aeroplanes, is unhappily prevalent.

III. STATESMEN AND JOURNALISTS

AT GENEVA, where men and women of all nations intermingle, with only bureaucratic functions to fulfil in the intervals between Sessions, there was, some time ago, an amusing and, on the whole, a good-humoured contest in ingenuity. The predilections of the various races were facetiously defined somewhat as follows:

> One Swiss—a pastry-shop
> Two Swiss—an inn
> Three Swiss—a Grand Hotel

Again:

> One Austrian—a Rumanian Jew
> Two Austrians—a Hungarian Jew and a Czech
> Three Austrians—the Anschluss

Of the Germans it was said:
> One German—a professor
> Two Germans—a beer-hall
> Three Germans—the goose-step

Of the English it was unkindly remarked:
> One Englishman—an imbecile
> Two Englishmen—a club
> Three Englishmen—a great Empire

The Russians were thus described:
> One Russian—a genius
> Two Russians—two fools
> Three Russians—anarchy

The French were treated thus:
> One Frenchman—a monologue
> Two Frenchmen—a conference
> Three Frenchmen (and women)—a ménage

The Scotch came off fairly well:
> One Scotchman—a savings bank
> Two Scotchmen—a game of golf
> Three Scotchmen—the British Government

Sometimes the jokes were more cryptic, depending on the special application of words. For example, the Greeks have earned an unenviable reputation at card games in the casinos of Europe. Therefore:
> One Greek—one Greek
> Two Greeks—two Greeks
> Three Greeks—three Greeks

Perhaps the satire on Americans will not be found too severe:
> One American—a millionaire
> Two Americans—a cocktail party
> Three Americans—prohibition

And so on, and so forth, *ad libitum* and *ad nauseam*.

Of course these facetious definitions have no serious significance. The most pointed of them were invented by citizens of the country to which they apply. Some kind of amusement must be found by the unhappy officials who are compelled to live in the rather dull town on Lake Leman. The newspapermen, when they have nothing better to do, send out messages announcing the fall of the peak of Mont Blanc. How many times the peak of Mont Blanc has fallen off is beyond computation.

Even when the statesmen are meeting in Geneva there is often a lack of liveliness. It is necessary to try to work up dramatic interest in the proceedings. Occasionally the dramatic interest is overdone. Once there was an especially dreary disarmament conference. It was represented as desperately bitter. At last the correspondent of a New York newspaper received from his editor a telegram couched in these terms:

"Remember you are reporting a peace conference, not a war."

On the whole newspapermen have a proper sense of their responsibility, and it is rare that their account of international affairs is seriously inaccurate. But while they do their job with commendable discretion, making the best of the tons of statistics and reports that are handed out, it may be doubted whether the new conception of open diplomacy always works out well. By open diplomacy it was intended that an end should be made of secret accords such as existed between European nations in the years which preceded and prepared the Great War, and which still exist as numerous as ever, though it is not in the best of taste to speak about them. It was not meant that every question, even in its preliminary stages, should be thrashed out publicly. When diplomatists are on the point of agreeing to a compromise it is surely wrong to arouse the public opinion of different countries on this or that aspect of the compromise and thus prevent an agreement. There is a good deal of spadework that should be performed as quietly as possible. Unhappily, since the war, statesmen have learned to live in the limelight. They chiefly wish to advertise themselves, and they proclaim every other week or so that they are on the point of discovering a fresh way of assuring peace.

Far too frequently this demagogic diplomacy is positively mischievous. For the sake of a little cheap applause Foreign Ministers deliberately surround themselves with journalists. They go to Geneva to be among the journalists. They would do better to stop at home but they would not be noticed at home. Then they complain of the journalists when indiscretions are committed. I am sure that more harm than good has been done by the diplomacy of the market-place, and that in prating of peace continually—instead of taking it for granted—we are making everybody think of war.

For the most part the press reports of European affairs—I can pronounce this verdict after a daily study of the European press for many years—are honest and helpful. When they are not, it is usually the fault of the politicians, who instead of exchanging written communications through the Chancelleries insist on meeting together spectacularly; and who, when they have directed attention on themselves for their own purposes, and have invited the press of the world to watch their movements, still think they have a right to complain if the press is not subservient and flattering, or if the record of their own folly injures them. Doubtless they would like to dictate all messages—though if they did they would suffer far more from their own mistakes. They appoint "spokesmen," to give out what is known as "dope." No self-respecting pressman is content with the rôle of official chronicler. Knowing his business, he does it thoroughly and independently. He is not the servant of the politicians or of the good eager ladies of the League who write to editors whenever correspondents tell unpleasant truths. If sometimes unwelcome revelations upset the plans of the politicians, the initial error is in seeking publicity for proceedings that would have been better conducted in private.

After watching the diplomatists in most of their meetings since the war, I unhesitatingly affirm that they are far less efficient and far louder than they used to be. They are more and more concerned with their histrionics and less and less with true peace. If they would remain in their Foreign Offices they might accomplish more effective work. Statesmen are the most undesirable of travellers. . . .

In the more remote countries of Eastern Europe the press would do well to reorganise itself. Sometimes its correspondents are paid anything but a living wage. They are, in a number of cases, on "space rates." If their paragraphs are accepted, they receive a fee. If they are not, then they go unrewarded for their work. This is quite indefensible. It is remarkable that wealthy newspapers and agencies should place the temptation to exaggerate and invent news in the way of poor casual correspondents.

Yet most of the news which comes from these sources is innocuous enough. It is, indeed, generally trivial. If it does not tell us anything worth while of the life of nations of which the correspondents are the accredited interpreters, it is mildly amusing in its repertory of oft-told tales.

For many of the Central and Eastern European stories are hardy annuals. The history of the traveller without trousers, for example, is history which repeats itself. I have grown to love it as an old friend. You have doubtless read it frequently, but I too must be allowed to relate it. It concerns a man (I do not know whether he is always the same) who, on the Turkish frontier, gesticulates frantically from the window of a compartment of the Simplon-Orient Express. When the guard asks for an explanation, he invariably declares that he bought a new suit of clothes in Constantinople, and to avoid paying customs duties he proceeded to change his clothes in the compartment. He threw his old suit out of the window before he opened the parcel of new clothes; but from that parcel the trousers were missing!

Generally the guard manages to find a pair of trousers for this unfortunate passenger.

Pierre Mille, the versatile French writer, once wrote a short story telling of a tragic Christmas in a Central European castle where a mysterious murder had been committed. . . . What was my surprise to find this fictitious episode in the news columns of several journals a week or so later!

As for the recrudescence of leprosy, it is a favourite topic. Despite the evidence of medical men themselves as to the non-transmission of leprosy, we are informed from time to time that somebody who bought a Russian fur or a necklace which came from the Near East, is afflicted with the dreadful malady. . . .

This kind of nonsense is better than the exaggerated ideas of their own importance that journalists who dabble in politics sometimes develop. There was one well-known editor whom I never met without having to listen to his account of his latest successful attempt to save Europe. Conferences were on the point of breaking up, but he invariably rushed to the hotel of the most obstinate statesman, dragged him from his bed, and, while the statesman shivered in his nightshirt, persuaded him that there was a way out. Then he dashed off to the hotel of the opposing statesman who met him in his pyjamas, and recounted his conversation with the first statesman. The next morning nightshirt statesman and pyjamas statesman met each other cordially, and all was well.

Variations on this theme are common. Happily most journalists laugh at themselves when they realise they are unduly boastful.

There is a good story told by one of my friends, whom I

will designate as G., about himself and two other friends whom I will designate as F. and B. G. was on good terms with Venizelos. D. had been well acquainted with the Russian statesman Witte. F. was accustomed to send private correspondence to President Wilson.

D. lay sick in his hotel. When G. heard of this he hurried round to cheer him up. The morning newspapers lay unfolded on the bed, and G. began to read them aloud to D.

When he came to the Russian news—the Revolution was in progress—D., forgetting his sickness, sprang up in bed and exclaimed: "There! That is exactly what I warned Witte would happen. Had my advice been taken . . ."

G., chuckling over D's vanity, took leave of him. In the street he met F. who was also paying a visit to D. "Have you seen the morning papers?" cried F. excitedly; "Wilson has issued a manifesto which is word for word as I suggested it to him."

G. went on his way in high glee. On the Boulevard he joined his wife, and laughed uproariously with her over the pretensions of his colleagues.

They sat on a café terrace. The newsboys were crying the afternoon papers. G. bought one. "Good Heavens!" he shouted. "Look at this! Venizelos has at last followed my counsel."

"And you wanted me to share your merriment about D. and F.," said his wife reproachfully.

It was one of this trio who, attending with me a dinner given by the late Ambassador Myron T. Herrick, was called upon to make a speech. In the course of his remarks, seeking an oratorical effect, he asked: "And what did Lindbergh say to you, Mr. Ambassador, as you sat on his bed on the night of his arrival in Paris?"

He suddenly realised that he had forgotten what Lindbergh had said, and therefore he converted his rhetorical question into a real question. "Tell us, Mr. Ambassador, what Lindbergh said when you were sitting etc. . . ."

The Ambassador had not the smallest recollection, so he replied: "Go on, it is your story."

The speaker paused, disconcerted. "I am afraid that perhaps I am betraying a confidence. I cannot repeat what he said without your permission."

"But you have it," said the Ambassador.

"All the same, I would rather that you told them."

"By no means," said Herrick. "Tell us what he said."

Everybody by this time understood precisely the cause of the contretemps, and there was a general cry for the observation of Lindbergh. The speaker might have joined in the merriment by frankly confessing that he had forgotten, but he preferred to gain time. "I feel that I should not give away a secret. . . . Well, there is Mr. ——, who also heard what Lindbergh said. Perhaps he will tell us."

Mr. —— shook his head. He did not know, and if he had known, he would not have spoiled the joke.

For five minutes F. endeavoured to induce somebody to finish his story, but his efforts were without avail. He had to finish somehow; the diners, headed by the Ambassador, were clamouring to know what Lindbergh said; and so, making a supreme effort, he revealed the secret. "Did he not say, Mr. Ambassador —did he not say—did he not say, as you sat on his bed—did he not say—'Well, thank God, it's over'?"

The anticlimax was irresistibly funny.

IV. LANGUAGES

MISS THEODORA BOSANQUET recently pointed out that no fewer than a hundred and twenty languages are spoken in Europe. Many of them are spoken by few people. Yet there are thirty-eight which are each the current language of more than a million persons. The difficulties of intercommunication are obviously increased; instead of diminishing languages are multiplying. It was thought an excellent thing to revive and foster the often forgotten culture of small nations. The peace-makers did not create the New Nationalism, but they encouraged it when they Balkanised Europe. While the tendency of Europe in the Nineteenth Century was towards unification, the tendency in post-war Europe is towards division.

German and Russian are the most widely spoken languages in Europe. After them come English, Italian, and French. Then there is Little Russian, Polish, Spanish, Rumanian, and Dutch. The ten next languages are still fairly important—that is to say, together they are almost as widely spoken as German. The hundred other languages together are not as widely spoken in Europe as French or English.

These are facts of immense importance. They go far to

shatter the hope of the formation of the United States of
Europe. They render travelling far less easy than it should be
in a rational world. While I rejoice in the breaking down of
national insularity, and believe in the virtues of travel, I nevertheless sometimes doubt whether we are not as ignorant of each
other's thoughts and purposes as ever. For the language barrier
is almost insuperable.

My friends Jan and Cora Gordon used to go a-vagabonding
in little known parts of Europe, mixing with the peasant folk,
writing, sketching, learning to play strange instruments; and
they prepared themselves by acquiring a smattering of a few
hundred words of each tongue they might be called upon to
speak. With these few hundred words they managed to make
friends with the simple common people, and obtained some
genuine insight into their mode of life, their reactions, their
character. But we cannot all go a-vagabonding, and although
a comparatively few words alone are necessary, still it requires
aptitude and perseverance to equip oneself for travel off the
beaten track.

On a recent tour of Europe I was particularly conscious of
linguistic difficulties. It is often said that with English and
French one can travel almost anywhere, and this is undoubtedly
true of the sheltered kind of travelling which most people
prefer. They take an international train on which the attendants smatter several languages; they call out to "Mr. Cook" for
help with their luggage on their arrival; they stay in a cosmopolitan hotel; and if they go shopping or sightseeing they
employ a guide. But this is not travelling—or at any rate, it
is travelling only in a narrowly limited sense. If one is to stay
among one's own people or among sophisticated foreigners, if
one is to carry one's house on one's back like a snail, and surround oneself with one's own emanations like a cuttle-fish, one
might almost as well stop at home. There are doubtless folk
who love the mere displacement, and relish the incomprehensible peculiarities of strange lands; but the intelligent traveller,
I think, likes least of all the journey, and the more exotic is the
flavour the more he deplores his lack of catholic understanding.

What is the alternative in a Europe fashioned like a crazy
quilt of shreds and patches? It is that the traveller should make
himself familiar with a number of languages. But not all of
us have time and patience and aptitude for the study of tongues
which, after all, will not often be needed. Proficiency in

German Athletic Youth

tongues can only be expected of men and women whose profession it is to observe, as diplomatists or writers, other peoples; and in point of fact many diplomatists make shift with very little, and most writers are content with sufficient knowledge to struggle through the front pages of the newspapers.

I do not blame them; if I did I should be blaming myself. Life is short, and languages are long. In my career I have met two men who spoke perfectly a score of languages; one of them, I was informed, could compose sonnets in Turkish! Much as I admired them I could not help recalling the well-known story of Herbert Spencer, who, when beaten at billiards, exclaimed: "Such proficiency is evidence of a misspent youth!"

When did they do their work? Could they do their work properly if they devoted their energies to the study of languages instead of life? Would not this habit of poring over words within four walls destroy their faculty of observation, their interest in their fellows? There are, of course, prodigies who are equally at home in the library and in the café; but, speaking generally, I should distrust the judgments of the accomplished linguist more than the judgments of the language-less man.

Some of the more enterprising smaller countries which are dependent on foreign trade or foreign visitors endeavour to teach their citizens German, French, English, Italian, in addition to their native tongue. Such is the case of Belgium and of Switzerland. When I was lately in Czecho-Slovakia I was glad to remark the keenness of the Czechs—who at first patriotically pretended ignorance even of German—to learn French and English. In Austria, too, there is a strong desire to become polyglot, in order to bring visitors to the truncated but beautiful country. But on the other hand there are extremely insular nations where one is helpless without a working knowledge of the language. Such for example is Spain; as soon as you reach the frontier town you find that few people know a word of French, and there are first-class hotels in the great cities where Spanish only is spoken.

Moreover, though educated men in the Balkans generally speak French, the foreigner must stick closely to the towns, for it is too much to ask the peasants to possess a second tongue. Hungary may be cited in this connection; in the higher circles French and English are understood, but then, Hungary is chiefly countryside.

Latin as a universal language is, I think, out of the question.
In spite of university traditions, most people instinctively feel
that it is somewhat absurd to learn a dead language, and it cannot be made a living language again until this aversion is broken
down. We are in a vicious circle. . . . As for newfangled
composite tongues they will never, in my opinion, make sufficient progress to have the smallest pretension to universality.
There is a proper prejudice against them. Why add still more
foreign languages to the world's great store—and ungainly
artificial languages at that?

English is my native language and therefore I should prefer
English to be adopted as the common tongue; but French is
surely better from many points of view. It is already the
second language of a number of European nations, and it has
qualities of precision and of regularity that commend it. It is
also easier to learn for most of the European peoples, especially
of the South and East. German seems to me impossibly alien for
the bulk of European nations. Italian, in spite of its Latin
origin and its beauty, is too local; and Spanish, though a great
language, is, from the purely European standpoint, too little
known outside Spain, the most non-European country in
Europe.

A great disservice was done to Europe at Versailles when
English was, owing to the linguistic deficiencies of Mr. Lloyd
George and Mr. Wilson, elevated to the rank of a diplomatic
language. French had been hitherto used for diplomatic purposes, but now it has a rival. The Versailles Treaty is in the
two languages, and in the process of translation absurd blunders
have crept in which might conceivably give rise to difficulties
of interpretation. We should have accepted what was the
custom, and have encouraged and extended the existing state
of affairs, instead of beginning a competition that can only
produce confusion. Now the Germans insist on the use of
their language in international assemblies—and, as there are two
Richmonds in the field, we can hardly refuse the entrance of a
third.

Unfortunately the League of Nations has become a Tower
of Babel. It would have been easy, had not foolish questions of
prestige arisen, to have decided that all speeches in the League
of Nations should be in one language. Those who could not
speak that tongue or understand it would naturally have been
ineligible as delegates. There would not have been the slightest

difficulty in finding competent delegates; but unhappily there was a stupid theory that Foreign Ministers should be induced to go to Geneva, thus converting the League of Peoples into a mere League of Foreign Offices, and it is notorious that Foreign Ministers are ignorant of foreign languages if not of foreign affairs. A splendid opportunity was presented of simplifying foreign relations and of advancing the cause of a common tongue. Not only was the opportunity lost, but the bigwigs of the League have, by insisting on the right to speak their national language, set back the clock, and rendered international understandings much more difficult than they were before the war.

Now I read of all kinds of proposals by which non-linguistic delegates—who have not the smallest right to appoint themselves or allow themselves to be appointed to international conferences—may be kept informed of the proceedings. Instead of successive translations, a telephone system may be inaugurated by which a team of interpreters will simultaneously whisper into a long line of microphones, while each delegate will wear a sound helmet. Or the speeches are to be thrown, as the orator proceeds, on perhaps a score of screens. Could anything be more ludicrous? Could anything be less inspiring? Could anything more emphasise the chaos which the League should have reduced to order? I must be forgiven if I suggest, as one of the earliest advocates of the League, that, in the matter of language, it has done bad work, and has strengthened the fences between nations.

* * *

I write this book with the hope of contributing something to a general understanding of the position and problems of European countries of to-day. For many years I have been a student of international affairs, and at times I have been placed in exceptional posts of observation. I have come into contact with a large number of persons, some of them prominent, some of them characteristic; and I have by no means confined my interest to those manifestations which are narrowly called political; on the contrary, I have tried to interpret politics in the light of social conditions and literary movements, in the light of popular sentiments and intellectual activities. In other words, politics—to employ this ill-defined term—are essentially human. So, in this book, which is not a travel book, there are travel pictures; in this book, which is not a book of memoirs, I draw on my memory of rich experiences; in this book, which is not a portrait gallery, there are nevertheless portraits of artists, scientists, and statesmen; in this book, which is not a book of diplomacy, there are answers to most of the questions which everybody is asking about Europe. I will tell my story in a personal manner—wandering from Spain to Italy, from Italy to Austria, and thence to Balkanised Europe, and finally to Germany—and at the end I will endeavour to sum up my views on the present situation and the future of Europe. Of these views I will permit myself to say that I have held and expressed them from the beginning, and many of them, though by no means all, which were most fiercely contested are now widely accepted.

PART II
SPAIN

I. AN AFRICAN COUNTRY

THERE is one thing that Europe knows well how to do: travelling is as comfortable and even as luxurious as it can be made. From Paris to Madrid is a twenty-four hours' journey, yet it is not wearisome.

The Sud-Express is a remarkable train, smooth-running, and provided with every possible convenience. You step aboard to your appointed compartment in the evening, go to bed, and wake up near the Spanish frontier, where you breakfast before you are transferred at Irun to the Spanish carriages.

The purpose of a recent visit to Madrid was to ascertain how the country stood after six years of Dictatorship. Spain is a land of mystery, and in nothing has it been more mysterious than in its attitude towards Primo de Rivera. In our newspapers we read accounts of army risings and student riotings; and communiqué after communiqué from the Government assuring us that nothing is happening only arouses our curiosity. Methinks he doth protest too much! Such volubility of optimism seems to betoken misgiving. The more the Marqués de Estella informed us that he meant to stay, the more we believed that he was about to resign.

Besides, there is an evocation in the name of Spain. We imagine that political changes must somehow be accompanied by violence. The sulkiness of artillery officers and the uproariousness of students are at once magnified into a revolution. My old servant was even alarmed for my safety. She pictured Madrid as a howling mob with knives and rifles; with tramcars overturned to form barricades; with machine-guns crackling from burning buildings. I was plunging headlong into multitudinous perils.

The reality was altogether different. It is strange how distorted are the images produced by press reports and the imagination. Even were Spain passing through a revolutionary period, I doubt whether it would be visible to the naked eye. Revolutions are of course scattered incidents; generally life goes on for the ordinary citizen without particular excitement and sometimes without particular knowledge of what is happening round the corner. Somewhere I have read an eye-witness's account of the battle of Waterloo. He found himself solitary in a dismal plain. It rained pitilessly. Somebody told him to march in a certain direction. He trudged through mud. Here and there was a hurry of men. He continued to trudge through mud. There was a vague sound of guns. Then there was more hurrying of men. . . . I will cut the narrative short, but finally the spectator was informed by a fugitive that he had been present at the battle of Waterloo. . . . That I suspect is about all the individual usually sees of great historic events. So that, even supposing Spain to be in what is described as a state of upheaval, I might at the best hope to witness a street row, and to hear a bullet whistle by my windows while I was quietly dining.

As it is, I can report no spectacle as unusual as a street row and no bullet whistled past my window. The interesting international exhibitions of Barcelona and Seville were uninterrupted by untoward events; and there were as many visitors as Primo de Rivera himself could have desired. Everything was calm on the Spanish front; whether Primo de Rivera now goes or stays is a political matter which may or may not occasion social perturbation. . . .

The British Minister in Portugal bore out my view that even revolutions are usually harmless, hardly noticeable things. "I have passed through seven revolutions in Portugal and in Russia," he told me; "and I suffered no inconvenience."

Spain is the least known of European countries. To the American and the English traveller Spain lies off the beaten track. France and Germany and Italy and Holland and Switzerland are, to the man of average education, lands which, still unvisited, are nevertheless understood. When he at last finds himself in these countries he is almost surprised to discover that the impressions which he had formed from reading, correspond to the impressions he receives by seeing. But of Spain he has only fantastic notions. He vaguely thinks of the Inquisition, the Grand Armada, the Conquest of Granada. . . . Exactly a hundred years ago Washington Irving went to gather material for his history in the old Moorish palace of the Alhambra. . . . The association of ideas extends to Miguel de Cervantes and Don Quixote, to George Borrow and his Bible, to bullfights and mantillas. There are gitanas and guitars, Virgins with magnificent bijoux, orange-trees and flowers, cigarette factories and dancers with castanets. . . . He has heard of the Escorial, the Kingly tomb, of the port of Barcelona, of the street processions of Seville, with huge images carried aloft, of the parks and Prado of Madrid, of the bridge of Toledo, of blue Cadiz and white Valencia. . . . But somehow Spain remains unknown though unchanging.

When Louis XIV tried to effect the union of France and Spain by placing his grandson on the Castilian throne, he exclaimed, "Il n'y a plus de Pyrénées!" For him the Pyrenees no longer existed. The Spanish Ambassador grandiloquently replied that this range of mountains had melted like snow in the rays of the Sun-King. They were both mistaken. The Pyrenees, though they are now easily crossed by the railway, constitute a barrier that implacably separates Spain from Europe. On my latest European travels I was deeply conscious of this separation. It came to me in divers ways. I had wandered in the space of a few weeks in nearly every country of Western Europe, and had pushed far to the East, and always had I felt at home. There were strange sights, but there were no secrets. But now I was conscious of a civilisation that is altogether alien. The feeling can be summed up in the assertion that, despite geography, Spain is not in Europe but in Africa.

The phrase is not original. I thought it was when I jotted it down in my notebook. But, like most travellers, I carry with me in my baggage a small library concerning the cities in which I expect to stay; and when at night I opened my valise the first book I read epigrammatically told me that Spain is not a European but an African country. It is hard to say anything new nowadays! I can only console myself with the reflection that my sensibility to differences is not less acute than that of my predecessors. Moreover, I am comforted by the corroboration. If it is true that Spain has features which remind one of Northern Africa, then it would have been inexplicable that others had not observed the fact before me.

A diplomatist with whom I dined in Madrid wittily remarked upon the Moorish character of Spain: "Mr. Ford, of automobile fame, tells us that history is bunk," he said, "and he is right. For, according to history, the Moorish invaders were finally driven from Spain by the end of the Fifteenth Century. You can see for yourself that this is not true. They have never been driven from Spain. Here is their architecture and their character; and, still more important in its ultimate consequences, here is their country—desert and sierra." . . .

Before we reached the frontier I was approached in the corridor of the train by a Spanish professor. "We lunched together, you may remember, before the days of Primo de Rivera, when King Alfonso XIII made one of his sojourns in Paris, at the Spanish Embassy. The Ambassador then, as now, was Señor Quiñones de León."

I remembered! The Embassy had been transferred to a new building, and the occasion was the house-warming. The Ambassador had taken me aside to explain that the King, who prides himself on being a draughtsman, had designed the garden and pergola. As in duty bound I admired the Royal garden and pergola. The King had likewise sent from his palace in Madrid a number of magnificent pictures which hung upon the walls of the Embassy in Paris: and these too I admired. . . .

"Times have changed," said the Professor, "I am now in exile —voluntarily—and I am to meet some relatives on the border. The Dictatorship is altogether bad. There has been blunder after blunder. Oddly enough, my sympathies are with Primo de Rivera against the juntas of army officers which would impose their will upon the Government. But, generally, the Dictatorship is a yoke under which Spain groans and which it intends soon to throw off. Certainly the former method of political rotation—the alternation of liberally-inclined Conservatives and conservatively-inclined Liberals—together with extreme Socialist and Syndicalist action—was producing little good. Yet the game of ins-and-outs is practised in most Parliamentary countries; and the Spanish Parliament was not suppressed because of the rotation of parties. No, it was suppressed because at last labour and liberal thought were becoming too advanced. Real reforms were recommended, and would have been put into operation, had not Primo de Rivera, with whom the King has seriously compromised himself, made his reactionary coup. Progress has been retarded, not accelerated. I am afraid that things will be worse before they are better." . . . He shook my hand sadly. . . .

The train stopped. The Professor got out. Was he right or wrong? That was the question which I was to endeavour to answer in Spain itself.

King Alphonso XIII

II. THE BLUE SKIES OF THE SPANISH
DARK

IT IS necessary to change trains at the frontier because the
Spanish railway lines are wider than the French. Why has
Spain not adopted the standard gauge? Various reasons are
given but the real reason is military. Yet it is almost ludicrous
to suppose that Spain could now, in spite of the troubled past,
come to blows with France. The disparity between the populations of the two countries is alone sufficient to assure peace; for
a certain equality, or supposed equality, is necessary between
belligerents. But, in addition, Spain has abandoned all military
ambitions. In the Great War it was neutral, and neutrality in
the Great War is often taken as a sign of decadence.

The conscript system nevertheless continues in Spain; I saw
a batch of young men assembling for their transportation to
barracks; they bantered each other as all young conscripts do,
but there was melancholy in their farewell to civilian life.

Soldiering in Spain is not serious. The rank and file are too
individualist; they never acquire the esprit de corps which is
needed to make good soldiers. As for the officers, they long ago
decided that the army offers a social career, and sometimes a
political career, but never a military career.

In Spain, as d'Annunzio picturesquely says, the booted tyrant with wooden sword may yet flourish; but the inefficiency
of the Spanish army has been amply demonstrated in Morocco.
While the French, under Marshal Lyautey, developed their
Moroccan zone, the Spanish totally failed. They were unable
to cope with the rebel bands of the Riff. Primo de Rivera him-
self counselled surrender. Finally, it was only the military help
of France which extricated Spain from the direst difficulties.
In Morocco, Spain lost the last vestiges of its prestige as a Great
Power; and if, some day, Germany purchases Rio del Oro and
Morocco from Spain, as is probable, the once mighty Colonial
Empire will completely disappear.

This incompetent army, beaten and disgraced, nevertheless
pretended to govern. It could not subdue the Riffans, but it
could suppress the aspirations towards freedom of the Spanish.
It gave its support to the authorities, on condition that its
commands were obeyed. It exercised a constant and conscious
political pressure. The army overthrew Governments, dismissed

Governors, blacklisted recalcitrant persons, nominated the officials, and generally reduced Spain to the sorry condition in which it stood, with men and money wasted in the Moroccan morass, with Syndicalism instituting an anarchist terrorism, with Catalonia pursuing a movement for autonomy, with impotent Prime Minister succeeding impotent Prime Minister, while Alphonso XIII amused himself at Deauville.

If Spain is infested with militarism, it does not follow that Spain is militarily powerful. On the contrary; the more militarism rules, the more ludicrous becomes the army.

In Spain the army has destroyed liberty; has blocked the path of progress. Eventually it made Primo de Rivera Dictator; but Primo de Rivera, instead of remaining the tool of the army, presently defied his creators. . . .

The change of gauge is only a trivial annoyance for the traveller, but it is a reminder of the folly of frontiers. There cannot now be the smallest strategic purpose in maintaining wider rails, but nobody—not even Primo de Rivera—has had the courage to denounce this particular lack of uniformity which was originally based on distrust. In the same way the Channel Tunnel which would unite France and England has been for many years opposed by military men, although England is no longer, in the old sense, an island, isolated from Europe.

My *compagnon de voyage* agreed that the Spanish gauge was maintained by mere conservatism. The reason had long ago been forgotten. "Look at those men with their little hammers hitting the wheels of the train," he said. "I once asked a railroad employee why it was done. He scratched his head. 'I don't know,' he replied, 'I've been doing it for thirty years, and nobody ever told me why.' Politicians are like that—except that there really is a reason for hitting the wheels of a train."

Astonishing that a few miles should bring such a transformation! On one side of the frontier French is the common tongue —though the Basques have their own patois. At Irun, the gateway into Spain, not even the newspaper seller in the kiosk at the station knows a word of French. Nor do the Customs officers. Almost everywhere else in Europe there is some transition. Here there is none. Almost everywhere else people make shift to speak other tongues. But the Spaniard has his own tongue, and that must suffice. It is a truly great language in which at least one of the six literary masterpieces of the world have been written. Yet I could not but remark that throughout Spain one is more completely lost without a smattering of the native language than in most other countries.

It is common to speak of Spain as the Latin sister of France and Italy. Nothing could be more misleading. France and Spain belong to different worlds. One is brisk and neat; the other suggests indolence and decay. One is a smiling garden admirably arranged; the other, in spite of its beautiful oases, is relatively deserted, and is, indeed, in some sense a desert. Geographical conditions as well as racial origins count greatly; and moreover, historically Spain missed the two mighty experiences of the Renaissance and the Reformation. Nominally France is a Catholic country, but in reality France has always been in revolt against the Church, just as much as the Protestant countries. Spain has stood still. It was the home of the Inquisition, and to-day it accepts a primitive superstitious Catholicism. My daily newspapers are filled with pictures of the Crucifixion. Most of them are sanguinary. There are also photographs of bullfights, equally sanguinary. It is quite impossible to imagine the front pages of French newspapers thus illustrated. In the streets one watches religious processions, with huge images carried aloft, with cowled penitents, who irresistibly remind me of the Ku-Klux-Klan.

Sunny Spain! The expression is fully justified. The sun brilliantly painted the high mountains with green grass, white blossoms, and golden gorse. In the distance was a sunny dome and a shining city. The donkey, the ubiquitous beast of Spain, made his appearance, standing patiently tethered in the fields or perambulating placidly with huge burdens on his back along the white lanes. Women with heavy pails on their heads turned to look at us. I lost count of the number of priests who filled the platforms of the railway stations. The whole atmosphere had suddenly changed. Out of the trim land of France, with its manifold activities, its utilisation of all resources of nature, we had come into the wider unutilised spaces of Spain, where life is more indolent, and in spite of the sun, more sombre. I had the sensation of coming out of the Twentieth Century into the Middle Ages.

Yet there were curious contrasts. Yoked oxen were not only drawing the plough across the fields, but were drawing carts along the roads. They were overtaken by swift automobiles.

One felt that the yoked oxen belonged to Spain, while the automobiles did not. Modernity has not left Spain untouched, but it has been superimposed on Spain without modifying the real Spain.

So we went for miles through country which had the air of being underpopulated. Each little town that we passed had hung out its washing like banners to greet us. From each storey hung long lines of washing. It was an everlasting washing-day. The better-class houses presented their verandas, their balconies, and their pergolas, where men and women can live in the sunshine.

My *compagnon de voyage* was an American, the Director of a great industry which had installed itself in Spain. The movement began long ago—before the war. German and British firms went to Spain. French firms followed. Now American capital is largely engaged. . . . One of the grievances against Primo de Rivera is that he is endeavouring to nationalise Spain. By tariffs and by taxes and by onerous regulations he makes the position of the foreign importer and manufacturer difficult. His friends explain that it is because he has taken this patriotic stand that influential foreigners are waging an economic war on the country. The peseta is depressed. The currency was quoted when I was there at a very low figure, and the foreigner was blamed.

"Do you find the Spanish workman good?" I asked.

"He is surprisingly good," was the somewhat unexpected reply. "Allowing for the climate he is an excellent workman. He is, of course, better in the North than in the South. The Catalonian is extremely willing to learn on American lines. The Andalusian is less industrious—but this is natural. What puzzles them is piecework. They turn out a large quantity of material, but my office rings every week with complaints. One workman is paid too much and another workman too little. The bookkeeping is atrocious. The percentage of mistakes is incredible. Figures seem to have little meaning. They are unimportant to the clerks, and thus it is not easy to keep accounts straight. But emphatically I should say that the workman is good while the executive is not sufficiently acquainted with modern business ways."

We were running through endless whitish plains with whitish hills in the distance, and whitish villages ever topped by the

square tower of a whitish church. After Valladolid, where, in
the year 1217, the Queen of Castile gave the crown to her
son, where in 1469 Ferdinand and Isabella were married, where
Christopher Columbus lived, where Philip II was born, where
the mighty Emperor Charles V sojourned, where the first of
the *Autos-da-fés* was celebrated, the dusk fell on the rows of
dark green parasol pines, with long twisted stems and bushy
heads; and the big boulders on the high plateau grew grey.

The red flames of the invisible sun made the scene more lurid
and more barren. There was a sudden chill in the air after the
hot day. More and more did one realise that Castile, which is
the heart of Spain, is largely an expanse of arid sierras—a
wilderness of sun-baked stones. But it is well to make the approach at nightfall, for then the desert is covered romantically
by the blue skies of the Spanish dark. It is a deeper blue than
one finds anywhere else on the Continent that enwraps these
ribs of an ancient buried world—a rich blue as of a dyed curtain—a blue out of which a few stars shine, and on which
sometimes are fastened the golden lights of a village, like jewels
on this deep blue curtain of night. There is magnificence in this
blue world; but it is a magnificence that is alien and African.
It is lonely and silent, but over this blue desert, that Dante
might have invented, the night slowly spread its benedic-
tion. . . .

Out of it rises Madrid almost painfully new and white. It is
perhaps the only great city of Europe which does not stand on
a river. (In point of fact, Madrid too has its river, but it is
tiny and utterly insignificant—unworthy even of a village—
and I have forgotten its name.) Despite its modern thoroughfares, its light and bustle, its grandiose buildings, it is as Spanish
as the rest of Spain. Yes, it is modern; it lacks the impressive
antiquity of Burgos and of Toledo; motor-taxis have in the
past few years multiplied in the streets and are driving off the
uncomfortable horse carriages; there are emporiums which resemble the Paris emporiums, and have French names; there is
the most elaborate post-office I have seen built in the style of a
huge cathedral and facetiously called "Our Lady of Communications"; cinemas, the newest form of communal building,
glare beside churches, the oldest form of communal building;
yet all these things seem to be accidental, and let Madrid try
to be as up-to-date as it will, it keeps the temper of old Spain.

III. MAÑANA

MAÑANA! The word is spoken in cafés and shops. To-morrow! There is no doubt that many people have become tired of the Dictatorship, and would welcome a change. But the change is for to-morrow. If you ask me when to-morrow comes, I can only reply that I do not know. "We shave gratis to-morrow," announced the enterprising barber; but when customers pointed to the sign he remarked that it plainly said "to-morrow," not "to-day." In *Alice in Wonderland,* too, it was jam to-morrow, but never jam to-day.

Primo de Rivera, when I was in Madrid, was issuing communiqués indicating his intention of resigning at some future date. But what date? The foreign newspapers took it for granted that it would be to-morrow. In Spain the communiqués were interpreted altogether differently. The Dictator would retire—but only when he had completed his task. An Ambassador in Madrid expressed his scepticism to me. Certainly the Dictator has moments of vacillation, but his tactics are to persuade his opponents that they need only wait patiently. Thus the edge of their attack is blunted. Moreover, every time he announces his impending departure, his friends organise a manifestation in his favour.

Surely, I remarked, if these statements are misleading to the public they are dangerous for him.

"Yes," said my friend, "you have only to compare the impression produced with that produced in Italy by Mussolini. Something unexpected may, of course, happen to Mussolini; but whatever may be the sequel there is no doubt that he means to stay. The Fascist organisation believes that he is in office for life, and this gives it an undisputed solidity. Now in Spain the followers of Primo de Rivera are hesitant. They are taught to be hesitant by their chief. Most of the leading members of the Patriotic Union are disgruntled politicians who were unable to obtain posts under the former régime. If the Dictator is to go in a few months, or even in a few years, they may judge it prudent not to commit themselves irrevocably."

And now at last the text of the Bill for the reform of the Spanish Constitution is tabled in the National Consultative Assembly. It is quite anti-democratic. Roman Catholicism is adopted as the State religion; and no public demonstrations other than those of the State religion will be tolerated. Naturally Primo de Rivera is obliged to restore those personal liberties which were guaranteed by the Constitution of June, 1876, which he improperly suspended; and once more we are promised, if a plebiscite of the people approves the new Bill, that Spaniards shall not be arbitrarily arrested, as they have been, that they shall not be obliged to change their domicile, as they have been, that they shall not be prevented by censorship from expressing their opinions, as they have been. The Cortes shall be a single Chamber; and shall consist of deputies appointed by the King; deputies elected by the people; and deputies elected by professions and classes. This is obviously not a political Parliament as Parliament has been understood for the past hundred years. As citizens the people have no determining voice in the conduct of affairs. As industrialists, as artisans, as intellectuals, they are allowed a limited share in the government, but as men with broader concern in the conduct of the State they have a greatly diminished place. Theoretically there is something fascinating in the proposal to give some degree of direct specific representation to different elements of the nation; but in fact, to appoint deputies purely on a class or professional basis is sadly to restrict the notion of citizenship. Deputies who have such a narrow view of their functions will be impotent "experts" expected to give advice only in a technical manner on technical matters. That this kind of Chamber can exercise real control over the Executive is improbable; and the composition of the Royal Council is purely reactionary, with its Archbishop of Toledo, Generals and Admirals of the Army and Navy, Judges, and Grandees.

Mr. R. A. Calvert who was Vice-Consul in Cadiz and afterwards in Madrid, summed up for me the forces for and against Primo de Rivera. For him are many of the officers of the army —though divisions have declared themselves in the army since Primo de Rivera showed his independence of this prop. For him are the priests of the Roman Catholic Church whose pay has been increased, and who have been treated with special consideration. . . . What is called "secular morality" has been denounced by the Spanish Archbishops as unorthodox, and a menace to ecclesiastical authority. Even when ideas of kindness to animals and good fellowship among men are preached in Spain, they are looked at askance as "modernist." Change of any kind is held to be undesirable. . . . Although Primo de

Rivera cannot possibly share these rigid views he has been politically friendly to the Church. He admitted the right of the Augustinian Monks and the Jesuits to issue diplomas in their Colleges, equivalent in value to those of the Universities, thereby lowering the scholarship standard. Further, the industrialists favour Primo de Rivera on the ground that he suppressed anarchy in Catalonia, and stimulated national industry. Strangely enough, the Socialists are friendly towards the Dictator. They point out that he has set up arbitration councils, and established public works. As for the King, whatever may be his private views, he does not venture to oppose Primo de Rivera.

On the other side are ranged the Universities which, protesting against ordinances of the Dictator, were promptly suspended. Blowing hot and cold, the Dictator exempted a number of Universities, and he then attempted to placate that of Madrid. Again, the artillery officers resented the abandonment of the tradition by which promotion was strictly based on seniority, describing as mere favouritism promotion by so-called merit. Now the artillery officers are drawn from the best families of Spain, and the Dictator's high-handed action in disbanding them, and in compelling them to take a new oath of loyalty to his régime, have produced bitter feelings. The old parties, both Liberal and Conservative, are deeply indignant at the abolition of Parliamentarism, and some of their members at least, including the King in their resentment, are inclined to Republicanism. Finally, there are the Syndicalists—those who favour direct action. Their numbers are growing, though their legal status is doubtful.

It should be added to this interesting tableau—as a distinguished Spaniard added, in conversation with me—that the people generally are restive under a system which gives them no part in politics. They like to express their opinions in cafés and in polling-booths, but are forbidden to do so. The newspapers are under a ridiculous censorship. "It is pure folly," said the Spaniard, "to clap the lid on all opposition for six years. Sooner or later there will be an explosion."

Yet when I was in Spain the active opposition was not very formidable. There was plenty of discontent but it had not reached the point where action is necessary. Nevertheless it is obvious that such a Dictatorship is at the mercy of a sudden incident. If there were a successful uprising anywhere in Spain, it is quite possible that the latent hostility would break out. But the Spaniard is not given to disciplined political manifestations. He is essentially a lonely figure—as solitary and fantastic as Don Quixote, or as comfortable and complacent as Sancho Panza—and Primo de Rivera. The old game of ins-and-outs was possible because of this lack of civic unity. The new game of Dictatorship is likewise possible for the same reason.

Even the Patriotic Union is not particularly strong. It encourages social spying. The Spaniard loves to gossip, but he gossips at his peril. If a social spy overhears animadversions on the régime, it it his business to report the offender to headquarters, and in the arbitrary state into which Spain has fallen, the lot of the offender may be unhappy. This, I think, is futile as well as irritating. Gossip is a good safety-valve, and if the Spaniard could only talk freely he would put off action. Mañana would still be his watchword. As he cannot talk, as he cannot criticise, as he is suppressed in the governmental scheme of Primo de Rivera, mañana may come more quickly than is expected.

It was inevitable that somebody should have recourse to the favourite sport of the Spaniard, and find a metaphor in bull-fighting. "The people," said one of my friends, "are prepared to look on impartially at the struggle in the arena. At first Primo de Rivera was the matador who dealt a masterly stroke at the Cortes. But now he is the bull. He is being teased and enraged. He reacts against his opponents with some vigour, though his rushes are somewhat too wild. He is, I should say, in the banderilla stage. The artillery officers and the students have managed to prick him. But the matador has not yet entered the arena. Who is the matador? He is not yet announced. If ever he steps forward, the public will applaud matador and bull. But it is, of course, always the bull which succumbs in the end, and Primo is now the bull."

IV. BEGGARS, BOOTBLACKS MANTILLAS

WHEN Primo de Rivera wished to show my friend Jules Sauerwein, an excellent Paris journalist, that there was no political crisis in Spain, he invited him to share his box at the opera. There was music, there was dancing; there were women smartly dressed and bediamonded; there were gallant men, clean-shaven, as in all countries since the invention of the Gillette razor; and, altogether, M. Sauerwein was favourably impressed by his glimpse of Tout-Madrid.

The General waved his hand airily. "This does not look like revolution or counter-revolution, does it?"

Certainly it did not, but an audience at the Madrid opera-house will presumably look exactly the same whether there is political discontent or not; and I found the argument unconvincing.

I did not sit in the box of Primo de Rivera, but I did find Madrid wearing its usual appearance. There are fine new streets and beautiful parks; and there are also ramshackle dingy quarters, picturesque but insalubrious. There are noisy street-cars which can hardly pass in the narrower thoroughfares and are continually blocking the traffic; and there are likewise pack horses, left unattended in the busiest streets, while their master delivers bread.

The number of beggars has been considerably reduced, say the friends of Primo de Rivera; but I found them plentiful enough. They delighted in the exhibition of their sores; one would display a leg swathed in bandages, another would make the exposed nerves of a stump quiver, a third would revoltingly reveal his ulcers. . . . The women invariably carried an infant in their arms. They were persistent to an incredible degree. Many of them sat on the steps of the churches, for church-goers are expected to be particularly generous. But they caught me at every street corner, and if I sat on a café terrace I was perpetually importuned.

Strictly, perhaps, the vendors of lottery tickets ought not to be called beggars, but I confess that I put them in the same category. How many lottery tickets are sold in Spain I do not know, but the number must be staggering. One sees them everywhere, and they are thrust unceasingly under one's nose. A lottery ticket is left on the café table, and the vendor refuses to take it up.

"Please do not molest me," I plead.

"But think, kind gentleman, of the great fortune which will come to you for a few pesetas."

In Spain the building of castles continues to be a favourite occupation. The poorest beggar builds his castle for himself, and another for you. They have no foundations, but they are so light that they never tumble down. Everybody will tell you tales of emigrants who left Spain penniless, and after a few years in South America returned home fabulously rich.

Nor is it possible to pause in the Madrid streets without a bootblack's offer to shine your shoes being followed by the instant unpacking of his brushes. He is kneeling at your feet and has begun his job before you realise it. One might easily spend a whole day in having one's boots blacked. . . . Francis Carco, who has written an amusing book on Spain, seems to have been unable to linger anywhere without being approached by an old woman with a young girl for sale. Everywhere he encountered winks and leers and crapulous proposals. For my part I missed this side of Spanish life, and I am certain that commercialized vice is less conspicuous (except in the ports) and less organised in Spain than in most continental countries. Perhaps one sees what one goes out to see. . . .

Work is started fairly early in the morning. I hardly know how the bourgeois classes of Madrid contrive to be so alert. Until lunch they labour indefatigably, and the midday relief does not come until 1.30 p.m. It lasts for two hours and during this break offices and shops are shut. Indeed, on entering a restaurant a few minutes before two in the afternoon, I and my companion found ourselves uncomfortably alone—except for an army of idle waiters. There is nothing more disconcerting than to lunch alone in a large restaurant. Happily in a quarter of an hour or so the place began to fill up, and we could talk without hearing the echo of our voices.

Incidentally I had in this restaurant a little lesson in Spanish pride—that peculiar pride which is shared by grandee and beggar. I had paid my bill, on which was marked ten per cent for service, but through force of habit I left an extra two or three pesetas on the plate. I was leaving, but suddenly found the waiter on my heels. He presented me sadly and reproachfully with my tip. Useless to explain that it was for him. He pointed to the bill. He had already been paid. With quiet dignity he made me understand that he did not accept alms. I will not say that all Spanish waiters are like this, but I could not help admiring the characteristic gesture.

Dinner is uncommonly late. In one Spanish house where I dined, the meal did not begin until well after 9.30. The theatres start even later, and the performances may last until one o'clock in the morning. If, as is the custom, one stays to take a cup of chocolate, one is not home before two o'clock. Yet the inhabitants of Madrid are abroad and brisk in the early morning. . . .

Going home by moonlight, the night watchman gives you his greeting. He walks about with his long staff and his dark lantern, a bunch of keys at his girdle. He can produce the identical key which will open your door. He watches over your safety while you are asleep. With his fellows he maintains the immemorial system of signals—lantern-flashing and whistling —which would mobilise the night watchmen of the whole city in case of need.

It is such details as these which persuade me that time has stood still in Spain, despite the introduction of modern inventions. In some respects the King is extremely advanced; he was, for example, a pioneer in automobiles. But he represents, nevertheless, an ancient family and one of the most ancient of institutions; he is, perhaps, the last survivor of Kingship as it was formerly understood. Spain has had its upheavals, but it has never had its revolutions like France. The French Revolution broke up the great estates and made the peasant a proprietor; Spain is still owned by rich land owners who keep their poor labourers almost as serfs on the soil.

Social life in Madrid is dull. This is the verdict that was pronounced by all those whom I was able to consult. But there was one Ambassador—who did not belong to the *carrière* and whose appointment was the result of a personal whim—who certainly enlivened Madrid while he was there. He insisted for himself on the strictest observance of etiquette, and one day when by some accident or misunderstanding a number of people had entered a room before the Ambassador they were asked to troop out again and reënter after him!

It was good to see how he enjoyed his position. An acquaintance of mine was with him in his motor-car when they were saluted by the Royal Guard. The Ambassador beamed: "Just fancy," he cried, "and I used to think that the Mayor of my home town was a big man!"

Of the position of the King, however, he seemed to be ignorant. One day he rang him up, as though kings are expected, like common mortals, to answer telephone calls. He would be content with no intermediary. So insistent was he that the King

MANTILLAS IN SEVILLE

good-humouredly picked up the receiver. These were the words he heard: "Say, I want you to use your pull to get a villa for me at San Sebastian."

My informant asserts—but here I am sure there is exaggeration—that on one occasion the Ambassador boisterously went up behind the King, slapped him on the shoulder and brightly exclaimed: "Hello, Al!"

In the most spacious of the Madrid thoroughfares, with chairs under the trees, I sat to watch the holiday panorama unroll itself. They say that the mantilla is vanishing, but on this sunny day seven out of ten of the girls and women who filed past, laughing in the sunshine, had donned the mantilla. How gracefully they carried these head-dresses of black lace which fell in folds to the hem of their gowns. Since feminine heads are bobbed in Spain as elsewhere, I wondered how it was possible to fix the immense combs from which the mantillas depended. I was informed that it is necessary to build up a structure of smaller combs to hold the gargantuan comb in place. However this may be—and this is a mystery of Spain on which I speak with no authority—the effect was truly elegant. Why, in normal life, do Spanish girls, who are so exquisite in their mantillas, ape the Parisian mode and wear the Parisian cloche hat? How wonderfully, when they are not trying to be in the fashion, do they appreciate the artistic use of black! Generally their robes were black, as their mantillas were black, though they might put a flower in their hair and sometimes wore coloured shawls. As for the capes and cloaks that figure so darkly in romance, there are still men who wear them. I understand that a Society of Lovers of the Cape has been formed, and is flourishing. Its object is to preserve the cape. Let us wish it success!

Thus it was that in the streets of the Spanish cities I looked in vain for signs of revolt. They existed no more than they existed at the opera. The visitor, whether he spends his time in the Real Museo de Pintura del Prado, that splendid gallery of masterpieces by Titian, El Greco, Velasquez, Goya, or in the Puerta del Sol, the Calle de Alcala, and the Plazas with their unceasing rumour of human activities, will fail to find evidences of political perturbations. Nevertheless it is inevitable that Spain, in the process of emerging from the old into the new, will experience a serious crisis.

V. PRIMO DE RIVERA

PRIMO DE RIVERA did not look to me like a Dictator. He is far from being theatrical. He does not affect sternness. He does not play the part of a military martinet, a solemn Cæsar, or a ruthless tyrant. On the contrary, he is gay and kindly in appearance—a bon vivant pretending neither to intellectuality nor force. He is tall, broad-shouldered, plump, rather red in the face, with silver hair and blue eyes. Socially he is regarded as a charming man of the world. There is in him unbounded vitality, but with all his energy he is amiable.

Until the Dictatorship gave him a sense of responsibility he was a notorious gambler. Perhaps in a larger way he is still. But when he was convinced that gambling was a vice which was particularly bad for Spain, he wiped out gambling. A man who has been intimately associated with him for many years told me that one of the closest friends of Primo de Rivera built a skating rink in order to turn it into a surreptitious gambling den—and not very surreptitious at that. He relied upon his highly placed friend to help him, or at least to close his eyes to the enterprise. To his surprise the General was adamant. Once he had decided that gambling had to go, he ceased to gamble himself or to allow his friends to encourage gambling. The proprietor of the skating rink was financially badly hit.

When this genial joyous man makes a decision it is immediately carried out. Bullfighting is not to be suppressed in Spain as is gambling; but when it was pointed out that at least children under the age of fourteen should not be admitted to these cruel spectacles, Primo de Rivera instantly agreed. Again, when it was represented to him that the real victims in the bullfights were the unfortunate horses, he decreed that horses should be given padded armour, so that the worst feature of the Spanish sport is largely obliterated.

The General prides himself on being a practical man. He does not hold himself up as an "intellectual." He does not discuss ideas or cherish ideals. His Dictatorship is necessarily weak because it is inspired by no mortal purpose. . . . But as a materialist he has certain likes and dislikes. First and foremost he regards himself as a patriot; and for the average politician who lacks patriotism, or who exploits patriotism, he has an undisguised contempt. There is in him nothing that is romantic and

PRIMO DE RIVERA

he does not pose as a hero. He is, in a word, an ordinary sort of man with perhaps a spice of recklessness, a little more vitality than the ordinary man. He is the stuff of which good policemen are made. His limitations are obvious but it is just because he is not really different from the man in the street, sharing his prejudices and his predilections, that the man in the street deems him to be either the worst or the best Prime Minister that Spain has had. Primo de Rivera is then a superior gendarme—superior in power, but not in intelligence.

His critics acknowledge that his reign has been relatively good-humoured. He has closed universities, he has exiled professors, he has disbanded recalcitrant army corps, he has imprisoned his adversaries; but he has spilled no blood. It is something to deprive a country of liberty—it may be that nothing graver could be charged against any man than to deprive a country of liberty. Yet the manner must be considered, and the manner of Primo de Rivera compares well with that of other despots. He became Dictator impulsively, continued with bonhomie, and does not want to hurt anybody. He even foresees the fragility of his work; for when he transformed the Chamber of Deputies into the meeting-place of the National Assembly he merely had a new plaque placed over the old inscription that can be taken down at any time without trouble or expense. Théophile Gautier said that Spanish reforms are like a coating of plaster on granite; and Primo de Rivera endorses this opinion.

No doubt the Constitution of 1876, which was liberal enough in theory, promising freedom of meeting and of speech, fell into decay. There was corruption, there was a total absence of political education. Fifty per cent of the citizens were altogether illiterate. The Church and the landlords were the real rulers of the people, and the politicians fought each other simply for office. There was an incompetent bureaucracy. There could be no progress where there was no continuity.

Throughout the Nineteenth Century Spain experienced a number of Dictatorships, and the army backed up the pronunciamientos. But after 1876 the rotative system was in vogue. Before Primo de Rivera, another general bearing his name had rebelled against governmental authority: rebellion is a family tradition. Primo de Rivera himself made little excursions against the government. When, during the war, he was Governor at Cadiz, he made the unauthorised suggestion that Spain should come into the war on condition that England exchanged

Gibraltar for Ceuta. He was recalled; but on another occasion he publicly advised the withdrawal of Spain from Morocco which has brought nothing but trouble on the country. Thus before he made his coup of September 1923 he had shown himself disposed to take his own course.

In 1923 he seized power because it was vacant. If in Catalonia there was anarchy, even in Andalusia there was a violent agrarian movement. Juntas of officers were formed, and without any opposition from the existing Cabinet, Primo de Rivera asked the King to sign a decree appointing a Directory. He dissolved the Cortes, suspended constitutional guarantees, dismissed officials. In three months, he said, he would purify public life. But two years later he abandoned the Military Directory, and composed a Cabinet of civilian Ministers. Nearly six years have passed; and there is no Parliament, no trial by jury, no liberty of the press. Spanish opinion is evolving very slowly from its indifference; it has grown weary of that kind of politics, which José Ortega y Gasset, a great intellectual leader of Spain, whose criticism and philosophy are remarkably penetrating, had described as indefensible and invertebrate.

Invertebrate it may have been, but I look in vain for anything which indicates that Primo de Rivera, cynical, without direction, second-rate in every respect, displaying no true statesmanship, has effected permanent improvements. Unless a greater man arises, there may again be chaos. The Spanish press, fighting with a stupid censorship, does not believe in the so-called reforms of the Dictator. It inserts the official communiqués because it must, and under them it prints the intimation that the publication of these communiqués is obligatory. Overwhelmingly the newspapers are against the man who refuses to them the right to express their views if those views are not in consonance with his.

Censorships are always stupid. During the war I recollect the struggles with the censorship in which I was myself to some extent involved. The classical example of stupid censorship is the blue-pencilling of the quotation from Kipling—"The Captains and the Kings depart"—on the ground that it might convey information to the enemy! In the same way the Spanish censor forbids perfectly harmless statements, and blacks out news that, rightly conveyed, would be favourable to the Dictator.

A foreign correspondent of great experience who has been

friendly to Primo de Rivera, and indeed friendly with Primo de Rivera, told me that when the Cuidad Real revolt of artillery officers had created the impression abroad that Spain was on the verge of revolution, and Primo de Rivera had contributed to the creation of that impression by the issue of statement after statement which could only emphasise the gravity of the revolt, he wrote a straightforward account of the facts, showing that nothing more than platonic protests had been made. Yet the censor stopped this telegram which would have reassured foreign opinion! The result of the censorship is that many irresponsible messages are sent from Spain, for anybody can telephone sensational information across the frontier, uncontrolled by the authorities, and uncontrolled by the sense of duty and of accurate presentation that is possessed by accredited journalists.

Worst of all is the order which calls upon the police to arrest anyone who "slanders" Ministers, or does not take a rosy view of the future of Spain. Clubs and associations which permit political discussions are closed. Registers are compiled in all official departments setting forth the degree of "political discretion" of each employee. Corporations suspected of hostility to the government are dissolved. The Patriotic Union compiles a black list of recalcitrant persons. After all, bonhomie may be compatible with tyranny.

VI. "NO LIKE, NO GOOD"

DEMOCRACY," said to me one of the ablest diplomatists it has been my lot to meet, "appears to have suffered many setbacks. But it is a mistake to suppose that the forward march is definitely checked. The temporary circumstances of to-day are misleading, whether we apply our attention to Spain or more widely to Europe. The whole flow of things is away from autocracy, and we should not be deceived by these phenomena which exist in defiance of the current."

And as I reread in my hotel room, glancing now and again at the midnight procession of penitents with lighted candles through the Easter streets, the observations made in *The Spectator* two hundred years ago by Addison on Dictatorships, I could not but regard them as topical. "Where the prince is a man of wisdom and virtue, it is indeed happy for his people that he is absolute; but since, in the common run of mankind, you will find ten of a contrary character, it is very dangerous for a nation to stand to its chance, or to have its public happiness or misery depend on the virtues or vices of a single person. But this is not all; an honest private man often grows cruel and abandoned when converted into an absolute prince. Give a man the power of doing what he pleases with impunity, and you overturn in him one of the great pillars of morality. . . . It is odd to consider the connection between despotic government and barbarity, and how the making of one person more than man makes the rest less".

Primo de Rivera cannot possibly represent the best elements of Spain, and indeed hundreds of artists, writers, professors, and the intelligentsia generally besides the politicians, have voluntarily gone into exile, while others have been arrested or arbitrarily deported. I have deliberately tried to say everything possible in favour of the Dictator, but I conclude that neither his character nor his ability are such as would persuade any reasonable man to put himself unreservedly in the hands of the General.

Nobody knows precisely what goes on in Spain, for much is done which is never reported. I was sitting after dinner in a Madrid drawing-room. My host glanced nervously at the door. "A veil of silence", he said, "has fallen over the land. The police might make an irruption into a Spanish family, and give any orders—for detention or for deportation; and except for the intimates of the family few people would be informed of what had happened. Were Primo de Rivera a pattern man, it would be monstrous that he should have such power. Even had he regenerated the country, loss of liberty would be a tremendous price to pay. It is not only the intelligentsia who are so treated. The present way of stopping strikes of working men is to send the supposed ring-leaders to towns a hundred miles away. How can they there take fresh roots? How can their family join them? I foresee confusion following the government of Primo de Rivera. True, he does not display the iron fist himself, but his Minister at the Home Office, Martinez Anido, does his bludgeoning for him".

In short, if you are a friend of the Government, you will be well treated. If you are not, you must not expect good treatment. I am reminded of a passage in Stevenson's "South Seas":

"The King, he good man?" I asked.

"Suppose he like you, he good man," replied Te Kop; "no like, no good".

I asked my host as I had asked others about the attitude of the King.

"It is not difficult to understand the position of the King. He has no personal practical experience of government. He has relied on his Ministers. And whenever he opposes the policy of Primo de Rivera, the Dictator threatens to resign. Rightly or wrongly, the King has a sudden vision of political confusion. What would become of his country? What would become of his family—for with his children suffering from an hereditary disease which invalidates them, there is a serious dynastic question, a question of the succession to the throne. He surrendered against the advice of his mother, the late Maria Christina, who stood for the Constitution and was afraid of the consequences of linking the fate of Royalty with the fate of Dictatorship."

Sanchez Guerra, former Prime Minister and a Conservative, lived in Paris. So serious did he consider the outlook that he left his comfortable home, and embarked on a hazardous adventure, hoping to restore the Constitution. The story goes that risings were prepared in twenty garrisons, to coincide with his arrival at Valencia. But his sailing was delayed, and telegrams were sent, in conventional form, advising the chiefs that "Josephine" would be two days late. The Spanish police is vigilant, and Spanish officers are talkative. Orders were given that nineteen telegrams were to be duly delivered, but the twentieth was held back. In consequence nineteen garrisons postponed their rising; and the twentieth, unaware of the postponement, acting prematurely, and in isolation, sprang the plot.

At first the laugh was against Sanchez Guerra. But he managed to place Primo de Rivera in a quandary. The Dictator did not wish to proceed to extremes, but Sanchez Guerra, prisoner on board the Canalejas, insisted on being tried for a capital offence. Were Sanchez Guerra acquitted, a blow would be struck against the prestige of Primo de Rivera. But conviction would be equally unpleasant for the Dictator who is afraid of drastic measures. Why would Guerra not say that he visited Spain for his health or entertainment? In that case he would be released. But no! he obstinately posed as the leader of the Opposition, well knowing that he was in no peril, well knowing that he placed Primo de Rivera in a dilemma. Cheap heroics but not without political value!

The dilemma of the Dictator increased daily. He did not know how to deal with the Opposition. If he gave it freedom he was doomed. If he repressed it he emphasised the one-man character of the government and widened the gulf between himself and the people. That gulf is indeed great. No wonder that sometimes Primo de Rivera wished himself well out of the Dictatorship.

But it is perhaps harder to escape from a Dictatorship than to institute a Dictatorship. As a result of his policy of supressing criticism, which is necessary and healthy in any community, Rivera got out of touch with public opinion. He was vaguely aware of his own unpopularity. How was he to let go? How was he to effect the transition from Dictatorship to Constitutionalism? He was frankly puzzled, and saw no alternative but to hang on. In the meantime he alienated himself from the confidence of the people, and relied more and more on coercion.

Prophecy is always rash, but it is clear that by violent or by peaceful methods the end of this experiment must soon come. It is to be hoped that Spain will not simply revert to the former régime which was marked by incompetence, impotence, and corruption. Spain has played a very minor part in European affairs, because it has not advanced as other nations have advanced. A new opportunity is coming to it, and it is to be trusted that it will avail itself of the period of change to develop a sounder civic sense. There are problems of an international order that Spain can help to solve, and it is time the peninsula emerged from its humiliating situation of neutrality. Spain has had a remarkable past. It has sunk into decadence. But it may well revive and have a useful if not a glorious future.

Above all, the chief political impression that I brought from Spain was that it is probably on this front that a breach will be made in the fortifications of the new autocracy that many people have seized the opportunity of postwar difficulties and uncertainties to build. Autocracy has reinforced its positions, and is rejoicing in the apparent defeat of Democracy. But the reaction from reaction has begun. It would be somehow fitting that Spain, one of the least progressive of European countries, should arouse itself and show the way to a fuller Democracy.

In any case the next few years will be exceedingly critical for Spain. It deserves our special attention, for it may indicate which way the world is going. Let us trust that Spain will march proudly in the ranks of modern nations.

VII. "DU SANG, DE LA VOLUPTÉ, DE LA MORT"

OF THE life of Spain the traveller who goes from San Sebastian to Barcelona, from Salamanca to Valencia (by the way, there is great pride in Spain at the popularity of the song "Valencia," by José Padilla—one man informing me enthusiastically that such a success had not been known for a century!) from Corunna to Granada and Seville—who sees Burgos and Valladolid, Zamora and Avila, and the grave of Torquemada, Segovia and Madrid and the Escorial, Toledo, Cordova, and Cadiz, and the rest of the cities of Spain, about which Edward Hutton has written the most delightful of books, will have many memories; but the chances are that if you ask him to name the spectacles which impressed him most he will answers: "Bullfights, processions, and the Cuadro Flamenco".

And the traveller is doubtless right. He cannot be expected to enter more deeply into the veritable life of Spain; while visions of beauty are fugitive and incommunicable. But the things that are communicable, and that remain, have in them something distressing. Maurice Barrès has expressed it in the title of his book "Du Sang, de la Volupté, de la Mort". There is blood and death and a strange voluptuousness in the most characteristic spectacles of Spain.

There is nothing truly joyous—not even the dancing. Melancholy and passionate energy alternate. The matador is a hero in his shining dress, but he awakens emotions that are at once primitive and jaded. The Spaniard, elemental as he is, has grown weary; his sensibilities must be violently pricked. In the religious processions too there is sadism. The romantic Spain, of pearl-like patios, with lovers twanging guitars in the moonlight, veritably exists, but it is steeped in dejection. Azorin— whose real name is Martinez Ruiz—has properly protested against the "picturesque" Spain shown to travellers: "If the traveller returned without having seen the conventional Spain of the guide-books, he would astonish his family." . . .

Hundreds of pens have described the bullfights. Some of them have been competent; but for the most part they have been, I suspect, incompetent. For to the foreigner the bullfight is, except in its broader aspect, incomprehensible. Imagine a man who has never before seen a game of Rugby football, or a

game of baseball, trying to set down a record of the hopeless
puzzle that these games present to the uninitiated. The very
points which appeal to the instructed must appear crazy to the
uninstructed. Unless one is by long residence in Spain almost
a Spaniard, it is well not to attempt to praise or to criticise the
bullfight.

For myself I confess that the Corrida de Toros has always
seemed a noisy, dusty, disgusting thing. Apart from its cruelty,
it is monotonous—that is to those who do not appreciate the
finer points of the game. Just as baseball might appear to be a
perpetual repetition of the same movements, so does bullfighting appear to be without variation. There is fierce drama, but
its elements do not change. One knows what the end will be.
One knows the precise stages that will lead to the end. Of course
accidents are possible, but they are rare, and I do not suppose
anybody goes to a bullfight in the hope or expectation of seeing
a toreador killed. No, it is the bull which must die: that is
decided in advance, and therefore there is no suspended interest.
He must be tired by the picadors and enraged by the banderilleros, and when he is sufficiently weakened there will be a few
passes and a dexterous sword thrust by the matador. The bull
is given no chance to save himself. It is all one whether he
shows fiery courage and skill or is a poltroon who merely wishes
to escape from the ring. In no circumstances is his life spared.
Thus although the details differ, there is no essential difference
between one bullfight and another. I have heard of people who
attend a successful musical comedy as many as twenty times;
but I cannot understand their mentality; once is usually more
than enough for me. I suppose they observe trifling modifications in the voice and gestures of the principal actors, just as
the bullfight aficionado observes trifling modifications in the
behaviour of the bull or his human antagonist. Yet to me, to
be condemned to witness a bullfight every week would be a
deadlier sentence than to be condemned to witness "Rose-
Marie" in a hundred performances.

While I am prepared to admit then that the Spaniard sees a
good deal that I have failed to see in the Fiesta, do not look
in these pages for a pastiche of Blasco Ibáñez. The torture that
is inflicted on the bull with spikes and darts is sickening; and
is not redeemed by the excitement of the combat. Worse still
is the terror of the horses that are forced to face the horns of
the angry bull. They are disemboweled and trample on their

THE ARENA

own entrails. The unspeakable horror of it all! It is true that
the new regulations for the protection of the horses are designed
to spare us such sights, but at the best bullfighting is a bloody
business.

About fourteen thousand people can enter the great amphi-
theatre at Seville. There is colour galore—the blue sky, the
golden sand, the variegated shawls, the white mantillas. The
onlookers are of all classes and they have come to delight in
the spilling of blood. The gorgeous procession, the time honoured ceremonies, prepare the way for the entrance of the bull
and his mad rushes at horses and riders. Then it is the turn of
the banderilleros, and finally the golden figure of the matador
flashes before the bull. With his muleta concealing his sword,
he cleverly avoids the murderous horns until the moment comes
to despatch the bleeding beast. . . .

Apparently however it is useless to try to suppress bullfighting in Spain. Reformers are nearly always unconsciously amusing, but particularly so when they are foreigners who come
from far-off lands to persuade a nation that they have been
doing wrong for centuries. I remember two estimable old ladies
who called on me; they had come, I think, from Ohio, in order
to convince the Spanish that they should give up bullfighting.
They were eager and sincere, and even managed to believe that
they had made some progress. They had, they told me, spoken
to quite influential persons, who were in sympathy with their
mission—in other words, who had treated them with politeness.

Thus if I state that the bullfight does not appeal to me, that
I find it brutal and beastly, it must not be supposed that I would
begin a new crusade. *Chacun son goût!* But it is good to note
that the wiser reformers are endeavouring, not to fight against
the bullfight, but to eliminate useless cruelties that give pleasure
to nobody.

Especially has the use of the petos, the padded coat for horses,
largely removed one of the worst features of the bull ring. I
understand that now one instead of six is the average mortality
of the mounts in a corrida. Yet the fright of the defenceless
horses is pitiful. They are so terrified of the bull that they can
seldom be induced to enter the arena more than three times.
Beating is ineffective. It is lamentable to think of the terror of
the poor beasts.

The Times correspondent in Madrid, Mr. de Caux, recently
told a capital story of a brave horse, Medallita. He seemed to

be fearless. Brought to the Tetuan Ring by gypsies, he was neglected for some time by the picadors, for he was old and blind in one eye, and generally ill-favoured. "Finally," says Mr. de Caux, "a picador rode Medallita out and at the first charge horse and rider were heavily thrown by a furious and powerful bull. Most horses thus treated lie stunned until thrashed to their feet by the long canes of the red-sashed *monosabios* (attendants). Medallita struggled up alone and when mounted again faced the bull quietly. This he did time and again, and at the end of the season he held the stupendous record of having been ridden against 38 bulls. No fewer than 70 pike-strokes were delivered from his back. Though terribly punished by falls and six times seriously wounded by the bulls, Medallita never once baulked or showed fear. He became the favourite mount of the *picadores* and when not in hospital was always in the ring. Last autumn the secretary of the Federación Ibérica de Sociedades Protectoras visited the Tetuan stable-master, El Cartagena (in common with gypsies, most men in the ring use nicknames) and offered to buy the horse. El Cartagena listened in silence to the request and then said: 'No, I will not sell him to you. I cannot sell such a brave animal. I will give him to you.'

"When they came to fetch Medallita to take him to a princely estate he was out doing an odd day's work ploughing. 'Look', said the ploughman; 'see how willing he is', and he showed, quite unconcernedly, how the *serreta* (cavesson iron) had bitten half an inch deep into Medallita's nose. His last wound, let us hope."

Although the young men of Spain are to some extent turning to other amusements, football, motoring, and other sports, the crowds which collect round the arena, sitting on the sunny or on the shady side, do not noticeably diminish, and pictures of the famous bullfighters cut from the pages of the journals which devote themselves to this entertainment, decorate the walls of thousands of Spanish homes. The visitor who comes to Spain may fulminate against the exhibitions, but almost invariably he asks at his hotel for the date of the next bullfight.

There are exceptions and an English friend of mine who has lived in Spain for twenty years, occupying important official posts, told me that he has never yet seen a bullfight—and does not intend to see one.

Both French and American authors—notably Henry de

A Nocturnal Procession in Easter Week

Montherlant and Ernest Hemingway—have recently been fascinated by this national entertainment.

*   *   *

The processions through the Spanish streets are gorgeous; they indicate the strong hold that religion still has upon the people. There is indeed in Spanish devotion a strain of what we should call superstition. I have seen poor peasant girls with incredible quantities of medals, scapularies, rosaries, holy images, hanging round their necks; in them they place their strange faith. There are pictorial representations of the Virgin Mary everywhere, and statuettes and crosses. . . . Probably no house of ill-resort is complete without its religious ornaments.

On Good Friday the old cabman suddenly stopped, took off his hat, and made genuflexions. "What is the matter?" we asked. He turned upon us a startled face. "Do you not know", he said solemnly, "that our Lord is dead?"

Into the churches the people were filing, and the policemen were hard put to it to keep order and to clear a passage. Everybody was dressed in black. And then, later in the day, the crowd in its Sunday clothes, held back by soldiers on foot and on horseback, contemplated with a sort of ecstasy the cortege of which the central figure was Christ on the Cross—a realistic piece of work carried on a long platform by a score of porters whose feet moved rhythmically under the long drapery of the platform. It was lit up by candles in silver candelabras. The sight was at once sumptuous and macabre. Agony was depicted in the lineaments and limbs; and it is on the agony of the drama that priests and people lay stress. Even the resplendent figures of the Virgin, carried aloft in golden mantle, brood sadly over the sorrows of the world. The Spanish have a strange and morbid love of horror. . . .

The newspapers, which reproduce the most celebrated pictures of the Crucifixion, choose those which insist most on the crown of thorns, on the wounding nails, on the deadly spear; nothing that can add to the impression of human suffering is omitted.

*   *   *

In the cafés-concerts, the Spanish dancing, in its utmost frenzy, seems to express not the joy, but the painful, almost unbearable sensuality of life. The sound of the guitar is pathetic. The beating of time with hands and feet, the noise of the castanets, the swaying of body, arms, and head, the trepidation of the whole scene, are convulsive in their effect.

"I am going to take a real Cuardo Flamenco to Paris, and then on a tour round the world," said an impresario to me. "Outside Spain there is no genuine unsophisticated Spanish performance. Here is extraordinary talent, among dancers and singers and guitarists; but abroad Spanish spectacles are prepared to the supposed taste of foreign audiences. If X. (a Spanish singer and dancer who is known in two continents) came back to Spain she would be laughed at. Yet it was in one of these cafés that she started on her career. Perhaps Spanish art is like certain wines which cannot be transported. But I will try".

I take this verdict for what it is worth. Certainly there is much sophistication; but Raquel Meller has not lost her Spanish character; and the wonderful Argentina, the most bewitching dancer of our day, who holds us enthralled, may have developed the Spanish dance to an expressiveness undreamed of in Spain—but Spanish it remains, Spanish in the nth degree.

*   *   *

In any case, there is for me a dark thread, hectic and morbid, which connects these three manifestations of the Spanish temperament—bullfighting, religious display, and café-concert gloom in gaiety.

VIII. MIGUEL DE UNAMUNO

IT IS this sentiment of tragedy in the life of man that forms the theme of the chief work of Miguel de Unamuno, one of the most interesting of living Spaniards. It was my good fortune to meet him on several occasions. He was in exile. He was obviously suffering from his exclusion from his native land. Yet, as he spoke in his quaint French, he seemed deliberately to seek to mingle the comic and the tragic in his speech. He is a learned don who has nothing of the professorial manner. Even in repose his countenance is ravaged. His eyes are grave behind his glasses. His black and white beard emphasises his somewhat heavy appearance. But when he speaks in staccato sentences, and gesticulates fiercely, he betrays a passionate intensity that is startling.

His philosophy is emotional. Imagination is for him more

than reason. "Reason," he says, paradoxically, "man shares with the animals. But only man is touched by poetry."

He advises us therefore to live in a continual whirl of passion and to be dominated by a passion, for only the passionate produce durable and fecund work. And as an example of the passionate man he takes Don Quixote. "Don Quixote has left us himself; and a living and eternal man is worth all the theories and all the philosophies. . . . He is a man of flesh and blood, who was born, who suffered, and who died."

That Miguel de Unamuno is a man on the pattern of Don Quixote himself there is no doubt: though, for that matter, all Spaniards are, in some degree, either Don Quixote or Sancho Panza. He was sixty years of age when he was driven out of Salamanca, where he had been teaching for thirty-two years. One day he wrote a letter criticising the Dictatorship. It was published in a newspaper at Buenos Aires. Quickly it found its way back to Spain.

A few days later, Unamuno, walking through the streets of Salamanca, saw a little group of townsfolk reading a poster. "What is it?" he asked. And a working-man, respectfully doffing his cap, replied: "Don Miguel, we read that you have twenty-four hours to prepare yourself for exile."

"Indeed," said Unamuno humorously, "then I must hurry home to pack my bags."

Nevertheless he went, after his stroll, to the University and conducted his class. There were present all his pupils, and the professors of the University. Unamuno calmly began to expound a Greek text which denounced the exercise of tyranny. . . .

The Salamancans turned out in force to witness his departure for the little island of Fuerte Ventura, for he was known and esteemed by them. They had listened to his discourses under an oak tree in the Salamancan fields; and they were sorrowful at his leaving.

The greatest blot on the Dictatorship of Primo de Rivera is, in my opinion, this deportation of Unamuno. World opinion was stirred, and a French editor decided to rescue him from his island-prison at all costs. Henry Dumay, the founder of the French Radical organ, the Quotidien, has since fallen into disgrace. It may be that there was a good deal to criticise in his management of the newspaper. But Dumay is certainly not lacking in ardour. It was a bold thing to establish the Quotidien.

It was a bold thing to fight the forces which always oppose an independent journal. Dumay succumbed in the end to attacks which, whether just or unjust, we need not determine. But before he succumbed he performed a memorable exploit which links his name to that of Unamuno.

He chartered a small vessel, and sailed in the teeth of bad weather for the Canary Islands. By various ruses, the guardians of Unamuno were outwitted and Don Miguel was able to take refuge on board the Dumay vessel.

When after a perilous voyage he arrived in Paris and was asked for his impressions Unamuno said: "The months that I have spent in splendid isolation have enriched me immensely. Now I go towards a new life."

Perhaps the most characteristic expression of Unamuno is this: "My mission is to shatter the faith of official Catholics, of Free-thinkers, and even of a neutral sect—to shatter faith in affirmation, faith in negation, and faith in abstention; to combat those who resign themselves to Catholicism, to Rationalism, or to Agnosticism; it is to make all who live restless in an unending search." He has no use for stereotyped creeds of any kind. Life is above creeds: it is to be lived. The journey is more than the goal, and to seek is better than to find.

His speech is a torrent which carries in its rapid course a multitude of things. They may be bad or good, but they come pell-mell from the very soul of this impetuous Spaniard. He does not talk for the sake of making well-bred conversation. He declines to be impersonal or trivial. He talks to utter his profound sentiments. For him everything, politics, philosophy, poetry, becomes a personal experience and a personal problem. He is concerned with himself as a man and not with a system. Doctrines are of no importance except in so far as they start wheels working inside Unamuno. In his poems, in his essays, in his stories, there is this exalted egotism that represents at its highest the Spanish temperament.

IX. VICENTE BLASCO IBÁÑEZ

VICENTE BLASCO IBÁÑEZ is more than a Spanish author; he belongs to the world. In France he was a familiar figure; I had opportunities of seeing him in Paris; and his last days were spent in the Villa Fontana Rosa at Mentone. Aston-

VICENTE BLASCO IBÁÑEZ

MIGUEL DE UNAMUNO

ishing success came to him; his novels were read in every country; and after suffering a long period of poverty, immense sums of money poured upon him. There is no romance that he has written, thrilling as many of them are, richly coloured, too richly coloured, as they are, which equals his own life.

If there is a new interest to-day in Spain, it is largely because of Blasco Ibáñez.

Yet the greater part of his existence was spent outside Spain. In many respects he was a truly representative Spaniard; audacious, extravagant, energetic. Regarding himself as a man of action, he yet wrote enormously, but he refused to rank himself among professional writers. In a letter which has often been quoted, he confessed his pride in being as little of the *littérateur* as possible: "I am a man who lives, and who, when he has the time, writes under an imperious necessity. I am thus pursuing the Spanish tradition, noble and virile."

He frankly rejoiced in his aureole of glory, and had almost a childish pleasure in magnificence. But it is to be doubted whether he cared for literary fame as such. A true force of nature, it was probably a matter of indifference to him how he expressed himself. After he had won everything that a man could wish, he threw himself with amazing vigour into the fight against the Dictatorship and against the Monarchy in Spain. I remember one small gathering to which he consented to come to expound his views—a gathering that was particularly humble, and could not reasonably be expected to advance the cause which he took up with such overwhelming enthusiasm. But what matter? He could express himself fierily. . . .

His contacts with Spain had worn very thin, and he might well have disregarded politics. He threw himself into the fight, after long absence, as a virtual stranger. Many people, in my opinion rightly, regard his polemical pamphlet against King Alphonso as a blunder; it is packed with errors. But again no matter; it was not the quiet enjoyment of his wealth that he wanted; his literary achievements did not satisfy him; it was action for which his robust temperament called. So he denounced the reign of Alphonso as impotent and destructive, and declared that he would not rest until it was destroyed. He compared his country to a lady of mediæval romance, imprisoned in a dark tower; every man owed it to the spirit of human freedom to attempt to liberate her.

"Between the King and me it is a fight to the death; I will get him, or he will get me." Thus he spoke.

Born at Valencia of bourgeois parents, he was sent to the university of the town, but he provoked his fellow students to rebellion and after tumultuous days fled to Madrid. There he became the secretary of the popular novelist Manuel Fernando y Gonzalez. But he was on the revolutionary side in politics, and was soon arrested. Back in Valencia, he divided his labours between literature and politics. He was sent to prison, but he came out impenitent, and he participated in a number of plots which failed. He took refuge in Paris, returning to Spain some years later in virtue of an amnesty. For ten years he worked as a journalist on El Pueblo. Every night he spent in a newspaper office, writing indefatigably, and putting the paper "to bed."

Besides his current duties, which were heavy enough, he wrote in this period the stories of life in Valencia on which his reputation was founded.

During the Cuban war he was openly for the independence of Cuba. Orders were given to apprehend him but he managed to hide in a fishing boat which landed him in Italy. After the Cuban defeat he returned to Spain: he was sentenced to four years' imprisonment but was released in 1898 on condition that he should reside in Madrid and present himself regularly to the police.

At the elections he was candidate. In Spain, as in various Continental countries, there is one advantage in being deputy— it is that a deputy enjoys immunity from arrest. Unfortunately this privilege, which was highly esteemed in the nineteenth century, when it made possible the fight for freedom, is not jealously guarded by European Parliaments to-day. It used to be extremely difficult to persuade Parliaments to suspend the immunity, but now the Chambers are only too ready, at the request of their Governments, to deliver up their colleagues to justice. This is true even of such countries as France. Moreover, the safeguard is practically abolished, in that the Governments, when they have a weak case, simply wait until Parliament is in vacation. When the Chambers are not sitting, the deputies are not "covered," and although there was a tacit understanding that nevertheless no action should be taken without the consent of Parliament, that understanding is now habitually broken. In this, as in some other respects, Democracy has suffered a setback since the war. But Blasco Ibáñez, elected deputy, enjoyed comparative safety for eight years, and he travelled extensively in Europe.

During these years he wrote some of his best known novels, no longer local in character but national. Yet he was still poor. Across the seas were the young flourishing countries of South America. He decided to tempt his fortune there and he succeeded. In Argentina, in Paraguay, in Chili, his inflammatory addresses were applauded by delirious audiences. High prices were paid for his lectures. But this was not enough. In Patagonia he became a pioneer, raising crops, breeding cattle, and building a town which he called Cervantes. It was a rude, dangerous life, and on more than one occasion the workers attacked Blasco. Alone he faced them, rifle in hand. He harangued them; he excused himself because he could not make gestures —otherwise the rifle would go off! His eloquence was convincing. . . . He founded a second colony, and amassed a considerable fortune. The new Conquistador prospered, but suddenly Argentina was shaken by a financial crisis, and he was compelled to sell out.

When the war began he was in Paris. With his usual energy, discontent with the neutrality of Spain, he flung himself into the service of France, writing week by week a history of the war, writing hundreds of articles for the Spanish and American newspapers, writing above all "The Four Horsemen of the Apocalypse." Few books of our time have had a more remarkable sale. Many hundreds of thousands of copies were printed and it is certain that if Spain remained outside the war, a Spaniard helped to determine the movement which brought America into the war.

His tour of the United States in 1919 was a triumphal procession. Two years later he visited Spain. Then came Primo de Rivera; and the novelist's protestation was so violent that once more, in spite of his fame, he was obliged to fly to France. It is curious that a Radical Minister, M. Herriot, consented, at the demand of the Spanish authorities, to start proceedings in France against Blasco Ibáñez for lèse-majesté—a crime committed on French soil against a foreign monarch. These proceedings did not actually reach the courts; they were ridiculed and eventually abandoned.

In his splendid villa, overlooking the blue Mediterranean, he lived until the end, framing bigger and bigger projects. For him the men of the Mediterranean were the salt of the earth. His lyrical passages on the Mediterranean in his novel "Mare Nostrum," state so well the old quarrel of the North and the South that I will quote them here: "The entire history of European man—forty centuries of wars, emigrations, and racial impacts—was due to the desire of possessing this harmoniously framed sea, of enjoying the transparency of its atmosphere and the vivacity of its life.

"The men from the North who needed the burning log and alcoholic drink in order to defend their life from the clutches of the cold were always thinking of these Mediterranean shores. All their warlike or pacific movements were with intent to descend from the coasts of the glacial seas to the beaches of the warm *mare nostrum*. They were eager to gain possession of the country where the sacred olive alternates its stiff old age with the joyous vineyard; where the pine rears its cupola and the cypress erects its minaret. They longed to dream under the perfumed snow of the interminable orange groves; to be masters of the sheltered valleys where the myrtle and the jasmine spice the salty air; where the aloe and the cactus grow between the stones of extinct volcanoes; where the mountains of marble extend their white veins down even into the depths of the sea.

"The South replied to the invasion from the North with defensive wars that extended even into the centre of Europe. And thus history has gone on repeating itself with the same flux and reflux of human waves.

"The Mediterranean peoples were the aristocracy of humanity. Its potent climate tempered man as in no other part of the planet, giving him a dry and resilient power. Tanned and bronzed by the profound absorption of the sun and the energy of its atmosphere, its navigators were transmuted into pure metal.

"Every type of human figure has sprung from the Mediterranean races—fine, sharp as flint, doing good and evil on a large scale with the exaggeration of an ardent character that discounts half-way measures and leaps from duplicity to the greatest extremes of generosity. Ulysses was the father of them all, a discreet and prudent hero, yet at the same time complex and malicious."

X. GOMEZ DE LA CERNA

AMONG the younger men Ramon Gomez de la Cerna certainly knows how to attract attention to himself. One day
in Paris a number of friends were convoked to meet him at a
banquet. It was agreed that there should be the briefest possible
speeches—of not more than two minutes each. But Ramon de
la Cerna turned up with a huge black satchel under his arm.
When he sat down he placed the satchel before him on the
table.

The organiser told me of his anxiety: "Everybody had been
informed that it was a purely social affair with opportunities
for conversation. The idea was to make the acquaintance of
Gomez, not to indulge in mutual laudations. And there, before
Gomez, was that wretched satchel, obviously bulging with
papers. I regarded it with dismay. It fascinated me throughout
the meal. I could eat nothing in my rueful contemplation of
the abominable satchel."

The chairman uttered a few words of welcome. Gomez rose,
took up the satchel, began to open it. There was nothing for
the diners to do but to bear with this Spanish guest who had
failed to appreciate the object of the gathering. They thought
with dismay of the possibilities of Spanish prolixity as Gomez
fumbled in the satchel. . . .

"I have considered the best reply I could make to your kind
welcome," he began, "and as there are present Englishmen and
Americans, besides Frenchmen, here it is!"

And he snatched out of the satchel an ingenious apparatus
such as, I suppose, conjurors use, unfolded it, shook it, waved
it, and lo! floating above the table were the flags of the United
States, England, France, and Spain.

On another occasion when his book on the Circus had been
published in French he came to Paris and by arrangement rode
into the ring of the largest circus in town seated on the head
of a gorgeously caparisoned elephant. The band played its
liveliest tunes, and amid the clash and blare of brass instruments, Gomez conducted his elephant round and round the
ring. He produced a long scroll of paper and proceeded to read
from it, and, as he read, it streamed behind him, lengthening
with every lap.

But these eccentricities are as much designed to amuse their author as to entertain the public. In his writings there is something of this quality—a perpetual surprise, the crash of cymbals. He is explosive. He is what Ortega y Gasset has called an Adamite—that is to say, like many of the most typical Spanish writers, he tries to write as though no one had ever written before him. He is the first that ever burst into that silent sea.

Jean Cassou, with Valery Larbaud the finest interpreter of Spanish literature in France (I first met him at a banquet to celebrate the award of the Legion of Honour to Larbaud) has described the Saturday evenings at Madrid over which Gomez presides. "Ramon has chosen one of the oldest cafés of Madrid for his exploits. To it he has devoted two books, each of them as big as The Bible, and in them he chants on every tone this refuge of idleness, this temple of friendship and of gossip. In a corner of the Pombo café, Ramon, in the night of Saturday, officiates; there he unites, for the joy of his friends, but especially for his own diversion, all that he can find of fools, of failures, of maniacs, of versifiers, of originals,—a vari-coloured menagerie, a burlesque court—and there he gives galas that are unique. The cries, the laughter, and the triumph of Ramon in that nocturnal fair, already convey an idea of the accent of his books, their mirthfulness and their diversity. I would add that the visage of Ramon (framed in side whiskers) offers, when illuminated, an evident resemblance to one of the most joyous artists of our time: the smile of Ramon resembles the smile of Douglas Fairbanks."

Certainly when I was in Madrid Gomez was ubiquitous. His books are conspicuous in the shop windows, and I could not buy a Spanish newspaper or magazine without finding a contribution signed by Ramon Gomez de la Cerna. As for his subjects, they are infinite and his fantasy is inexhaustible. . . .

XI. SALVADOR DE MADARIAGA

SALVADOR DE MADARIAGA is a Spanish writer whom I am happy to have met—a critic, essayist, poet and novelist. He lived in Paris and later in England where he is, I believe, a professor at Oxford. For some years he held an important official position in the League of Nations at Geneva. With a remarkably quick intelligence and a perfect knowledge of European languages he has penetrated the spirit of each nation, and is, in my opinion, one of the best interpreters not only of

Spain but of France and England. Spain has given birth to
many international men—of keen sensibility, of insatiable
curiosity, of marvellous adaptability—and an excellent representative of this type of citizen of the world is Salvador de
Madariaga.

On one accidental meeting—we were both of us wandering
about Europe—we discussed the outlook ten years after the
war; and I found in this sharp-faced eager man an uncommon
mixture of critical judgment and enthusiastic idealism. His
desires do not blind him to the realities; but his sense of the
realities does not dampen his desires.

How clearly he saw that a new spirit is needed in world
affairs! He believed that the League of Nations, not because it
is sacrosanct, not because it is perfect, but because it does
supply a centre around which our aspirations can cluster, and
does provide machinery to coördinate our efforts, is the hope of
the world.

Common sense is the foundation on which this distinguished
Spanish professor would build the League—not on some vague
new religion in which the saints would be the officials of
Geneva. He would not, like so many of the amiable ladies who
visit Switzerland at regular intervals, erect a cathedral with
niches in which should stand effigies of M. Briand, Señor
Quiñones de Léon, Sir Eric Drummond, Lord Cecil, Sir Austen
Chamberlain, M. Bénès, and the rest of the saintly figures in
the new hagiology. I for one refuse to accept these men as
prophets, priests, and apostles; and they will certainly wear no
martyr's crown.

The League is not a body designed to give periodic thrills to
politicians, social workers, busybody ladies, and the rest of
the strange self-satisfied motley throng that one finds at
Geneva. Much of its perfervid and obviously unreal oratory
may become positively dangerous; its operations should be
followed with a critical eye, and ill-regulated sentiment, vague
ideology, and amateurish diplomacy, should not be allowed to
meddle with delicate matters which demand the most careful
handling.

Let us consider the League, says Madariaga, not as a religion,
not as a wonderful institution in which ecstatic idlers can find
fresh emotions, but as a well-conceived organisation to be used
soberly and sensibly to promote world coöperation and to
assure peace.

Reason is the basis of the League, not sentiment. That is what the Spaniard plainly enunciates. And although many people have criticised Spain for its neutrality in the war, it is possible that Spain chose the better part, and that neutrality was the first step towards a higher conception of international relations. But Spaniards have seen that mere abstention is not enough. Some positive action is needed. And it is not without significance that Spaniards have been particularly conspicuous and helpful in the practical work of the League.

In his recently published book "Disarmament," Salvador de Madariaga expresses admirably this view. "Our work," he says, "is not negative and destructive; it is positive and creative. We do not want to destroy war. We want to create peace.

"For peace is no negative state which turns up through the mere absence of war. Peace is not going to come about by mere bleating. The work of peace is hard work, the hardest work of all. For we shall not obtain a state of peace unless we keep in check the herd of wild beasts which we harbour in our individual and natural heart—the tiger of which Mr. Baldwin spoke with his unusual candour, yea, the tiger and the dog as well, and the swine also, not to forget the donkey—all the zoo which is in us must be kept rigorously in leash every day and everywhere. Like the price of liberty, the price of peace is eternal vigilance, but also eternal activity.

"A hard work for every day. The world is not going to conquer peace and then sleep on its laurels and roses; for the instincts of war are ever alive and so the reasons of peace must be ever awatch. A point which peace-bleaters usually forget, for they see peace as a rest between men, while peace is the organisation of men for the fight against the evils of war by coöperative means. No institutions, no coöperation; no coöperation, no peace.

"Nor is it possible to rely on fear of war, for fear never stopped man at the gates of folly. And, moreover, the folly of war usually begins with exhilaration, just as the delirium tremens of the drunkard is born in the delights of the first frothy cups. Easier, ten times easier to drift into war than to defend peace against the ever-recurring attacks of the war disease. The world must know that if it wants peace, it must work hard for it."

It is on that excellent note that I would leave Spain. Something was perhaps learned in neutrality; while Spain sat back, watching the folly of mankind, curiously immune from the fearful infection which enfevered the rest of mankind, it witnessed, as none of us who were in the thick of the strife witnessed, the dreadful folly of it all. We were absurdly killing each other; while Spain watched from some corner of Sirius. The ghastly unreason of war impressed the best thinkers of Spain; and they determined to devote their energies to a more permanent construction of peace. Of such is Salvador de Madariaga, and his example proves that Spain is not effete, after all; that his country, or at least his countrymen, have yet a high rôle to fulfil on the European stage—a rôle which is nobler than that of mighty monarchs, like Philip II, whom men have hitherto admired more for their material power than for their moral purpose.

PART III
ITALY

I. PERSONAL MEMORIES

IT IS personal experiences which determines in large part our attitude towards nations; and sometimes the decisive experience is trivial. Thus a score of my friends have told me with indignation that they have been disgracefully treated when travelling in the Italian trains; they have actually been requested, somewhat brutally, according to their account, to remove their feet from the cushions of the carriage! One of them, who was particularly obstinate, was escorted to the police station. . . .

From this it will be judged that my friends, almost without exception, esteem highly the privilege of putting their feet on railway carriage cushions. They are annoyed with the nation that interferes with this elementary liberty. They immediately rush to unfavourable conclusions when they learn that the foreigner as well as the native is expected to keep his feet on the floor. Fascism for them is the Barbarian invasion of Rome.

I do not know how to explain the fact that this particular grievance against Italy has been repeated to me so often. Perhaps there is a fashion in grievances, as in hats. Perhaps there has been some world-wide conspiracy to take these railway regulations as a symbol of Fascist tyranny.

On the other hand, sympathisers with Fascism have assured me, over and over again, that as a result of the Mussolini régime the Italian trains run according to time-table. For them that is the miraculous performance of the Dictator; the outstanding consequence of the abolition of the former political groups is that you need not be late for your appointments.

It may be that both adversaries and advocates of Fascism are right. It may be that one should always judge by little things. The Italian train service is symbolical. Those who stand for freedom deplore the new Italy with its objection to muddy boots. Those who stand for efficiency rejoice in the possibility of arriving at their destination at a given hour.

For myself, I find my love of Italy considerably influenced by a number of insignificant incidents. At least they are insignificant from the public point of view. But what they mean to me! Do you remember, my dear W., my dear Y., that delightful journey in a one-horse carriage up the steep, rich hillside; and how you leaped out and leaped into the carriage in sheer lightness of heart? I remember, and foolish as it may be, the memory of that perfect Italian day touches me, so many years later, to tears. The beautiful blue sky, the beautiful springtime green of the hillside, the beautiful reddish valley, and the beautiful deserted village hanging in ruins far above the valley—precisely what there is in this picture to affect me so deeply it would be hard to say. But, of course, you were there, my old friends, with your beauty and your youth, and in this particular Italian landscape, no better and no worse than many other Italian landscapes, brightened by your presence, I felt more profoundly than I had ever felt before the inexpressible beauty of things. While you were gambolling I was silent and still; for I was afraid lest my slightest motion should break the spell. . . .

Many are the memories which Italy stirs; it is for most of us the most personal of lands. I could write of the rude inscriptions of lovers on the crumbling stones of a venerable church; of the house amid the crooked streets where the warmest hospitality alternated with the fiercest fights; of the wise girl in the railway buffet who . . . But that is a story which may be told.

She spoke to us in English, as she could speak to German travellers in German, Czechs in Czech, French in French; and my companion struck up a sudden friendship with her. (We were both alas! many years younger than we are now!) We ate the macaroni of the railway buffet day after day; day after day she told us of her life, her thoughts, her hopes; sincerely enough, but always with an unnecessary touch of melodrama. She would steal behind my companion's chair, and whisper; she would glide away as though afraid of detection. Of this commonplace passing acquaintance she wanted to make a romantic intrigue, mysterious, dangerous, thrilling. She would slip little innocent notes under my companion's plate; notes thanking him for the flowers he had brought, or excusing herself for having been called away on the previous day. My companion, entering into the spirit of the play, which would doubtless provide pleasure in the retrospect as well as in the present, left a note in his serviette, asking her, in flowery language, if she would be gracious enough to accompany him, on a free afternoon, on a short excursion, and declaring his respectful admiration for the girl of the buffet. Solemnly, when we went for our next meal, she tiptoed in the empty room to our table, like a conspirator, put her finger on her lips, dropped, as if by accident, a card on the table, and vanished.

We read it together (perhaps I ought not to have taken my share of the secret missive). "I thank you, dearest and kindest sir," it ran, "for your gentlemanly intention and your lovely words, which I like very much, but I cannot believe them."

I trust my companion has kept this card; I like to think that the maid of the buffet, now presumably a Roman matron, still consoles herself for the humdrumness of life by the recollection of those daring days of high romance. . . .

But less romantic, and yet equally significant to me was my adventure with an obliging Italian bank manager; and to it I can attach a considerable moral.

I had gone to Italy for professional purposes, and had need of relatively large sums of money. I had made arrangements with my bank to notify a number of its correspondents in Italian towns that I should be allowed to draw on them. This method, in the circumstances, seemed to be the most convenient.

But I too had reckoned without the lateness of trains and the labour unrest which, before the days of Mussolini, rendered travelling in Italy hazardous. When I presented myself at one of the corresponding banks the clerk looked glum. He had never heard of me or my arrangements. There was a great search among documents, but nothing concerning me could be discovered.

"What then am I to do?" I asked somewhat angrily; "I cannot afford to wait—I must find the money somehow."

The manager hastened to me, smiling but grave. He was exceedingly courteous and placatory. He promised that something should be done immediately.

He remained with me while another search was made, making pleasant conversation. When the negative result was reported to him, he smiled again and he said (I can recall his exact words, for they appeared to me to be so extraordinary):

"You see, no notification has reached us. But it does not in the least matter. A letter has doubtless gone astray. There is a strike of railway men, and it is not surprising that there is some confusion. But since you have given your orders, they shall be respected. Will you be good enough to draw on us for whatever amount you need now? It will be a pleasure to pay you. If tomorrow you should want more, it shall be given to you. It may be, of course, that we shall get the letter by to-morrow, but if not it will not in the least matter."

This manner of conducting business amazed me. In spite of my need I could hardly bring myself to take the money. I have been in many countries, and I have had many temporary monetary difficulties, but never have I been invited, except in Italy, to draw upon an inexistent account without furnishing guarantees of any kind. I do not suggest that this experience is typical. Perhaps for aught I know it had never happened be-fore and will never happen again. But it happened to me, and I cannot think of Italy without thinking of this incident.

What does it denote? Probably it denotes nothing at all. We all remember the English traveller who, arriving at Boulogne, and observing a red-haired woman, wrote in his notebook: "French women have red hair."

Yet foolish as it is, I have somehow contrived to persuade myself that the Italian character is indicated in this astounding treatment of me by an obscure Italian bank manager. For the Italian is natural. He is not a creature of routine. Even a bank manager is liable to act impulsively. I cannot explain why he believed me, but, believing me, he did not hesitate to behave like a human being and not like a bank manager. It is quite inconceivable that a French official would have taken the smallest risk unless he were covered by every kind of paper demanded by the rules of the service. Without personal knowl-edge of me no English banker would have been so lax, though with personal knowledge he would have set aside the strict rules. But nowhere in the world outside Italy would instinctive trust have overridden lack of papers and lack of personal knowledge. I cannot resist the temptation to say that Fascism itself can only be a transient expression of Italian character because Fascism is founded on discipline.

II. DYNAMIC AND INDIVIDUAL

THE Italians are dynamic; it is not for nothing that we asso-ciate anarchism with Italy and that we associate mass dis-cipline with Germany. My bank manager was an anarchist in the ultimate sense of the word. Perhaps he is a Fascist to-day, but if so it is only because Fascism is a living inspiration, and when that living inspiration has left, Fascism will break up, and the Italians will again become individual anarchists.

The Italian man, however cultured, however rigidly trained, is essentially primitive. He exists as a human being and not as a member of society. He grows simply as a tree grows. He has the most ancient of traditions—like the tree; but he insists on being himself—like the tree. History does not contradict this peculiar Italian individuality. Italian unity may be unquestionably true but such unity is the simultaneous expression of individual desires, not a principle imposed from above. The great movements for Italian emancipation were possible because individuals were worked up to white heat, and pursued individually the same passionate aims. Certainly Italians have known how to combine, but it is rare that these combinations have been nation-wide. After all, Italy is, even to-day, composed of more distinct communities than any other country, and Italian is a rather loose generic term which embraces Florentines, and Milanese, and Venetians, and Neapolitans and Sicilians, and so forth. The Italians are a mixture of races, just as they were when Italy was divided up, in ancient days, into Kingdoms and Republics, and when each city was distinctive and administratively separate from the rest. We still speak of ancient Rome rather than of the ancient Roman Empire. Rome extended its influence over other Italian cities neither more nor less than it extended its influence over non-Italian cities. Something of this feeling has been expressed by many writers on Italy, and if I recollect aright, Keyserling lays particular stress on it.

If it is possible to reduce Italy to a number of cities, it is further possible to reduce those cities to a number of families. For family life is exclusive as it is exclusive nowhere else. I have never lived long in Italy, but all my Italian friends—and I have had many—and all my non-Italian friends who have lived long in Italy, agree that family life is more jealously guarded from outside influences than that of any other European country. One can stay for a score of years in Rome and be intimately acquainted with nobles and politicians and officials and the middle classes and the masses, meeting them in assemblies and in clubs and getting on the most confidential relations with them; and still, at the end of a score of years, realise that one has rarely if ever been invited to cross the threshold of an

Italian household and to mingle intimately with an Italian family. On this point there is unanimity.

I am told by Anglo-Saxons that they have been conscious of similar conditions in other so-called Latin countries—notably in France. Possibly I cannot speak with authority on this subject, for I have personally found the French family to be far less exclusive than is generally supposed; and I must therefore presume that my experience has been exceptional. What is sure is that the Italian family is remarkably reserved, and that from the domain where the woman reigns interlopers are rigorously barred.

And if one can reduce the city to the family, so one can reduce the family (and here we complete the circle) to the individual. Italy at all times has been distinguished by unusual men who did not conform to existing conventions. In England and in Germany—to take only these two countries—the leading men are generally ordinary men. They correspond to our ideas of the English or German type. Sometimes one is inclined to assert that only the conventional man can truly succeed in these countries; he must not shock and startle; or perhaps it would be better to say that he must be surprising only because he is more conventional than the conventional, because he represents conventionality *in excelsis*. He must be the embodiment of national prejudices. He must be trained to think along certain lines, to act in accordance with preconceived ideas. If he is not mediocre he is suspect. A Disraeli may eventually impose himself by dint of long efforts to disguise his eccentricities, and to make acceptable as merely harmless peculiarities the manifestations of an exotic temperament. If he does succeed it is in spite of, and not because of, his idiosyncrasies. His originality is a drawback. But the Gladstones achieve the same success almost without effort. The Baldwins rise to eminence because they are plain and honest and do not differ noticeably from their compatriots. I do not intend this as a criticism of the Peels and Palmerstons who are excellent men for whom I have much admiration; I only mean that they are conformists and not non-conformists; they owe their strength to their ordinariness and not to their extraordinariness. You will see the same lesson in the popular newspapers which do not represent the men and women who are held up to public esteem as men and women who are alien in their thoughts and habits. If they smoke the plebeian pipe or take manual exercise such as anybody might take, if despite their high rank they darn the family socks, these things are recorded as virtues. And so, of course, they are; it is good for society that its conspicuous men and women should set the pattern of conventional behaviour.

But Italy loves the theatrical. It is attracted by public personages who do nothing without a certain flamboyancy. It perpetually gives birth to men who are different. This is true in the realm of art as well as in the realm of politics. Italy gave us the opera. It was the true mother of Christianity. It was the originator of Imperialism. Europe owes the experience of the Renaissance to Italy. Cæsar, Raphael, Michael Angelo, Leonardo da Vinci, the Medicis, the Borgias, the Garibaldis, the Popes, the Giolittis, and the Mussolinis—these are a few only of the typical untypical figures which have in all ages made Italy a fount of life for the world. Incomparably Italy, which was not even nominally a nation in the modern sense sixty years ago, has been and is the renovator of mankind. It is at once eternally old and eternally new. Spengler speaks of the life and death of nations, as though they were organic entities, and sometimes nations indeed seem to advance from youth to age. There are today in Europe nations which are dying of senile decay. But despite Spengler's analogies, which are far from being universally true, Italy does not decay: Italy is deathless.

III. A TEEMING LAND

ITALY is as vital to-day as it has ever been. It is a teeming country, situated in three different climes, and while its monuments of antiquity are to be visited, it is its present activity that most strongly impresses the traveller who is not the slave of his guide-book. Old Rome may be a glorious memory, but Italy does not nourish itself exclusively on memories. Latin is no longer a living language, but Italy is a living land. The capital surges heedlessly about the vestiges of the past. Florence with its bridges and pearly light is as thriving to-day as it was in its heroic days. Milan is industrious around the Duomo, its lace-like cathedral which mingles Lombard, Gothic, and Renaissance styles. Venice, which espoused the Adriatic, and is the dream of lovers, is still a reigning queen. History speaks from the stones of Italy, but life perpetually springs anew. It is no wonder that men and women pass through the great Alpine gateway into Italy with literary and artistic reminiscences weaving endless patterns in their minds; but they would do well to beware lest the past blinds them to the present.

Milan, whose population is nearly a million, may now be reckoned the leading city of Italy. Although Rome is the seat of government, in my own most active days it was to Milan that the principal newspapers looked for the bulk of their news; and it is from Milan that most of the great modern movements have come. It is said that Naples will again overtake Milan as the largest city of Italy, but it will certainly not overtake it in importance. Rome comes third, with a population of something under nine hundred thousand; Genoa fourth with a population of over six hundred thousand (it was there that Mr. Lloyd George endeavoured to undo the work of Versailles in a great but unhappily unsuccessful conference); Turin fifth with forty thousand fewer inhabitants; and then Florence, Venice, and Bologna, a rich modern city with the oldest of universities. They should all figure on the tourist's itinerary; yet, if there are Italian cities which, by their associations, mean more to the foreigner than Milan, there is none which means anything like so much to the Italian. It is wealthy, it is enterprising, it is up-to-date. It stands in the centre of a prosperous region where, until you reach the lakes and the hills of Northern Italy, you will find many scores of factories. It offers a strong contrast to the more artistic cities though it is well dowered with art treasures. One fact is sufficiently significant: a quarter of the industrial wealth of Italy is invested in Milan. Lombardy is the silk capital of the world, and it also pursues a thriving industry in cotton, iron, and steel.

One of my anti-Fascist friends—an Italian Count who was imprisoned for a political offence, who lost his fortune, but who immediately regained it by his mechanical inventions—used indeed to complain that Italian industry was becoming too concentrated in the temperate North. "Mussolini," he said, "is always pursuing colonial aims. He has declared that Italy must expand or explode. But before he tries to colonise more remote territories he should turn his attention to Southern Italy. There he would find a suitable field for colonisation." Against this it must be urged that the sub-tropical climate of Southern Italy is not suitable for industrial enterprise.

Be this as it may, Milan is a bustling city. It seems to be full of banks and motor-cars. The streets are modernised; it is one of the most important international railway centres in Europe, since the Simplon and the Saint-Gothard lines lead to it, and the Orient Express takes this route. Moreover, with the continually growing use of aerial locomotion, it is at Milan that converge the principal air routes. Among the evidences of up-to-dateness is the extraordinary development of the telephone service which is hardly matched anywhere else in Europe.

Its Music Conservatory and the Scala opera-house, dating from 1778, where the greatest musicians of the world have appeared, preserve the unrivalled musical traditions of the city; and its university and its art galleries save it from the reproach of sacrificing its former fame to modernism.

It is not my purpose to write of lovely Naples, with its bay looking towards Vesuvius. "To know Naples," writes Clive Holland, an authority on travel in Europe, "one must live there." See Naples and die, runs the old tag, but if there is any city which should make one love life, it is Naples, bathed in brilliant sunshine, rejoicing in its exquisite curves and colours, its green avenues and blue sea. The stately dignity of Florence, all towers and domes and open squares, has made it beloved of Anglo-Saxon visitors and residents, and by the golden Arno dwells an English and American colony. Indeed such colonies are scattered all over the peninsula, and from Italy there reaches us the best work of a number of English and American poets and novelists.

Rome itself, on its seven hills, is perhaps best appreciated if one forgets the guide-book approach, and comes upon it with a fine start of surprise. I do not suggest that old Rome should be neglected—it is impossible to neglect it—but merely that one should remember that Italy is undergoing one of its periodical renaissances and must not be regarded merely as a museum of antiquities.

It is chiefly its political renaissance which has interested the world. Yet nominally little is altered. Italy is still legally under the régime of a constitutional monarch. The head of the state is King Vittorio Emanuele III who has reigned for thirty years, and who does not appear to resent the authoritative methods of Benito Mussolini and the Fascist party. Fascism insisted on a new directing intelligence but was not anxious to shatter the constitutional fabric. Nevertheless it swept away Parliamentarism which had, indeed, in Italy, shown itself incompetent, corrupt, unrepresentative. The elections in Italy were always manufactured by the existing government, which exercised pressure on the prefects and mayors, and by menaces and promises assured majorities. A similar state of affairs prevails or has prevailed in most of the European countries which pretend to Parliamentarism, and in these countries, as formerly in Italy, the Chamber is an undisciplined, ignorant, and practically useless body. Certainly I hold no brief for Mussolini, but it is a mistake to confound the interests of Democracy with the interests of an unruly, irresponsible and dishonest Parliamentarism. Nobody who observed events in Italy before the change could doubt that Parliamentarism was doomed.

Apart from the indefensible character of the Italian Parliament, it is as I have elsewhere suggested, theoretically unfair to assume that Dictatorships necessarily indicate the decline of Democracy. Governments are determined by circumstances; and it is curious to observe, as Lucien Romier has observed, that along the Mediterranean all the independent nations have some kind of authoritative régime—with the possible exception of France, where, however, Caillaux sought exceptional powers and Poincaré obtained them *de facto* though not *de jure*. From Spain to Turkey there are Dictatorships: Primo de Rivera at Madrid, Mussolini at Rome, King Alexander at Belgrade, Venizelos (though he respects the Republican forms) at Athens, Mustapha Kemel at Angora.

What is the reason for this curious Mediterranean phenomenon? Certainly it is not confined to the Mediterranean—Russia, Poland, and Baltic States are also in the hands of one or several men who impose their will—but the contempt for words and the demand for action have been displayed more prominently and more generally in the South than in the North. There are in the North more accidental, casual, disguised, half-hearted, or usurped Dictatorships; but in the South there is open Dictatorship often fully accepted by the people.

There is not one reason; there are several. The Eastern tradition, and the Latin tradition, are authoritative; whereas the tradition of the Protestant North lays greater stress on the rights of the individual, who must have the liberty of exercising his own judgment whether it be in matters of religion or of the State. Doubtless, too, the relative illiteracy of the population of the South and East has its effect. But at bottom it was insecurity that called Dictatorships into being—political insecurity, economic insecurity, social insecurity. Dictatorships may represent the instinct of self-preservation.

Lucien Romier remarks that the territories which are washed by the Mediterranean are about equal in area to the United States of America; but they contain a population twice as great. Yet their commerce is not a third of that of the United States. Overpopulation and poverty are two important factors in most of the Mediterranean lands. Hence the need for strong control, the maximum of organisation, the minimum of wasted efforts. . . .

In the case of Italy the partial closing of the doors of the United States to immigrants has intensified the demographic problem. Italy is practically without colonies—for the Libyan possessions of Northern Africa are poor and undeveloped— and although the density of population is lower than in Great Britain or Germany, it is apparently, in the present state of industry and agriculture, too high for the temperate clime of the country. Spain is empty enough, but then Spain is arid and in decay. France, the neighbour of Italy, is relatively under-populated and is prosperous. No wonder that Italy looks with envious eyes on the fair land of France; and that some parts of France—particularly the Midi—are already half Italianised.

IV. RELATIONS WITH FRANCE

THERE have been cultivated on both sides of the Alps sentiments of hostility. It is useless to make peace on the Rhine if it is only to foster antagonisms on either side of the Alps.

Both France and Italy have been greatly to blame. Bitter articles were written against Italy in the French Radical newspapers. We were presented with the curious paradox that those of the Left who were foremost in striving for a *rapprochement* between France and Germany, were the most implacably opposed to a *rapprochement* between France and Italy; whereas those of the Right who resisted the Franco-German *rapprochement*, clamoured for a renewal of friendship with Italy. Thus I am tempted to ask whether there really exists a pure pacifist. Your mildest pacifist is always ready to make war on somebody, while your wildest militarist is always ready to make peace with somebody. Labels are usually misleading, but they have rarely been more misleading than in the case of the so-called French pacifist. By pacifism he meant a certain attitude towards the defeated enemy, but he did not answer for his attitude towards a victorious ally. Indeed he was not consistent in respect of defeated enemies; for while Germany was to be helped, Hungary was to be suppressed. One must therefore come to the conclusion that a real pacifist is rare.

Men like or dislike this or that country for various reasons, personal, philosophical, or political—and that is all. France is particularly inclined to express its likes and dislikes violently. It is a Crusader by nature. It cried, "Down with Mussolini!" exactly as it had cried, "Down with the Kaiser!" and afterwards, "Down with Lenin!" Briand's movements were jealously watched. He could take as many meals as he pleased with Stresemann, but not with Mussolini. So there was incident after incident on the French frontiers and in Tunisia. No attempt was made to dispel the gathering clouds. The Italian press denounced the French in the most heated language, and Mussolini went about uttering general menaces whose particular application it was not difficult to guess.

Then came the battle of the treaties. Italy challenged Yugo-Slavia by taking Albania under its control. France signed a treaty with Yugo-Slavia which, as interpreted by the Italians, was tantamount to a warning that at a given moment France could, if it pleased, turn loose on Italy the most ferocious fighters of the Balkans. Thereupon there was much criticism of these pacts, which are contrary to the spirit and the letter of the League of Nations, and divide Europe into opposing camps.

Everywhere there was alarm, and it was impossible for France and Italy to continue their manœuvres on the diplomatic field. In both countries there was a demand for reconsideration of a serious situation. There are grave problems which will require the most delicate handling; but if it was possible for France and England to liquidate their quarrels in 1904, and if it was possible for France and Germany to arrive at some measure of accord after the war, there are no insuperable obstacles to a Franco-Italian understanding to-day.

The fundamental facts about Italy are that there is what is generally regarded as a superabundant population, there is a lack of raw materials, there are inadequate commercial outlets, and there are insufficient Italian colonies. France, which is under-populated, has the second largest colonial empire in the world. In these conditions it was easy for Mussolini to build a vast and ambitious foreign policy. France's control of, or at least association with, Balkanic States, in which Italy would like its own influence to be predominant, helped to direct Italian sentiment against France; while France is also supposed to have thwarted Italy in the Adriatic and in the Mediterranean. There is a good deal of point in the Italian contention that Italy's relations with Albania, for example, do not directly concern France, and normally could scarcely be developed in such fashion as to involve Italy in a conflict with France. The pact may be perilous inasmuch as it arouses Yugo-Slavian jealousies. But what interest has France in supporting Yugo-Slavia? On the other hand, the French pact with Yugo-Slavia would obviously bring France almost automatically into war with Italy if Italy and Yugo-Slavia were embroiled. Italy has certainly sound arguments in favour of its contention that it is more naturally interested in the Adriatic and in the Balkans than is France. In the Adriatic there must be free passage. In the Balkans, Italy must be allowed room for economic expansion. It is not understood why France should endeavour to interfere with Italy's guardianship of Albania, which stands at the mouth of the Adriatic; and it is not understood why France should endeavour to range the Balkanic countries in what is potentially an anti-Italian League.

In the Mediterranean, Italy feels that it has the strongest claims to be considered the leading Power. Are not its shores washed by the Mediterranean; and, on the southern banks, is there not Libya? But France too is a great Mediterranean Power. Part of its coast-line is on that sea, while Morocco, Algeria, Tunisia and even Syria, which it holds under mandate, lie along this great basin. Spain also must be considered, while Great Britain seeks to command the Gibraltar gateway and the Egyptian exit by the Suez Canal. Italian claims to "Mare Nostrum" are unquestionably exaggerated; but it is not surprising that Italy should have asked for participation in the government of the International Zone of Tangiers.

With regard to Tunisia, France is the Power in possession and cannot be removed. Yet it is the Italians who chiefly colonise Tunisia. The Italians were there before the French. They helped to develop Tunisia. They still, greatly outnumbering the French settlers, contribute to the prosperity of the protectorate. There was a convention which regulated the position of the Italians in Tunisia; but it was denounced by the French as the war was ending in September, 1918. The status of Italians in Tunisia is unsatisfactory. They have to be vigilant lest they are robbed of their nationality. Their property rights are restricted. Here again, if I am rightly informed, the French are disposed to make changes in the laws for the benefit of Italian nationals. Again, Italy considers that it has grievances in Libya, and requires a readjustment of the southern frontiers.

There has been talk of the transference of the Syrian mandate, now held by France, to Italy. This is, in my opinion, an idle demand. There is no prospect of the voluntary surrender by France of such a mandate. Occasionally it is suggested that Germany and Italy, which are both to all intents and purposes deprived of colonies, should unite in the demand for a redistribution of the territories which the more powerful Allies allocated to themselves after the war. It is to nobody's interest that the Franco-Italian quarrel should be envenomed. It is to everybody's interest that it should be ended before it is too late.

V. GIOLITTI

OF THE pre-Fascist politicians Giovanni Giolitti was undoubtedly the ablest—if by ability one means mastery of wiles and stratagems. For many years he could be the Prime Minister of Italy almost whenever he liked, and when he was not he was the power behind the Prime Minister. He came and went; for a perpetual incumbency would naturally have been intolerable. It did not much matter; in the periods in which he was out of office he was as occultly influential as when he was in office. If one possesses a house it is not for the purpose of making it a prison; there are exits as well as entrances which it would be folly not to use. So it was with the Italian ministries; there were doors by which Giolitti left, but the ministries nevertheless belonged to him.

A robust giant he was, dominating by his presence as well as by his prestige, but when the war broke out he was already ageing. Italy, according to its commitments, should doubtless have been neutral, but circumstances forced it into the war on the side of the Allies. Giolitti was already in the first stage of eclipse. He made the mistake of standing for Italian neutrality, and when, in the flush of patriotism, he was beaten, he fell into unpopularity. Once national feelings were inflamed he was suspected and accused of disloyalty if not of treachery; and in the spy and treason cases which multiplied in France after M. Georges Clemenceau became Prime Minister, his name was frequently heard as that of the arch-pacifist. In those days pacifism was the synonym of pro-Germanism.

During the peacemaking at Paris he was still out of office. It was Signor Orlando whom I saw at the head of the Italian delegation—one of Giolitti's former ministers, it is true, but now under the influence of Baron Sonnino, who was frankly an Italian Imperialist. Orlando was a lawyer of great distinction, but he never impressed me as possessing a strong personality. He was purely an advocate, and, what was worse, he was unable to win his case. In these Paris proceedings he was singularly subdued. Although he was one of the Big Four, he made a poor fourth, after Wilson, Lloyd George, and Clemenceau. Perhaps he was too modest in his claims. Instead of endeavouring to command Europe he merely tried to command the Adriatic. He failed so badly that he went out of the conference slamming the door behind him. For once the American President took up an uncompromising attitude. He stiffened his back against the proposal to give Italy not only the Dalmatian coast, peopled by Yugo-Slavs, but the port of Fiume, which the Yugo-Slavs demanded as a necessary port. Of course Italy's claim to Dalmatia was supported by a secret treaty which the Allies had signed as the price of Italy's help in the war. But the Allies treated secret treaties as scraps of paper. Lloyd George calmly proposed to postpone Italian questions until German questions were definitely solved; but Sonnino, acting through Orlando, checkmated him and demanded a Dalmatian decision before consenting to peace with Germany. Mr. Lloyd George said, "If you hold us to our pledge we are bound to agree to your possession of Dalmatia, but we shall refuse Fiume which we have not promised you." Mr. Wilson said, "I am tied by no secret treaties. You shall have neither Dalmatia, which would be an abomination, nor Fiume, which would be an outrage." Italy was furious. The annexation of Fiume was placarded in Rome. Wilson launched an appeal to public opinion over the heads of the diplomatists, and in high dudgeon Orlando and Sonnino left Paris. In Italy they were greeted with wild approval. A little later Gabriele d'Annunzio made his most memorable exploit, capturing Fiume for the Italians.

There is no doubt that the Allied treatment of Italy was unjustifiable and from the diplomatic standpoint worse—it was tactless; and it may be that this flouting of Italian nationalism because Italy was relatively weak, determined the subsequent vicissitudes of the Italian nation which oscillated from sacred egotism to confused Communism and then to Fascism.

In the turbulence of the Italian spirit, humiliated, and as it thought cheated, Giolitti saw his chance. This was in July, 1920, when he was approaching his eightieth year. After his retirement his name had been cleared of the most dreadful charges, and it shone forth again as a symbol. His country was in chaos. Anarchy had come out of Italian sacrifices. The man who had been called a traitor, the man who had warned Italy against war, was asked to liquidate the consequences of the war. Salandra, who was responsible for the intervention of Italy on the side of the Triple Entente, who signed the declaration of war against Austria, was discredited. Sonnino was bitterly blamed for Italian misfortunes. Orlando had never had a real following.

Discouraged, disappointed, indignant at the non-fulfilment of so many promises, believing that it had suffered in vain, Italy turned to Giolitti, who had always counselled neutrality. The mediocrity of the interventionists had been manifested, and Italy accepted again its former Dictator—for Giolitti, too, had been a Dictator; that is to say, he had manipulated Parliament, and had not suppressed it, but he had exercised personal power almost as strongly as Mussolini was later to exercise it. He had flattened political doctrines, reduced the parties to impotence, cleverly resorted to every combination, won the confidence of the House of Savoy, and assured the re-election of those deputies who were his vassals.

The Italian régime?—it was Giolitti! He was the real King of this Kingdom of Comrades.

It is the fashion to rail against Mussolini; but let us not forget that in the time of Giolitti dead men voted for Giolitti's candidates, and living men who were opposed to Giolitti's candidates were prevented by violence from voting. Let us remember too that Mussolini at least shoulders his responsibilities, whereas Giolitti, whenever he encountered difficulties, quietly retired and left his adversaries to flounder in difficulties of his making.

How was it possible that this strategist of the lobbies should seriously face the frightful problems which followed the war in Italy? He could not; his "come-back" was short-lived; he succumbed to the attacks of his enemies, and was out of office in the crucial days that preceded the Fascist march on Rome. Only once more did he attempt to return; he spoke out in the Chamber against the Fascist ostracism of non-Fascists and against the iron press laws of Mussolini. It was in vain.

VI. NITTI

SIGNOR NITTI played a brief but prominent part on the diplomatic stage. I met him at San Remo where the so-called statesmen of Europe were again in conference, and for a moment I looked upon him as the man who, if circumstances favoured him, might lead the world back to sanity. Things had gone from bad to worse. Statesmanship seemed bankrupt. The Alliance was breaking up. America had a powerless President and an implacable Senate, and was withdrawing from European affairs. Britain had a coalition which was dissolving. No clear voice was heard. France had lost Clemenceau, who at least held the country to a consistent course; and France was beginning to veer with every wind that blew, without a firm-handed pilot at the helm. Germany was fast sinking, splitting asunder between the rival factions. Russia seemed to present a model to the Western world, because at least it had a stable government with some sense of direction, but Russia was remote and was in dire distress, and had been so desperately assailed for its misdeeds that to speak of it as possessing a pattern Government (without, of course, expressing an opinion upon the form or the policy of that Government, but only regarding its ability to govern) would have been rank blasphemy. Who would tell the truth, who would place realities before the peoples? Journalists had, of course, done it long ago, but then journalists who are heard with interest if they write with vigour are never taken seriously.

Signor Nitti's chief merit lay in his readiness to catch up the phrases of the journalists—not, of course, the conventional journalists content to follow in the wake of the foreign offices, but those who showed a certain independence in analysing the situation. I cannot pretend that he displayed more originality, more power of expression, more clairvoyance, than his colleagues; but, at a critical moment in present-day history he decided to utter those journalistic paradoxes which a few years later were political commonplaces.

When I first encountered Signor Nitti, the fortunes of his own country were at their lowest ebb. Nobody troubled about the opinions of Italy which was left to play alone in its own backyard of the Adriatic. People shrugged their shoulders about d'Annunzio, who was parading in his pasteboard helmet and waving his buckram sword in Fiume. Orlando had not survived the duel with President Wilson, in spite of the Sonnino-inspired sonority of his patriotism. Diplomatically speaking, Italy was out of the picture. Internally, it was in desperate straits. In spite of certain territorial gains it was undoubtedly to be classed as among the defeated nations—for the defeated nations, of course, were not all attached to the enemy group of Powers. Imperialism, in spite of the quarrel with the Yugo-Slavs, had lost ground; for bread and coal are more important to the plain citizen than the political possession of a few towns inhabited by other peoples. Hardly anybody spoke of aiding the unfortunate country which had held Austria at bay. The lira had fallen in value much lower than the franc, though not so low as the mark or the Austrian paper crown.

Signor Nitti as he sat at San Remo among statesmen who took no notice of him, smiling cheerfully as though the troubles of his country and the difficulties of his Cabinet could not affect his *joie de vivre,* struck me as being endowed with about the same amount of political intelligence as an Italian tenor. He looked like an Italian tenor. He was fat and round-faced, with a little tooth-brush moustache, and a rather meaningless expression, an imperturbable good humour, which took no count of circumstances or of his company. This comfortable air of *bonhomie,* though it might predispose one towards him as a person, could hardly convince one of his qualities of statesmanship. And yet Signor Nitti suddenly became the leader of European politics. He dared to say things that were positively startling.

If Signor Nitti did this it was because he possesses good, honest, sound common-sense. He did not search out devious ways. He did not cudgel his brains to find a demagogic justification for an obviously absurd policy. He just saw that Italy in particular and the world in general were in bad case. He just saw that they wanted raw materials that Russia could supply, and manufactured articles that Germany could make; and he asked himself why they should not have these raw materials and these manufactured articles that they needed so much. It

seems simple enough now. And yet all the brains of all the
Cabinets had turned away from this straightforward solution.
They had been engaged in the quadrature of the circle; they
had wondered how they could have the advantages of peace
while keeping the hatreds of war; they had wondered how they
could treat half Europe as an eternal enemy and yet enjoy the
products of those countries. They wrestled night and day with
the problem of eating their cake and having it, of killing the
goose that lays the golden eggs and collecting the eggs in
abundance.

It will always remain to Signor Nitti's credit that he was the
first of the men in power to preach sympathy and clemency
for the vanquished, to declare that the reconstruction of the
vanquished countries interested above all the victors. If they
owed reparations to their conquerors it was assuredly by their
prosperity and not by their impoverishment that they could
acquit their debt.

I think the reason why Signor Nitti was so superior to the
rest was because he is too good-natured, too easy-going, in a
word, too fat, to brood over his national grievances, to nurse his
anger like an hysterical woman, to sulk and ruminate over the
wrongs done to Italy. It was not so much a question of intelligence as of mental health and a body not given to vapours.

I will not inquire how far Signor Nitti was pushed by the
pressure of events in this direction. There was much in his parliamentary position that made such a policy of coöperation
imperative. A policy of metaphors—"barbed wire," "barba-
rians," and so forth—would have been completely disastrous for
Italy. Epithets are not a substitute for action. Headlines cannot
give back riches. In a Europe which permitted itself the luxury
of abuse, the Socialists of Italy saw that ruin was imminent
and would not allow any more wasteful attempts to subjugate
other nations.

To Signor Nitti I owe a personal debt. He published in his
book "Europe Without Peace" a document which had been
privately circulated in 1919 by one of the leading members of
the Peace Conference pleading for a clean peace in Europe. It
showed that Germany was to lose immense territorial possessions, was to be disarmed, was to be deprived of raw materials,
was to pay Arabian Nights reparations, and it suggested, quite
mildly, that the Allies should be "moderate." It is without interest to repeat the arguments of this document which every-

body accepts to-day. But it so happened that the author of this document had expounded his views to me; and without disclosing his name I had written them as those of a High Authority to be published in the old green Westminster Gazette, edited by my friend J. A. Spender. Instantly there was an uproar. This "moderation interview," as it was designated, alarmed the men who clamoured for a blood and thunder peace. Over three hundred Parliamentarians called on the supposed author to explain. The supposed author immediately repudiated these opinions, and as I was not in a position to reveal his name I was compelled to smart under the implied accusation of having "faked" the message for three years. But when Nitti revealed the existence of the circularised document it corresponded, except in minor points, with the views expressed in the "moderation interview." The very language was substantially the same. After consulting J. A. Spender as to the propriety of vindicating myself, I disclosed the whole circumstances. The case was clear, and in second Parliamentary debate it was not I, but the statesman who questioned my veracity, who suffered. A few weeks later the minister fell.

VII. GABRIELE D'ANNUNZIO

GABRIELE D'ANNUNZIO, supreme Italian poet, acted. When Wilson denied claims, d'Annunzio thundered against the prominent teeth of the American President and then went off to seize Fiume. He had always endeavoured to put colour into his life as into his books.

In the old days he lived a good deal in France—at Arcachon, under the pine trees, where he paced restlessly with his gambolling dogs; at Paris where, in the war days, he became a familiar figure. His advocacy helped to bring Italy into the war. There is no stranger personality even on the crowded Italian stage where strange personalities abound.

And now the poet has become a Prince: Principe di Monte Nevoso, Prince of the Snowy Mountain. The Italian authorities drove him out of Fiume, but they nevertheless profited by his exploit to obtain Fiume, and they recognised their indebtedness to him by offering him a fine historic mansion.

D'Annunzio, poet, playwright, novelist, aviator, politician, patriot, warrior, has lived his life greatly. He could not, with all his picturesqueness and energy, have become a Mussolini; he

GABRIELE D'ANNUNZIO

does not possess the solidity of the Duce. Mussolini doubtless poses, but he poses to some purpose; whereas d'Annunzio poses for the sake of the pose.

Yet Benjamin Crémieux, the black-bearded genial French-man whom I take to be the greatest authority on modern Italian literature, rightly draws a distinction between "the d'Annunzio of the Italians and the d'Annunzio of foreigners." There is an "international d'Annunzio" who has become legendary. Crémieux explains that the international d'Annun-zio is relatively simple, because only a few of his novels and a few of his theatrical pieces—notably "Le Martyre de Saint-Sebastien" originally written in French for the slim, long-limbed, extraordinarily beautiful Ida Rubinstein, whose per-formances were, as I saw them, plastic poems—have become known outside Italy. He has impressed the public imagination by his dramatic appearances, and by his princely gift of language in a dozen amazing manifestos. But the "d'Annunzio of the Italians" is, says Crémieux, much more complex, much richer, much more original, and he is not only the greatest artist who has carried the Italian colours since 1870, but his contribution to Italian letters has been the most important since Manzoni and Leopardi. With this verdict of Crémieux many people will not agree, for d'Annunzio has made many enemies, political and literary. Nevertheless if the vogue of d'Annunzio is passing, and d'Annunzio is now too old to renew his youth, it is well to remember the immense and indeed unique place which he occupied for so long.

"D'Annunzio,"—I quote from Crémieux—"is the great national poet of Imperialist Italy. And, in spite of the apparent contradiction, he is the writer who has best assimilated in his work all the thought and sensibility of the Europe of his epoch, from Nietzsche to Tolstoi, from Ibsen to Dostoiewski, from Baudelaire to Walt Whitman. (I am not responsible for the in-clusion of Walt Whitman among the Europeans.) He is the first truly non-classical great writer of Italy. He it is who has acclimatised in his country, in the midst of the literature of professors, the notion of a literature of exception, and the notion of the liberty and rights of the artist, with all that they comport, in daily conduct as in literary production, of au-dacity, of excess, of challenge to bourgeois taste, of stylisation, and of individualism!"

It is not generally realised that d'Annunzio is approaching

his seventieth year. He was born in March, 1863. Somehow he contrives to give an impression of remarkable youthfulness, and the young men of Italy, who are now inclined to regard him as demoded, are not as ardent as their elder. When he was sixteen years of age he wrote his first published verses. His tragedies were at first coolly received. He entered Parliament as a deputy. A few years before the war he was ruined, and went into exile. After the Fiume adventure he retired to Cargnaceo, above Gardone, on the Lake of Garda.

Dictatorship as Dictatorship does not win his approval. When Unamuno was expelled from Spain, d'Annunzio denounced, with flaming scorn, the unimaginative Primo de Rivera. From time to time his great phrases flash round the globe. So it was when Eleonora Duse died in America; he issued a splendid command that her body should be brought back to Italy for state burial.

The admiration of Eleonora Duse for d'Annunzio is well known. There are elements of tragedy in the adventure. The first time they met was in her dressing-room in the theatre at Rome. She had been playing La Dame aux Camélias; as always she had put her soul into the performance and she was exhausted. D'Annunzio spoke three words only: "Oh, great inspirer!" and he fled. That was the beginning of an unhappy idyll.

They met again at Venice, moving in their gondolas on the sunlit canals. There followed a tormented friendship. Duse produced his pieces, but though she was personally acclaimed the dramas of d'Annunzio were criticised. The financial sacrifices that the superb actress made to enable d'Annunzio to construct his theatre are notorious. It is recorded that when she was playing his pieces in South America, with indifferent success, she telegraphed to him every day large sums which represented his share of imaginary receipts. Sad it is to think that she was obliged to appear on the stage old and sick and poor. On her American tour, in Pittsburgh, she died. Difficulties and disappointments, moral and material, had followed this glorious and incomparable artist all her life.

What memories must people the white-frescoed building with the green shutters, and must accompany d'Annunzio on the terraces which descend to the lake among the cypresses, the oaks, and laurels! It is not a sheltered artistic existence that d'Annunzio has passed in a study. He has been a moment of the Italian consciousness. He has put much of himself into his books, but his life has been fuller than his books. When he was in exile, and his career appeared to have ended, and he seemed to have fallen on flat, unprofitable times, he still doubtless dimly foresaw that he was to be the principal actor in his own epic.

His ardent spirit was not that of the *littérateur* who weaves around himself a web of words. He wanted to break the winding shroud of phrases, and to soar, a winged hero in the storm and sunshine, over a heaving world. There grew in his brain the conviction that he was reserved for a great destiny. What glorious career awaited a man, who had persuaded himself of his splendid mission, in a humdrum age, it was hard to foresee, and the Man awaited the Hour, wondering dimly when the Hour would come and in what questionable shape, but ready to tingle into more terrible life than any of his own passionate creations. Whatever volcanic forces were in the people of his imagination were in him, slumbering uneasily and demanding their release. But how? What was left for a man of poetic action to do?

And so, whether he wrote in French or in his native Italian, his lyricism was but a prelude, a preparation, for the greater lyricism of his life. Symbolist, he sought a new kind of art, an art which should be a synthesis of all the arts. His preoccupation was to make his personages move in accordance with the laws of music, and to depict them in pictorial or statuesque attitudes. The laws which governed these personages, governed d'Annunzio.

He is, in his rôle, without flaw. I only wish I could admire him as he deserves to be admired—as a marvellous poet in action. But alas! the poet has no place in politics; and a *beau geste* which satisfies every artistic convention, a situation which is theatrically impeccable, may have the most disastrous results for the world. No one with a feeling for æsthetics can fail to applaud Nero. What sublime tragedy that Rome should flame like a torch! What admirable appreciation of the dreadful beauty of the spectacle that appalled less artistic souls!

But we cannot afford to burn down Rome, or as d'Annunzio would have us do, burn up the world in order to provide the appropriate stage setting for a poet.

In the serene sky the world war broke, and d'Annunzio realised, not that he was Italian, but that he was Italy. Henceforth he was to personify his country in all its fierce, flaming beauty and pride. His entrance upon the scene was a tremendous success. He had caught the exact moment. In that unique hour he stood uniquely for Italy. His exploits in the air when he flew above the battle, quickly made him a legendary hero.

His later enterprise, when with a few thousand men he took possession of Fiume, his designs upon the Dalmatian towns were pitched in the heroic key. But they revealed a singular lack of the sense of realities. What Italy needed most was not new buccaneering expeditions, not a crusade of Nationalism, but peace, and protection from Revolution, and the friendship of its Allies. These sword-and-cape adventures, these grandiloquent speeches, had for background a dark confused curtain; and for auditorium a howling theatre.

Of all the representatives of Nationalism-Gone-Mad, d'Annunzio was the supreme example, because he was inspired by a poetic insanity which abandoned all pretence at prudence. He scattered with incoherent prodigality his splendid words. He fulfilled his baneful romantic rôle.

He was born in an age when the new Italy should be prepared to play soberly its part in Europe, when the adventurer who age after age has been a frequent figure in the multitude of little Italian States, was giving place to the business man, to the professor, to the engineer. This was an inopportune moment for the prancing imagination of a d'Annunzio.

VIII. MUSSOLINI

THOSE of us who frequented international conferences after the war, met the rather shabby journalist Benito Mussolini. He was, for example, at Cannes, the correspondent of his own journal, "Il Popolo d'Italia." Nobody took any particular notice of him. Apparently as a newsgatherer he was not very successful. He had no access to the official sources of information, and he appealed to his English and American colleagues for some knowledge of what was happening.

Now one could draw up a list of the members of the Italian Government somewhat as follows:

Prime Minister......................Benito Mussolini
Minister for Foreign Affairs...........Benito Mussolini
Minister of the Interior..............Benito Mussolini
Minister of Colonies.................Benito Mussolini

Mussolini

Minister of Corporations. . . . . Benito Mussolini
Minister of Aviation. . . . . Benito Mussolini
Minister of Marine. . . . . Benito Mussolini
Minister of War. . . . . Benito Mussolini
Minister of Public Works. . . . . Benito Mussolini

Etc., etc. . . .

It should not be difficult to convoke a meeting of the Italian
Cabinet. A quorum would be amply constituted by Mussolini
alone. As I write, only five posts remain in other hands, and it
may be that before the publication of this book the Dictator
will have taken them over. If a Minister does not agree with the
majority in the Cabinet—that is to say, with Benito Mussolini
—he is called upon to resign. It is quite inadequate to describe
Mussolini as the apex of the pyramid of the State. He is the
whole pyramid.

He is photographed perpetually—apparently the hall-mark
of greatness to-day. One of the most amusing—though irreverent—pasquinades that in spite of Fascist discipline circulates
at Rome—in the salons, the cafés, the offices—is as follows:

When he died Mussolini went straight to Paradise. The arch-
angels and saints hurried to meet him at the gates, and to
escort him to the Throne. Saint Peter, in a black shirt, raising
his hand in salutation, presented him to the Eternal Father.
He remained silent and brooding. The Madonna offered him
flowers, but he took no notice. The Holy Dove alighted on his
arm, and he accepted the homage without comment. Finally,
the Eternal Father, troubled, took off his triangle and placed
it on the head of the Dictator—who mutely acquiesced.

"Poor creatures that we are!" cried Jesus; "may we ask what
the Duce desires?"

And Mussolini thundered:

"The photographers!"

As for his admirers, they are unrestrained in their eulogies.
In the "New York Herald" I read an astonishing article by the
Countess Solito de Solis, a Californian woman who married
an Italian pianist, on "the only genius that the war has produced." I am sure she will forgive me if I borrow two or three
paragraphs:

"I am so often asked: 'Have you met Mussolini?' My heart
swells with pride and I answer—'Yes, I have had that great
honour.' 'What is he like?' my friends ask. 'Well, he is not

like any other man living.' . . . He is tender and gentle, he speaks with the most wonderfully soft and refined voice, he is so aristocratic and natural and oh, what eyes; they look straight through you. The eyes are the mirror of the soul, and we surely see this great man's soul in his eyes. They are black and powerful, and remind one of the eyes of a saint. Have you ever noticed that nuns have different eyes from us ordinary human beings? I suppose it is because they are superior beings. That is the reason perhaps why his eyes are so different to ordinary eyes.

"Of course I was nervous, who would not be in front of such a man? My friends were surprised at my being nervous. 'You,' they said, 'who have known so many royalties. There are few women like yourself who have had the great honour of having received a king at dinner in your own house. You, who have wined and dined royal princes and grand dukes, ambassadors, etc., you say you were nervous.' Yes, all that is true, but a man of Mussolini's quality is very rare and you feel his greatness in the atmosphere. . . .

"What a marvellous listener he is. He let me talk on and on, he was interested in all I said, made many comments and once or twice I thought those great eyes would jump out of his head.

"My friends asked me—'What does he look like close by?' Goodness, how curious you are, you want to know everything. Well, he looked positively fascinating with his riding breeches in a shade of soft reddish brown and his high boots that made him look very English."

Nobody has preached the doctrine of energy and practised it more than Mussolini. Yet Mussolini is not a freak in modern Italy. The explosive kind of personality which he has revealed was already revealed by writers and painters. D'Annunzio was a forerunner of Mussolini. Marinetti, the apostle of Futurism, who amused those of us who knew him in Paris or Milan with his incredible vigour, was also a forerunner of Mussolini; and there is some affinity between the idea that animated Futurism and the idea that animated Fascism. But in spite of his romantic exterior, Mussolini is uncommonly shrewd and, at bottom, sober. . . .

The beginnings of Mussolini were difficult. I have seen the report of a meeting of the Geneva Council dated March 4, 1904, in which is given the reply of M. Odier to M. Wyss who had put a question as to the reason for the expulsion of the Italian citizen Mussolini from the territory of the canton.

"Mussolini," said M. Odier, "is a former Italian teacher, who is now occupied in spreading Socialist revolutionary propaganda. He was arrested in July, 1902 at Lausanne for vagabondage, and at Berne in 1903 for a political offence. Because of his activities at Geneva Mussolini has placed himself in a situation justifying expulsion." He accused Mussolini not only of speaking and working on behalf of revolutionaries, but also of falsifying his papers.

We must not judge Mussolini for his youthful errors. His temperament is revolutionary, and a revolutionary temperament may express itself equally well in revolutionary Socialism or revolutionary Fascism. Mussolini is belligerent by nature. When the Socialists in Italy stood for peace, Mussolini, then editor of the "Avanti," stood for war and was expelled from his party.

The father of Mussolini, a blacksmith, was Republican and anti-Clerical; he was extremely violent, and one day, when the local election results displeased him, he broke the ballot boxes, and was sent to prison. From his father Mussolini inherited his instinct for rebellion. His mother was a schoolteacher renowned in her own circles for her orderly virtues. From her Mussolini doubtless inherited his constructive qualities. In the paternal home the glowing pages of Victor Hugo were read aloud. The young Benito was influenced by other French writers—the Socialists Babœuf and Proudhon. If he read Karl Marx, he preferred the idealist Socialism of the French authors to the scientific Socialism of the German. Nietzsche also influenced him, besides the Italian economist, Vilfredo Pareto, who declared that all systems are errors, all theories prisons. Georges Sorel, the French philosopher of Syndicalism, who is better known in Italy than in France, also appealed to him.

Nor must one forget, among the formative influences of Mussolini, that of the French Emperor, who was at least half Italian—Napoleon. It is easy to trace in the acts of Mussolini the mentorship of Napoleon. An American girl who was engaged to teach Mussolini the English language used to tell her colleagues of the numerous volumes on Napoleon which Mussolini had annotated with such phrases as "Superbly played," "A fine stroke," "This is where he went wrong," "Admirably conceived and executed," "I think he made a mistake here," and so forth.

There is a strange kind of idealism which thinks itself realism.

It expresses itself romantically. It prides itself on breaking down illusions. While the ordinary spell-binder substitutes glamorous words for things, the extraordinary spell-binder pretends to substitute things for glamorous words. Mussolini contrives to be elevated, and not cynical, when he denies human kindness, brotherhood, and love; he proclaims that with the rapid multiplication of philanthropic works for the alleviation of the miseries of men and animals in our century, there exist profounder, higher, and more vital impulses which are opposed to this humanitarianism. War is not caused by the caprices of monarchs, by race hatred, or economic rivalries: it is produced by instinctive feelings. Did not Proudhon utter the paradox that war is of divine origin?

So does Mussolini reveal himself. In denouncing mysticism he becomes mystical. Economic, artistic, intellectual, political, or sporting interests, binding nations together, cannot prevent the outbreak of war. While there is increased interchange among peoples, greater diffusion of common culture, the establishment of an international economic system, the peoples nevertheless tend to isolate themselves, both psychologically and morally. There is a new Nationalism. . . . He stated in one of his speeches the guiding lines of his policy:

"You will have the opportunity of realising that more valuable than my words will be the acts of my Government, which, in all that it does, will be inspired by and will keep before it these three fundamental principles:

"First: The nation, which is an undeniable reality.

"Secondly: The necessity of production, because greater and better production is not only in the interest of the capitalist but also of the workman; since the workman, together with the capitalist, loses his livelihood and falls into poverty if the productions of the nation do not find a market in the trade-centres of the world.

"Thirdly: The protection of the legitimate rights of the working classes."

He justified the use of force on behalf of Nationalism. "My desire," he said, "is to govern, if possible, by consent of the majority; but, in order to obtain, to foster, and to strengthen that consent, I will use all the force at my disposal. For it may happen that force will bring about consent and, if that fails, there is still force. With regard to all the requirements of government, even the most severe, we shall offer this alternative:

'Accept in the spirit of patriotism, or submit.' This is my conception of the State and of the art of governing the nation."

The methods of Fascism cannot be condoned—the bludgeoning of adversaries, the forcible administration of castor oil, political murder and arson, imprisonment and exile. Whatever excuses may be found for the earlier outrages, they were utterly abominable; and they were continued long after there could be the smallest necessity for them on any conceivable ground. Of the assassination of the deputy Matteotti, which shocked the conscience of mankind, it is difficult to acquit Mussolini himself and certainly high officials of Fascism were implicated in this outrage.

But it may be suggested that this is an exceptional incident, a regrettable outcome of misdirected zeal. Let us take then a more typical example. "The New Statesman," to which I have had the honour of contributing for many years, gave an account of Fascist methods long after Mussolini was strongly entrenched in power. Here is a plain tale of the brutality practised on a highly distinguished Italian thinker in March, 1924.

"In our issue of March 1st we published an article by Professor Guglielmo Salvadori, of the University of Florence, on 'Fascism and the Coming Elections.' Professor Salvadori certainly attacked Signor Mussolini's policy; but nobody could suggest that he overstepped the limit of fair political criticism as understood in civilised countries, and the burden of his argument was a demand that the law should be respected. We were warned that if we put his name to his article he might be murdered by the agents of Mussolini; but as a brave man he wished his name to appear, and so we decided to print it. We now learn, not from the Professor himself, but from some of his English relatives who can speak without fear of further reprisals, that he has been punished most brutally for the honest expression of his opinions. A band of armed Fascists visited his house and demanded an explanation. This he offered to give at their headquarters. He went there and was received by a dozen or so Blackshirts, first with gross insults and menaces and then with blows. They hit him repeatedly on the face and head and turned him out bleeding, to be struck again—this time with leather-covered canes—by another band at the door. His young son, who was waiting outside, rushed to his father's rescue, and he too was hit and thrown to the ground. The two got away, but were followed by their tormentors, who presently came up with them and once more beat them over the head with their sticks. Policemen looked on without interfering. They were only saved by a passing officer, who deputed two soldiers to escort them home. Since then the Professor has been assured that he will escape further molestation so long as he breathes no word of criticism of the Fascists' activities. Such is Fascism!"

Hundreds, perhaps thousands, of similar incidents could be related.

For my part I am unable to declare myself against Dictatorships in all circumstances. It may become an indispensable method of government. But for gratuitous barbarity no single word can be spoken.

But Fascism was given its opportunity because existing previous governments had shown themselves unable to save Italy from disintegration. I travelled in Italy in the worst days which immediately preceded Mussolini's march on Rome. All responsible Italians to whom I spoke shook their heads sadly, and deplored the breaking up of institutions, the lack of patriotism, the conflict of classes, the economic disorganisation, the financial chaos. The mass of the people had become apathetic. There were quarrelsome factions. Bureaucracy was inefficient. Everybody had grievances. There was no leadership. Things were going to pieces.

Towns like Milan fell into the hands of singularly ineffective Socialists. A poor-spirited Communism made some progress and tried to imitate the example of the Soviets in Russia. Committees took over factories and found themselves incompetent to run them. Revolutionary schemes, like Governmental schemes, proved abortive. There was neither organisation nor cohesion. There was only inertia in chaos; and the experiments which occasionally broke the inertia were ludicrously futile.

In this lamentable state of affairs, when Italy was crumbling to ruins, Mussolini suddenly emerged, and collected around him a little band of men who were, in many cases, war veterans. The backbone of the first Fascist forces were old members of the Arditi—the shock troops of the war, who had thrown themselves into battle bomb in hand, dagger at belt, with supreme contempt for death. Fighting desperately they had sung their hymns of war. Around this nucleus Fascism was formed. It proclaimed its intention of saving Italy. It became fiercely anti-Socialist. Its members wore black shirts. They took vows of discipline. At first they were really in peril and they did not

shrink from peril—on the contrary they paraded ostentatiously
in uniform in the midst of Socialists and Communists. The success of Fascism is largely due to this contempt for danger that
marked its earliest adherents.

The black shirt was a symbol of an adventurous spirit. If
the early Fascists practised violence it was repaid; and one
would not complain of the blows that were then given and
taken had not the Fascists, when they became masters, continued their violence though safe from retaliation. In his usual
grandiloquent, self-glorifying manner Mussolini has described
Fascism at this time:

"Fascism, unique lighthouse in a sea of cowardice, of compromise and of foggy, plum-coloured idealism, had engaged
itself in battles; it was overpowered by mere blind multitudes.
I was the bull's-eye of the target of the Government of Nitti.
He unloosed against me all his hounds, while his journalists
tired themselves in vain to note down my contradictions in
political matters. The Socialists, mindful of my moral and
physical strength, covered me with their vengeance and their
ostracism. . . .

"I had an effect on my soldiers which seemed to me almost
mystical. The boys saw in me the avenger of our wronged Italy.
The dying said, 'Give us our black shirts for winding sheets.'
I could not remain unmoved when I knew that their last
thoughts were of 'Our native land and the Duce.' Love and
songs bloomed. A revival of youth filled with Italian boldness,
swamped by their virile male beauty the unrestrained rages of
irresponsibles; painted out the fear of the Socialists; obliterated
the ambiguity of the Liberals. . . ."

The movement—for Mussolini refuses to call it a party, since
it is anti-party—grew slowly. It nearly succumbed for want
of money. But it did grow and presently it became an organised
military force which spread throughout Italy. After the street
fights the Fascists prepared real expeditions. They took possession of towns that had been controlled by Communists. There
is no doubt that they showed courage and discipline and that
they were well directed.

The Government looked on helplessly. At last Mussolini felt
that the hour had come to take the decisive step. He marshalled
his army; they mustered over a hundred thousand men; they
wore tasselled caps and black shirts; they carried carbines and
triangular flags. With Mussolini at their head they marched to

Rome. The populace cheered them. The King saluted them. It would be interesting to speculate on what might have happened had the King opposed them. Mussolini had Republican leanings, and it is possible that had the King not ranged himself with Fascism Italy would now be a Republic. It is also possible that Fascism would have been crushed in a terrible civil war. On the whole, it was well perhaps that the King put himself on the side of Mussolini, and Mussolini on the side of the King.

Not long ago an Italian came to me with startling news. "There is," he said, "a Fascist plot to kidnap the King and to proclaim Mussolini Emperor."

"Nonsense," I replied. "Mussolini is not a madman. At present he has no trouble with the Monarchy. But if he suppressed the Monarchy a powerful Royalist party would immediately spring up in Italy."

Apparently that was how Mussolini reasoned. A little later my Italian informant came to tell me that while it was true that some irresponsible Fascist had worked out such a scheme as he had indicated, Mussolini had forbidden its execution.

And now my correspondent writes to tell me that Mussolini contemplates the transformation of the Kingdom of Italy into an Empire, with the King as Emperor and himself as Imperial Chancellor.

IX. AN ESTIMATE

I ASKED my friend, Dr. Paul Cremona, certainly one of the most judicious commentators on Italian affairs, sincere, unbiased, to give me his considered opinion on the Italian political situation. It will be seen that he does not share the prejudices of anti-Fascists, but neither does he rush into the excesses of zealous pro-Fascists:

1. In 1925 the opinion held abroad was that Fascism was only a passing phenomenon, destined only to a short life; but it is now recognised and admitted that the Fascist régime is more firmly than ever seated in the saddle, and that no change is to be expected in Italy. This view is fully shared by me.

2. I notice, not only in London, but also in Paris, that the campaign conducted by the adversaries of Fascism against the Mussolini régime has lost much of its sting and is no longer finding that response which was noticeable in many quarters

two or three years ago. This, of course, does not mean that there is approval of the Fascist methods of government, but, in my opinion, it shows (a) that the alarming reports on the trend of Italian affairs spread by anti-Fascists are being taken less seriously and given less credence than was the case two or three years ago, and (b) that there is a growing tendency outside of Italy to give greater attention to the most recent Fascist reforms, and more especially to the Fascist syndicalist legislation, and to see the practical result of their application before passing any definite judgment on Fascism.

3. A question which has been put to me is: What will become of Fascism when Mussolini is no more? This is one of the points which is at present attracting great attention outside Italy, and there is much speculation as to the eventual choice of Mussolini's successor. No precise answer to the question can be given to-day. Its importance, however, can be realised by the fact that the Fascists themselves, who hitherto had refused to give the slightest consideration to the matter, are now thinking and talking about it, and the recent law on the Grand Council principally aims to ensure the continuation of the Fascist régime. It must not be forgotten that the whole machinery of government arranged by Mussolini pre-supposes that the reins of government should actually be and should remain in the hands of one man, possessing authority and prestige above everybody else. If such a man were not to be found—and certainly to-day no Fascist statesman can claim that distinction —then the machinery will not work and will by degrees break into pieces. This seems to me to be one of the greatest dangers of Fascism, a danger common to all autocratic governments; it is realised by all, but no one dares to face it and still less to suggest a solution to the difficulty. The law on the Grand Council may perhaps avert the confusion which will necessarily arise when Mussolini disappears from the scene, temporarily enabling the Fascists to hold their present strong position, but it leaves the problem unsolved.

4. It is, however, in the intricate field of foreign problems that we are mainly interested. The Fascist Government seems to have inherited from previous Administrations the principal characteristic of their foreign policy, namely, its inconsistency. One day, for instance, Italy seems to be on very friendly terms with Germany, and the very next day you notice a sudden

change in attitude. On many occasions you hear that Italy will
stand by its former allies for the integral application of the
Peace Treaties, and on other occasions you will see Mussolini
giving his influential support to the Hungarian campaign for
the revision of the Treaty of Trianon. While, therefore, it is
possible to make a fairly accurate forecast of the future foreign
policy of Great Britian, France and Germany, it is extremely
difficult, in the case of Italy, to base one's judgment of its
future conduct in foreign affairs on its past or present attitude.

5. The guiding principles of Italy's foreign policy as they
appear to me to-day are:

(a) To assert most vigorously and whenever opportunity arises
that Italy to-day ranks among the Great Powers of the world;
it expects to be treated as such by all nations, big or small.

(b) To proclaim the necessity of Italy's "pacific" expansion
and to insist upon the need of new outlets for its excessive
population.

(c) To maintain that in the partition of German colonies at
the Peace Conference of 1919 it was most unfairly treated by
Great Britain and France, and that if ever there shall be a redistribution of mandates it has a better right than Germany to
receive the charge of overseas territories.

(d) To oppose the political union of Austria and Germany.

(e) To prevent all other States, and especially Yugo-Slavia,
from interfering in Albanian affairs, and to consider any such
interference, direct or indirect, as a serious menace to its vital
interests in the Adriatic.

(f) To defend by all means in its power, and if necessary by
war, its present privileged position in Albania.

(g) To consider any action of foreign Governments on behalf
of Italian subjects of other nationalities, (German, Yugo-Slav
and Greek) as a violation of its sovereign rights and as an interference in its domestic affairs.

(h) To do its utmost to defend the national status of Italians
living in foreign countries.

(i) Italy does not sincerely believe in disarmament, which it
regards as advantageous only to those States who are rich and
powerful.

(j) It has little confidence in the League of Nations, and will
almost surely refuse to bring before the League any serious
dispute which it might have with another power.

(k) It favours the revision of the Peace Treaties so far as this revision affects other countries because it hopes to gain advantages therefrom.

(l) Italy will never renounce one inch of its territory and would be ready to go to war to defend its new boundaries.

(m) There are several territories which even to-day Italy regards as "irredente" (unredeemed), and upon which it holds a claim of a more or less sentimental nature. These are Corsica, the French Riviera, Savoy, Dalmatia, Malta, and, to a certain extent, Tunisia. Italy, however, will not go into war with France, Yugo-Slavia or Great Britain just to gain possession of these territories, but, in the event of war with any of these powers, it will, if victorious, demand the annexation of such territories.

6. It cannot be denied that relations between Italy and France are not satisfactory, and it is difficult for one who perceives the strong anti-French feeling in Italy to feel optimistic about the future of Franco-Italian relations. Fortunately, however, the points of difference between the two Latin countries are not so serious as to justify a recourse to war for their settlement; but there are many examples in history which teach us that when bad feeling exists between rival nations, an incident of minor importance may lead to war. I do not think that there is any possibility to-day of an armed conflict between France and Italy, but at the same time, I strongly believe that the interests of peace could better be served by a timely and honest denunciation of a potential danger to peace than by ignoring events which might easily lead to serious international complications. The persistent campaign in the Fascist Press against France, and the "war spirit" of the Fascists, have undoubtedly created a situation which, although not yet alarming, is a cause of anxiety to observers of Italian affairs. People here are being daily taught to look upon France as the country which is opposing Italy's "pacific" expansion and is responsible for all the diplomatic difficulties which Italy is encountering in its forward march. While friendly references to Italy appearing in the French Press are hardly ever reproduced by Italian newspapers, all articles hostile to Italy published by the French Socialist and Radical papers are given the widest possible publicity, being described as truly representative of French public opinion.

7. If the French and the Italian Governments were really animated by goodwill and by a sincere desire to remove the obstacles for a close understanding between them, it would not be difficult for them to come to an agreement. After my return to Rome some French newspapers prematurely announced that the French and Italian Governments were about to sign a treaty for the settlement of their differences. The cold reception given by the "Giornale d'Italia", an organ notoriously in touch with the Italian Foreign Office, to the alleged terms of the coming Franco-Italian arrangement shows that Italy still maintains its claims to the rectification in its favour of the Libyan frontier and to the modification of the status of Italian subjects in Tunisia. An arrangement on these two very important questions may eventually be reached between Italy and France, but relations between the two nations will not really improve until they seriously make up their minds to replace their mutual suspicion and mistrust by sincere goodwill. In Italy's case this suspicion and mistrust of its neighbour is more marked than that shown by France, but it would not be fair to put all the blame on Italy for the present unsatisfactory condition of Italo-French relations. Pacts of friendship are valueless (as the Italo-Yugo-Slav Treaty of 1924 has shown) unless they are accompanied by mutual goodwill. Incidentally, I may add that an amicable settlement of Franco-Italian differences would certainly be followed by a substantial improvement in Italo-Yugo-Slav relations.

8. I have referred in a previous paragraph to the "war spirit" at present noticeable in Italy. A perusal of Mussolini's speeches during the last few years should suffice to show what he thinks about peace and war, disarmament, etc. He has succeeded to a remarkable degree in convincing his followers of the truth of his theories, which they have adopted as their own. Especially among the young members of his party (who know nothing about the horrors of the last war) he has a large number of personal followers. His frequent threats to other nations and his warlike speeches should not be taken too literally. The speeches are mostly made for home consumption, but one must admit that he has cleverly raised the problem of Italy's need for expansion, and that in many countries there is now a movement in favour of Italy. "Obviously something must be done for Italy" is the conclusion arrived at by many with whom I

have discussed the problem, and who fear that one day Italy may pass from words to action.

X. PIRANDELLO

TWICE it has been my privilege to meet Signor Luigi Pirandello, unquestionably the Italian author who has achieved the widest fame in recent years. He is one of the youngest of Italian writers. If one counts by years he has long ago passed middle age; but one must not count like that. The dramatist who was approaching his sixtieth year before he conquered the world vibrates to all the influences of his time. He is overwhelmingly modern. Like the psychoanalyst, he is obsessed by the mysterious relations of the subconscious and the conscious. What is real and what is imaginary? Can the frontier be drawn as definitely as we have been accustomed to draw it? Is it not as untraceable as those frontiers the statesmen of Versailles foolishly thought they could set down on paper?

It would seem that personality is much more definite than a nation, that you can draw a line round a man if you cannot round a country, and declare that inside the line is the whole man and nothing but the man, while outside the line he does not exist. The psychological map-maker knows better—that is to say, he knows that he does not know. It is impossible to delimitate the spirit. It is impossible to say where we begin and where we end. It is impossible to draw the boundaries between being and non-being. No definition can be given of reality and imagination. It may be that the creations of the brain are truly alive, while we who think we are alive are merely dead pieces of mechanism, like those dead pieces of mechanism which generate electricity.

In fantastic paradoxes like these does Pirandello revel. I was well acquainted with his extraordinary theatrical achievements in which he insists on the validity of imagination, on the sanity of insanity, before I met Pirandello; and I half expected to find a wild-eyed, half-crazy individual hovering like a ghost on the border-line which separates the visible world from dreamland. No, that is not correct; I am tricking myself into a conventional error. I was perfectly well aware that the artist who is capable of profound psychological analysis must be particularly sane. To deal with the eeriness of things requires an especially cool temper. Moreover, experience has taught me that an author rarely looks like an author—or at least not like the particular kind of author he is. Nevertheless, it is true that vaguely I had thought of Pirandello as a Pirandellan personage—a strange emanation from one of his own plays. . . . However this may be, Pirandello soon showed me that he is totally unlike a Pirandellan personage.

He is a quiet-looking, grey-bearded little man, entirely conventional in dress and manners. One notices his agate eyes, but they are all that is distinctive. His white hands, rather plump, lay on his lap. He made no gestures. He spoke softly. He was unobtrusive. He wore an old-fashioned black tailcoat, and looked for all the world like a little provincial lawyer.

This stocky little man was the great Sicilian who has been described as the most original theatrical genius since Ibsen. He has mystified the whole world with his subtle distinctions between thinking and being. He has carried illusion to a higher point than it has ever been carried before, for he has almost persuaded us that illusions are far more substantial than that which we generally regard as substance.

He talked without much zest on commonplace subjects. He seemed exhausted, but there was a glint of humour in those agate eyes.

"Yes, the grotesque side of things interests me, if indeed it may be called grotesque," he said; "but I did not pay much attention to the theatre as a form of literary art until after the war. Obviously the stage is the proper place for my conceptions. I do not know whether anyone else has tried to put them on the stage."

"Your characters are so intensely alive," I said; "they must cost you a tremendous expenditure of energy."

The agate eyes lit up. "I have put myself into them," said Pirandello simply. "They are my impressions of life which have taken flesh and in whose veins flows real blood."

For the rest there is not much to recall of our broken conversation. He paid a tribute, I think, to Max Reinhardt whose industry is incredible and whose art is incomparable, and he expressed appreciation of Bernard Shaw, who, in his turn, has hailed "Six Characters in Quest of an Author" as the most extraordinary drama of modern times—perhaps of all time.

Pirandello was born in Sicily in 1867. His father tried to prepare him for a business career. The family owned sulphur mines and was relatively rich. But young Pirandello preferred Latin

PIRANDELLO

MARINETTI

and Greek to arithmetic and book-keeping. He had his own way, and he pursued a classical education at Palermo and afterwards at Bonn.

Financial disaster fell on the family; I understand that the wife of Pirandello was afflicted; Pirandello himself was seriously ill for many months.

It was in this period that he received those impressions of insanity and sanity, of actuality and illusion, which serve as the texture of his subsequent plays. For it is in insanity that the partition between actuality and illusion, thin at all times, is definitely broken down.

In his novel, "The Late Mathias Pascal," he has already adumbrated this method. The dissociation of the personality forms the theme of all his plays, but he treats the subject in a most diversified manner. The personality is something. It is a thousand somethings. It is nothing. We are conscious of being. We feel we are unique. But in fact when we try to form a precise image of ourselves the reality escapes us. Which is the real "I"? Is it the "I" which I present to this or that interlocutor in these or those circumstances? Or is it the "I" which I present to another interlocutor in different circumstances? Or is it the "I" which corresponds to my own conception of "I"? Oliver Wendell Holmes put the point neatly and humorously in one of his Breakfast Table Talks. Pirandello puts it more tragically, and at the same time more philosophically. On the foundations of this simple doctrine—that the personality is elusive, that it is not stable, that it changes in changing conditions, that it is not the same for one observer as for another—Pirandellism is built. We should not be judged by a single action performed by somebody who has apparently no relation to ourselves. We may be not only Jekylls and Hydes, but a hundred Jekylls and Hydes. Those who are most consistent in their personality are madmen, who pursue their fancies without regard to the opinions of others or the contradictions of circumstances. And perhaps the characters of novels and plays, truly created, with an immortal and immutable life, are far more real than living and changing men and women.

It is fantastic enough; but in constructing his plays Pirandello contrives to throw light on great human problems. He is not merely a manipulator of grotesque marionettes. There is a profound humanity, a poignant pity, in the humour of Pirandello. He teaches us that man cannot live without thinking his life, that his tragedy lies in the discrepancy between his image of himself and the image of himself fashioned by others. Although Pirandello never forgets his thesis, he is such a marvellous dramatist that we never, while his dramas are being enacted, regard them as allegories. We admire his ingenuity, but we are above all gripped by his story.

To the writer—or to anyone with the urge to write—who has ever endeavoured or been tempted to create a personage, Pirandello becomes especially interesting. We have been obsessed by fictitious personages clamouring for existence. They cry to us to be delivered from some dark limbo. They are personages in quest of an author. They are our dream-children who suffer if we deny them a separate existence. How many authors are quite unable to control their characters when once they are born! The characters do what they please; they go their wilful way without regard to artistic laws. . . . Pirandello has felt the appeal of his dream-children more consciously than others, or at least he has expressed his sensations more clearly than anybody else. His Characters pleaded to be written. He had to write to free himself of an obsession. Born in his brain, they were not his creatures. They had a separate potential life, and they obliged him to give them their dramatic functions.

It is true as the critics have said that in Six Characters Pirandello has expounded his single subject. Yet he does not repeat himself. He is inexhaustible in resources. For my part I thought that, hallucinating as the Six Characters were, Henry IV revealed a finer technique. It is a marvellous tour de force—if ever that hackneyed phrase can be applied. From beginning to end it is almost a monologue but it is never monotonous. The madman is no longer mad. In his lapse into lucidity he commits a crime; and there is nothing for it but to resume his mask of madness. The madman is sane, and the sane are mad; he is mocking them and they are humouring him. . . . In another play a woman who has woven a legend of martyrdom about herself finds herself stripped bit by bit of the fiction which made up her whole life. Without her fictions she is a poor miserable naked creature. . . . Always is there this clash of illusion and reality, and the reality is that which we are accustomed to regard as illusion and the illusion that which we are accustomed to regard as reality. Always are we shown the isolation of the individual; we are stricken with a sense of the transitory;

we are puzzled by the lack of clear identity; we are disconcerted by the discontinuity of life. Always is the human desire
for fixity of form at odds with the eternal flux of life. We
clutch at straws, but the current rushes headlong; our attempts
at crystallisation are perpetually defeated.

The elements of this philosophy are, in expression at least,
characteristically modern. That is why I described Pirandello
as one of the younger men. He has caught up the thoughts of
many of the "moderns." As Crémieux remarks, there is the
vitalism of Bergson, the subconscious of Freud, the relativism
of Einstein, the subjectivism of Proust; but these things make
up something new—Pirandellism.

We are acquainted in France, in England, in America, with
an amazing number of Pirandello's works, but they do not
represent the quantity as well as the quality of his extraordinary production. He pours out his novels and plays with
dazzling speed. There must, I suppose now, be nearly four hundred novels and plays, short or long, signed by Pirandello. Some
of the best of them have been written in a few days. He has
invented for himself a system of abbreviated writing in which
he sets down his sentences; it is a system which few people
understand; and it is the son of Pirandello who transcribes the
mysterious signs.

XI. EXCLUDED

ONE of Mussolini's pet ideas is the establishment of an
Italian Academy similar in character to the Académie
Française. It was difficult to execute the project and it hung
fire for more than three years. But I gather that now Italy too
has its Academy and that the honour of presiding over the
Italian Immortals has fallen on Senator Tommaso Tittoni, the
eminent statesman and learned scholar. This fact clearly gives
a Fascist colour to official literature and scientific research, for
Tittoni is one of the ex-officio members of the Fascist Grand
Council.

Always do such academies make for the sterilisation of the
intellect. It has been so in France where, from the days of
Richelieu to our own, the Academy has been strictly conservative in its influence. Its function is to stabilise—that is to say,
to imprison art in the accepted forms. The greatest French
authors were either not elected at all to the Academy, or were

elected for reasons which had nothing to do with their real
work, or were elected after they had ceased to be innovators
and had become stereotyped. On the other hand, mediocrity has
always had a conspicuous place in the Academy.

It is therefore not surprising to learn that just as Emile Zola,
Alphonse Daudet, Frédéric Mistral and Georges Courteline
were barred from the French Academy (to say nothing of
Molière and Balzac and Baudelaire) so the Italian Academy has
omitted the most illustrious exponents of modern Italian
thought. On the first list there was no mention of Gabriele
d'Annunzio. Perhaps d'Annunzio is too personal to be acceptable to any Academy; and it is difficult to imagine that he
would allow any Academy to smother him with its slimy excre-
tions. Nor did I find the name of Guglielmo Ferrero. Perhaps
this too is not surprising, for if the historian of ancient Rome
and the philosophical commentator on current affairs is widely
read abroad, and possesses a deserved influence outside Italy, he
has never been accepted wholeheartedly in his own country.
He is not looked upon with a friendly eye by Fascism. He does
not think as an Italian but as a citizen of the world. He writes
what he believes to be the truth, not the Fascist version of the
truth. . . .

Again Benedetto Croce, philosopher, historian, critic, was
not chosen. Yet he has had an enormous influence over his own
century while refusing to follow the intellectual fashions. He
too is a non-conformist—a rebel to accepted thought. Accordingly he has had to fight against the university circles and he
has repeatedly alienated his own disciples. Erudition as such he
denounces as insufficient. Sensualism and mysticism and empty
rhetoric he abhors. He is an independent champion of spiritual
values. Incidentally he is anti-Fascist. When he (as Senator)
made an illuminating speech on Mussolini's Vatican policy, it
was not reported in the Italian newspapers, and my own copy
of it came as a circular.

Giovanni Papini who was converted to Catholicism after the
war, is likewise left out. He has changed his views frequently
but he has preserved in his transformations the ardour of the
unsatisfied searcher. Revealing his doubts and living his moral
life in his pages, he becomes a sort of cross-section of an epoch.
After his conversion he wrote a Life of Christ, highly coloured,
extremely personal, revolutionary in spirit, that made him
world-famous.

Another who is omitted is Ugo Ojetti, an acute observer of contemporary men and things, a suggestive critic, an excellent chronicler. Then there is Grazia Deledda who is doubtless not included because she is a woman. In 1927 the Nobel prize was awarded to her for her stories of the Sardinian peasantry. She observes simply and sets down her impressions with refreshing directness.

If Fascism becomes a permanent social system will it produce a definite type of literature? Will there be a Fascist manner in writing? It is doubtful. At first there was revival of Futurism in the arts, endeavouring to identify itself with Fascism in life. That period has passed. As Fascism consolidates itself it turns academic. Fascism as such may be as barren as Bonapartism.

Mussolini himself aims at a vigorous, vivid, and even brutal style, though it is puffed up with false grandiloquence. In the newspapers this style is regarded as Fascist—though certainly it was not invented by Fascism. But it would be difficult to point to any specific Fascist contribution to literature. On the contrary, Fascism is turning from Modernism to Traditionalism.

For some time in France and other European countries an Italian review in the French language entitled 900 was read with interest. Its influence, however, was largely negative. It opposed the doctrine of art for art's sake; it was against Romanticism, against Realism, against sentimentality and æsthetic refinements; it was against lyricism and formalism, and the whole hotchpotch of isms that have led literature into impasse after impasse. What was it not against? This movement was directed by Massimo Bontempelli. A rival movement is directed by Ardengo Soffici; for him Italy is not ultra-modern but anti-modern. There are a number of other movements, polemical and noisy enough, but these literary quarrels, though they may be amusing, are not important.

Benjamin Crémieux excellently points out that the persistence of "fragmentism"—made up of impressions, things seen, immediate notations, detached pages—"is in part due to the fact that the literary production of Italy appears first in the daily papers. Italy is almost without literary or semi-literary periodicals. . . . Apart from book form the Italian writer has no other outlet than the third pages of the dailies, or the illustrated magazines which depend in general on the dailies." He sees the influence of the "third page" in the descriptive or autobiographical "fragments" which distinguish present-day Italian literature.

XII. FUTURISM

FUTURISM has played its part; it seemed to be sterile in the arts, but it has been productive in life. Energy, destructive rather than constructive, may be fatal in art; but it is essential in life. So while the artists were hurrying up cul-de-sacs, the men of action, who think life itself a worth-while adventure, were learning much from Futurism.

Filippo Tommaso Marinetti, the Futurist chief, may not improperly be described as the father of all the eccentricities that have manifested themselves in modern art, and of the vitality that has manifested itself in modern life. Some of these eccentricities are obviously idiotic. Others, however, have added something to our knowledge of æsthetics and of life. Whatever has actually come out of the experimentation of our time, it was good that there should be experimentation. It was good that these explosive forces should have shaken us out of our complacency. You may think what you will of Cubism and Dadaism and Surrealism and Vorticism and Expressionism and I do not know how many other isms, but it was necessary to take a fresh attitude, to make a violent effort to escape from the conventions in which we were becoming mummified.

My acquaintance with Marinetti was purely Parisian. In the French capital I came upon him on diverse occasions. Always was he provocative. He had a veritable genius for creating a tumult. His fiery manner, his strident voice, his incessant gesticulation, seemed to set electric currents in motion. Everybody was soon gesticulating, shouting, disputing. . . . I remember one occasion in particular. We were crowded into a tiny room awaiting Marinetti. We were calm enough and indeed there was no reason why we should be excited. But he entered; his long figure conveying a challenge; his head thrown back; his moustache upcurled; his eyes flashing defiance. Instantly there was an uproar. It is impossible for me to say why. His very presence produced perturbation. When he began to talk he did not, as I recollect, say anything that should logically have aroused us. But arouse us it did, and soon he was crying above the commotion, shrilly dominating the confusion which swelled and broke and swelled again. I have a vision of his head on a long muscular neck waving like a scarlet plume above the battle. I have a vision of his hands angrily shaken like banners. But what it was all about I completely forget.

It was in Paris that Marinetti spent his student days, and to Paris he constantly returned. Yet his accent was anything but French. His Italian pronunciation was in itself at once humorous and irritating. Yet his verbal ingenuity in the French language is extraordinary.

Futurism is not doctrinal but dynamic. In his manifestos Marinetti proclaimed the necessity of escaping from the past which had become a prison. In letters and in life Futurism professes horror of peace. The first Futurist meeting at Milan, nominally artistic in purpose, opened with cries of "Down with Austria!" Marinetti himself sought danger. He plunged into the war as an officer of artillery. Futurism called for an acceleration of the rhythm of things. It denounced all that was old and known. It emphasised the value of the individual. It set no bounds to ambitions and human desires.

Man can multiply himself and magnify himself by machinery.

The poetry of Futurism consisted of Words in Liberty. Syntax was destroyed. Adjectives and adverbs were abolished. Objects and images were confounded. Punctuation was suppressed. Mathematical signs were employed. Ugliness was permitted but solemnity was banned. Intuition replaced intelligence. The most daring comparisons were used; a lively fox-terrier, for example, became boiling water; a trench of bayonets became an orchestra.

We should, cried Marinetti, be drunk with life and life should be drunk with us.

Marinetti argued that if a really living person with lyrical gifts tried to tell his experiences of an earthquake or a revolution he would not take the trouble to construct periods; he would throw out the essential words without apparent order. He would use a sort of "telegraphese" corresponding to his internal vibrations. Similar expression on the printed page presupposes a typographical revolution. Marinetti also indicates the necessity of a suggestive orthography, of verbal deformation; and perhaps he may therefore be taken to be a forerunner of Mr. James Joyce.

He declared himself especially hostile to all the paraphernalia of fatal women, moonlight, memories, nostalgia, eternity, immortality, picturesqueness, solitude, twilight, ruins, pessimism, and that patina which he called the filth of time.

Before me is a Futurist manifesto on the art of noise. It is addressed to Pratella, a Futurist musician, and it records that with fists and with sticks the first performance of Futurist music was defended in a theatre of Rome. . . . Antique life was silence. In the Nineteenth Century, with the invention of machinery, noises began to be heard. To-day noises dominate the sensibilities of men. Normally nature is quiet, and tempests and avalanches are exceptional; but men learned to make noises. Primitive peoples attributed to the earliest sounds drawn from pipes or chords a divine origin. As music developed mere sweetness was sought. Later, dissonance was admitted. Now every kind of noise should be arranged by the musician in a new art.

Beethoven and Wagner have, continues the manifesto, appealed to us for many years. Now we are sick of them. That is why we take far more pleasure in combining ideally the sounds of tramways and of crying crowds than in listening to their harmonies. The sound of a few violins is ridiculous when we are acquainted with the sound of underground railways and electric saws. So, I gather, the music of the future will be produced mechanically, and will be composed of steam whistles, crashing trains, the percussions of Nasmyth hammers, the whizz of aeroplane propellers—the whole scale of sounds that has been brought to us for our delectation by mechanical invention. It is not mere imitation which is demanded, but a fantastic association of varied tones which will awaken emotions by their sonority or their shrillness. Instead of a few musical notes we will be able to combine, some day, twenty or thirty thousand different sounds.

Marinetti likewise invites us to develop the art of tactilism—that is to say, to learn how to obtain emotions from the sense of touch. We can, for example, have tactile tables on which we can enjoy various categories of tactile values. We can successively touch silk and velvet, metals, sandpaper, wool, wire, brushes,—obtaining caressing sensations, piquant sensations, fresh sensations, soft sensations, warm sensations, cold sensations, and so forth. He proposes tactile cushions, tactile divans, tactile beds, tactile shirts. He even proposes tactile rooms, in which sensual pleasures would be provided by marbles, mirrors, metals, electric wires. More complicated still are his tactile streets which I do not quite understand, and his tactile theatres in which audiences will place their hands on long rolling ribbons and thus receive rhythmic tactile sensations.

All of which is nine parts nonsense. Nevertheless, in painting, in literature, in music, in life, the influence of Marinetti has been prodigious. It has not been sufficiently recognised. We can laugh at particular aspects of Futurism, and doubtless Marinetti has his tongue in his cheek. But there is a most serious side to Futurism. It has served to make us aware of the changes of a vibrant world.

XIII. THE POPE

MANY times has it been said that the salient fact of the new Europe is the revival of the Vatican as a world power. Benedict XV was openly accused, in the allied countries, of favouring Germany during the war; and whether the accusations were well founded or not it is certain that the Vatican suffered by its silence; it permitted the terrible slaughter to go on for four years without effectively raising its voice, without imposing its authority. An inexperienced observer might well have supposed that the war was a death-blow to the spiritual, after the temporal, power of the Vatican. Yet soon afterwards Papal influence in European Chancelleries greatly increased, and the Vatican must to-day be reckoned among the important diplomatic agencies of the world.

It is in large measure to the present Pope, Pius XI, that this unexpected result is due. The Church may have lost adherents in several Central European countries, but it has planted its emissaries everywhere. Pius XI will be remembered as a political rather than an ecclesiastical Pope. He is doubtless intelligent, but he is obstinate and more personal in his action than some of his predecessors. He has, in my opinion, made many mistakes. His intervention in French politics has been marked. The Nuncio in France, contrary to all precedents, eulogised, as doyen of the diplomatic corps, the diplomacy of M. Briand in the Elysée Palace on the occasion of the New Year reception. The French bishops, on the instructions of Rome, refused to marry or bury pious Catholics whose only offence was that they were, politically, Royalists. The "Action Française", a Royalist newspaper read by many Catholics, was put on the index—as though one can assume in advance that unpublished editions of the journal will be doctrinally unsound! Clearly the Pope has resolved to go outside his religious functions and to favour political and diplomatic designs which will help to restore the Vatican to an influential place in world affairs.

On his election in 1922 he was comparatively young. The need of an energetic Pope, who would rise to the height of a great opportunity for inspired and sagacious service was felt by the Cardinals. The peoples had madly tried to destroy each other, and to some extent they had succeeded. Now they had returned to sanity, and saw in the principle of universal justice a better objective than individual profit which could only be secured by general destruction. They still kept their notions of Nationalism and had indeed sharpened them, but they had begun to realise that another orgy of Nationalism in action would mean universal ruin. Could Vatican diplomacy help in the ardent yearning for pacification? Could the Pope bring, as he had announced, the Peace of Christ in the Reign of Christ?

He cannot do it by pettyfogging intrigues, by subtle combinations, by the turning of one countenance towards this nation and another countenance towards that nation.

Cardinal Ratti, Archbishop of Milan, knew a great deal about European politics; before his elevation he had served as Nuncio at Warsaw. He is, of course, an Italian by birth, but he is acquainted with many tongues, and he talks with American and English visitors in their own language. Short in stature but sturdily built, he had, until he was imprisoned in the Vatican, kept himself in excellent physical condition by his favourite sport of mountain-climbing. A friend of mine who was recently granted an audience tells me, however, that, deprived of his former exercise, he has become pale-faced and unhealthy in appearance. Although he may now leave the Vatican the prolonged confinement has considerably aged him.

The election of a Pope is a tremendous event which brings to Rome not only Cardinals from the ends of the earth but hundreds of newspapermen. The more experienced newspapermen write their stories in advance—graphic descriptions of the proceedings which they have copied from old files and which they hold in readiness for the moment when a thin column of white smoke goes up from a little tin chimney by the Sixtine Chapel to announce to the beholders that the Cardinals are in agreement. One journalist amused me by his cynical confession that his work had been done—with the exception of the name—before he began to watch for that thin column of

THE POPE

smoke. His colleague did not find the confession so amusing, for
he had taken the pains of first informing himself and of then
rushing his story by cable, only to find that his account, while
it was doubtless truthful, was useless because it was belated.

The Swiss Guards, in multicoloured uniforms, stand by the
bronze doors—and the rest of the guards and gendarmes in the
Papal service picturesquely parade. The Cardinals are shut up
like jurymen when once they have gone into conclave; their
food is sent in to them by a revolving box; and they sleep on
little iron bedsteads. All the entrances are locked, and for several days the Cardinals are cut off from worldly influences.
Outside patient multitudes wait; their eyes glued to the tin
chimney. It is the custom to burn damp straw with the ballot
papers if no decision has been reached—and so the smoke from
the chimney is dark. When it is white the choice has been made;
and presently a Cardinal makes the announcement from the
balcony of the Basilica.

This time the world was wrongly informed for the name of
Ratti sounded like Tacci, and before the error was discovered
it had been cabled round the world.

It was significant that Pius XI came out on the balcony to
bless the assembled crowds in the square. He set a precedent
which was soon interpreted as an indication of his desire to
escape from the conventional prison of the Popes.

Another precedent was set—though presumably not with
the consent of the Pope—when a cinematographic film was
taken of Pius XI walking in the grounds of the Vatican. Let me
tell the story (for which I in no way vouch) as it was told to
me by the operator:

"I had received a telegram from the American company for
which I was acting, telling me that I must get a moving picture
of the Pope. This was a tall order, but I decided to do what I
could. My job might depend upon my enterprise.

"So I flew to Rome and without much difficulty obtained an
introduction to an official of the Vatican. We went to lunch
together and I boldly made an offer of ten thousand dollars
for the right to take a picture. As I understood, the offer was
accepted.

"But presently I heard that an Italian company had obtained
some sort of promise, which it described as the exclusive right
to photograph the Pope. This complicated the situation, and I
entered into negotiations with the Italian company. I found

that the arrangement was exceedingly vague, and did not amount to much. Nevertheless I asked what sum would satisfy them to surrender whatever rights they had. They demanded three hundred thousand lire.

"Thereupon I replied that I must consult my firm before paying such a large sum. They agreed to a short delay.

"In the meantime I took another course. I got in touch with an officer of the Papal Guards, and gave him a thousand lire. We hit upon a plan by which I was to stay in my hotel until the last moment in order not to arouse suspicions, for if I was recognised my purpose might be divined. Accordingly I stayed in my hotel and never showed myself.

"In the early morning, while it was still dark, I changed into guard's uniform. My apparatus was carried in various sections into a little box-room almost completely dark; and I too was smuggled into this box-room which overlooked the grounds.

"There I remained, scarcely daring to move, from five o'clock in the morning until five o'clock in the evening. I had a few sandwiches to eat and something to drink in a flask.

"Everything passed off well though those were the most uncomfortable and anxious hours I have ever spent. I got my picture in the late afternoon and made my escape.

"Had I instantly disappeared suspicions might once more have been awakened. I hung about my hotel, showing myself ostentatiously, but an assistant was flying in an aeroplane across Europe. He arrived in a French port just in time to catch a ship which was leaving for the United States.

"That is how I obtained the first cinematographic film of the Pope."

A well-known correspondent was wont to chuckle over a somewhat gruesome experience. He was in Rome without any particular mission but it occurred to him that he might be received in audience by the Pope. Word came to him that he would be received with others at an appointed hour, and it was intimated to him that he should on this occasion don the swallow-tailed open-fronted coat which is reserved for evening wear in England and the United States but is worn ceremonially on the Continent at all hours of the day.

He had no evening clothes in his baggage. Where could he procure them? He was directed to a second-hand clothes shop and there without difficulty he hired the necessary garments.

But what garments! They were greasy and far too big for

him. Still, they had to serve, and in spite of their musty smell he attired himself for the reception.

As he was kneeling with his companions, awaiting the entrance of the Pope, feeling ill at ease in coat and trousers which did not fit, and increasingly conscious that he was ridiculous, it suddenly flashed upon him that dead men in Italy were laid out before their burial in just such hired clothes. The conviction grew upon him that he was wearing the garb of a dead man!

It was a ghastly thought. The sweat broke out on his forehead and he was utterly confused. At this moment the Pope presented his ring. In a sad state of perturbation he seized the hand of the Pope and impressed upon it a resounding kiss that awakened echoes. Everybody was startled. How he left the sacred presence he told me he hardly knew. . . .

Certainly he had not the assurance of the American who had, twice in his life, been received by the Pope. "Your Holiness," he said, "I am the more overjoyed in that I was admitted to audience by your father, the late Pope."

It was not an American, but a man of another nationality, with an imperfect knowledge of French, who, talking to me in France about the Pope—*Le Saint Père*—repeatedly referred to his Holiness as *Le Sacré Père*—a phrase which has an altogether different and highly irreverent meaning!

XIV. THE DUCE AND THE CHURCH

WHEN this year (1929) the Lateran Treaty and the Concordat between the Vatican and the Italian Government were signed, and the Pope was free to walk abroad after a voluntary imprisonment of nearly sixty years, I could not resist the temptation of writing: "In Rome there is a Pope with sovereign rights, a King with Imperial traditions, and a Dictator with unlimited ambitions. For the ancient city on the Tiber, whose geographical area is a quarter of that of Paris, this appears to be a plethora of powers. In the nature of things equality will be difficult to maintain, and the European press is probably right in suggesting that either the Vatican will become the vassal of the Quirinal or the Quirinal the vassal of the Vatican."

Since then Signor Mussolini has spoken; he has declared that it is not Fascism which will be subordinated to Roman Catholicism. He has set the Fascist doctrine against the Catholic doctrine, the Italian State against the Italian Church. Thus the Italian Dictator plays the classic game of blowing hot and cold. When the premature and perhaps unjustified rejoicings which followed the reconciliation subsided, he took care to point out that the reconciliation did not imply any lowering of the Fascist flag. The national conscience has never been so strong and it is precisely because Nationalism is put first that Signor Mussolini can afford to put Catholicism second. In 1871 the offer of "guarantees" to the Church was a sign of weakness on the part of a new nation which was somewhat afraid of the consequences of its own temerity. In 1929 the Lateran Treaty is a proof that the State is sufficiently aware of its power to be able generously to accord sovereignty over an insignificant area of Rome to the Roman Pontiff.

It is not surprising that the observations of Signor Mussolini provoked a violent reply from Pius XI. It was immediately suggested in the Continental press that this controversy about the predominance of Catholic or Fascist tenets might mark the beginning of a fresh quarrel which would again change the relations of the Holy See and the Italian Government. "In fact," wrote the "Temps", "the question is whether in Italy Catholicism will be Fascist or whether Fascism will be Catholic." In the domain of education in particular the Church cannot recognise any teaching which it does not approve; but in the making of a "new race of Romans" Fascism must come into collision with Catholic creed and policy. Mussolini will certainly not yield on the fundamental point, which is that Fascism postulates that everything must exist "by the State and for the State."

Will Italian legislation be brought into harmony with the Concordat or will the Concordat be accommodated to the Fascist conception of the State? There will be some practical compromise, no doubt, in spite of the dialectical opposition that has already manifested itself, since theory and practice are not necessarily consistent.

Mussolini justifies the preëminence of the State over the Church not only philosophically but historically, affirming that it is to Rome and the Italian genius that the Catholic Church owes its universality; if the Roman Empire had not sheltered Christianity it would have died like many other religions which had their birth in Palestine. This thesis is peculiarly offensive to the Church which asserts the Divine character of its message. Not Latin protection but Heavenly protection is, both historically and philosophically, the buckler of the Church. Yet this kind of theological debate may not have much importance; it may prove to be purely verbal. What is of more concern is the Fascist "interpretation" of the Concordat.

"In three months I have seized more Catholic journals than in the preceding seven years," said Mussolini. M. Maurice Pernot, an able writer on this subject has explained the causes of the Catholic discontent that rapidly succeeded the first outburst of joy. Cardinal Gasparri held the Concordat to be a model and the Pope himself affirmed that it alone was sufficient to justify the Lateran accords. It makes Roman Catholicism the State religion; recognises the marriage sacrament; provides for religious instruction in elementary and secondary schools; authorises the existence of Catholic organisations; and so forth. But in examining these Mussolini concessions, one soon finds that they are almost worthless; and that Mussolini is right in bluntly intimating that he has surrendered nothing of consequence, but has received everything for Fascism.

For if Catholicism is the State religion, other cults are equally "admitted"; if Catholic marriages have civil effects, so have marriages according to other rites; if religion enters the schools, it is Fascism which proclaims its intention of forming citizens, with or without the Church, in its own mould, for Fascism and not Catholicism is the doctrine of the State; while as for Catholic organisations it is doubtful what will be tolerated since the Duce has warned the Church that he will not permit the "resurrection of parties and organisations that we have destroyed forever."

XV. ITALIAN UNITY

WHEN, after the war of 1859, in the course of which Italy, with the aid of French troops, had ejected the Austrians from Lombardy, Cavour established, in the Italian Parliament, which sat at Turin, the principle of the transference of the Court and Government to Rome, the ancient capital, he encountered enormous and seemingly insuperable difficulties. Rome was not legally an Italian city—it was not even situated in Italian territory. It was the Papal city, situated in Pontifical territory. To make it the capital of Italy it was necessary first to dispossess the Church.

Against this measure Italian consciences rebelled. Napoleon III proposed a compromise by which the Italian Government would nominally recognise the States of the Church and by which the States of the Church would effectively surrender the actual administration. The Pope declared his "absolute and irreducible" opposition to any infringement of the rights of the Holy See and this refusal was unanimously endorsed by the Catholic Bishops convoked to Rome to pronounce on the proposition.

Moreover Pius IX launched his encyclical letter in which he reproved "modern ideas of liberty and democracy"; he issued his famous Syllabus condemning modern errors. In 1869 he proclaimed the temporal sovereignty of the Pope, regarding Kings and Governments as his delegates.

The situation was perplexing, but Napoleon III, while posing as the Liberator of Italy, continued to defend the Pontifical States against the Italian Government, until the Franco-Prussian war of 1870 obliged him to recall his soldiers. The Italian Government executed the project of Cavour and troops under General Cadorna entered Rome by the Porta Pia. A popular plebiscite authorised the annexation of Church territory by Italy. Thereupon the Pope shut himself up in the Vatican and considered himself a captive.

His successors, Leo XIII and Pius X, continued to repulse the offers of Italy to provide indemnities and guarantees. Benedict XV, however, began to envisage the possibility of an understanding with Italy. Pourparlers were indeed discreetly proposed by Cardinal Gasparri, but before the question could be seriously discussed Benedict died.

He was succeeded in February, 1922 by Ratti. The name chosen by the Milan Archbishop—Pius—was of ill omen; it seemed to indicate that he repudiated the overtures of his predecessor and reverted to the implacability of Pius IX and X. Yet shortly after his accession to the Papal throne, it was apparent that he was disposed to search for a solution.

Mussolini was described as the "providential man," but it is probable that in any event, whatever Government had ruled in Italy, a treaty would have been concluded very much on the lines of that which was negotiated this year, not because circumstances had changed, but because the Vatican was sick of its own sulkiness. If Mussolini was ready to seize the chance of performing a spectacular feat, the Pope was willing to break the deadlock at all costs.

The Pope merely claimed a nominal sovereignty; he wished to have full and entire possession only of Papal buildings and grounds. He would be content with a relatively small indemnity. He desired a Concordat such as the Vatican has concluded with other countries. These were demands that could, without undue difficulty, be conceded by Italy, and however arduous and prolonged may have been the negotiations on details, it was inevitable that an agreement would eventually be reached.

I remember writing an article to this effect more than five years ago; and it was printed in my book "Those Europeans," published in 1924.

Yet the conclusion of the accord was beautifully timed by Mussolini and his own diplomatic prestige is undoubtedly enhanced. Whatever might have happened in other circumstances, it is an excellent argument in favour of the superior statecraft of Mussolini that he settled the Roman question which his predecessors had failed to settle and thus completed the work of Cavour, unfinished until the Church officially recognised the United Kingdom of Italy. Moreover, the date of the settlement was significant. It preceded the plebiscite that was being taken in Italy on the Mussolinian régime; and enthusiastically the Catholic forces ranged themselves with the essentially Fascist forces, and secured for the Duce a remarkable triumph which accusations of political jerrymandering cannot successfully reduce.

The stage-setting was excellent. Mussolini had an extraordinary dramatic instinct. Yet he nearly overdid things. His personal advantages and the advantages of Italy were apparent. The advantages of the Church were not so apparent. Therefore, there was strong criticism of the accord by Roman Catholics in all other countries than Italy. Such criticism was chiefly based on the supposed dependence of the Pope on Italy. The so-called Papal independence is guaranteed only by Italy.

M. Charles Maurras rightly points out that Italy is the power against which the Vatican has always wished to be guaranteed: it is the power from whom guarantees have hitherto been refused; yet it is Italy which guarantees the Vatican, and there is not, for the Church which claims an international status, the

smallest international guarantee. Naturally the Quirinal would
never have accepted an international guarantee, which would
have operated against Italian sovereignty; and if the Vatican
wished to bring an anomalous position to an end, it was bound
to take its guarantees from the hands of Italy, and from the
hands of Italy alone.

Nevertheless, other Catholic countries, which regret the
Italianisation of the Roman Catholic Church, foresee with some
dismay the further Italianisation of the Roman Catholic
Church, which the appointment of a few more non-Italian
Cardinals—lollipops to children—cannot disguise.

Is not the Pope diminished as a petty Kinglet whose domains
are municipally administered by the Rome authorities? Would
not his authority be greater if it were purely spiritual, and is
there not incompatibility between the conception of universality and the conception of geographical delimitation?

A writer in the French Catholic paper "La Croix" argued:
"It is necessary that the Pope shall be free, and it is necessary also
that his liberty shall be manifested clearly in the eyes of the
Catholics of the whole world. To assure his complete and evident liberty the existence of Papal territories, absolutely independent, is required. The Pope cannot live on the territory of
another sovereign. That is why he demands the proprietorship
of a territory, however restricted, where he alone is master.
How can one conceive his sovereign independence if the
property in which he finds himself is subjected to a foreign
power?"

This argument is excellent in the void; but it is vitiated by
the fact that the Papal possessions in fact constitute a tiny
enclave in the midst of a modern Kingdom—a tiny enclave
which is dependent on every side, in which no political power
can be exercised, whose simplest public services are assured by
the Italian authorities, which is completely at the mercy of
Italy! What strange sovereignty is this? Was there not some
sentimental value in the very captivity of the Pope, voluntary
as it was; in his halo of martyrdom; in his unceasing protest to
Christendom?

Yet it exists, the new Vatican City—a City which is unique.
There are a number of small states in Europe. There is a Republic of San Marino, with its thirty-eight square miles and a
population of twelve thousand, claiming to be the oldest State
in Europe; and existing on friendly terms, consecrated in a

treaty, with the Kingdom of Italy. In the Pyrenees is Andorra, a tiny community which comes under the joint suzerainty of France and the Spanish Bishop of Urgel. Its six thousand inhabitants occupy 175 square miles. There is the Principality of Lichtenstein, on the Upper Rhine, a territory of fifty-three square miles, governed by one of the most ancient families of Europe. Scarcely less anomalous is the situation of the Grand Duchy of Luxembourg, which is neutral territory, though Luxembourg has nearly a thousand square miles. For purposes of comparison it may be recalled that the very small countries of Europe, such as Albania, Denmark, Esthonia, Latvia, and Lithuania, are from twenty-five thousand to thirty-five thousand square miles in extent.

The Vatican City cannot even be put beside San Marino, Andorra or Lichtenstein. It covers an area of just over a hundred acres! Were it not for its buildings, it would make a good-sized golf course!

The citizens of the Vatican City probably number about five hundred. The smallest public building or concert-hall could contain them.

It is therefore somewhat farcical to regard the Vatican City as a State. If it be true that the Roman Catholic Church girdles the globe, and that the Pope has more subjects than any President or Monarch, there is something irresistibly comic in the insistence on temporal power.

And even over his few acres the Pope has no real sovereignty. He could not, if he wished, close the Piazza di San Pietro to the Italian public, or exclude the Italian police. He could not, if he wished, make the art treasures of the Vatican City inaccessible to visitors. Of course he would not wish these things, but the point is, that in the very heart of his temporal State, he is far less master than a landed Earl is master of his domains.

Mussolini has been ironically pleasant about the citizenship of the Vatican State. He has suggested that the ideal position for a sovereign is to have no subjects. He has said that nobody can be born a subject of the Pope, for births in the Vatican City are impossible!

So citizenship must be made to depend upon "permanent residence," and "permanent residence" is restricted by considerations of space and the pleasure of the Pope.

Criminals may not, of course, be afforded refuge in the Vatican City. The Vatican City will look to the Italian State for its water supply, its railway station, its post-office, and so forth. Yet the Vatican will, as a token of its authority, issue stamps and coins!

XVI. A POLICY OF PRESTIGE

THE Pope may now go abroad, transporting his sovereignty wherever he travels; he must be treated with the highest honours, as a sovereign, in Protestant as well as Catholic countries; and he will undoubtedly produce a powerful impression on the public imagination, stimulating unprecedented zeal among the faithful, and determining a revival of Catholicism. In the spiritual sphere Catholicism has lost ground. In Hussite Czecho-Slovakia, for instance, the authority of the Pope is seriously challenged by millions of Catholics. In France, the best Catholics are grieved by the disabilities placed upon them if they happen to hold political views which are now condemned (on French territory only) by the Vatican. Diplomatically, the Vatican has made great strides since the war, and its representatives will now enjoy official immunity, prestige, and extra-territoriality. It is to be remarked that the number of Ambassadors and other diplomatic representatives at the Vatican has quintupled, while the Papal Nuncios have multiplied enormously. Even France, proud of being a "lay" Republic, has now an Ambassador at the Vatican, and receives a Nuncio at Paris, and having need of the diplomatic support of the Pope, tries to forget the old anti-clerical feud.

As for the Concordats that have been concluded since the succession of Pius XI, they have followed each other without interruption—Latvia, 1922; Bavaria, 1924; Poland, 1925; Rumania, 1927; Lithuania, 1927; Czecho-Slovakia (in the form of a modus vivendi) 1928; Portugal, 1928; Italy, 1929; and it is understood that there is to be a Concordat with Yugo-Slavia and another with the German Reich.

It will be observed that some of these countries at least are by no means profoundly Catholic. Doubtless the Concordats, if they authorise Catholic action, limit that action. Doubtless diplomatic relations with the Vatican are not always intended to facilitate the diplomacy of the Vatican, but rather to keep it in check. But whatever may be said to the contrary, whatever reservations one may make, it is unquestionable that Pius XI has set out to regularise the position of the Church in as many countries as possible and to give to the Church a new temporal standing in Catholic and non-Catholic countries by means of diplomatic representation.

How is this new standing to be used? It is claimed that in the political realm the Church is governed by mediæval conceptions which exclude the idea of nationality and there is a saving clause in the present accords by which the Vatican will not be a party to "temporal competitions" unless it is specifically asked to exercise its peaceful influence.

A Cardinal Nuncio is reported to have said: "All that is Catholic is Italian, and all that is Italian is Catholic." It does not much matter whether the epigram was uttered. It is an exaggeration in both senses, but it has elements of truth. The majority of the Council of Cardinals, the officials of the Roman Church, and most of the missionaries, are Italian by nationality, as is the Pope; and it is difficult to believe that they will not be influenced by Italian ambitions, now that the "frozen enmity" of the Vatican and the Quirinal has been thawed.

Outside Italy there will be two Italian representatives at many Chancelleries—an Italian Ambassador and a Papal Nuncio, who, it is to be presumed, will generally work along the same lines. Coöperation of this kind will increase both Italian and Papal influence. It is possible that the Vatican designs will be forwarded by the *rapprochement* with the Quirinal, but it is equally probable that Italian designs will be advanced.

"The place of Italy in the Vatican is twice vacant," said an Italian newspaper when France resumed relations with the Vatican; that double vacancy is now filled. And in the Balkans, and in Central Europe, and in the East, and wherever Italy is in rivalry with other nations in its bid for hegemony, the friendship of the Vatican, the activities of the Vatican representatives and missionaries, will undoubtedly be precious.

The question has arisen whether the Vatican as a State is entitled to become a member of the League of Nations. In spite of temporal sovereignty, it is as a religious organisation that the Church must be regarded, and if one religious body may sit in the League why not other religious bodies? Why not, for example, the Salvation Army which is international in its activities? And what of Methodism? And what of the Jewish community? They may not possess the material status of the

Vatican, but everybody knows that material status to be largely fictional. Why should the moral authority of one church be set above the moral authority of another?

I imagine there would be clamorous protests from all denominations were the Roman Catholic Church to pretend to a seat on the League Council. But I do not think the claim will be seriously put forward, for the Vatican could hardly be content with less than first place, and if it took sides in the lobbies, and was beaten in the Council, it would be humiliated.

Now the policy of Pius XI is a policy of prestige; and he will not plunge lightly into temporal quarrels where his influence can be put to an immediate and decisive test. That would be, in effect, a policy of humility; and the Roman Catholic Church, though it often blunders, will surely avoid this gross blunder.

The Roman Catholic Church will endeavour to remain an ecclesiastical League of Nations; and the League of Nations will doubtless remain a lay Vatican.*

* The most impartial and illuminating account of the Roman situation is to be found in "Le Partage de Rome" by "Pertinax", the ablest of French diplomatic journalists.

PART IV
AUSTRIA

I. CHEERFULNESS BREAKING IN

FROM Paris to Vienna is a good day's journey, and from Vienna to Berlin, or Berlin to Paris, is a much shorter journey; yet the difference between Vienna and Paris is nothing like so great as the difference between Vienna and Berlin. Certainly on my recent visit I discerned some of the old traces of depression, but on the whole Vienna is bright and smiling, and has regained its former grace and charm. Berlin has run to experimental excesses, and there is much in its lack of restraint, its blatancy, its brutality, expressed in its startling architecture, its noisy amusements, even in its spirit of enterprise, that shocks an observer of my temperament. But Vienna has kept its ancient culture. It has a sense of measure. It is the capital of Central Europe, and lies half-way between the Extreme East and the Extreme West of the Continent; yet it is, as much as Paris and London, perhaps essentially more than Paris and London, a Western city—a Western city with a window to the East. For its roots run deep down in the traditions of the Holy Roman Empire. Berlin is *nouveau riche*; Vienna, despite the collapse of the monarchy, has all the quality of true aristocracy.

The very coins seemed symbolical. Some of them were stamped with the head of Schubert. To be sure, the Centenary of Schubert was celebrated not long ago, and thus a special occasion was offered for the striking of his effigy. Nevertheless, it is difficult to imagine the head of Shakespeare on an English shilling; and it appears to me that the Austrians have a peculiar consciousness of what constitutes their national glory. Possibly, as Keyserling remarks, the Austrian is of weak character and lacking in practical ability, but he is tactful, good-natured, Mozartian, and *spirituel*. In the far-off days of the ancient Empire, when the Germanies were a loose conglomeration of States, which the French and other rulers endeavoured to keep divided and independent, the overlordship of Austria was exercised not by violence but by tolerance. The rise of Prussia was the manifestation of the opposite forces of the Germanic spirit. There is, indeed, no stronger contrast than is furnished by Berlin and Vienna, and the historic contrast can be appreciated as clearly as ever to-day.

Doubtless there has been a good deal of exaggeration about

the pre-war oppression by Austria of the various races which made up the ramshackle Empire. The component parts had always a certain freedom. Some had their Diets. Such compulsion as they suffered was the inevitable consequence of a bureaucratic system which insisted on centralisation; and old bureaucratic systems, strongly entrenched, tend to become autonomous, and to outpass the intentions of the nominal rulers. It was softness rather than hardness which brought about the disruption of Austria. Germany should have foreseen the destruction of its ally, and would have foreseen this result had it possessed a Bismarck. It is, of course, possible to suppose that the shattering of Austria was, at least unconsciously, an agreeable prospect for Germany; but in any case it should have been apparent that, while German unity would be welded by the war, Austrian unity demanded increasing decentralisation and unbroken peace. Defeat was obviously fatal, and the unfortunate Karl, realising the truth, feebly attempted to secure a speedy peace, and by his feebleness contributed to the victory of the allies.

As we, my companion and I, rolled along through Southern Germany and at Salzburg approached the magnificent hills of Austria, I recalled an amusing cartoon of the days of Francis Joseph which illustrates the Austrian love of decoration. It represented the French Ambassador, Philippe Crozier—an estimable, soft-spoken gentleman of the old school, whose company I found always agreeable; he was covered from head to foot with medals and ribbons, and there was not an inch of room for other regalia. But the Emperor stood before him, perplexed, with an immense plaque in his hand; his face was more wrinkled than ever and his little eyes were puckered; he pulled his moustache which ran, a tributary stream, into the broad favourites of his cheeks.

"I see no place for this Order with which I would reward you," he said.

The Ambassador reflected. A bright idea struck him; "Qu'à cela ne tienne, Sire," he exclaimed. And, turning round, he lifted up the tails of his Ambassadorial coat!

The brightly clad Austrian officers were, in those days, decorated; the performances at the famous opera-house were brilliant, with jewels on uniforms and on women's gowns. It is true that, for ten years before the end, the old Emperor, crushed under an almost unprecedented weight of domestic tragedy, had renounced public life as much as possible, and that the court was regarded as comparatively dull; nevertheless the Viennese aristocracy made of the capital a glittering centre of social activities. Had all this gone? Was Vienna as it had been pictured, the dead city that it became after the war, when the Empire was broken up, when the Republic was declared, when the krone crashed day by day in its precipitate downward course?

I was pleasantly surprised. Vienna is itself again—or at least makes a brave show of being itself again. We came to it at night, and it was lit up as Paris, which is called La Ville Lumière, has never been lit up. Throughout my stay the dominant note was one of cheerfulness. The theatres, big and little, the magnificent opera-houses, the music-halls and the cabarets, were crowded, though the foreign invasion had not begun. There were new plays and musical comedies. The cream overflowed in one's cup as in a shaving mug. The women were stylishly dressed. The Kartnerstrasse and the Ring were thronged; and I wandered about with delight among the palaces, in the parks, and by the river, finding everything gay and sparkling. The smart uniforms have certainly gone, and the Court life has gone—part of the Messe or Fair was housed in the old Imperial stables—but there were music and amusement galore; while the intellectual life of Vienna is as intense as at any time since the University was founded six centuries ago. My companions were Viennese students, *littérateurs*, politicians, and they were keenly aware of modern movements though profoundly aware of their history. The past of Austria has been of the greatest importance to Europe; and the importance of Austria, politically and intellectually, in the European scheme, has by no means ended.

II. GEMÜTLICH

RARELY have I stayed at a better equipped and more friendly hotel than the celebrated Bristol, and I am told that the others—the Grand, the Imperial, the Ritz, and so forth—are equally up to date and truly helpful to visitors. It was good to stroll down to the Cathedral of St. Stefan, to peep into the churches and the museums, to admire the wonderful statues, the handsome shops, and to participate in the café and the open-air life. After the débâcle Vienna has become cheerful and charming—the most cheerful and charming city in Europe. If one were to sum it up in a word one would say that Vienna has again become Viennese.

They were agreeable days that I spent in Vienna, but now and again little evidences of poverty would obtrude themselves. Against the rich background of sumptuous mansions, of animated races, of crowded entertainments, there would suddenly appear traces of financial embarrassment. I was walking with a man whose name is well known in the literary world; he has written many worthy works, and that night a new play of his was to be produced. I hailed a taxi. He stopped me and waved the taxi away. I looked to him for an explanation, since he had agreed that we had better take a cab.

"That is an eighty groschen taxi," he said. "We shall soon find a fifty groschen taxi. The eighty groschen taxis are only for careless strangers."

So we saved about two pence. It appears that there are two kinds of taxis. One of them is supposed to be a little more roomy than the other. Originally they were private automobiles, which were converted into public vehicles when their owners had to sell them or ply for hire themselves. Certainly there is now very little difference, but it is still customary to have the two sorts of taxis, the starting fare of one being slightly higher than the starting fare of the other.

I observed the clothes of my companion; they were threadbare. At a reception that evening, at which other "intellectuals" and their womenfolk were present, I observed again that the womenfolk, in spite of their elegant appearance, were wearing dresses which had obviously been turned and titivated. This class at least has not fully recovered from the terrible hardships that were experienced. Its earnings are relatively low, and economy is as necessary as ever.

Yet what a proud show Vienna makes!—its Burg Theatre with its view over the Ring, formerly the old walls of Vienna, and now its boulevards; its beautiful Volksgarten, its Rathaus Tower, its Belvedere, its picture gallery, its palace dating from the Thirteenth Century, into whose courtyard the populace was permitted to enter and watch the sovereigns through the windows. . . . And the Prater Park with its chestnut trees, its café tables, its orchestras playing Strauss waltzes, Hungarian melodies, and Wagnerian operas! And the Stadt Park, into

FRAU SACHER

which poured students, laughing girls, and comfortable-looking bourgeois.

We went of course to Sacher's. There the Viennese were dancing light-heartedly, while a man, carrying an instrument like a garden hose, went round and round the room, spraying a somewhat unpleasant perfume into the air. We were joined at our table by two students. One of them was an American boy from Chicago, though his father was an American from Vienna. The father had vivid recollections of his medical training in Austria, and had sent his son to follow in his footsteps.

"But I would not be doing so well," he told us naïvely, "I might have gone to the devil, had it not been for Walther. Walther has found a home for me with friends of his family—a gemütlich family."

Gemütlich! The word is repeated again and again. It seemed to me to be the favourite expression in Austria, and it denotes a quality that is essentially Austrian. Gemütlich—good-natured, comfortable, cosy, homely; it has a dozen translations, but none of them really expresses what the Austrians express by gemütlichkeit. It sums up the character of the Austrians, and their moral ideals. True, there have been severe criticisms of the Austrian character, none more severe than those of Austrians themselves. Kürnberger assailed his countrymen as follows: "Gemütlich, you call it, eh? It is cowardly, slack, slovenly, faint-hearted, uncourageous, forceless, nerveless, without energy or power of resistance. You are an effeminate people, you are not a manly race. Don't call yourselves Germans. The Germans can say No. The Germans can stand up for themselves. But no Viennese has ever, face to face, said No!"

Which only proves once more that virtues may be vices, and vices virtues, and that words can be used in a complimentary or a derogatory sense. For my part I like the gemütlichkeit of the Austrians; it is a lovable quality; but it has doubtless brought misfortunes upon them, just as the opposite quality has brought misfortunes on the North Germans.

"Is it not so, Walther? Walther has saved me from squandering money. There are so many temptations for a young man in Vienna! Walther has taught me many things—have you not, Walther?"

Walther was mildly flattered at the praises of his young American friend. Walther is twenty-two or twenty-three years of age, but he has the gemütlich gravity of a man of forty.

He is already almost bald, and such hair as he has is close-cropped. He is fair and blue-eyed; almost an albino. But beneath his quiet speech and his humble manners there is concealed the real spirit of the Austrian student—a strange mixture of seriousness, and, on occasion, recklessness. Walther is the typical Austrian student.

Across his face there is a characteristic sword slash. I asked him if he had fought a duel.

"Why, yes," he said, hesitatingly. "But I think it is better not to belong to the duelling clubs. I am from the Salzburg University. Oh, yes, there are still duels of students; it is very foolish perhaps, but it is traditional, and even the war has not put an end to it. It is not really dangerous. The swords are rubbed in alcohol, and a doctor as well as the seconds are present. It is thought good form to have a sword slash across the face."

He was passably content with his sword slash, but that did not prevent him from soberly pursuing his studies. Of Salzburg he spoke with subdued enthusiasm, and of the wonderful voyage along the Danube from Lintz, with the old castles dominating the valley. "It is as finely historic as the journey along the Rhine, though the castles are smaller," he said, with his blend of pride and humility.

"The difference between the Germans and the Austrians," he ventured, "is the same as that between the inhabitants of New York and of Chicago—or the inhabitants of London and of Manchester." His meaning was not quite clear, for none of these towns even faintly recalls Vienna or Berlin. But I took it that he intended to evoke contrasts, without indicating the nature of the contrasts.

I looked round Sacher's. Its famous mistress was still in charge, though she was shortly afterwards to relinquish the establishment which has been known to European travellers for I know not how many years. Frau Sacher was the friend of princes and students alike. Everybody in Vienna will tell you of the black cigars which she smoked and of the autographed photographs of celebrities which she possessed. Everybody will tell you how she permitted the *nouveaux pauvres* to dine without paying when Vienna was passing through its most severe tribulations; and how her property was respected during the period of rioting when nothing else was spared. . . . Well, Sacher's has certainly no aristocratic air to-day; its habitués are

of the student and bourgeois classes, with the inevitable sprinkling of gay girls. . . . Perhaps there never were so many
Grand Dukes as is pretended at Sacher's; any more than there
were at Montmartre. Every European capital has this kind of
legend; it did no harm, and you could persuade yourself that
your neighbour was a Balkanic potentate, while he could persuade himself that you were one of the numerous Germanic
Kinglets. . . . Dining out and dancing was thus thrilling in its
possible encounters. They have all of them, Archdukes and
Counts, been to Sacher's, and have tasted Frau Sacher's own
torte—layer upon layer of cake—and her Fürstpückler—the
best ice-cream in the world. . . . Now Archdukes and Counts
are rare, and Frau Sacher has retired.

III. A WORLD'S PLAYGROUND

THERE is always for me, and, as I suppose, for many others,
a veritable magic in the words: Lilac-time. In my own
garden the long dreary days are suddenly routed when spring
comes marching under the banner of lilac branches. And on
the banks of the blue Danube—blue it is, and the old phrase
cannot be omitted—the coming of lilac-time works a charm.
The winter is rigorous; double windows, which are built everywhere, do not suffice to keep out the cold; the rivers are frozen
over, and there are great snow drifts in the valleys and on the
hillsides. Then a delicately tinted wand is waved, and Austria
is glorious with sunshine.

There are flowers everywhere; in the gardens, and in the
hotels, and in the shopwindows. Lilac bushes blossom in the
Viennese parks, and climb up the slopes to the Wiener Wald.
It is not too much to say that lilac-time in Austria compares
with tulip-time in Holland.

Impossible to escape the feast of lilac—if anybody could
have such a strange wish! One looks upon lilac from the café
terraces of the Ring; while if one can discover a horse-carriage
and be driven slowly round the town and up the hills one will
pass through groves of lilac trees, and look down on a city
adorned with the blue and white flowers. The fleeting impression repays a long journey. . . .

This is only one of the many inducements held out to tourists by Austria. For Austria now wants tourists. Once it suf-
ficed unto itself; it had over fifty million inhabitants; now it

has fewer than seven million of whom nearly two million are congregated in Vienna. Austria is making a definite bid for foreign guests; it is devising attractions for them; it is organising travel bureaus, drawing up programmes of entertainment with an eye on the visitor. It is fairly successful, too, for I am told that hundreds of thousands of foreigners have come to stay for longer or shorter periods in Vienna alone, while the Tyrol and other resorts are growing in popularity. "Austria should become the world's playground. That is a title at present held by Switzerland but there is no reason why our country should not share the tourist traffic."

I found this kind of conversation rather pathetic. Not once nor twice but many times and by many different people were these suggestions made to me. Sometimes I could hardly prevent myself from protesting, on behalf of Austria, against the Austrians.

"What! you propose to turn the heart of one of the oldest European Empires into a holiday resort, living sleekly on the bounty of visitors?"

Yet, in fact, there are few countries which are so favoured by nature as Austria. Vienna itself is encircled by delightful forest, the Wiener Wald, where the townsfolk love to picnic. Pleasant vales, and low hills, and great snow-clad peaks, six thousand feet in height, form a varied and lovely landscape. The longest of the European rivers flows through this changing scenery, and one perpetually comes upon old ruins on steep rocks contrasting with the quiet country-houses over which grows the vine. There are hundreds of places of historical interest, such as the Imperial residence of Schönbrunn, now a public museum, the castle of Kreuzenstein, with its reminiscences of the Thirty Years War, Mayerling where the Crown Prince Rodolphe ended his life in mysterious circumstances, the Semmering pass with its pine woods, Salzburg famous for its musical festivals, and Innsbruck the chief town in the Austrian Tyrol. The Tyrol offers facilities for winter sports, such as skiing, skating, bobsleighing, and ice-hockey. The pure air of the mountains and the brilliant Alpine sunshine are wonderfully exhilarating. It is true that the journey is longer than the journey to Switzerland, but nevertheless Austria sets itself up as a real rival.

Summer and winter Austria is rich in interest; and moreover the Austrians are a friendly folk; nowhere have I met with more kindness and genuine hospitality. Peasants and towns-people alike are extremely courteous and will take pains to make the foreigner feel that he is welcome. Yet Austrians who extolled their country as a new Switzerland admitted that it would be necessary for the Austrians to learn languages. In Switzerland, even in the smaller resorts, the Swiss speak English, French, Italian, and German. If Austria thus conceives its rôle, it must likewise learn foreign tongues.

No greater injustice was done in the peace-making than the attribution to Italy of South Tyrol. It is inhabited almost exclusively by Austrians. Yet, easy-going as the Austrians are, they are almost ready to forget this injustice, and to exist on friendly terms with the Italians. Indeed, Austrian friends of mine, who lived under the Italian occupation, had only good words for the soldiers of the Peninsula. Italians and Austrians should easily understand each other. They have many interests in common. While Austria has need of the Italian port of Trieste, Italy has need of transit privileges to Germany across Austria. When Vienna was starving, Italy behaved with far more consideration than any other of Austria's neighbours.

But then came the awakening of nationalism in Italy, and the Austrians were deeply distressed by its workings among their lost compatriots. They informed me, with as much indignation as they are capable of, that they could have forgiven everything except the dragooning of Mussolini. On the tombstones in South Tyrol inscriptions must not be chiselled in the German language, but in Italian. Surely it is almost a sacrilegious decree, and one well understands the sadness of the Austrians in recalling it and similar facts. But even in this respect Austrian indulgence soon displays itself.

IV. THE TADPOLE

VIENNA has reconciled itself to its fate as the large capital of a small country. I had political talks with representative men, and I came to the conclusion that Austrian ambitions are not political. There is no great regret for the vanished order of things except in so far as Austria is financially hit. The old aristocracy, now dispersed and impotent, and sometimes sulky, naturally deplores the shattering of the former régime which was profitable to them, but the people are perfectly content to be a small nation, provided they can find the wherewithal to live.

What is it to be a small nation? It is certainly not necessarily unpleasant for the individual citizen. On the whole the happiest countries in Europe are those which are the smallest. Rich little Holland, progressive little Denmark, happy little Switzerland, are examples of countries which seem to have no cares. The big country has usually a desperate struggle to manage its own affairs, and it engages in a still more desperate struggle to manage the affairs of its neighbours. France, Germany, Italy, are uneasy countries. Either they want more territory and prestige, or they are afraid of losing territory and prestige. *Noblesse oblige!*—and among nations high rank brings perpetual embarrassment. The so-called Great Powers are jealous of every triumph, are watchful, envious, sensitive, and ready to become panic-stricken or blatantly patriotic.

Unfortunately for themselves and for Europe in general, a number of the new, or the newly reconstructed smaller nations, are disposed to catch the infection of the larger nations, and to cultivate ambitions, foster fears, and develop animosities. On a lower scale they lead the same anxious existence as the Great Powers. In this they are extremely foolish. Were they to take Holland, Denmark, Switzerland and even Belgium, as models, they would be wise; as it is they remind one of the fable of the frog that would puff himself up to resemble the bull.

The Great Powers are, for the most part, like certain Society personages who are constantly preoccupied with questions of precedence, and who vie with each other in social display. Some of the lesser powers are like social climbers, whose interest in each other is chiefly directed to clothes, motor-cars, and the success of sons and daughters. But Austria is willing to live by itself without regard for worldly rank. It has its musical and intellectual traditions, which are second to none, and they are enough.

This is, I think, one of the most remarkable phenomena of the post-war Europe. Perhaps there is not another nation on the Continent which lost by the war that complains so little; and certainly there is far more complaining among those which gained. The others fret because too much has been taken away from them, or grumble because they have not received enough, or whine because they are not entirely secure from aggression.

Austria accepts the settlement philosophically, and only asks to be allowed to make a livelihood.

The astonishing thing is that no nation suffered such utter defeat, such complete loss, as Austria. It was at the head of a mighty Empire—one of the five or six greatest powers in Europe. Now it is, politically speaking, nothing. Now it is, territorially speaking, insignificant. Yet Austria is less troubled about its position than is, let us say, Czecho-Slovakia, which was formerly a subject of the Austrian Empire. It does not trouble about its reduction from one of the largest European States to one of the smallest European States. In this it is unlike its neighbour and old partner Hungary; for whereas Hungary is enraged and restless, Austria is placid and patient. Hungary still hopes to recover its former rank. Austria, in its most secret thoughts, never dreams of rebuilding the destroyed Empire. It has no desire to extend its territory, which now includes only Lower Austria, Upper Austria, Salzburg, part of Styria, Carinthia, Voralberg, and part of the Tyrol. Perhaps I should make a reservation in respect of Southern Tyrol, but if Italy treated the inhabitants of Southern Tyrol passably well even these lingering doubts would disappear.

Is this state of mind to be praised or blamed? I think it is to be praised, for in any event the Treaty of Saint-Germain could not now be substantially altered. Yet many people have shaken their heads sadly over the apathy of Austria. They would have preferred to see it react strongly against misfortune, deserved or undeserved. Other countries, they point out, have, whether by truncation or expansion, had their national consciousness stimulated, and it is to the discredit of the Austrians that they should meekly bow to the inevitable.

For some time after the partition, when the prospect was gloomy, Austria was prepared to lie down and die. It was faced with difficult economic conditions and it declined to assert itself; so that the peace-makers, looking with dismay on the spectacle of a people of between six and seven millions condemned to extinction by their arbitrary decrees, hastened to help Austria, and to persuade it that it had still a fine future if it would only accept the coöperation of its former enemies.

Poor Austria was left, when Czecho-Slovakia, Italy, Poland, Rumania, Yugo-Slavia, and Hungary, its partner, had been given all the land that they could persuade the peace-makers to carve out of the Empire, a curious helpless tadpole-like coun-

try with a huge head and an elongated tail. Nearly a third of
the population of the country was crowded in the great capital
—a capital that had developed to correspond to the needs of
an immense administrative area. Now this tadpole-like head
corresponded to no administrative or commercial needs. It
might be compared to a splendid mansion whose master had
lost his entire fortune. . . .

Vienna therefore became an anomaly. It was monstrously
disproportionate. Imagine London suddenly becoming merely
the capital of the Southern Counties, or Paris of the Ile-de-
France and Normandy. The function of Vienna had gone, its
raison d'être had been destroyed. It was an enormous parasite,
drawing its substance from a totally inadequate countryside.

Moreover, Vienna was altogether different from the provinces which were left to Austria. Those provinces were purely
German. Vienna, like all great cities, was cosmopolitan. It was
a cultural centre, and to it had come Czechs and Poles, Magyars
and Italians, Yugo-Slavs and Jews. Now they would stay at
home in their newly constructed countries, and its Universities
would be deserted, and its musical institutions would suffer, and
its scientific reputation would diminish. So at least it seemed.
As for its commerce, it found all doors shut to it—doors which
before had merely separated one room from another, but now
separated one country from another.

Chaos had been created by the sledge-hammer peace-makers,
and the Viennese threw up their hands helplessly. There was
famine, there was complete misery. Even among such easy-
going people as the Austrians, a Revolution was invited by the
impossible conditions produced by short-sighted politicians at
Paris. If ever diplomatists played the game of the Communists,
they played it in 1919. That Europe is not altogether communistic, in spite of the folly of the peace-makers, is due to
the good sense of most European peoples. Austria showed particular good sense, and the Socialist Government, with Communistic tendencies, did not succeed in imposing its authority
on the country. Whatever Vienna might say or do, the provinces, inhabited by pious Catholics, refused to be guided by a
godless capital. For a moment there was grave danger lest even
the component parts of tiny Austria should fly asunder—this
part uniting with Switzerland, and that part uniting with
Bavaria, and other parts affirming their regional autonomy,
leaving Vienna isolated.

The redness of Vienna was at no time a fast colour. There were always more Christian Socialists, Pan-Germanists, and other Conservatives, than Social-Democrats. The Socialists were held in check, and for governmental purposes there has been a series of coalitions. Extremists at both ends of the political field have been reduced, and a moderate régime has been established. As I write, the Christian Socialist party is the strongest, and it endeavours to hold an even balance. It has given several Chancellors to the State, among them the most prominent figure in Austrian politics, Ignaz Seipel, who is professor and priest. The party is content to preserve the *status quo,* though it has dallied with the idea of monarchy—not very seriously— and with the idea of union with Germany.

Dr. Otto Bauer and Dr. Karl Renner are the leading members of the Social-Democratic party, which has nearly as many members as the Christian Socialist party. It, too, favours union with Germany. As for the Pan-German party, which may be regarded as Centrist, it is relatively weak in numbers but extremely important in influence; it is, of course, Nationalist and is strongly in favour of union with Germany.

V. THE ANSCHLUSS

THUS we see that, politically, practically everybody is in favour of the Anschluss—union with Germany. The real alternative is federation with the other Central European States —that is to say, to some extent, a reconstruction, though with vital modifications, of the old Empire. Such federation appears very remote.

I found everybody in Austria sympathetic to the Anschluss, not because Austria would thus form part of the great German Reich, but because the union with Germany would solve the economic problem. The Austrians do not anticipate subservience to Berlin. The Anschluss, as they conceive it, would be merely a convenient arrangement that would permit them to live their own lives. But there is not, in my opinion, any acute demand for the Anschluss. It is regarded as an ultimate necessity, but it is not something for which immediate sacrifices are to be made. The *laisser-faire* which distinguishes the Austrian is to be seen here as elsewhere. In good time the union will be accomplished, but there is no need to hasten the day.

It is well to consider this question of the Anschluss seriously.

Sledge-hammer diplomacy in Central Europe may have helped to win the war. It may hereafter jeopardise peace. A number of politicians and journalists considered that the solution of Continental problems was to break up the old Austro-Hungarian Empire. They mapped out new States which were just as ramshackle and arbitrary as the old patchwork Empire, and which offered the additional inconvenience of multiplying disputes with the multiplication of frontiers. The Balkans were brought to our doorstep. We now begin to see the consequences of this clumsy work. It was illogical to smash up the Austrian Empire and not, at the same time, to smash up the German Empire. On one side was left a great and powerful nation, and on the other side was left a fragmentary and helpless country whose racial affinities with its big neighbour urged it to join the Germanic Federation.

But this was precisely what the Treaty of Versailles forbade. The treaty-makers imagined that by putting a few phrases on paper they could make water flow uphill. Having, in pursuance of their policy, reduced Austria to a little thing, having created for it the irresistible attraction of Germany, they blandly proceeded to reconcile the contradiction by condemning in solemn phraseology the natural union.

Article 80 of the Treaty of Versailles stipulates that Germany will strictly respect the independence of Austria within the frontiers fixed by the Allied Powers, and will acknowledge that independence to be inalienable except with the consent of the Council of the League of Nations. In the Treaty of Saint-Germain, which was signed by Austria, there is a similar clause forbidding the Anschluss.

If an appeal were made to the League it is certain that the League would express its veto. Some of the League members might support the alliance, but there would be nothing like unanimity—indeed there would be an overwhelming majority against the Anschluss. If the Austrian people were of one mind and if Germany were powerful enough to dictate to the rest of Europe then might the Anschluss be achieved. As it is, the agitation for the Anschluss may be productive of trouble, and at the best is already giving rise to uncertainty and uneasiness.

In 1919 it was plainly pointed out that Austria, in its reduced form, was probably not self-sufficing. Vienna as one of the great European capitals, is dependent upon a prosperous proportionate country. Diplomatists, who do not place conscience among their more important assets, became conscience-stricken. Though the Empire was shivered, even those who shivered it had misgivings, and have not been without sympathy for their victim.

In point of fact, there has been a progressive assimilation of Austria by Germany. There is a growing consciousness of the affinities of the two countries. Thus the Austrian code has been copied from the German laws. The same military rules for mobilisation have been adopted, and the same uniform. The telegraphic, telephonic, and postal relations enjoy the same internal tariff. There is a close customs understanding. Industries are associated in cartels. The intellectual organisations of Germany and Austria are working in common, and professors, authors, and musicians belong to the same societies.

When in November, 1918, just after the Armistice, the provisional assembly of Vienna pronounced in favour of the attachment of Austria to Germany, the allies urged that it would be paradoxical that Germany, after losing the war, should add six and a half million inhabitants to its population, and 83,000 square kilometres to its territory. France would be alarmed, numerically inferior as it already is, by the creation of a Greater Germany. Nor is this all. Other diplomatic considerations are still more important. Such a Greater Germany would have a common frontier with Italy nearly 300 miles in length. It would reach down to within sixty miles of the Adriatic. Either Italy would have to ally itself with Germany —and this is, having regard to the ambitions of Italy, highly improbable—or the rivalry of Italy and Germany would become dangerously acute. In the first case Italy would be dominated by Germany, and Europe would be seriously perturbed. In the alternative, Italy would perhaps successfully endeavour to raise a coalition against Germany.

As for the Little Entente, it could not remain indifferent. Opinions may differ about the strength of the Little Entente in view of Italian intrigues. Yet Czecho-Slovakia could not consent to be caught in a pair of pincers, and be surrounded, except for its Eastern extremity, by German territory. It would do everything to move the Powers. France and Italy would probably stand by it and Rumania and Yugo-Slavia would be compelled, as a matter of life or death, to oppose a new German *Drang nach Osten*—the push Eastwards—which would be possible by an arrangement with Hungary, whose territorial aspirations are ardent and have been encouraged in unexpected quarters.

Thus it is difficult to see how European diplomacy can accept the policy of the Anschluss, which would have incalculable consequences. Austria is denied the right, in the superior interest of Europe, to dispose of itself. But the moral is clear. Such a refusal of the right of self-determination (much vaunted in 1919) demands a counterpart; and if Austria is to live alone it is entitled, in all fairness, to economic concessions. Let it not be forgotten that, with the restricted domestic market of Austria, the Austrian industrialists must export 70 per cent of their products. It becomes a duty, as well as good policy, if the Anschluss is prohibited, to facilitate Austrian commerce with Central Europe. If there were fewer rivalries and jealousies in the Succession States, and a sensible view, apparently generous but really enlightenedly selfish, were taken, it should not be hard to turn Austrian sentiment against the conversion of the proud and historic city of the Hapsburgs into a mere chief town of a German province.

Some kind of reorganisation in Central Europe is obviously necessary. The French, alive to the risk that their diplomacy was running, at one time evolved a scheme whereby a Danubian Confederation would have been set up. It was far too difficult. It would have necessitated the detachment of Bavaria from Germany, and the "disannexation" of the Rhineland. Into this combination Austria would, according to the calculations of the Quai d'Orsay, have entered. Catholicism was to have been the common link. It was sought to pit Danubian Catholicism against Prussian Protestantism. In articles which I wrote at the time I fully exposed the fatuity of this plan. Indeed, the French did not persist. They have had no consistent policy, but only a sentimental and instinctive horror of the Anschluss.

M. Maurice Turpaud has recalled the history of the economic union of Bavaria with Prussia a century ago. The French Minister at Munich in 1828, the Comte de Romigny, warned the French Government against the activity shown by Prussia in assembling the small German States in a Customs Union. He predicted that if the French did not make counter-propositions and give Bavaria the advantages that Prussia was prepared to give, Munich would be compelled to turn to Berlin, and the economic union would be the prelude to a political union. Paris paid no heed to these advertisements, believing that Metternich would find some means of counteracting Prussian policy. Nothing was done, and Bavaria adhered to the Prussian economic system. Thus, remarks M. Turpaud, the disaster of 1870—and, perhaps one should add, of 1914—was rendered possible by French apathy in the early part of the nineteenth century.

The situation to-day is not dissimilar. I fail to find, however, any positive and practical programme. There is plenty of vituperation. There is plenty of negative protest. That is all. The best observers have sufficiently affirmed that Austria cannot remain isolated. It is the most peaceful community in Central Europe, but it is, if sensible steps are not taken, the most likely to cause war. Two of Europe's leading statesmen—M. Bénès and M. Briand—are reported to have issued the warning that "the Anschluss means war." It behoves them, then, to find an alternative; and it is only in the economic sphere that it can be found.

VI. TOLERANCE

THE most conspicuous trait of the Austrians is their good-humoured tolerance. Doubtless some of the "oppressed" races, which have now become independent nations, will not agree; but their dissent would be chiefly political. They had genuine grievances, arising out of the system of government and their own consciousness of nationship, but, if the régime was bad for them it was bad not because of any deliberate desire to "oppress," but simply because it was bad.

In my conversations with leaders of Austrian thought I particularly observed this tolerance. There were no angry outbursts; there was a placid acceptance of things as they are, or when they could not be accepted, a mild expression of the wish that they should change.

So it was, for example, with Doctor Ernst Benedikt, the editor of the *Neue Freie Presse*, one of the most important Viennese newspapers. On the Anschluss he took the view that I have already set out—which is everybody's view—but he would not have events precipitated; there is no bitterness in his lamentation over the fate of his country; in good time a way will be found. Meanwhile, Austria would like another loan. . . .

Even when Italy was mentioned, he retained his composure.

He was far from nursing resentment against the Italians. The desecration of the tombstones?—It was, of course, unfortunate, but it would be better were the Austrians of South Tyrol to refrain from provocation. They had been too abusive, and abuse could only bring retaliatory measures upon them. "Of course," said he, "it is not surprising that they protested vehemently, but what good did that do? Since they are under the Italian government, they must submit passively. That is the way to obtain better treatment. Our authorities have intimated as much to them, and now things will improve. The Italians are not really unfriendly to Austria and the Austrians. It is absurd for them to have any fear of the comparatively few Austrians who come within their jurisdiction. Czecho-Slovakia is not afraid of the millions of Germans in their midst, and it has accorded them full liberty, so that there is hardly a German problem in Czecho-Slovakia to-day. Why then should Italy be so intent on Italianising the Austrians of South Tyrol?"

This kind of a speech was typical. Nothing struck me more than the absence of animosity.

I do not think anybody better embodies the Austrian desire for accommodation than Dr. Benedikt. He would have peace with all the neighbours of the little country. Particularly, since economic considerations must be paramount, friendship is needed with Czecho-Slovakia. The Austrians are too inclined to regard the Czechs with disdain, as lacking the high culture of Austrians, but this feeling is happily diminishing. It is natural enough that Czecho-Slovakia, in spite of its ancient history, should be looked upon as a parvenu among the nations, but Czecho-Slovakia has made good, and is prepared to break down the tariff barriers which operated so seriously against its neighbour. . . .

So he purred pleasantly. . . . Goodwill to all men. And I think he is perfectly and temperamentally sincere.

Other well-known publicists—and I spent some time with a score of them—struck the same note of friendliness. Among them I remember Dr. Lippe, who nevertheless vigorously defended the policy of the Emperor Francis Joseph. It had never been the design of the old Emperor to treat unfairly any section of his subjects. He had allowed them to enjoy partial autonomy. Undoubtedly he was a good hard-working King; and if he, unaware of modern changes, thought of the people of the Empire as *his* people, and had an old-fashioned notion of the majesty of his office, he was simple-minded and single-minded in his conception of duty. A reserved old man, he tried to be regally courteous. If he was not a brilliant monarch, he possessed sound common sense, and he had a remarkable memory. Certainly he lacked a broad outlook, and as he grew older he hesitated to take the initiative, relying more and more on his Ministers who were mostly mediocre. But even the Czechs respected him for his honest intentions, his blameless character, his personal kindliness. . . .

The Wilsonian doctrine of self-determination seemed to give substance to grievances which were certainly not greater than are those of the Germans, the Slovaks, the Croats, and the Slovenes to-day under their new masters, the Czechs, and the Serbians. . . .

He added that certain journalists—some of them English—fed the flames of discontent because they were not treated with the consideration that they thought due to them by the Austrian Court. "But how could they expect the great Austro-Hungarian Empire to flatter them, to pander to their vanity? It is an evil thing to pursue a sledge-hammer policy out of pique."

Whether one accepted his view or not, it was entertaining to hear him expound it. The voluble little man, with hair brushed over the bald spaces of his cranium, his kindly intelligent eyes gleaming behind his glasses, would have had me believe that before the war everything was for the best in the best of possible worlds. But there was no malice in him, and he wished the Czecho-Slovaks well.

A not dissimilar opinion of Francis Joseph is set forth by Professor Redlich, the authority on Austrian history and political institutions. He blames Francis Joseph because he cared too little for public opinion and cared too much for the House of Hapsburg. On the whole he was conservative, yet if he was convinced that reform was desirable and offered no danger to the dynastic supremacy he would accept it. For sixty-seven years he was a magnificent anachronism. He stood for the idea of Absolute Monarchy, but he was personally amiable. He had the pride of his race, but his own tastes were simple. Nobody can deny his stoicism in the face of tragedy. He was tried in a fiery furnace; bereavement followed bereavement, disappointment succeeded disappointment; but he went on with unshaken courage. What he lacked was imagination. He was industrious, and within his limitations able, but he could not foresee the results of his actions. When he issued his ultimatum to Serbia in 1914 he did not realise the tremendous consequences to Austria and to Europe. He probably saw only the supposed necessity of inflicting condign punishment on the nation which was responsible for the assassination of the Archduke. . . .

Thus there is everywhere a wish to judge everybody and every nation tolerantly.

The politicians themselves are mild enough. One reads in the newspapers of demonstrations in the Viennese streets, with the parties glaring at each other and ready to come to blows. There are alarmist speculations in advance, and one pictures Vienna bathed in blood. But, in fact, the parties parade, Socialists and Catholics, in perfect amity; and there is seldom a real clash. The other day President Miklas, himself a Christian Socialist, gave a tea which brought together the leaders of the parties; and I noticed that it was the subject of comment in the Press that Catholics and Pan-Germans and Social-Democrats munched sandwiches and rusks together, and chatted pleasantly. I do not know what is the purpose of such social items. For my part I find it hard to believe that Austrians behave otherwise than munch their rusks and chat pleasantly together.

VII. MONSIGNOR SEIPEL

UNQUESTIONABLY the outstanding politician in Austria of recent years has been Monsignor Seipel. This priest has governed the country with extraordinary discretion. Self-effacement, one would imagine, is hardly a quality to be found in a Chancellor. If a man places himself at the head of a State, he is not likely to be a man of exceptional modesty. Yet Mgr. Seipel truly shrank from publicity, and went to his office on the Ballplatz by tramcar like any city clerk. He likes to pass unnoticed, this black-coated, thin-faced, pale, thoughtful man, who looks for all the world like an elderly curate in a town parish.

He is frail and sickly; before he accepted office his precarious health obliged him to take long periods of repose; but when he threw himself into public work he never abandoned his desk; politics were the only cure which he would undergo.

Monsignor Seipel

He is trusted by the people and esteemed by his opponents. When he became Doctor of Theology thirty years ago, he was appointed lecturer in the Vienna University, and later in the Salzburg University. He has written on theology. There was little in his career which appeared to prepare him for the rôle which he was, late in life, to assume. For that matter there is little in his present life which appears to be compatible with his occupation. Content with his simple cell in a suburban convent, he is assiduous in his devotional exercises. Nothing is more astonishing in contemporary Europe than the ascendancy of this ecclesiastical figure, apparently unfitted for political strife, and yet a match for the wily and bellicose leaders of the Second International.

His manner is insinuous. He is not given to plain speech, but takes refuge in subtle reservations. It is difficult to seize his precise sense. Every sentence is a studied blend of affirmation and denial. It is full of nuances. The meaning is elusive. If, for example, you think you have pinned him down to definite assertion of the necessity of the Anschluss, you will find that his advocacy of the Anschluss is conditional; union with Germany would be desirable if it were accepted by the countries which it concerns—or rather if it ceased to concern other countries. Everything is contingent on something else; one can speak of desiderata, without implying that they are immediately demanded. Thus, whatever Mgr. Seipel seems to want—if he wants anything—is for an undetermined future; it is an eventual possibility, a hypothetical prospect, something which may be realised at an ulterior date. . . .

It would be difficult to conceive a politician who differs more radically from the common picture of the Dictator. To some extent every real politician in power must be a Dictator. That is his function—to make an end of vacillation, to decide and to act. There is no country which does not possess its Dictator, and the most democratic countries have the greatest need of a Dictator. But while democracies expect their rulers to make up their minds for them, there are various methods of performing the job. All Dictators, of course, pretend to be carrying out the will of the people, and, in so far as the people have a will, they are right, for it would be impossible to impose authority against the will of the people. But while Mussolini boldly proclaims Italy Fascist, and regards himself as the supreme representative of Fascist Italy, Seipel works in a quieter

manner, and endeavours to divert attention from his own
personality.

When he retired momentarily from the arena of action he
did not go under compulsion; he announced that he considered
his personality an obstacle to an understanding among the
parties; his object could be better attained without him. . . .
So he came and went, almost furtively, gliding in and out. He
would prefer to be unnoticed, to move like a ghost in the
avenues of government. But his black silhouette casts a long
shadow whether he is in his office or in his cell.

In his own party his influence is predominant. When other
men are nominally Chancellor, it is Seipel who guides their
hand. So it was when Mayr and Schober were his henchmen.
Had they succeeded in restoring Austria to economic health,
he would have been well pleased to remain in the background.
But they failed, and for the first time in centuries a priest
became Chancellor. He is no Richelieu, no Mazarin, but he is
as efficient as either of them.

He it was who secured the League of Nations' loan which
stabilised the Austrian currency. He went personally to Rome,
Berlin, and Paris, to persuade the authorities that it was in the
interest of Europe not to leave Austria in despair. He worked
largely through Sir William Goode, who has done more excellent work in the restoration of Europe than any man I know.
Goode was originally President of the Austrian Section of the
Reparations Commission, and when he saw that Austria needed
outside assistance, and that it was folly to badger it for payments, he resigned from the Commission, which then came to
a speedy end. He was invited to become financial adviser to
the Austrian Government. To present the true case of Austria
to the different nations required great patience, for war passions died slowly. Finally, he managed to convince the creditors
of Austria that they should relinquish their prior claims on
Austrian assets, in order that they might serve as the guarantee
of a loan.

In those days I saw a good deal of Sir William Goode, as I
did of Sir Arthur Salter, at the head of the Financial Section
of the League of Nations, and I greatly admired their tact and
sound judgment. Goode allied joviality with shrewdness, and
he was indefatigable in his advocacy of the Austrian cause. The
opposition of the Little Entente was comprehensible enough,
but while these countries pressed Austria there was no hope of

escaping disintegration. The first thing was to promote friend-
lier sentiments in the nations of the Little Entente.

Seipel deserves immense credit for his handling of the situation. He brought a spirit of friendship into the Austrian parties
and into the Central European nations. So it came about that
though in appearance he is cold, encouraging neither popularity
nor affection, yet this frigid priest-professor-politician aroused
both popularity and a veneration not unmingled with affection.

When he was shot in 1924 he mustered up his strength to
point to the man who had succeeded in wounding him gravely,
and to cry to those who were maltreating the assassin:

"Above all do not hurt him; he, too, has tried to do his duty,
though he is misguided." . . .

VIII. DANSE MACABRE

LOUIS, the bar-tender, produced the banknote for several
milliard kronen. "With that in my pocket-book I can
imagine myself a rich man"—and this production of worthless
paper, with an appropriate remark, seems to be the principal
joke of the Austrians.

I sympathised with Louis. "But by the way," I asked, "how
does it come about that you have a French name?"

"It is not French," he said, "it is international. Louis is a
name that is recognised in every language. Of course my real
name is Ludwig, but Ludwig is specifically German. So I adopt
the international form of the name."

This bar-tender told me that his life savings had been swept
away. They were, he assured me, not negligible, for he had been
in the luxurious bars of all the cosmopolitan cities; and he was
about to retire when the *danse macabre* of the krone began.
He was obliged to start again. Yet he said all this with a cheerful air, as though it were a minor mishap that must be expected
in the métier of bar-tender.

"You take it lightly now, but it must have been pretty awful
to go through that experience," I said, to encourage him to
talk.

And then he launched forth on a description of those days
when the krone was falling to zero. "It was nothing like so
bad as in Germany," he remarked, rather proud of the relative
superiority of Austria in the monetary crisis. "But it was bad
enough. Everything was sold at ridiculous prices—furs, jewels,

tapestries, and pictures—and the foreigner who happened to be in Austria snapped up incomparable bargains."

While the housewife was asleep the purchasing power of the money in her purse diminished. At night she might have enough to purchase the next day's meal. In the morning the sum would be insufficient. One man was tempted to buy something and went to his hotel to get the money; when he returned to the shop the price had doubled.

A resident of Austria, obtaining his income from England, paid on an average less than a shilling a day for his rooms during that period. He took four friends to dine in the best restaurant of Vienna—and the best cuisine in Vienna is very good; paying with an English pound note, he received a huge handful of change. . . .

Such incidents seem humorous now, but it does not require much imagination to realise the dismay of Austrian families in finding themselves suddenly penniless. No wonder that they went so far, in spite of their tolerance, as to mob one disgusting traveller who ostentatiously flung away millions of kronen in paper money in the principal streets of Vienna.

Even after the Austrian schilling (roughly worth about two-thirds of the English shilling) had taken the place of the worthless krone, and there was stabilisation of the currency, the well-to-do Austrians were denied whipped cream, which they love, with their fruit or coffee in public places. There were still children starving, and it was properly felt that cream should not be publicly eaten. This self-imposed hardship emphasises Austrian kindliness, for the men as well as the women eat cream and cakes in Austria as they do nowhere else.

The worst feature of all was the unprecedented growth of prostitution. The most respectable girls, without money, and unable to find work, promenaded the streets and infested the fashionable hotels. . . .

As for suicides, they were frequent. I remember how I was shocked at the news that a professor and his wife, who had worked devotedly on behalf of the children, found themselves forced by poverty to end their days. Indeed there are still an unusual number of suicides every year, which may be attributed to the nervous strain of those days as well as to poverty.

Anomalies continue. House rent, for example, has not changed as monetary values have changed, and in some cases the tenants continue to pay on the basis of the old krone. The

Social-Democrats defend this practice, and the unfortunate landlords are still unable to obtain anything like their old revenues.

I went to see a friend of mine who lives in Vienna. He inhabited half a splendid mansion. The high-ceilinged rooms, richly decorated, panelled, and painted, were as spacious as the reception halls of a palace. The furniture consisted of pieces that would not have been out of place, one would have thought, in a museum. House and furniture surprised me, for they appeared to be far beyond my friend's means as I had known them.

He explained: "I am living in the mansion of one of the richest and best known members of the Austrian aristocracy. He is ruined, and he is doing what many others are doing—that is to say, he has let to me half his house and furniture. In the other half he lives himself."

"Would it be impertinent to inquire how much you pay him for the use of his property?"

"Not at all. I pay fifty dollars, or, in round figures, £10 per month."

Still, things are righting themselves, and the old paper money can be bought from hawkers and from shops as a souvenir of tragic days that in retrospect have become a huge joke. In the end, the notes actually cost more to print than they were worth, and breweries bought them up to use them as labels on beer bottles. When silver coins were struck again, the Austrian Government made the mistake of putting too much silver in the coins, and before the error was discovered Poland had purchased great quantities of the Austrian schilling for the sake of the silver.

It is not only the vanished krone that has become a joke. Outside my hotel a street pedlar with a rubicund face was selling funny little green hats with enormous feathers. It is too bad that the green feathered hat, which one used to find so picturesque, has likewise become a joke.

IX. MUSICAL PREËMINENCE

BUT the Austrians are inclined to make fun of everything, even of their famous musicians. Of Richard Strauss I heard many amusing stories. Thus you may, if you are fortunate, be shown the handsome apartments of the greatest living

Austrian composer, and finally be taken into his bedroom: "Here," the lady guide will say with bated breath, "is the room in which the great Richard Strauss will die." It is probably a unique experience to stand reverently, by anticipation, in the future death chamber of a living celebrity!

The Viennese are especially proud that Richard Strauss and Felix Weingartner and Frantz Schalk direct their operas. Vienna's predominance in music is undisputed; a century ago Gluck, Haydn, Mozart, Beethoven, and Schubert, lived and composed in Vienna, and their houses are pointed out. There are many memorials to the Masters. A love of music is inculcated in every Austrian child; and even during the darkest years of the war the Viennese sought solace in attending concerts and operas.

The ubiquitous American jazz has not lessened the vogue of the lighter forms of Viennese music, and Vienna still supplies the world with its operettas. Franz Lehar and Oskar Straus have an international fame; and their forerunner, Johann Strauss, gave us the best of those graceful waltzes which hold their own despite fox-trots, tangoes, and one-steps.

The opera performances start early; the Viennese willingly forego their dinner to attend these performances; but they see no reason why they should not eat between the acts. So, after listening to Marie Jeritza or Lotte Lehmann, the good bourgeois regale themselves, in the beautiful buildings, on sausages and sandwiches.

One name stands out from the long list of great executants of Austrian origin—that of Fritz Kreisler. As an ardent admirer, I would wish to mention him here, though he later took up his abode in Berlin. There are few capitals in Europe in which he has not played; I have myself listened to him in several European cities. As for America, he has toured it over and over again. He is easily the most celebrated violinist of our time; and Paderewski hardly exceeds him in renown.

Over forty years ago he was the youngest pupil ever admitted to the Vienna Conservatory, and when he was ten years of age he was the winner of a First Prize. Paris, too, has some claim in his making, for he studied in France under Delibes, and there won the Prix de Rome at the age of twelve.

There is perhaps no good reason why a violinist, who has the most perfect technique, and whose loveliness of tone is unsurpassed, should, if his country is at war, obtain privileges that

RICHARD STRAUSS

are denied the humblest peasant and the simplest artisan. If the theory of exemption for merit in the arts is admitted, it would carry us far. Everybody who has the smallest pretensions to skill in writing, painting, or music, would feel that he should escape the ordinary obligations of citizenship. For my part I am opposed to conscription in any form, but if it is practised it is difficult to admit exceptions; and the average run of artists have no special claims to consideration whatever. They imagine themselves to be superior persons in inverse ratio to their importance. Those who are absolutely null are the most insupportable. As a class they are insufferable; and the hangers-on of the arts should certainly not be excused from any civic services. I would exempt ten honest artisans for one worthless artist. . . .

Yet the case of Kreisler brought home to many people the stupidity of war; one was shocked to learn that this man, who possessed unique gifts, which were valued highly by men and women of culture the world over, was exposed to the perils of the trenches. It was not for the sake of Kreisler that we felt this; it was for our own sake. We felt, without any thought of nationality, which appears absurd when it is applied to arts and artists, that it is criminal to run the risk of prematurely depriving the world of its rarer elements of beauty. In point of fact Kreisler was wounded on the Galician front, but happily he recovered; and his playing, when I heard him again this year, had lost nothing of its strength and charm. . . .

In the larger cafés—or beer-halls—I have listened to musical programmes of a higher quality than are given in the majority of concert halls in London and New York. They are directed by conductors of real ability and some fame. The musicians, on their daïs, perform for the audience of beer-drinkers on their benches, as earnestly and as skilfully as many highly reputed orchestras in other capitals. I count the musical evenings in Viennese cafés as among the most interesting I have passed.

But there are also the folk songs which are an unfailing delight, especially in the suburban inns—guingettes the French would call them—at Grinzing. On sunny slopes hang the purple grapes; the vines clamber over trellis-work; and on wooden benches, at rude tables, sit men and women of all classes and of all ages, drinking the new wine, and listening to the players and singers on a small platform. Nor are they content merely to listen. They join in the refrains. The merriment is simple

and hearty. The songs are old and new, and often they have a
political or a satirical cast. In Vienna itself there are cafés
which imitate the *guingettes* of Grinzing; they imitate them
well, and one sits under purple vines, drinking the Grinzing
wines, listening to the quartets and joining, if one can, in the
choruses. My companions at least, one a Viennese student, another a man of letters, roared lustily; and I felt that the world
was good, in spite of wars and bankruptcies. . . .

As for the theatres, they also have a tradition which is well
maintained; and I noticed that English plays are freely produced. There were translations of Shakespeare, Shaw, and
Wilde; and when I was there plays by a younger American
were particularly successful. Max Reinhardt spends six months
of the year in Vienna; I do not know how he manages to run
several theatres in Berlin, in Dresden, in Vienna, and elsewhere,
perpetually inventing new methods of presentation and taking
his companies abroad.

The wonderful collections of art treasures in Vienna are
valuable just because they are collections; and I can imagine
nothing more foolish than the proposal to distribute them
among the Succession States, on the ground that as these States
formed part of the Austro-Hungarian Empire, they are therefore part-owners of the Viennese museums! Nobody would
have benefited by the scattering of collections which have
grown slowly throughout the centuries and have become an
organic whole.

Vienna, stripped of many things, must be left its cultural
supremacy in Central Europe.

X. REJUVENATION AND BEAUTY

IN THE sciences, as well as in the arts, Vienna is supreme.
The professors do not welcome publicity. Yet their studies
are extraordinarily suggestive, and sometimes their experiments, of a sensational character, are exploited by the newspapers. For example, we are told that it may be possible to
transplant eyes, and certainly amazing results have been obtained in the case of fish, frogs, and rats. Beetles would appear
to suffer no inconvenience in being given new heads for old.
It seems to be possible to change the sex of fowls. On these
matters I cannot pronounce.

A good deal of attention has been rightly attracted to the

rejuvenation methods of Professor Steinach, to which Gertrude
Atherton refers in "Black Oxen."

Steinach has proceeded on entirely different lines from those
followed by Dr. Voronoff in France. Voronoff has employed
the glands of monkeys, with surprising effect, not only on
animals but on human beings. He has obtained a more vigorous
breed of sheep with thicker wool and he is said to have given
a new lease of life to ageing man. I have heard Voronoff, in
whom there is nothing of the charlatan, expound his theories
convincingly; but in some respects Steinach's work is more
significant.

He, too, tried the effects of transplantation, but he afterwards simply tied the vasa deferentia, thus increasing the tissue
of the interstitial cells (which he named the puberty gland)
and stimulating the production of hormone.

There has been a storm of objections, not merely scientific,
but sociological, psychological, and religious. Into these con-
troversies I cannot enter, but there is much evidence that vaso
ligation produces rejuvenation. It is unfortunate that the
sexual aspect of this operation has been emphasised, and that
less has been said about the alleged increase in mental alertness
and physical endurance. The sexual aspect has always been regarded by workers in this field as a subsidiary phenomenon. . . .

During the war the audacity of the surgeons knew no
bounds; and afterwards plastic surgery was applied to women
who wished to increase their charms. If men wounded in the
war could be made presentable by the process of cutting and
grafting, why should not women suffer on behalf of beauty?
Il faut souffrir pour être belle, is an old French saying, which
now has a more specific meaning. Yet there is surely a difference between operations intended to enable a man to earn a
living, and operations merely intended to minister to feminine
coquetry.

However this may be, it is in Vienna that the practice of
plastic surgery has been most highly developed. One professor
announced that he could remove superfluous fat—and did so.
Patients are not lacking in these days when plumpness is somehow considered disgraceful. Women are prepared to make any
sacrifices to fashion. Formerly, rotundity was desirable. To-day,
slimness is obligatory. The mode issues its ordinances which
nobody dares to defy. As a mere man I can understand changes

in dress, but I cannot understand changes in physique. It is easy to discard the crinoline, but it appears impossible to discard fleshly curves, which were once reckoned charms, but are now thought ugly. . . .

Since the war there has been an amazing outbreak of materialism. We pay more attention to sports and bodily exercises; we pay more attention to sexual matters; we likewise talk a great deal more than would have been deemed decent a few years ago about eating. Gastronomy is elevated into an art—the seventh or the ninth or the thirteenth, or whatever it is in these days when we pretend to have increased the number of the arts. I cannot sit down in the smallest dinner party without hearing prattle about the *cuisine*. Women who are entirely ignorant of how an omelette is made, pose as authorities on food and wine. They are acquainted with the latest pretentious restaurant, to which "gourmets," who cannot distinguish between good and bad cooking, snobbishly go. They are exploited—as, of course, are the men—by profiteers who are equally ignorant of the *cuisine*, but who realise that there is money to be made by opening a restaurant which they call an Auberge, or a Rôtisserie, or a Relais, and which they decorate rather quaintly. An immense literature has sprung up on this subject, and generally it is good form to concern oneself with the new "art."

By a curious paradox, however, this mode exists simultaneously with the mode of slenderness. Nobody dares eat today as heartily as in the days when one was content to be a good trencherman without talking about it. A real gourmet of twenty years ago would have put to shame the false gourmets of the present generation. He not only knew when food was good, but he ate that food with relish. Nothing amuses me more than to observe that my fair neighbour at the dinner table, who makes gastronomy her principal theme of conversation, scarcely touches her food. She is afraid to touch it, for if it is *bon ton* to be a gourmet, it is also *bon ton* to be thin.

But this is not all. Semi-starvation may do the new generation of gourmets little harm; they are ridiculous, but otherwise estimable. In addition, however, they have recourse to plastic surgery.

The other day the case was recorded of a woman who lost a leg as it was being carved to the right proportions. It was not, let me hasten to say, in Vienna, but in another European capital where doubtless the sculptors in flesh and blood are not so skilful. She was good-looking, but her legs were not as elegant as she wished. Has not somebody said that the murder of a woman with thick ankles is justifiable homicide? If skirts had not been so short it would not have mattered; but the poor girl, worried about her shapeless limbs, found a doctor who undertook to reduce them. After spending an hour and a half on the operating table, one of her legs was certainly reduced. But infection set in, and presently she was informed that she must choose between her leg and her life. . . .

The leg was amputated and she recovered. Then she brought a suit for damages against the doctor. Her counsel contended that a surgeon was not entitled to perform operations with a purely æsthetic purpose. The risk was too great. The human body was sacred and should not be mutilated without reason. It was not sufficient that the patient demanded an operation; there are a number of operations which are often demanded, but which are specifically illegal.

The defence of the doctor was simply that there was no carelessness, that the operation was not forbidden by law, and that it had been carried out with every care. The Court, despite its condemnation of the vanity of the woman, returned a verdict against the doctor.

The general view will probably be that plastic surgery, if it involves risks, should not be practised. There are, it is true, comparatively negligible operations which are permissible. There is that which consists in making an incision in the skin over the ears and under the hair in order to tighten the skin. "Face-lifting," I believe it is called. It takes out all wrinkles. One woman whom I knew who had thus been treated looked extraordinarily young, but I could not help remarking the contrast between her face and her hands. The hands, badly wrinkled, told her age. So far as I am aware, no method of "hand-lifting" has been thought out.

Another kind of operation which was brought to my notice was the removal of breasts. Boys will be boys we used to say, but the modern version of it is that girls will be boys. Dancers who undergo surgical treatment of this kind, may be regarded as making a sacrifice to professional efficiency. A stranger case was that of a sportswoman who has won several athletic championships and is a crack automobile racer. Questioned by newspapermen she admitted that she had submitted to such an operation. She said:

"For me, who lead an active life, it was like a sixth finger. A sixth finger is embarrassing and one has it cut off. That is logical. There is no question of æsthetics or of eccentricity. Sport and business are my whole life, and I am not concerned with the rest."

Frivolity and seriousness are strangely blended in Vienna. Beauty specialists abound, some of them known the world over. It amused me to read in a Viennese newspaper an account of a beauty parlour which is worth literal reproduction:

"I visited one of the largest and best known schools for the enhancement of feminine pulchritude in Vienna. The salon and the individual booths are attractively decorated, and the charming proprietress makes it a point that her operators shall be young and pretty examples of the art they administer. After a two months' course the student is either given the privilege of a position in the salon or a diploma with which she can open a shop of her own. Mme. —— specialises in facial massage, and manufactures her own preparations with the help of skilled physicians and chemists. This charming and vivacious woman spends the forenoon in her factory and the afternoon at her big establishment. She even edits her own newspaper and is now planning to open branches in other cities. And here is a secret —she has procured the Austrian rights for the Steinach rejuvenation mask. Mme. —— advises that every woman over thirty should watch herself before the damage is too advanced to be easily corrected. . . . There is a special orthopedic nurse who does nothing but 'slenderise' feet and ankles."

XI. FREUD AND ADLER

SOON after the war I used to meet Americans—they were almost exclusively Americans—who would tell me that the chief object of their voyage to Europe was to go to Vienna.

"Why Vienna?" I would ask.

"Well, I want to be 'siked'," they would reply, "and Vienna is the only place in which to be 'siked'."

The word puzzled me at first and then I realised that it was a new slang for designating the process of psycho-analysis and should probably be spelt "psyched." They were, for the most part, perfectly normal men and women. They suffered from

SIGMUND FREUD

nothing, except from idleness, which gave them too much leisure to think about themselves. At last they had heard about psycho-analysis, and particularly about Dr. Sigmund Freud. It had taken many years for the teachings of Freud to reach these leisured folk, but they actually discovered that they, too, possessed inhibitions, and the unconscious mind, and other curious things that may produce unhappiness and folly and genius. They considered themselves abnormal beings. They had dreams which might be given an obscene interpretation, and they looked to psycho-analysis to release hidden and suppressed forces, to eradicate perverse desires of which they were hardly aware, and to explain themselves to themselves.

So there was a steady stream of these foolish folk to Vienna. There still lives Freud, who has been called the father of psycho-analysis; he no longer lectures and he now receives few patients. His theories have, however, been adopted by a host of practitioners, and, as is inevitable, there are, among these practitioners, charlatans as well as serious disciples. There is much that is bad as well as much that is good in his exposition of psycho-analysis. Some of his doctrines appear to be fatuous, while others are illuminating. But when the dross is washed away doubtless a great deal of gold will remain, and Freud will be properly appraised as a remarkable pioneer in a necessarily obscure country.

There is a reaction against Freud. The University, in which he taught, turned against him. Many who found that he was inspired and inspiring, now find that he is nonsensical. But popularity and unpopularity are of little consequence. Freud will be always remembered as the man who applied psychology to daily life, and revealed dark secrets of the prison house. Neither those who trooped gaily to Vienna to be 'siked,' nor those who scornfully dismiss Freud as discredited can decide on the true value of his teaching.

I recall amusing verses which were entitled "The Jung Idea":

> The young things who frequent picture palaces
> Have no use for this psycho-analysis;
>   And although Doctor Freud
>   Is distinctly annoyed,
> They cling to their old-fashioned fallacies!

Yet Freud, if he no longer enjoys the transient and ignorant hero-worship of a few years ago, has unquestionable claims to his place as a thinker who has thrown light on the fantasies and delusions and complexities of the mortal mind. Thousands of people imagine themselves to be neurasthenic and seek to be cured by psycho-analysis; but presently the current terminology will be rejected, and people will forget their imaginary ills. These exaggerations are of little importance. Freud can only be judged when he is neither fashionable nor unfashionable. That he made mistakes can hardly be denied; it is impossible, in my opinion, for the ordinary man to read a Freudian work without being startled by passages which betray an amazing credulity, an extraordinarily simple faith; but it is equally impossible not to be struck by passages which suggest the penetration of genius.

"What is new in Freud," said one distinguished scientist to me, "is not true, and what is true is not new." But this is an unfair verdict; for although one "knew" everything that Freud teaches long before Freud, one knew it vaguely and did not realise its importance. Freud has expressed many things clearly and systematically. He has perhaps pushed his theories too far and has seen morbidity where there is no morbidity— unless the whole of life is morbid. He has insisted, as I think, far too strongly on the rôle of sex in life, especially in early life. He has arbitrarily and falsely interpreted dreams, gestures, and memories. Nevertheless he has found many keys to behaviour and has been the foremost and most courageous worker in a peculiarly difficult field.

The danger of falsification at once arises when observations are reduced to a system. Healthy instincts are, for those who perpetually treat maladies of the soul, too easily converted into maladies. One admires Freud for his long years of research, his perseverance in face of fierce hostility, his thoroughness, his modesty, his simplicity; but one must not take him on trust.

It is thirty years ago since he began to expound the principles of psycho-analysis. In 1909 he went to America with Jung, his favourite pupil. Nobody was more surprised than Freud himself that his name should be on every tongue. His lectures, his treatises, were translated into all languages. His classes were crowded by eager students. When he finally triumphed he was about fifty years of age; he remained as unassuming as ever. He possesses a remarkable power of expressing himself with exceptional clarity, without affectation, without recourse to scientific jargon, with an almost childlike simplicity.

Dr. Paul Farez, an able French writer, asserts that the psycho-analysis of Freud, which was originally a method of psycho-exploration, has unfortunately been transformed into a sort of religion, and he gives the best summary of its credo that I have seen: "In the depths of our unconscious mind move instinctive aspirations. . . . To safeguard the ego a censorship institutes itself. In the name of education, manners, tradition, the moral conscience controls these instincts, rectifying some of them, tolerating others, and driving back those which it reproves. But, although repressed, these instincts are not without force. They demand satisfaction. Sometimes they are content with an imitative compensation. Or they are purified, idealised, sublimated—carried into moral, æsthetic, or intellectual channels. Often they insinuate themselves in automatic actions, dreams. . . ."

Thus the dream is not meaningless; it is a safety valve; it may be the key to the mysteries of the unconscious. It may explain various maladies which could be cured were their causes brought to light. In the system of Freud sex is the basis of everything. Even the infant in the cradle is dominated by the libido. No wonder that Freudism or Pan-sexualism, has been called by Kroepelin "the metaphysics of pornography"; and that Professor Blondel sees in it "obscenity promoted to the rank of a science."

It is almost needless to add, for all readers who have followed the trend of modern literature, that Freudism has had an enormous influence over the writers—especially the post-war writers—of every country. For the most part the influence has been unhealthy, for the writers have not understood, or they have used Freudism as a cloak to cover whatever is morbid, perverse, indecent, in their thoughts and language. But, on the other hand, the curiosity about the springs of human action, the determination to reveal the truth about human nature, has inspired profound and penetrating works of fiction which are vastly superior to those which contain a ready-made and conventional psychology.

Dr. Alfred Adler is the author of the phrase now used in and out of season—"inferiority complex." The workings of the inferiority complex are curious. It may be that the victim will become meek, timid, subservient; or it may be that, reacting against his secret distrust of his own capacity, he will become audacious, pompous, authoritative. An excellent example of inferiority masquerading as force is presented by Louis XIV of France, the most magnificent monarch of his age. I was induced to write my biographical study of the King because I discovered that in every phase of his life there was confirmation of Adler's theories. Adler was kind enough to express his appreciation and to recognise Louis as an excellent illustration of his teaching. It may be recalled that Louis was oppressed and suppressed by his mother, Anne of Austria, and Mazarin; that he was a dull, neglected, uninstructed boy; that he was deprived of common necessaries; that he was pursued by Condé, and trailed, during the troubles of the Fronde, through France in the wake of armies. Yet the moment Mazarin died, this unpromising youth asserted himself. He asserted himself in such an exaggerated manner that he betrayed his misgiving. While a well-educated normal Prince of his age would have relied on his ministers, Louis dismissed them; he defied Europe; he began his "wars of magnificence" which were to end in disaster; and generally he demonstrated a sense of weakness that was obliged to save itself by a grotesque assumption of strength. In his love affairs, how-ever, he showed the other side of his character; he chose, for the most part, the lowly, the ill-favoured, with whom he was more at home than with the *grandes dames* of the Court; he enjoyed their gratitude, he was flattered and exalted. When he fell into the hands of more designing women, of similar rank to his own, he was a poor bullied creature. . . . But I must not repeat my thesis; suffice it to say that it does, in my opinion, help to justify the contention of Dr. Adler that a large propor-tion of our virtues as well as our vices, our strength as well as our weakness, our triumphs as well as our defeats, our habits, our character, our actions, are determined by a sentiment of in-feriority whose origins are to be found in the difficulties and pains of infancy. These ideas are particularly of interest to educationalists and social workers. It is, of course, not a novelty to affirm that the child is father of the man, but Adler's books and lectures are filled with suggestive thought on this subject. For a number of years he has visited America, where he has had the opportunity of expounding his views and of making in-numerable friends.

Dr. Philip Lehrman, the well-known psychologist and pro-fessor of psychiatry of New York, who has studied in Vienna, sensibly estimated the position of this science in a recent talk:

"The realisation that all mental difficulties begin in childhood, has greatly increased the task of the pedagogue, who now finds himself charged with the double responsibility of assuring the mental well-being as well as the mental development of his charges.

"The psychiatrist finds it necessary to call on the pedagogue and the latter can qualify only if he is psycho-analytically well-informed.

"Humanity could not easily accept the idea that most of its mental activity is unconscious, and is dominated by instinctive forces over which it has no control.

"Gradually, in the past thirty years, psychiatry and finally the other mental sciences utilised Freud's discoveries, so that now there is hardly a branch of our knowledge of humanity which does not owe the major part of its development to psycho-analysis. Thus we find that besides psychiatry, sociology, anthropology, and last but most important of all pedagogy, have to rewrite chapters of their sciences in the light of psycho-analysis.

"The road to the knowledge of psycho-analysis is not an easy one. Self-analysis is essential before one can understand others. For this reason there is a need for institutions where such instruction can be had. The psycho-analytic institutes in Vienna and Berlin have served as models for the newly-formed institutes in London, Budapest and New York."

XII. LITERARY LIFE

THERE is little that calls for special attention in Austrian, as distinct from German literature. This does not mean that Vienna has failed to contribute its part to the post-war literature in the German language; on the contrary, it has been particularly active, and there has been an immense stirring of curiosity, a greater liberty of spirit. "Expressionism" in Austria was rather a movement of revolt than a literary doctrine, and this revolt was not confined to the younger men. It was a revolt against family traditions, social conventions, tyranny in every domain—an affirmation of individuality. It had an explosive force, but it was incoherent and destructive rather than constructive. New paths were being opened, but it would be hard to say where they lead. . . . Nothing I think is more amusing than recent efforts to range writers with the sheep or the goats, for with the sheep are placed men who are classicist

in style, monarchist in opinion, and Roman Catholic in religion—that is to say, authoritarians in every sphere—together
with men who are avowed rebels. What distinguishes the writers
who are to be accepted as sheep from the goats? Human dy-
namism perhaps? But that is romantic, or, on occasion, realist.
In short, the revolutionaries do not know what they want; and
they admit all kinds of writers into their ranks. Dadaism and
similar excesses raged in Austria, and art as such was denounced.
It is impossible to indicate what expressionism expressed: it was
mostly disorderly subjectivity.

But now there is a return to more detached methods. So far
as one can generalise, writers endeavour to look at the world as
it is, and the new naturalism is as coldly critical as expressionism
was hotly delirious; after the surrender to exasperated sensibility, comes the calculated recourse to unlyrical intellectual-
ism. It is nevertheless wrong to represent either Austrian or
German literature diagrammatically. For the sake of convenience one can say that there was a confused clamour of revolutionary anger, and afterwards a patient investigation of material causes and consequences. But in fact these things exist side
by side. The Expressionist period had its value. Perhaps little
that is of literary importance remains, but it was a stimulant.
It has had a tonic effect. Intellectual realism makes for dulness,
but it has been a powerful corrective.

This is not my own verdict, for I would be incompetent to
pronounce; but the verdict of the most enlightened critics with
whom I discussed Austrian literature to-day. There is—and this
is obvious to everybody—particularly to be observed, both in
Austria and in Germany, a strong literary reaction against the
war. The stupidity, the horror, the tragedy of war, have been
exposed relentlessly in a number of novels as well as in essays;
and generally the authors have chosen to eschew fulmination,
to avoid rhetoric, to refrain from such references to the bigness
of the conflict as might dramatise and exalt it. They have
chosen to show it in detail; to reveal its drabness, its monotony,
its senselessness; they take individual cases in their dismal daily
experiences. A simple man, helpless and alone, is the pitiful
creature of blind relentless forces. He hardly knows what is
happening to him, and the instruments of his misery are just
as ignorant. It is a grey picture that is painted, all the more distressing by the absence of vivid tones.

Vienna is veritably the home of creative as well as of critical writers. In this respect it differs from Berlin. In Berlin the critics live, but the creators are not, for the most part, to be found in the capital. Vienna is both critical and creative. A few men—Stefan Zweig for example—are at Salzburg and other provincial towns; but they are the exceptions which prove the rule.

Zweig is a remarkable creator as well as critic, but his exploitation of Ben Jonson raises a curious question of literary ethics. He wrote a German version of Volpone (Jules Romains afterwards turning it into French). But he suppressed the most characteristic and picturesque personages of Jonson; and cut out scenes of rich flavour; and presented a dénouement which was certainly undreamed of by Jonson. An adaptation is not a translation, but how far is it permissible to borrow the work and change the ideas of an original author? I am told that Zweig read Jonson's play, was greatly impressed by it, put it, as he thought, in his bag, and went off to a quiet retreat to translate it. When he arrived he found that the volume was not in his bag. So he set to work to write from memory. If this be true he has a prodigious memory, though it has betrayed him on important points. If it be not true, he has falsified, while using, an old author.

Zweig represents the cosmopolitan spirit of Austrian criticism. His studies of Dickens, Balzac, Tolstoi, his translations of Baudelaire and Romain Rolland, his own romances, all reveal that he has a fine dramatic sense, that he is well acquainted with modern psychology, that he is exceedingly catholic in his studies and outlook.

I was taken one day in Vienna to a café—the Imperial—where betting men congregate, and there amid the hubbub was a famous Viennese writer, calmly pursuing his work on a marble-topped table, apparently oblivious to the noise and bustle. He demanded no ivory tower in which to imprison himself; no solitude from which to survey his soul and the world. He scribbled away amid the betting men some book which will be translated into half a dozen languages. . . .

To be strictly accurate he was not an Austrian but a Hungarian. Moreover he had lived for some time in Russia. Again, he was a Jew. These facts have more than a personal significance. A surprisingly high proportion of the intellectuals at Vienna are Jewish. A fair percentage of them are not Austrian in origin. In several cases they have been subjected to Russian influences.

Often did I hear the term Hungarian Jew employed contemptuously in Vienna. Anti-semitic prejudices still linger, and the Jews are blamed for all that is disorderly and disruptive in modern writing. But this antagonism is of little practical importance. The Jews have brought the most distinctive note to Austro-German literature and it is absurd to rail against them. . . .

René Fülop-Miller is one of these Austrians of mixed origins; everybody was talking about him, and I was told that the forty-year-old man with the soft eyes, broad forehead, and square chin, was born in Transylvania of German father and Serbian mother; was brought up as a Hungarian; studied in Paris; travelled in Asia; and obtained Austrian citizenship. He made Europe better acquainted with Gandhi, and then with Lenin—comparing and contrasting these great revolutionary leaders. . . .

The outstanding figure in Austrian letters is that of Jakob Wassermann. He suffered for a number of years the direst poverty—his friends tell me that when he was thirty he was literally starving. Now he is recognised as one of the greatest novelists of our time. His plots and personages are unconvincing; it is the philosophical content which gives value to his work; his constant message is the oneness of mankind.

Then there is Arthur Schnitzler, sad and lonely; his life has been broken twice by tragedy; with his scepticism there goes a cultured melancholy.

Hugo Von Hofmannsthal, in whose veins flow Italian and Jewish, as well as Austrian blood, is the supreme dramatic poet of Vienna, playing colourfully with images, confounding dreams and realities. He wrote the librettos for Strauss' operas; a collaboration of musician and poet which is probably unique.* Rainer Maria Rilke I sometimes saw in Paris; he drew his inspiration from French letters. Franz Werfel best represents the storm and stress of our time in his violent poetry. Siegfried Trebitsch, poet and novelist; the dramatist Richard Beer-Hoffmann; Hermann Bahr, formerly director of the Burg Theater —these are a few of the men who, conspicuous in Viennese literary life, have become known far beyond the confines of

---

* As I write I learn that Von Hofmannsthal has died of apoplexy on hearing of the suicide of his son. The loss to letters is immense. Tragedy strangely pursues Austrian authors.

the little land that was left by the peace-makers to perpetuate the name, the fame, and the culture of Austria.

XIII. COUDENHOVE-KALERGI

WHEN there is so much vague talk of the United States of Europe—by which apparently is meant an economic union against the United States of America—it is natural that attention should turn on Count Von Coudenhove-Kalergi who from Vienna launched the idea of a pan-European movement. Certainly his hope is to break down Nationalism, not to set up Continentalism.

It is strange how the most excellent conceptions can be distorted to evil ends. Thus diplomacy generally makes the friendship of peoples the pretext for dangerous alliances. If we are not careful the economists will make of the demand for the abolition of tariff frontiers in Europe the basis of an anti-American policy.

There is no more curious international figure than that of Coudenhove-Kalergi. His family was originally Flemish. Then long years ago it established connections with Southern Europe. So while the first part of his name comes from the Low Countries the second part of his name comes from Greece. His father was a distinguished Austrian who was sent as Minister to Japan. In Tokio the present Count was born of a Japanese mother. He lives in Vienna and is married to a famous Austrian actress; but by some freak of map-making he is officially a Czecho-Slovakian subject.

Perhaps these racial admixtures, these national anomalies, helped to suggest the pan-European movement to Coudenhove-Kalergi. Quaint things sometimes happen in Europe. They are inevitable in a continent of thirty odd countries. Thus a friend of mine, a well-known art critic in Paris, was actually born in Holland. He married a French woman. A few years ago he became a naturalised Frenchman. Now the position, as I understand it, is that he who was born in Holland is a French man, while his wife who was born in France is a Dutch woman. And how many Europeans have lost their nationality altogether— are *heimatlos*?

The suggestions of the Count are not of course new. In the Eighteenth Century there was already eloquent advocacy of the constitution of a homogeneous Europe. In the Nineteenth

Century Victor Hugo wrote in favour of the United States of Europe. Behind the League of Nations, though its chief founder was President Wilson, and its scope is nominally world-wide, there was a dim notion that European countries should, to escape destruction by internecine strife, realise their essential singleness. But practical proposals have been lacking.

Coudenhove-Kalergi makes practical proposals. He would at least have customs frontiers abolished. He would at least have compulsory arbitration for the whole continent. He would at least have some loose form of federation. But apart from these political measures, whose application appears remote and diffi- cult, he would foster a new European mentality. He would have Europeans think of themselves as Europeans and not as Englishmen, Germans, Italians, and Czechs. He would make them aware of their common civilisation. Less stress should be laid on national differences and more stress on the general similarity of the continental peoples.

Utopian? The Count in a recent declaration points out that forty years ago the governments of the American Republics met in a pan-American conference to lay down the foundations of a common organisation of the American continent. That conference was followed by others and the pan-American Union was founded. It has preserved the peace of America; while Africa, Asia and Europe have suffered from terrible wars. When Bolivia and Paraguay almost came to blows it was the pan-American Union which prevented a conflict.

Europe then, he says, should follow this example and ten years after the signing of the Treaty of Versailles should con- voke the first pan-European conference. The ten years of so- called peace have not brought repose to Europe. There are still quarrels about the settlement; there are still alliances and counter-alliances; there is still a piling-up of armaments; there are still hatreds and fears, bitterness and oppression. In short, there is an armistice rather than peace in Europe.

The time has come therefore to make a new attempt to reconcile European peoples and to organise, politically, eco- nomically, and culturally, the divided continent. European solidarity should be established by a pan-European society which would not hinder but would help the larger task of the League of Nations.

Is this practical politics? Are there not too many languages, boundaries, and interests, in Europe, for a purely European

Count Coudenhove-Kalergi

society to have the smallest chance of success? Certainly at first
sight the prospect of the most infinitesimal progress along these
lines appears negligible. But there has been a sudden crystallisation of feeling that the economic prosperity of the United
States of America is due in large part to the extent of territory
in which there are no tariff barriers. Business men begin to ask
seriously whether the welfare of Europe does not lie in co-
operation. At present European countries are engaged in a tariff
war that brings no advantages to any of them. Would they not
all benefit by a general accord?

An object-lesson has recently been given by the exhibition in
business centres of a map of Europe on which were shown in
relief not the mountain ranges of Europe but the tariff barriers
of Europe. It furnished a striking argument. The strength of
America is the division of strength of Europe, was proclaimed
by Chambers of Commerce. Unfortunately the underlying reason of much of the agitation was the desire to take retaliatory
steps against America which threatened to raise its tariffs. That
is an undesirable motive. Europe should indeed remove its internal tariffs which injure European trade, but it should not do
so with the object of economic warfare against America.

The leaders of the United States have expressly stated their
hope of seeing the barriers to trade on the continent of Europe
broken down. It is to the interest of America that the European
standard of living should be improved. The nearer it approaches
to the American standard of living, the better it will be for
the whole world. America can help, and there is little doubt
that if the problem is properly approached America will help.
There is need for coöperation between Europe and the United
States.

What Europe should aim at is economic unity built upon
reason and not upon resentment, built upon coöperation and
not upon competition. It is useless to cease multitudinous trade
warfare merely to begin trade warfare between continents.
Europe's purpose in putting its house in order should not be
the destruction of the American house. Rightly conceived, the
prosperity of one should not be at the expense of the prosperity
of the other. By all means let us strive for European unity—
political as well as economic—but let it be in full accord and
sympathy with the United States of America.

PART V
"BALKANISED EUROPE"

KAREL CAPEK welcomed me in perfect English. Well-groomed, elegantly dressed, the slim, clean-shaven young man, who is famous in every civilised country, surveyed me keenly as he put out his hand; his deep-set eyes gleamed humorously.

"I suppose you are just dropping in on us," he said. "Have you been to Hong Kong lately? When did you take your last trip to Sydney?"

I protested that I am a poor traveller preferring to go by easy stages; and that in general the Anglo-Saxon, though he ventures abroad, is methodical, cautious, and leisurely in his movements. "But you," I said, "you run over to England and before we know you are there you have published a book which tells the English people more about themselves than they have learned after centuries of residence in the little island."

"Yes," he replied, "but then the British never stay long enough at home to see their own country. They are like men who work in the city and have their house in the country, and only go home at the week-end between two trains, and remain in complete ignorance of their own village. How can the British know anything about themselves and their own land, when they are always abroad?"

Thus he talked quickly, jestingly, betraying, even in casual conversation in a club in Prague, his unfailing liveliness. His small boyish face, slightly aslant, lit up as he spoke. "Yes," he admitted, in response to a remark that I made, "Czecho-Slovakia, with an intense consciousness of its nationhood, is a cosmopolitan country, and Czech literature, which has wrongly been described as local, is in the broadest sense European. We, no more than the British, wish to confine ourselves within our own frontiers."

But if the old reproach of insularity against Great Britain is not incompatible with British love of travel, it seems to me that Czecho-Slovakia, in making the acquaintance of the wider world, is truly making its own acquaintance.

"And helping to make Czecho-Slovakia known to the wider world," observed Alès Broz, an able Czecho-Slovakian diplomatist, Editor of the Central European Observer, to whom I am indebted for the most courteous hospitality.

Czecho-Slovakia is aware of the necessity of making itself better known abroad. Notable Czechs found it amusing, as we sat in their splendid club house, to recall that at one time even the peace-makers were ignorant of the whereabouts and composition of the proposed composite nation.

"Is it a new hair-oil?" asked one of them, who was addicted to facetiousness.

Even France, which has since strongly supported the little republic, would not admit that there was such a thing as Czech nationality before the war. A Czech friend of mine was a student at Paris in those far-off days; and he insisted on registering himself as a Czech. But the description was not accepted by the authorities; and eventually he was obliged to declare himself an Austrian.

During the war M. Briand himself was extremely vague about Czecho-Slovakia though he smuggled Czecho-Slovakian claims into an Allied manifesto. As for Mr. Lloyd George, it is notorious that at the Peace Conference he had the haziest notion of Central European geography.

Since then the little country, well guided, has neglected no opportunity of putting itself in evidence. This is a perfectly proper purpose and indeed is obviously necessary. It is not enough to consolidate the republic; it feels compelled to play a more conspicuous rôle than is strictly justified by its size and its situation, in order to accustom the world to its existence.

No wonder that the Czechs are particularly proud of Karel Capek, who, perhaps, has done as much as President Mazaryk and M. Bénès to acquaint the world with the fact that old Bohemia is not part of the Austrian Empire, but is the predominant partner in a little Slav republic, with its own language—a language in which great literature is being written.

Czecho-Slovakia would probably never have been born had not the Czech language been kept alive. While Czecho-Slovakia was still under the rule of the Hapsburgs, Czech poetry, Czech novels, Czech dramas, Czech criticism, were a conscious inspiration. They were the central fact in the struggle for independence. Now that independence has come, the Czech language as a medium of expression has solidly established itself.

The population is Slavic with a difference. Many of the

characteristics which we attribute to the Slavs have disappeared. Here are Slavs who are not dreamy and introspective. They are practical and laborious. Yet, though they are Germanised Slavs, they have nevertheless not altogether escaped from the influence of Russia. There are typical Russian ideas in many of the books produced in Prague. When I was there everybody was talking about Frantisek Langer, whose play "Periphery" made him famous throughout Central Europe. He was an officer in the Czecho-Slovakian army in the war, and was, I believe, sent to the Russian front. Certainly his story of a man who tries to unburden his soul by confession, but whose confession is, to his dismay, scouted as imaginative, bears the marks of Russian thought.

For that matter, Capek's Robots in R. U. R., highly symbolical, representing the process of mechanisation of the proletariat, are doubtless Russian in inspiration. Yet this does not mean that Czech literature lacks independence. On the contrary, though it has borrowed some of its characteristics from Russia, and others from Germany, and again from France, it has blended them and impressed upon them its own authentic seal.

With their liberty restored to them, the Czechs strive with considerable success to regain their old reputation of intellectual eminence. They were at first inclined, as was natural, to overemphasise their nationalism, but they always realised that it was not enough to be Czecho-Slovakian—if they had ceased to be Austrian it should be to become European. In them is a profound Slavic sense of seriousness and social piety. There is a deep humanity, allied with earnestness, in all they do. Their fantasy does not exclude irony. Their cleverness is not incompatible with lyricism. Capek is intent on a thesis, and he works it out with effective theatrical technique, but he contrives to stir the emotions. He is an intellectual, but he is also an artist. He deals in abstractions, but he does not forget life. He studies social problems, but they become human problems.

One should carefully watch Czech literature, for, with the sudden release of energy, it may give us new masterpieces. On my visit I was accompanied by a publisher who was given this advice by a young Welsh student who was educated at the Prague University, and who knows the Czech language like a Czech: "If you, as a publisher, wish to pick up bargains, there is no finer field than Prague. The Czech writers have, with a few exceptions, not yet achieved international fame, for their language is not read outside their own country. But they are doing wonderful work which has a broad appeal, and they should be translated far more freely." I am sure it is good advice.

In the beginning the reaction against Germany was so strong that the Czechs refused to speak the German language. They apparently expected foreigners to address them in their local tongue, and however respectable may be the national feeling which imposed Czech as the official language, it was pretentious to ask foreigners to have any knowledge of it. In reality German is generally understood, and it was absurd for shopkeepers and policemen to gaze blankly on those who addressed them in German. That foolish prejudice has vanished. But although German is used side by side with Czech, an effort is being made to spread a knowledge of French and even English. I was taken to the spacious city hall to hear a lecture in French. The subject was perfectly indifferent, and, one would have imagined, boring to Czecho-Slovakians; it was on the beauties of Sweden. Yet to my astonishment the large hall was packed by eager men and women. Doubtless they were willing to improve their acquaintance with Sweden; but chiefly they were anxious to improve their acquaintance with French. Nearly all the educated Czechs that I met spoke English, too. There are in the streets policemen who can speak several languages and who are anxious to serve as interpreters. In short, Czecho-Slovakia is paying special attention to languages. This is part of its effort to know the wider world and be known by the wider world.

The little country is favoured, from the point of view of tourism, in that it possesses over five hundred natural springs; and some of its spas, notably Marienbad and Carlsbad, are second to none in Europe.

II. THE GOSPEL OF WORK

PRAGUE lies between Vienna and Berlin, and is a convenient stopping place for the traveller in Europe. But even if it were not such an excellent stage, if it were far more inaccessible, it should on no account be missed from any European itinerary. For it is one of the oldest, most beautiful, and most industrious cities on the continent. Rich in historic memories, it is astir with men and women who, liberated from the Austrian yoke, are determined to justify their liberation.

Travelling is rarely monotonous. It is always enlivened by humorous incidents, though sometimes the humour is macabre. So it was as I sat in my corner of the Czech carriage. Two German-Americans were in the corridor. They were talking volubly. "You leave it to me, kid," said the elder of the two. "We are in a first-class carriage with second-class tickets. But the second-class carriages are full, and we are not going to pay any more. Let me deal with the inspector. I'd fight like hell for a dollar!"

Presently the conductor of the train approached them. Speaking in German, the elder man explained and expostulated, pleaded and bullied. His voice roared through the train. Finally, as I gathered, he and his companion were permitted to remain in the corridor until seats could be found for them elsewhere.

"I've come back to settle about the family grave," said the loud-voiced American after the conductor had left. "It was purchased for eighteen years only, but now I've bought it over again."

"That was good of you," said his quieter companion. "So now they can sleep peacefully for some time longer."

"Oh well, I can afford it. I had a big stone put over my father's grave. Of real marble. That high! I bought it during the inflation for fifteen dollars, and oh, boy! you couldn't get a stone like that to-day for two hundred dollars!"

"Would they have taken the stone away if you had forfeited the grave?"

"Why, yes. But I saved it. Now I've only to write my mother's name on it."

The rumble of the train drowned their voices, and I watched from the carriage window the changing colour of the evening sky on the snowy uplands—a delicate pink merging into pale blue. But presently I caught bits of the conversation of these German-Americans returning to the Fatherland.

"You take my advice. Don't ever look at a cremation. I thought it was the best way though it was expensive, but gee! how the corpses move! They look like they want to get out. . . . Well, it was easier like that to bring them over. . . ."

The conductor returned. He had found seats for them. So they departed and I saw them no more.

The train stopped at a little wayside station. There was a clamour of sausage-vendors. Everybody seemed to be getting out of the train and rushing to the steaming stalls on which hot saveloys were ready for the travellers. The hot saveloys were snatched up, two by two, and placed on pieces of greasy paper. I watched the scene for some time with amusement, but at last the appetising odour and the spectacle of everybody eating saveloys was too much for me. I, too, leaped from the train, tendered a small Austrian coin, was given an immense quantity of small change in Czech money, and hurried back to my seat with the steaming saveloys. . . . Yes, they were undoubtedly good. . . .

Even as we circled between the hills and the forest, fascinated by the colour of the evening snow and the dignity of the tall trees, we became aware that the gospel of Czecho-Slovakia is work. There is beautiful countryside, but wherever a little town springs up its purpose is conspicuously utilitarian. Occasionally these little towns are positively ugly in spite of the reputation of Czech peasant art; uniformity and cheapness of aspect mark the rows of houses, and the unfinished streets are without charm. In spite of the different landscape, I was constantly reminded of the little factory towns of Lancashire. Doubtless from the economic standpoint, the comparison is not unflattering. Czecho-Slovakia is still in process of making, and its people are bending their energies to industrial development.

As for Prague, I think I have never seen so much building in any city of considerable size. Impressions are sometimes wrong, and it may be that, by various accidents, I am led into exaggeration. Possibly I passed and repassed the same building operations. Possibly my particular quarters commanded more than their proper share of building operations. Possibly my brain registered this particular feature of Prague too vividly, and, having twice observed building operations, refused to notice anything but building operations. I am prepared to make every allowance, but it remains true that there are in Prague many building operations, and that they are typical of Czecho-Slovakia. Conscious growth, industrious accretion—here is the keynote of the little State which came into existence as a separate entity ten years ago.

The streets seem to ascend and never to descend in Prague. I realised this as I went to my hotel on my arrival. I was about to take a cab at the station, when a well-meaning official of the Y. M. C. A. approached me.

"Nobody ever takes cabs in Prague," he said. "They are too dear. I see you are a stranger. May I ask what hotel you are going to?"

I told him. "I am going in that direction," he said. "It is quite close. Let me help you with your bags."

He took a valise and I carried another bag. We went up the streets that ascend and never descend. We appeared to walk for miles. I was streaming with perspiration and nearly exhausted. But he kept assuring me that we were almost at our destination.

On the way he told me something of the extraordinary activities of the Y. M. C. A. in Central Europe. I could not help asking him if the organisation has no political or economic purpose, but he assured me that its object is purely social and philanthropic. Certainly whatever is to be said for or against it, its agents are well-meaning. But I wish they had not stopped me from taking a cab!

In spite of its large buildings Prague does not strike one as a capital. It wears the air of a provincial town. The hotels are rather poorly equipped, offering an unfavourable contrast with those of Vienna. It was not yet ten o'clock, but the hotel could not provide me with dinner: the best it could do was to send a plate of excellent ham to my room.

III. A ROOFSCAPE

EARLY the next morning I received a telephone call from the Foreign Office. More, a motor-car, in which was a Foreign Office official, was presently at my door; and I accepted an invitation to inspect the city and be introduced to some of the leading citizens. Let it not be supposed that I write with the smallest irony; on the contrary, I am grateful for the kindness that was shown to me—exceeding that of any other city I have been in. Obviously there was a propagandist desire, but it was an intelligible and an intelligent desire. There was in it nothing offensive, nothing restrictive; and my hosts appeared chiefly concerned to point out to me the old rather than the new Prague.

What a wonderful place it is, with its antique turrets and gables, its picturesque steeples and balconies, its bridge built by the old Bohemian King, and its palace on a hilltop from which one looks down on the quaintest of roofscapes in Europe. No, I do not cavil at the attentions of my guide; I merely mention the fact that Czecho-Slovakia thus welcomes its guests, because it is significant of the Czecho-Slovakian wish to make the country known and esteemed by the world. It is a fact of importance. It has both a political and a human meaning. Czecho-Slovakia shows its gratitude to the citizens of the nations which gave it independence—there is a statue to President Wilson in Prague, though there is, I believe, not yet a statue to President Wilson in America—and by its enterprise it seeks to justify its independence.

Every step one takes in old Prague, capital of the ancient Bohemia, brings back a point of history. The memory of the great Charles IV is particularly venerated, for he, in the Fourteenth Century, by his French affinities, counteracted the influence of German culture; he founded the University of Prague; politically, economically, and intellectually, he consolidated his Kingdom. And after him came a professor, John Huss, who gave noble and undying traditions to the Czechs. He denounced the mundane character of the Church, and to-day Czecho-Slovakia is, in matters of religion, as strongly impregnated as ever with Hussite ideas. But he did more: he helped to fix the Czech language, to shape the national spirit, and to give to his countrymen their love of intellectual integrity, of political and religious independence. Huss, the forerunner of Luther and Calvin, was burnt at the stake by the ecclesiastical powers. . . .

Even after Bohemia came under the domination of the Hapsburgs, and Vienna was substituted for Prague as the seat of the government of the Empire, the rulers sometimes selected Prague as their principal place of residence. In the Seventeenth Century Bohemia revolted against the Hapsburgs, but the Czechs were defeated and their nobles were exiled, their religious, political, and national liberties were strangled, and the administration was confided to foreigners.

Then began the decline of Bohemia. Jesuits and dragoons imposed Catholicism on the people; an alien nobility replaced the ancient families; Vienna flourished at the expense of Prague; the Czech language survived only in the speech of common folk in country districts. Yet Bohemia always remembered its days of glory; and in the Eighteenth Century there was re-awakened

a desire for national freedom and a determination to achieve
it. It was a long and seemingly hopeless task, and a real opportunity of enfranchisement did not come until the Great
War of 1914.

As I stood by the great Gothic Cathedral of St. Vitus on
its high hill, and looked on the vast Palace of the Hradzin which
is now the residence of President Mazaryk, I was reminded that
exactly a thousand years ago, St. Vaclav, Duke of Bohemia,
who is known in English-speaking countries as good King
Wenceslaus, lived and reigned in Prague. They were preparing
the fêtes which would mark the anniversary of the hero of our
best-known Christmas carol.

Listening to these legends of rulers who were friends of the
poor, who identified themselves with their people, I felt that,
despite the passage of time and building operations, I was
veritably in a land of legend. Prague with its strange roofs
and domes seemed to be a city of fable. There the mediæval
has survived as it has survived nowhere else. One sees it all from
this height, and the vision is unforgettable. But equally interesting is the stroll through the narrow streets. A row of one-
storey houses, whose roofs slope at all angles, is still known
as the Street of the Alchemists. It is difficult to believe that
it is real. It looks like an old engraving. In the nearby cloisters,
sandalled and hooded monks go placidly about their business.
The little market-places have surely not been changed since
their foundation. The statues which are built into the Charles
Bridge, and the Russian church, and the Jewish synagogue in
the former ghetto, and the grand gateway and the gardens, and
I know not how many churches, and the University, make up an
amazing and story-book spectacle. The Russian touch is there
and the Gothic touch; Baroque and Renaissance architecture
are intermingled.

And when the hour strikes, grave-bearded men as well as
boys, run to see the bronze figures moving in the mediæval
clock of the old Town Hall. They tell strange legends of this
remarkable piece of horology, whose dial shows the hours, days,
nights, months, years, the setting and rising of the sun and
moon, the situation of the planets and all the astronomical
signs, and whose mechanism enacts an allegorical drama of
life and death. They say that its ingenious maker was invited
to make similar clocks in other towns; but the rulers of ·the
city, proud of their clock, had his eyes put out. The construc-

tor asked only to be led once more to the clock to repair it. But, his request granted, he removed, unnoticed, one of the most important springs. The blind youth prophesied that in the year when the clock should go again, there would be a great war. . . .

But amid the old there is the new; and Prague has many fine shops. Here you will find a window filled with garnets, the beautiful stone which is peculiar to Czecho-Slovakia. There you will find the famous Bohemian glassware. Folk industry has been well organised, and Czecho-Slovakia makes toys, lace, ceramics, fancy goods, carpets, hangings, linen, dyed wool fabrics, and embroidered articles of all descriptions. The old handicraft secrets are not forgotten. They are indeed applied more methodically, and the artistic products of Czecho-Slovakia are fresh and vivid. In various towns there are industrial art schools which are admirably managed; they do not suppress, but, on the contrary, encourage the popular fantasy, naïve and pleasant, and the creative capacity of the people.

As a young country it would be strange if Czecho-Slovakia did not reflect all the European genres in the plastic and graphic arts. So far as I can judge, there is more eclecticism in Prague than in Paris. I observed every variety of pictural "ism." Certainly the younger artists are doing good work, but it is not, so far as I can see, very distinctive.

In music, of course, Czecho-Slovakia holds a high place. Smetana and Dvorak are the idols of their compatriots. Smetana, who lived from 1824 to 1884, was inspired by the romantic past of the country. Dvorak (1841-1904), who may be described as the pupil of Smetana, reverted to a more classic style. Fibich (1850-1900), was subjective. The following generation was led by Josef Foerster, Novak, and Josef Suk. With their roots in national tradition, they are alive to the musical development of the Western nations. The younger men, who form a group in Prague itself, definitely attempt to escape from the influences of Wagner and Strauss, Debussy and Massenet.

The opera-lover in search of novelty should certainly go to Prague. There it is possible to listen to operas that are entirely unknown to the regular opera-goer of Western Europe— to repeat the experience day after day for a fortnight. Smetana, in spite of modernism, remains the favourite composer of the Czecho-Slovakians, and it is in epics of patriotism, with something of peasant humour and of simple melodrama, that the people revel. The men in the Mozartium are skilful, but with all their perfected technique, they cannot impress the public like Smetana and Dvorak, or even Janacek, who collected and transposed the Moravian and Slovak folk songs.

IV. PRESIDENT MAZARYK

EMIL LUDWIG pays an astonishing tribute to the President of Czecho-Slovakia: "If I were asked to name him who, among living men, deserves the highest rank, I should say Mazaryk the Czech." And he explains that for many years this man dreamed of a people, which should be his people, and finally created it. He is at once a visionary and a constructor; rarely is a man who theorises practical; seldom has a leader such an opportunity as came to Mazaryk.

He lives there in his palace on the hill at Prague which, for him, is the geographical heart of Europe. And it is true that almost exactly Prague is the central point of Middle Europe. That is why Czecho-Slovakia plays a predominant part among the Danubian nations. That is why it is the leader of the Little Entente, though it is smaller than Rumania and Yugo-Slavia. That is why Poland is drawn towards Czecho-Slovakia. That is why Germany treats the tiny nation with particular respect. That is why Hungary regards it as the chief stumbling-block to its ambitions. That is why France endeavours to control the policy of Czecho-Slovakia—which does not, however, surrender its independence in spite of its gratitude.

An old grave man, exceedingly simple in his manners, Thomas Mazaryk, the father of his country, looks what he has been all his life, a scholar and a thinker. He was Professor of Philosophy in the University of Prague; but he was also prominent in the movement for Czech liberty. In politics, in the narrower sense, he was not greatly interested, and when he was elected member of the Parliament of Vienna in 1891, he soon resigned. Fifteen years later he was again elected. The authorities looked upon him as a troublesome person; for he opposed the annexation of Bosnia and Herzegovina; and he was always on the side of liberty.

His sympathies with the oppressed were strengthened by his American association. He married (fifty-five years ago) a young American woman, Charlotte Garrigue, while he was a student at the Leipzig University.

When the war broke out he organised the movement for independence. First he went to Holland, then to Italy, then to Switzerland, then to London, then to Paris. Everywhere he was a missionary for his country. Not long ago a plaque was put on the façade of the house in the rue Bonaparte in Paris where Mazaryk and Dr. Bénès established themselves. There were the headquarters of Czecho-Slovakia. There was the nation born. Its army was raised in 1917, and when everything was well under way in Western Europe, Mazaryk went to make an appeal to the great Slav sister nation, and to weld together on Russian soil his compatriots in an effective army. From Russia, despite his advanced age, he went to the United States, crossing Siberia and going by way of Japan. America received him warmly and took up his cause. The Czech National Council was recognised. Then came the crash of the Central Powers. The republic was proclaimed and Mazaryk was elected President by acclamation. His entry into the capital of the new republic was triumphant. Although the President may normally hold office only for seven years, Mazaryk was made eligible for life.

No life of devotion to an object could be more completely recompensed. Yet the war brought personal losses to Mazaryk. His son was killed in battle, and a few years after the war the death of Madame Mazaryk was attributed to the hardships she had suffered.

Mazaryk, the head of the Czecho-Slovakian republic, which he more than any other man founded, has wider views than those of a narrow nationalist. He is first a Czecho-Slovak, second a Slav, third a European, and fourth an apostle of the unification of all mankind. Soon after the war he made a notable contribution to the Slavonic Review, which I filed because it expresses the man and his views better than anything I have read elsewhere. Here are a few passages:

"Man cannot have any other programme than the welfare of man. The humanitarian programme means sympathy with all men, in spite of differences of language, nationality and class, and at the same time a conscious effort for the unification of all mankind."

That is his general outlook. On the increasing importance of the Slav peoples in the life of Europe, President Mazaryk

PRESIDENT MAZARYK

says: "German publicists and political thinkers are studying the Slav nations very carefully. Eighteen universities in Germany have announced lectures on all branches of Slavonic literature, history, ethnography, philology. In Western countries, in France, Britain and Italy, more attention is now paid to Slavonic problems than formerly, but still infinitely less than in Germany.

"The Slavs were estimated before the war as numbering about 150 millions. At present we have no official census of all the Slav nations, and I therefore quote the figures given by Professor Niederle for the year 1900.

Russians (with Little Russians and White Russians)	20,000,000
Poles	20,000,000
Czechs and Slovaks	9,800,000
Serbs, Croats and Slovenes	10,050,000
Bulgars	5,000,000
Lusatian Serbs	150,000
	139,000,000

"By 1910 the same authority estimates them to have increased to 156,000,000. In any case the Slavs make up more than a third of the population of Europe; if united, they would be the largest nation.

"The German nation is the largest in Europe next to the Russian. Germany has to-day a German population of 61, Austria of 6, Switzerland of 2½ millions.

"The Slav nations, although each has an ancient literature peculiar to itself, have nevertheless preserved many common linguistic traits which serve as natural links binding them together. They easily understand one another, and this is a considerable advantage for literary and practical intercourse.

"Geographically the Slavs do not form a perfect whole, since the Rumanians and Magyars separate the northern from the southern group. But in this respect the Slavs are no worse off than the Latins. Proximity has rendered possible very close relations between the different Slav nations.

"The fact that the Slavonic nations have now been liberated and politically re-organised, does not strengthen political Pan-Slavism. For precisely as a consequence of its liberation each

has been set separate tasks of reconstruction, in which its kins-
men can only render very limited assistance."

It is apparent that President Mazaryk's political thought is
not as exclusively pro-French as it is often represented to be;
that he is keenly aware of Germanic influences; that his Slavic
consciousness does not lead him to postulate a Slavic unity that
does not truly exist; and that his ideal is the peaceful association of all European races in the immense human family.

V. DR. BÉNÈS

DR. EDUARD BÉNÈS has been, throughout the years of
conception and the years of realisation, the right-hand
man of Mazaryk. Part of his education he received at Paris;
and he shows a greater leaning to France than his master and
mentor. The younger man was particularly active during the
propagandist period in France. He came to Paris unheralded,
and lived obscurely in Paris after a romantic and perilous escape from Austria. Sometimes it is remarked that Bénès too
conspicuously delights in his appearances at such ceremonies
as the signing of the Peace Treaties and the Kellogg Pact. And
it is true that he is obviously, and rather naïvely, pleased to be
among the representatives of the Great Powers on memorable
occasions. But it is natural enough that he should rejoice when
he compares his present situation with that of 1915, when he
was a fugitive, an exile, modestly pleading for his people who
were nominally enemies and unrecognised as a separate entity
by the Allies. Certainly he has kept some of the marks of his
humble origin; and it is even said in Central Europe that the
real difficulty of an understanding between Czecho-Slovakia
and Hungary lies in the contrast between Bénès, a son of the
soil, and Count Bethlen, an aristocrat of the soil.

He lived in a poor chamber in the rue Léopold-Robert, and
he took his meals (which cost 1 franc 50 centimes) in a little
restaurant in the same street. My own apartment at Mont-
parnasse looked over the abode of the apostle of Czecho-Slovakia, and I still experience some emotion as I pass through
the short street. Mazaryk himself occasionally took his meals
in the same restaurant with the young man who had become his
pupil, his confidant, and his collaborator. A few years later the
seat of the National Council of Czecho-Slovakia was installed

Eduard Bénès

in the rue Bonaparte (still on the left bank of the Seine) near the apartment of Marshal Lyautey.

That was a period of almost incredible activity. Bénès worked feverishly. He furnished the French official services with information received by way of Switzerland, and he also made friends with a number of excellent French journalists, among them Auguste Gauvain, the veteran writer of the "Journal des Débats," and Jules Sauerwein, of the "Matin." While pursuing his propaganda he had to gain a livelihood, and this was not always easy.

Then there was Milan Stefanik, an aviator whose patriotic and heroic career tragically ended when, after the liberation of the territory, his aeroplane fell in flames on the frontier. Stefanik had an old acquaintance with Anatole de Monzie, a brilliant French lawyer and politician, and presently he found himself in contact with the most influential French circles. Perhaps these social relations were more effective than journalistic propaganda; and shortly Bénès was furnishing French salons, through Stefanik, with confidential memoranda. The good ladies of Paris were thrilled at the thought that they were being let into war secrets.

Nor must I forget Stefan Osusky, later the plenipotentiary minister of Czecho-Slovakia in Paris, whom I was privileged to know—an indefatigable, highly cultured, and congenial man. He had been a propagandist in Chicago and also in London, and he brought fresh encouragement to the little Paris group.

Those war years I, too, passed in Paris, and, brought as I was into daily contact with the fluctuating fortunes of battle, realising how desperate was the plight of the Allies—it was worse in 1916, the year of Verdun, than in 1914, the year of the Marne, and was worse still in 1917, the year of the fruitless offensive, of military mutiny, and of civilian discontent—I cannot but have an unbounded admiration for the calm confidence of the Czecho-Slovakian group. Their faith in the issue was unshakeable. They had linked the fate of the future State with the fate of the Allies, and not only was the Allied victory doubtful, but it was by no means clear that the Allies would recompense Czecho-Slovakia for its fortitude. The Allies were not disposed to break up Austria-Hungary even in the event of their complete triumph. Clemenceau had no desire to be diverted from his business of making war by nebulous diplomatic speculations. Not until the spring of 1918, when Germany delivered its last great blows on the Western front, did the Tiger take up that implacable attitude against Austria which brought about the collapse of the composite Empire of Central Europe. President Wilson had pronounced for an Austro-Hungarian federation, and only at the last minute did he make his formidable response to the despairing appeal of an exhausted Empire. Doubtless his demand for "the self-determination of peoples" was primarily due to the advocacy of Mazaryk. Nevertheless it was the tenacity of the Paris group which made the resurrection of old Bohemia possible, and it was at Paris that a provisional government proclaiming the independence of the nation was established. It was France which first recognised this government.

To Bénès, therefore, must go much of the credit for the creation of Czecho-Slovakia; and to him must be attributed the solidity of the bonds which connected the Yugo-Slavs, the Rumanians, the Poles, and others who had taken refuge in France. They became conscious of their common purpose, and thus laid down the foundations of the Little Entente, that combination of Czecho-Slovakia, Rumania, and Yugo-Slavia which appointed itself the guardian of the *status quo* in Central Europe.

Dr. Bénès afterwards denied that the union of his own country with Yugo-Slavia and Rumania was intended as a mark of hostility towards other nations. But there can be no doubt that originally the formation of the Little Entente was an expression of distrust of contiguous countries.

As the danger of a violent revision of the treaties disappears, the Little Entente must find a constructive policy if it is to continue to exist usefully and effectively. The way must be prepared for a better all-round understanding, as distinct from an exclusive understanding between the nations which benefited in the peace treaties against nations which were reduced by the peace treaties.

In itself an alliance of the nations which gained, against the nations which lost, is undesirable, but if such an alliance is genuinely regarded as the first stage towards wider coöperation, then it may prove to have a steadying and upbuilding influence in the welter of jealousies and alarms provoked by the war.

As feelings of revenge decline it is seen more clearly that economic arrangements are the chief need of Central Europe, and will meet nearly every requirement. With Austria there is no reason why the barriers should not be broken down. Even Hungary, smarting under a sense of injustice, could be placated. There is a strong movement for recognition of Russia, though this would imply acceptance of the Bessarabian frontier. The path has been traced by the Pact of Paris and by the subsequent Litvinoff Pact which, in this aspect, may properly be regarded as a pledge of peace between Russia and Rumania as well as Russia and Poland.

Whether Czecho-Slovakia should come into the orbit of France or of Germany is a much-debated question, to which the Czechs reply that they are not the satellites of any country. Yet historically they have a predilection for France—a Bohemian king fought for France and was killed at the battle of Creçy; and to France the new nation is conscious of owing much.

Czecho-Slovakian trade is with Germany and as economic forces gradually prevail over sentimental traditions, Czecho-Slovakia, while keeping its identity, must necessarily undergo a change. Bénès has been overanxious perhaps to assert the personality of the republic. At bottom, it is not politically inclined; though it is not surprising that in these earlier years it should have been given an unjustifiable political rôle. It was particularly active (and often irritatingly active) in the League of Nations, regarded as the common buckler of the smaller nations. I do not suggest that its helpful League activities will diminish, but it is not now so necessary to use the League as a shield; and in so far as its League activities imply the playing of a political game that will sometimes range Czecho-Slovakia against other nations, they will doubtless be exercised more judiciously. For the prestige of Czecho-Slovakia is sufficiently established, and its only policy should be to live independently on friendly terms with its neighbours.

The racial constitution of Czecho-Slovakia might have brought great difficulties. The country is composed of three former Austrian provinces, Bohemia, Moravia, and a part of Silesia; and two former Hungarian provinces, Slovakia and sub-Carpathian Ruthenia. The former Hungarian provinces are relatively poor and uncultured. Moreover, five races are to be found within the frontiers of Czecho-Slovakia. They total (in round figures) fourteen millions. The Czechs number eight millions, the Slovaks two and a half millions, and the Ruthenians (who, living separately and scarcely affecting the life of

Czecho-Slovakia, may be set aside) five hundred thousand. The real minorities are the Germans and the Magyars. They number over three million, and they raise a troublesome and potentially disruptive problem.

Inquiries I made (not in official quarters) convinced me that the German inhabitants of Czecho-Slovakia have comparatively little cause of complaint. Doubtless they had at the beginning, but they have now parliamentary representation, and two of their leaders are members of the Government. They hold important posts—one of them is Minister of Justice, and the other Minister of Public Works. There is no reason to suppose that the German minority will not settle down with the Czechs, or that it will be subjected to any serious disabilities.

Hungary was regarded as the most dangerous neighbour of Czecho-Slovakia, but this belief in the aggressiveness of Hungary is passing. Dislike of a neighbour is usually the effect of fear, and the Czecho-Slovakian Government and people have begun to realise that they have little to fear from Hungary. The population of Hungary is very much smaller than that of Czecho-Slovakia, and even if the Little Entente did not exist, it is difficult to imagine a successful attack by the Magyars. I learned that President Mazaryk himself would not be indisposed to come to some reasonable arrangement, which would include territorial modifications, with Hungary, provided Hungary demonstrated its peaceful purpose. If Hungary were entirely peaceable, and the two countries were on the best of terms, it would not really matter whether there were territorial modifications or not, for everything could be adjusted by economic treaties. Be this as it may, the true obstacle to an understanding lies in the sharp distinction between the Hungarian land régime and that of its neighbours. Hungary is, in contrast with its neighbours, backward in this respect, and agrarian reform is badly needed to bring it into consonance with other Central European countries. But on the Czecho-Slovakian side there is a genuine movement in favour of the abandonment of grudging politics, and concentration on economic development.

VI. HUNGARY'S GRIEVANCES

MY MANY Hungarian acquaintances have invariably been most delightful. They awaken my sympathy. But it does not follow that I approve of an irredentist policy which, it seems to me, can only result in disaster if it is pushed to its logical conclusion. Count Bothmer-Bothmer, in reply to some recent observations of mine, wrote to remind me that by the Treaty of Trianon the area of Hungary is reduced by over seventy-one per cent, while the number of its inhabitants is reduced by over sixty-three per cent. He argued that it was folly to expect the Hungarians to accept this situation.

Certainly Hungary does not accept the situation, and in this it is encouraged by powerful outside influences. Lord Rothermere, for example, has been greatly moved by the unquestionable wrongs done by the Allies to Hungary, and his newspaper campaign stirred up a good deal of feeling.

Fundamentally, Lord Rothermere is right. But, in the present state of European sentiment, territorial changes can only be effected by force of arms. The first and essential condition of treaty revision is the allaying of suspicion. A better atmosphere must be created before calm discussion is possible. I do not know whether it will ever be possible. It is hard to suppose that Rumania, Czecho-Slovakia, and Yugo-Slavia, will voluntarily surrender substantial portions of their acquired territory to their despoiled neighbour. At any rate it is clear that nothing can be done by peaceful means until Hungary's neighbours are persuaded of Hungarian pacifism.

The problem is indeed difficult. However it is put, it resembles a vicious circle. Hungary will smart under a sense of grievance until land is restored to it; and Hungary's neighbours will not consent to restoration until the mistrust aroused by manifestations of Hungarian grievances has disappeared.

The only solution—it is better to put this bluntly—appears to be a new war in which the Little Entente would be defeated; a new set of peace-makers, ignoring the work of the peace-makers of Versailles, might then re-allocate Central European territories. But such a war would not be local. The Great Powers would again be engaged. Strife deadlier than that of 1914-1918 would disrupt Europe. . . . Is that what anybody wants?

For better or for worse, we have to accept the settlement at least for the time being, as France accepted the loss of Alsace-Lorraine in 1871, trusting that the future will bring fresh means of adjusting disputes. To be perfectly frank, I see no machinery at present in existence by which unjust frontiers can be changed. I do not, of course, mean that small concessions cannot be made; and in fact I was informed in Central Europe that such concessions were favoured by some of the chiefs of the Little Entente, provided they would produce a more satisfactory state of affairs. But, in their nature, concessions of this kind must be comparatively trivial. They cannot be more than symbolic. They cannot give Hungary its ancient boundaries, or even give Hungary those tracts of land which contain Magyar majorities. Theoretically, the League of Nations has the power to revise the post-war arrangements, but in practice the League would be shattered were it to attempt to alter the *status quo*. For the League is composed of members who are deeply interested in the maintenance of the *status quo*, and of others who, though perhaps not directly interested, have cast in their lot with the profiteers of the war.

The dilemma is obvious. One cannot defend injustices, but if the redressing of injustices involves the probable employment of arms, then the crusader for justice is taking grave risks.

On the whole it is advisable to make the best of a bad job, and strive for economic accords which will largely obviate the inconveniences of political blunders.

Were the economic barriers broken down in Central Europe, and there were free interchange and intercommunication, it would not matter overmuch whether this or that piece of land were called Hungarian, Rumanian, or Czecho-Slovakian. Doubtless this is a counsel which can be challenged by those who think abstract justice is superior to European peace, who place the self-determination of peoples above all other considerations, who would rather that the heavens fell than that the principle of nationality should be violated. Doubtless it is a cowardly policy, but, if the alternative is destruction, it may be preferable to be ranked among the cowards.

Responsible Hungarians themselves recognise the gravity of the issue. The other day I met in an official reception a distinguished Hungarian diplomatist, high in the counsels of his government. Jocularly I remarked: "I see by the papers that you are engaged in a terrible conspiracy against the peace of Europe."

He did not joke; he looked uncommonly serious and replied: "I wish less were heard about Hungarian claims. Even those of us who are most anxious to redress Hungarian wrongs are perturbed by the agitation that has swept Hungary, and has alarmed the Little Entente, and has placed the Great Powers on different sides. We are being pushed too far and too fast."

We discussed the prospects. Hungary, reduced by more than two-thirds, passed through a period of unprecedented misfortunes. It swung from Bolshevism to Nationalism. It was plunged into bankruptcy. It was befouled by scandal after scandal: its former dignitaries were convicted of forgery; it was arraigned before the bar of public opinion on charges of gun-running; it gained the reputation of being the most bellicose nation in Europe; it was the bugbear of the Chancelleries.

The wiser politicians saw the necessity of obtaining once more the confidence of the world. They bent their energies towards pacifying their own people and placating other peoples. Thanks to the devotion of Sir William Goode, and the sagacity of Count Bethlen, they obtained financial assistance which put their country on its feet. They had a solid government, essentially conservative, though it was agreed that the dynastic question should be left in abeyance. They endeavoured to avoid an aggressive policy that could only provoke alarm. Without abating their pretensions, they judiciously refrained from asserting them.

Their relations with their neighbours were lacking in cordiality but they were improving. Then there was started the campaign for a revision of the territorial clauses of the Trianon Treaty. Once more Hungary was the best-hated nation on the Continent. The Little Entente, which was dissolving, was again welded together. Throughout Central Europe there was a reawakening of Chauvinism. Hungary was ostracised and menaced. It was told what kind of government it should have. Its sense of oppression was intensified, its political stability was undermined. It was disillusioned, and it oscillated between despair and anger.

This was the unfortunate effect of ill-timed diplomacy. It would be well for Hungary to set aside the idea of rash adventures, and to settle down, despite its genuine grievances, to a long period of patient work. For the present dreams of aggrandisement are futile and dangerous. Hungary must try to forget its quarrels with Rumania, Yugo-Slavia and Czecho-Slovakia which hem it in. If it accepts the diplomatic patronage of Italy, it must beware lest Italy uses it as a cat's-paw in the Italian bid for the hegemony of the Balkans. It must strive first and foremost to build itself up, to consolidate itself as it is, to live in amity with its neighbours, and to subdue the firebrands in its own midst.

VII. PRESIDENTS AND PRETENDERS

BUDAPEST is by common consent one of the handsomest cities in Eastern Europe; it is also one of the gayest. The approach by the Danube is marked by a score of historical sites; memories of Turkish invasions, of the exploits of the Polish King Sobieski, of Napoleonic campaigns, are evoked. The city itself, with its palatial buildings on the quays, with its great suspension bridge, offers a beautiful spectacle. It is less than sixty years ago since the two towns Buda and Pest were united; since then the joint city has enormously developed. But while it not only possesses its independent Parliament but was formerly a royal capital—for the Emperor of Austria was also the King of Hungary and wore the crown of St. Stephen—it is now temporarily without a King.

But it is still a Kingdom—a Kingdom without a King. It has not surrendered its right to a Monarch. On the official communications which came to me was the reminder that Hungary has not changed its status. The functions of the King are being exercised by a Regent—Nicholas Horthy, who was an aide-de-camp of the Emperor Francis Joseph, who was Admiral and Commander of the Fleet, who served as Commander-in-Chief of the National Army when the Communist Revolution was headed by Bela Kun, and who, on the re-establishment of order, was appointed to his present post.

How long will he occupy it? The French have a saying that it is only the provisional which endures. Probably he will be in no hurry to surrender his place.

Indeed this man with nose like the beak of a hawk, with hard mouth, with steely eyes, was called upon by the unfortunate Karl to surrender his seat in the autumn of 1921; and he refused. The unhappy Karl, who did not deserve the misfortunes which he inherited, made an unsuccessful attempt to regain the throne of his ancestors. It was poorly prepared and it was better that it should fail. Had it been more cleverly timed and more skilfully arranged, the dilemma of Horthy would have been greater. For the restoration of the Monarchy then would unmistakably have meant the renewal of war. The Little Entente would have crushed Hungary again, and, although the world was weary, it is possible that other nations would have joined in the strife.

Yet he is there, in the stead of the deposed dynasty, and he represents an absent and unknown King. The Budapest Palace stands imposingly, overlooking the Danube, on its hill. There, stronghold after stronghold was razed by successive waves of enemies. The present structure was built by the great Empress Maria Theresa, though less than forty years ago the exterior was reconstructed in Baroque style with additions and improvements. The room of King Stephen I—or St. Stephen—is richly adorned with portraits in majolica, depicting incidents in the life of the saintly King, while the magnificent fireplace is also of majolica. In this palace are the Crown jewels.

So Admiral Horthy whom his countrymen regard as the saviour of Hungary from Bolshevism remains Regent. He is not a popular man. He is stern and unbending. Moreover, though he is now supreme in the social hierarchy, he is not really aristocratic at all. Hungary is essentially an aristocratic country; the Magyar aristocracy is proud of its origins. Why then should a member of an obscure family have risen to these heights? Why should his wife, a farmer's daughter, a milkmaid, as she is described, be Queen-by-Proxy of proud Hungary?

The eldest son of the late Emperor Karl is the Archduke Otto, still a boy in his teens. Yet he is the candidate of the Legitimatist party to the throne. The Awakening Magyars have another candidate—the Archduke Albrecht, son of the Archduke Friedrich and the Archduchess Isabelle. He is a young man of thirty odd years, who served as lieutenant in the war. His father was Commander-in-Chief of the Austro-Hungarian armies. Cousin of Otto, he traces his descent from Arpad who led the Magyars into Hungary eleven centuries ago. There came to me many stories of his intrigues with the Italian authorities, with the Papal authorities, with other pretenders such as Prince Rupprecht of Bavaria and the German Crown Prince.

Ringleader in the gigantic counterfeiting conspiracy designed to ruin the French financiers and permit the placing of the Archduke Albrecht on the throne, was Prince Ludwig Windischgraetz, scion of one of the oldest Austro-Hungarian families. He has had a remarkable career. He saw active service in the South African and Russo-Japanese wars. He shot big game in Africa. He was the confidant of Karl. He was mixed up in strange transactions with Germany. A reckless gambler, he lost heavily, and he sold his heirlooms and precious pictures. Finally came the crash when the forgery plot, in which were curiously intertwined the threads of a Monarchist plot, was disclosed. This is assuredly not the last of Monarchist plots in Central Europe.

The scene shifts back to Paris. There live the Count and Countess Michael Karolyi, of infinitely more distinguished birth than Horthy. The Count was the first President of the Hungarian Republic. He was driven out of office by the Bolshevik Bela Kun, who, in his turn, was driven out by Horthy.

While Horthy is Regent, Karolyi is an exile. A price is set upon his head. Were he to cross the frontier he might be assassinated with impunity. When the father of Countess Karolyi died, Horthy refused to lift the ban, and the Countess was a notable absentee from the funeral of Count Andrassy. When application was made for permission to visit the United States, there was official opposition. Karolyi was permitted to land only on condition that he refrained from public speaking. He obeyed the order but in Canada he made a speech. Later the State Department cancelled the passport of the Countess Karolyi.

It is affirmed that Horthy used his influence to strew these obstacles in the path of Karolyi. The Hungarian Government has behaved ungenerously towards a man who had already suffered greatly. Once he was exceedingly rich. His family had immense landed possessions. His property was sequestrated and the Count was hard put to it to obtain a livelihood.

We sat together one evening in a little public resort in Paris. "It is the literal truth," he told me, "that I cannot see my way ahead financially for more than a month. I am unable to obtain funds and every hindrance is placed in my way."

"But the Countess?" I questioned. "She has still her magazine of antiquities by the Étoile?"

He shook his head. "I do not take the money of the Countess," he said proudly. "Whatever she may gain is for herself."

He is a tall, dignified man, extremely intellectual. He speaks perfect English as well as French, and, I believe, German, but his voice is thick and husky. His palate was shot away, if I remember rightly, in an attempt on his life. . . .

Suddenly he became grim. He took a revolver from his pocket and placed it on the table: "I am not concerned about my life," he declared, "but if I am again attacked it will go hard with my assailant."

The father of Karolyi was an Ambassador, who was one of the representatives of his country at the Congress at Berlin in 1878. The present Count was born in Budapest three years earlier. He was educated in various countries and he travelled extensively. By hereditary right he was a member of the House of Magnates. Later he was elected to the House of Deputies and he was conspicuous in pre-war politics. During the war he foresaw the defeat of the Central Powers and he endeavoured to save his country. In his view the Austro-Hungarian Empire should have made a separate peace with the Allies and so have endeavoured to preserve the Dual Monarchy. His counsels were heeded, but too late. When the collapse came, he was called upon to form a Cabinet. He abandoned the Royalist cause; the downfall of the Hapsburgs was inevitable. As Prime Minister he negotiated the Armistice, and when Hungary was set up as an independent Republic he was chosen as President. Had he succeeded it would probably have been recognised that his policy was of immense European value. But he failed, and he became the most hated man in his country.

Like many others who have led a revolution, he discovered that when once revolutionary forces are set in motion they cannot be controlled. Half measures are useless. Bela Kun preached Bolshevism and he won the ear of a public that was angry and despairing. Bolshevism was a disease that threatened all defeated countries, and even some of the victorious ones. The reproach against Karolyi is that he unnecessarily yielded his place in March 1919 to Bela Kun.

He explained to me that he was in no way responsible for the momentary triumph of Bolshevism. "My purpose was to save bloodshed. I was informed that resistance was useless. I had to take a decision—I had to fight or to give up the keys of office. Whether my decision was right or wrong may be a matter of opinion, but I acted for the best in accordance with my information and my judgment."

The Bela Kun Government was quickly suppressed. Karolyi was accused of endeavouring to enlist foreign sympathy against the Conservatives.

The Countess Karolyi, after various adventures in European capitals, directed a little establishment near the Bois de Boulogne. "In other days," she explained, "I bought beautiful things as a collector. Now I use my knowledge of art and antiquities to earn a living."

"Nothing," she said, "can give an idea of Budapest in the winter which preceded the attempt to establish a Soviet government. People were dying of cold and of hunger. There were political intrigues. . . . Perhaps it is more amusing to sell antiquities than to meddle with politics."

Vivacious, handsome, elegant, the Countess Karolyi was, before the war, interested in the feminist movement, and she was regarded in the privileged social world as quixotic. She was on the side of the oppressed, she was on the side of justice. During the war she founded at Budapest a club with pacifist tendencies. . . . In exile the Countess Karolyi set to work—guiding tourists on the Adriatic, running a little restaurant for refugees, assisting in the making of motor-cars at London, trying her hand at dressmaking at Paris, lecturing in the United States until this method of earning a livelihood was closed to her. . . .

It is an amazing story. In the Magazine of Antiquities, its walls hung with blue drapery, among the old *meubles* and the bronzes and the 'silver work, Countess Karolyi passes her days after an extraordinarily romantic and tragic existence.

VIII. COUNT BETHLEN

BARON KORANYI, one of the ablest representatives of the Hungarian Government abroad, was a friend of mine for some years, and I particularly admired the dexterity with which he made the best of a bad job when scandal after scandal might have discredited Hungary completely. I do not think I am exaggerating when I say that he revealed, in difficult circumstances, higher qualities of statesmanship than anyone else I have known, with the possible exception of Dr. Leopold Von Hoesch, who obtained the confidence of Poincaré even during the occupation of the Ruhr.

He was no fair weather diplomatist. His work in winning some degree of French sympathy for Hungary was constantly being upset by the Nationalist firebrands at home. At the best it was a most delicate task, for France was deeply committed to the Little Entente, which naturally displayed the utmost animosity towards Hungary. Moreover, Italian friendship with Hungary almost excluded the possibility of French friendship with Hungary. Yet he persevered, undaunted, and he obtained an exceptionally high personal standing among official personages, who did their best to forget the follies of his country.

But it is perhaps his financial ability that is most marked. He steered Hungary through the dangerous years when the Reparations Commission was still pressing for huge payments.

One day, when I congratulated him upon some concession he had won, he said: "Everybody now looks upon me as a financier. But when I was a young man I had a reputation as a writer. My novels were popular. All that is now forgotten. Perhaps it would have been better had I kept on writing. . . ."

There was something wistful in this confession of his secret ambition. Many of us are not satisfied with what we have done. We think rather of what we might have done. The writer would have preferred to be a diplomatist. The diplomatist would have preferred to be a writer. What we have seems so tawdry. What we have not seems so rich.

This little man, invariably affable, after studying at Budapest, Heidelberg, the Sorbonne, and the London School of Economics, began his career in the Hungarian Ministry of Finance. He was made Minister of Finance after the Bolshevik troubles had subsided. The country was in a deplorable condition. The war, the revolution, and the Rumanian occupation, besides the reduction of Hungary to pitiful proportions, made a complete economic reconstruction indispensable. There was, of course, inflation, and a fall of the currency. Baron Koranyi took a firm stand against the proposal of a capital levy. He resigned rather than put it into force, and in fact the capital levy made Hungarian confusion more confounded.

It was in 1922 that he came to represent his country at Paris. At once he won French sympathy. Throughout negotiations which lasted for two years and more, I was personally in constant contact with him and Sir William Goode. As a result of these efforts, reparation obligations were set aside, and the financial rehabilitation of Hungary proceeded under the auspices of the League of Nations, with the Bostonian, Mr. Jeremiah Smith, acting as Commissioner-General.

In these strenuous days it was my privilege to meet Count Stephen Bethlen, the Prime Minister of Hungary, to discuss the situation with him, and to help in some degree in the forwarding of his reconstruction policy which depended upon external assistance.

He is a descendant of a Prince of Transylvanian territory which has now been incorporated in Greater Rumania. He is simple in his tastes, mild in his manners, and soft in his speech. Of all European statesmen I have known, he best satisfies my idea of the cultured gentleman. Somehow he reminds me of Balfour. There is nothing haughtily aristocratic in his demeanour. It is not by force that he would impose himself and his policy. It is by amiability. There is, then, something paradoxical in the spectacle of the country that is regarded—and rightly regarded—as the most bellicose in Central Europe, nourishing schemes of revenge, being governed by the most charming Prime Minister on the Continent.

His ancestors withstood the assaults of the Turks on Christendom, presenting themselves as a shield against the infidel. From these rude generations of warriors comes a polished diplomatist. Yet Bethlen, too, can be hard and implacable, persistent and unswerving in his purpose.

With his customary pliancy there goes a clear consciousness of his aim. He will adapt his methods to circumstances, but on essentials he is unyielding. When a foolish agitator with a grievance struck him on the cheek at Geneva, he smilingly turned the other cheek. It was not Bethlen who was injured in his quiet dignity: it was the apostle of physical violence.

Behind him are the peasantry and the middle classes. For years he has been virtually unchallenged as the leader of the Hungarian nation.

Budapest is often called Judapest, for a large proportion of its inhabitants are Jewish; half the doctors, half the lawyers, half the journalists and writers, and generally half the intellectual classes of Budapest, are Jews. The Jews form a large proportion of the landowners, and they have an enormous influence over factories, banks, and business houses. Against them there is a good deal of feeling; but Bethlen has tried to discourage Jew-baiting, directing his efforts towards the suppression of internal quarrels. For Hungary, unity is essential.

The unity of Hungary is easy to achieve inasmuch as there is comparatively homogeneity of race. Nearly ninety per cent of the population is Magyar. About seven per cent is German. No wonder that the patriotic sentiment is strong. Eight and a half million people are animated by the desire to extend Hungarian boundaries. If they cannot hope to get back all that they lost, they demand at any rate the return of millions of Hungarians who are now living under Rumanian, Yugo-Slavian, and Czecho-Slovakian jurisdiction. Before the war

Hungary was partly bounded by the Carpathian mountains, and the rivers Danube and Drave—with the provinces of Slavonia and Croatia beyond. Hungary was then certainly not united. It included three million Rumanians, two million Germans, two million Slovaks, nearly two million Croats, over a million Serbians, half a million Ruthenians. The Magyars were roughly half the population, but they were predominant. They believed themselves to be superior, and in many respects they were. Obviously, in the event of defeat Hungary would be greatly reduced. It cannot complain that subject races have been taken from it, but it does complain that Magyars and Germans have been put under alien rule. If they must let Slavonia and Croatia remain with Yugo-Slavia, and are relatively silent about the small Austrian gains, and even about the Banat, now held by Yugo-Slavia and Rumania, they are indignant at the loss of Slovakia and Transylvania. It is certain that if opportunity serves they will make a bid for a readjustment of frontiers. They look to Italy for help and they have not been rebuffed. They even look to Poland though Poland has interests in common with its fellow Slav countries. They woo Great Britain and have succeeded in arousing unofficial sympathy. Hungary is one of the danger-spots of Europe though at present it seems to be helpless.

Bethlen is well aware of the difficulties, and although he cannot resist the push of national sentiment, he will not lightly embark on a perilous adventure. He tries to preserve sagacity in a country which has a single national aspiration. This aspiration is shared by the *intelligentsia,* by the Roman Catholic and Protestant clergy, by the peasantry, by the aristocracy. Everything in Hungary tends to foster that aspiration. The historic sense is cultivated, Hungarian literature and art are narrowly Hungarian, sport is irredentist. . . . Yes, even Hungary's encouragement of such games as football is not without its menace and when I hear men of goodwill in Central Europe declare that if Hungary beats Czecho-Slovakia on the playing field it will not want to beat it on the battlefield, I remain sadly unconvinced. . . . The resurrection of Hungary has become a creed. It is repeated in the schools and in the churches.

The case was put as follows:

"Religion makes an appeal in Hungary because it promises the necessary spiritual preparation for the great struggle. Morality is accepted as a means of increasing the nation's physical strength. Every holiday is a reminder of past glory and an exhortation to future heroism. . . .

"In shopwindows patriotism is preached. The seed-merchant arranges his seeds in suggestive maps; the book stores are aflame with sermons. Education is extended to rural districts hitherto neglected, in the belief that an educated peasantry will have more heart for the sacred struggle. . . ."

Here is surely one of the most significant social facts of present-day Europe. An enormous responsibility lies upon Bethlen and whoever may be his successor. The Hungarians have shown themselves to be a hardy race of fighters ever since they came over the Carpathian passes at the end of the Ninth Century. They have a formidable fighting record and they are obsessed with the wrongs done to them. It will require a steady hand and a wise head to keep them from bringing disaster on Europe. Yet how can their demands be stifled? Recently Bethlen, in unveiling a monument to the Unknown Soldier (for every country has its Unknown Soldier now), remarked that Hungary could not accept the Trianon Treaty. Instantly the Little Entente protested. But Bethlen replied:

"Surely the Little Entente cannot make us say that the Trianon Treaty is just when we know it is unjust. Hungary will always endeavour to invoke Article 19 of the Covenant, which provides that if the Treaty proves to be unjust or impracticable, revision may be requested from the League of Nations.

"The Little Entente cannot deprive us of this right. There is nothing unfriendly about our attitude. We are for peace and are using peaceful methods in protesting against what we will always say is an injustice to Hungary in the Peace Treaty."

IX. PROPAGANDA

PROPAGANDA is in the blood and bones of Eastern Europe. I do not propose to specify the countries which practice this art with some naïveté, but I will relate a few incidents which have come under my own observation. I was discussing with a European diplomatist a violent campaign against a certain nation which was being conducted in various European newspapers.

"It is quite unnecessary to take any notice of it," he said

airily. "It is all inspired by one journalist, who could not get what he asked from the country he now attacks."

I expressed my incredulity.

"Oh, but I assure you it is true," he said, surprised at my challenge. "I can give you the exact details."

"It is quite impossible," I replied. "He would not have the audacity to write against a country which had refused his propositions."

He assured me most earnestly that nevertheless such was the case. According to his story the polemist had suggested that he should be given a salary to "write up" the country in question. A smaller sum was offered. He refused it. Then he went elsewhere and was duly rewarded.

Whether it be true or not I do not know. Certainly circumstantial evidence was offered to me. But it is of little consequence whether one believes this tale or not. It is sufficiently conclusive, in a more general sense, that my informant, who holds a responsible position, should himself believe the tale and treat it as a matter of course. The practice of paying for propaganda is recognised. . . .

On another occasion the representative of an Eastern community, which was anxious to obtain perfectly legitimate advantages, remarked to me that it was an expensive business to make known its claims. I pretended not to understand. Thereupon he produced for my inspection a lengthy list of journals.

"So much space on the front page costs so much," he said. "On the second page it is cheaper. Here is the scale of tariffs."

"Surely it cannot help you," I said, "to have paid articles in these sheets if everybody knows they are paid?"

He shook his head. "It may be that you are right. But it is the practice and we must submit to it."

"But it is for the governments to judge; and they cannot be influenced by a mercenary press?"

"I doubt myself whether they are seriously influenced, but others believe that the repetition of our case, in no matter what kind of press, must have some effect."

A friend of mine, perfectly honest, told me that one day the emissary of a minister who had just taken office came to see him. He was embarrassed and took time to come to the point. My friend, observing that he had something to say which he could not resolve to say, at last remarked:

"It is clear that you have a communication of some delicacy. Please be frank."

The emissary no longer hesitated. "The truth is," he said, "that the minister has no available secret funds, and we are compelled to cut down our list. I found your name on it, and knowing you as I do I cannot believe that you require pecuniary inducements to write in friendly fashion about us."

The suggestion was staggering. My friend demanded to be shown that portion of the list which concerned himself. There was his name, and the sums which he was alleged to have received. He had received nothing, and he became indignant. No proposal had ever been made to him, for his character was sufficiently known.

"Please do not get angry," said the emissary. "I was astonished to find your name and I thought it better to inform you."

"Then how does it come to be there?"

"It is perfectly obvious," gravely replied the emissary, "that my predecessor has been putting these secret funds into his own pocket. He has accounted for his peculations by placing you and others on the list."

One country made many presents of "caviar." "Caviar," in this connection, was not always the roe of sturgeon. It was a euphemism for more substantial gifts.

The photograph of a contract between a European country and a well-known newspaper was offered to me—for a price. As I am not interested in pillorying individuals, I declined to purchase the so-called "proof of corruption."

Twice in my own career it has been suggested that I should be "compensated." Once the compensation was to take the form of a small "pension."

"It puts you under no obligation," I was informed. "You will continue to express your own opinions. There is no question of bribery. We merely wish to reward you for your excellent services."

"But I have rendered none!" I exclaimed. "On the contrary I have consistently denounced the abuses of your country."

"That does not matter," was the reply. "Please speak of us as you judge best. We do not ask you to change your opinions, but if you will be good enough to look at facts and figures, which we should be happy to supply, you will be able to write with still more authority. But you would, I repeat, be under no obligation."

Again I was asked if I would not give a lecture in an Eastern city. For this address I was to be paid a fee out of all proportion to its value. My expenses, too, were to be paid. This was a more subtle form of bribery, but bribery I considered it to be. I could only politely refuse.

After the matter was settled I asked why the authorities thought it worth their while to offer me such a fee for a lecture that could be of no use to them. I could not speak their language. I had not the smallest pretensions to express the views of anybody but myself.

An explanation was fairly enough given to me. "We had no intention of conferring favours on you. You would be conferring a favour on us. It would be a proper price to pay for your loss of time and for the trouble we should put you to."

"But what do you get out of it?" I insisted.

"Well, you are a publicist, and we should have received you with honours, and have called attention in every possible way to your presence in our city. All this would be recorded in our newspapers and paragraphs would appear abroad. Something at least of what you said would be distributed broadcast!"

I was still unable to see the utility of such items. Then I was told that, rightly or wrongly, the country set much store on every kind of publicity. The authorities, wisely or foolishly, measured the standing of their country by the amount of advertisement it could procure. Press cuttings were apparently measured every month, and if they exceeded a certain length then the country was deemed to be making progress.

"It is really cheap to induce publicists and others to give lectures, for we could not have so much written about us directly, and if we could it would be more expensive."

I found it amusing to learn that ministers were gratified when so many feet of copy were devoted to their country. It seemed absurd that the success of a country should be judged in the same way as the success of a musical comedy actress. Yet, assuredly, there are men whose idea of rulership does not soar beyond such paltry methods. To make their people happy is of secondary importance. To have their States talked about is the true criterion.

There are writing men who properly do not seek, and who would refuse, the "decorations" which are so freely distributed by certain European countries. I do not, however, in the least reflect upon those who think they are entitled, without any thought of reward or of influence, to accept these foreign honours.

But I trust that a more serious appreciation of national needs is replacing a ridiculous system of publicity, artificial and, as I think, futile.

X. GREATER RUMANIA

RUMANIA, a Latin island surrounded by a Slavic sea, was one of the principal profiteers of the war. In 1913 its population was well under eight millions. To-day its population is seventeen and a half millions. No wonder that, ten years after its reconstruction, it celebrates its anniversary with great rejoicings.

It is stronger in every way—though nothing like as strong as it should be, had it been well governed. Militarily it is admirably placed; it is protected by the Carpathians, the Danube and the Dniester. Economically, it should improve, in spite of extraordinary mismanagement, if it can only forego the Bratianu restrictions on foreign capital employed in its development. The soil is wonderfully rich; cereals are grown in immense quantities; there is produced coal, iron ore, copper, lead, aluminum, salt, and crude petroleum. The possibilities in respect of oil seem unbounded. It is believed that oil lands cover an area eight times as great as that which is now exploited. Just after the war, it was possible for oil to be brought to Black Sea ports from America and sold more cheaply than Rumanian oil; and although it is true that the wells suffered greatly during the war, yet this strange situation was due to financial quarrels. Happily, Rumania now appears to take a more sensible view; and Rumania should grow vastly in importance in the Balkanic scheme of things.

Transylvania, Bessarabia, the Boukovine, and the Banat, brought to Rumania more wealth, but they also brought the problem of racial minorities. Bessarabia is claimed by Russia, to which it formerly belonged. Transylvania is claimed by Hungary, and for a number of years, at almost every international conference, we have listened to interminable wrangles as to the amount of compensation which Rumania should pay to Hungarian landowners for property confiscated under the Rumanian reform act. The sum in dispute is not very large, and Rumania would do well to settle, instead of providing Hungary

The Rumanian Royal Family

with the means of keeping alive a dangerous quarrel. In none of these regions is there a real Rumanian majority. There are Magyars and Germans and Ruthenians and Jews with some Serbians and a sprinkling of Gypsies.

With Czecho-Slovakia, Rumania is on excellent terms, but it is by no means sure that Rumanian relations with Yugo-Slavia, the third member of the Little Entente, would stand the strain of a European crisis. Italy, antagonistic to Yugo-Slavia, makes overtures to Rumania. Poland also appears friendly to Rumania. With Greece, Rumania has common interests, and these were expressed in Royal marriages which failed however to strengthen the dynasty, either in Greece or in Rumania. Prince George, the son of the Greek King Constantine, married the Rumanian King Ferdinand's daughter; but Greece is now a Republic. Prince Carol of Rumania, the heir to the throne, married Princess Helen of Greece, but he had love affairs which were recorded in the press of the world, and eventually he was barred from the succession. On the death of Ferdinand, it was Carol's little son, Michael, now eight years of age, who took his grandfather's crown. The Dowager Queen Marie, exceedingly beautiful and talented, of whom I have written in my book of Paris memories, is now a somewhat effaced figure. It is by no means impossible that Carol will some day make a bid for the throne.

With the coming of the peasants to power, a republican movement was feared. But Dr. Julius Maniu, their leader, now Prime Minister, strikes me as an able and sagacious man. He succeeded the Bratianus who had been all powerful in Rumania for many years and who are described as the real makers of modern Rumania. The Bratianus, who displayed remarkable qualities, though calling themselves Liberal, acted with tyrannic ruthlessness. The death of King Ferdinand was quickly followed by the mysterious death of Jean Bratianu, apparently in the full vigour of manhood; and his brother Vintila was not masterful enough to retain control. Maniu has shown prudence as well as authority. It is to be hoped that the passions of recent years are dying down.

Russia, in the Litvinoff Pact, which was a regional application of the Kellogg-Briand Peace Pact, has solemnly renounced war both with Rumania and Poland. It cannot yet be said that Greater Rumania is consolidated; there is still much corruption, there is still much discontent, there is still economic confusion.

Agrarian reform as adopted by Rumania may be good in itself, but the unfortunate small-holder is badly hit if there is a poor harvest; he cannot hold out; he has no capital; and in Rumania there is no organised system of credit to help him. As his land cannot be taken away from him, he has nothing to pledge, and if his crops fail he may have to pay as much as thirty per cent interest on his borrowings. Since the small-holder possesses four-fifths of the land in Rumania it will be appreciated that agricultural difficulties are inevitable.

The peasants—that is, eighty per cent of the population—are now in power; they are a formidable force; we shall see what they can make of their opportunity.

Out of the many Rumanians whom I have met I will select three. There is first—*place aux dames*—Hélène Vacaresco. If she is Rumanian, this vivacious woman is also cosmopolitan. At innumerable international gatherings I have seen her. She is rightly renowned for her eloquence; she is witty and poetical, earnest and indefatigable.

I am told that when she was a girl, King Ferdinand wished to marry her; but for reasons of State the match was deemed impossible.

She comes of an old and famous Rumanian family, her father holding high place in the diplomatic service. In her earliest years she became acquainted with the courts of Europe. Queen Victoria received her as a guest, and she has remained a friend of Queen Alexandra. Her governess was English and she was educated chiefly in France.

The companion of Queen Elizabeth of Rumania, whose pen name was Carmen Sylva, Mademoiselle Vacaresco wrote exquisite verses which won the approval of the Royal poetess.

She has been everywhere and knows everybody. In a dozen countries she has worked on behalf of the feminist movement—and on behalf of peace.

Panaït Istrati is an entirely different type of Rumanian. He is direct and even brutal. Certainly his early life, as he himself describes it in autobiographical pages, was a series of struggles; and he would have us consider him as a worker who, self-educated, now tries to set down his experiences and his impressions. When he was thirteen years of age his schoolmaster asked his mother what she intended to make of the boy. "He must learn a trade or go into service." The teacher replied: "That's a pity.

King Michael of Rumania

Can't you send him to the lycée?" "No, Sir. I am a poor widow woman who does daily washing for a living."

But the boy was not displeased to escape from school. He worked in a cabaret. He became a vagabond. Gaining his livelihood in every available menial manner, he went from Greece to Turkey, found his way to Egypt, had an unhappy time in Naples, and finally came to France.

Misery has left its traces on his countenance. His thin hatchet face, pinched and drawn, his keen unquiet eyes behind big round glasses, tell something of his tale of suffering. His thin nervous frame speaks of privations. Yet his expression is the serious expression of a student; and sometimes his face lights up with a peculiarly sympathetic smile, revealing gold-stopped teeth.

Success, even some celebrity, have only served to sharpen his irony. I asked him to sign one of his books for me, and with quick mockery of his own fame, he said: "Forgive me if I make a mistake in spelling your name, for it will surely increase the value of the book!"

Never has he forgotten his humble origins. Never has he lost his pity for the oppressed. When he went to Russia he shocked many of his admirers by espousing the cause of Bolshevism which, in his view, had done a great deal for the outcast. His opinions may not be accepted but nobody can fail to be moved by his deep humanity. Myself, I think of him as the Gorki of Rumania.

In all the trades which he practised he found time to read. In all his wanderings he contrived to procure books. When he was a sign-painter in Switzerland he was still ignorant of French, but he bought a cheap copy of Fénelon's "Télémaque," and with the aid of a dictionary struggled to understand it. The walls of his dingy bedroom were covered with French words as he noted them. Voltaire and Pascal, and afterwards Romain Rolland, completed his education. By this time he was a labourer in a garage. The labourer in the garage wrote a pathetic letter to Rolland relating his life. Rolland did not receive it at that time, and it was returned by the post. When in despair Istrati tried to commit suicide at Nice, the letter was found in his trunk and it was brought to the notice of the great writer who immediately sent an encouraging response. Then it was that Istrati began to write his memories of his strange life and revealed his gifts of story-teller and poet.

The third figure is that of Prince Antoine Bibesco, member of one of the most representative families of Rumania. He is, of course, in the diplomatic service, but since every Rumanian of culture is also a writer, the Prince has produced a number of plays which have been particularly well received in the critical world of Paris.

Paris is, indeed, his real home, as it is the second home of many Rumanians. Whether his diplomatic functions take him to England, to Russia, to Spain, or to the United States, he finds time to return to the house on the Ile Saint-Louis, wherein gather the most brilliant young men and women of many lands. His wife, Elizabeth Asquith, a talented writer with several clever books to her credit, shares his remarkable gift for entertaining, and together they attract all who are vitally interested in the arts and in politics.

This well-groomed, clean-shaven, aristocratic young man has an exceptional knowledge of the world, a subtle receptive mind, a rare talent for friendships, an acquaintance with all that is being said and done in literature and in diplomacy. For me he stands out as the true type of the cultured cosmopolitan Rumanian, acute and supple in a degree that is characteristic of his race.

XI. YUGO-SLAVIA'S DISUNITY

I REMEMBER how my attention was attracted in the hot days of July 1914 by a flaring newspaper poster on which were printed these words: "To Hell with Serbia!"

That is how many people felt about the country to which the Austro-Hungarian Empire was presenting menacing notes demanding reparation for the murder of the Archduke in the little town of Sarajevo. Serbia * was looked upon as savage and quarrelsome. It was backed up by its big Slav sister, Russia.

Russia, with its Balkanic interests, was linked to France, and France had an entente with England, and the Austro-Hungarian Empire, whose prospective King had been killed, was the ally of Germany; and so everybody was obliged to come into a stupid and atrocious war.

Once the fighting began it was quickly agreed to forget the

* Mr. George Harrap, the well-known publisher, told me that in a book issued by his firm fifteen years ago, the name of the country was changed from Servia to Serbia. The Servians, who had long objected to the "v," became Serbians. Newspapers welcomed the change, and the new form soon figured in diplomatic documents. But why not Slab instead of Slav, and Slabonic instead of Slavonic?

sentiment so vigorously enunciated in the words: To Hell with
Serbia!

As a result of the war it was agreed to recognise Serbia as the
nucleus of a new Kingdom—the Kingdom of the Serbs, Croats,
and Slovenes, usually called Yugo-Slavia. These Southern Slavs
escaped from the domination of Empire, but though (absorbing
little Montenegro) they form together a State with a population of over twelve millions, they have not yet been able to
settle down. The Croats (and the smaller body of Slovenes) are
discontented.

The case of Yugo-Slavia is not exceptional: for nations are
usually composed of disparate elements. But this amalgamation
of Serbians, Croats, and Slovenes has been, so far, a failure.
The Croats in particular had expected some kind of autonomy,
and they vigorously protest against excessive centralisation.
They have a higher culture than that of the Serbians, for they
belonged to the highly civilised Austro-Hungarian Empire,
while the Serbians, until comparatively recent times, were subjected to the less civilised influence of the Turks. So the Croats,
coming in a subordinate rôle into the Triune Kingdom, have
simply jumped out of the frying-pan into the fire.

King Alexander decided to dispense with Parliamentary rule,
asserting that the process of welding the component parts will
be accomplished more easily by autocratic than by democratic
methods. The Belgrade Parliament had become a bloody battle-
ground of Croats and Serbians; the leader of the Croats,
Raditch, had been shot in the Skupstina. Twenty-four Ministries of the most diverse kinds have been tried during the past
ten years and have failed to bring unity to Yugo-Slavia.

It was in the second year of the war that a committee was
formed on which Croats, Slovenes, and Serbians sat. It was not
dissimilar from the Czecho-Slovakian committee which was
directed by President Mazaryk and M. Bénès, to proclaim the
desire of the Czecho-Slovaks for independence. Professor
Troumbitch, chief of the Croat National Party, was the moving
spirit of this committee. When Serbia was hard pressed by
Austria-Hungary, its Government fled to the sea coast and
eventually took refuge in Corfu. Thus there were two organisations which stood for the Yugo-Slavian cause. There was the
Government of the old King Peter, and there was the committee of Professor Troumbitch. M. Pachitch, the Serbian Prime
Minister, invited Professor Troumbitch to discuss the situation

with him. In July, 1917, they agreed upon a declaration. They recognised the desire of the Southern Slavs to form a single nation. But there were reservations. The Serbs, the Croats and the Slovenes were willing to come under the same flag, but that flag, said each of them, should be its own. They were ready to accept a single King; but they stipulated that they should practise different religions—the Serbians being, for the most part, members of the Orthodox Greek Church; the Croats and the Slovenes members of the Roman Catholic Church; while in Bosnia and Herzegovina there were Mohammedans.

In other words while the three branches of the Slav countries were prepared to come together for common purposes, they were desirous of keeping their individuality. They were determined to escape from the domination of Austria-Hungary, but they were not prepared to come under any other domination. Serbia actually existed; but that was no reason why the Croats and the Slovenes should be simply annexed by Serbia. It was not a Greater Serbia that was called for. It was a veritable coöperation of three peoples.

Unfortunately, matters did not develop as the Croats expected. Belgrade was the existing capital, and it was at Belgrade that after the war the deputies assembled to frame a Constitution. There was much unpleasant manœuvring, and the Croats were unfairly treated. They felt that they had not played their part in the making of the Constitution, which was suitable only for a highly centralised country. There was considerable dissatisfaction. That dissatisfaction has grown steadily. The Croats and Slovenes consider that they have been improperly sacrificed to the Serbians. They resent being placed under the Serbian administration which compares unfavourably with the former Austro-Hungarian administration.

On one side, therefore, are Croats and Slovenes accustomed to a higher civilisation—a Western civilisation. On the other hand, are the Serbians accustomed to a lower civilisation—an Eastern civilisation. Yet it is the Serbian civilisation, the Serbian methods, which are imposed upon the former members of the Austro-Hungarian Empire. The Croats, properly handled, would ask nothing better than to live side by side with the Serbians; but they strongly deprecate the predominance of the Serbians; and if the new Kingdom is not to break up, with incalculable consequences for the Balkans, and indeed for the whole of Europe, it is necessary that the three branches of the

KING ALEXANDER OF SERBIA

Slav family shall be reconciled quickly. It is of the highest importance for the peace of Europe that the Yugo-Slavian nations should be welded. Internal strife may mean external strife. Internal peace will help towards external peace.

King Alexander who, like his namesake, cut the Gordian knot, is one of the youngest of European sovereigns. He is not without ability and is fairly well liked by the three peoples whom he would make into one people. Perhaps he may be described as the living link between the Croats and the Serbs. But it would be well to note that he is praised by the Croats because it is thought that he will help the Croats to realise their ideal—that is to say, to shake themselves free of Serbian domination. He has a heavy responsibility; it may turn out to be a bad business for a King to become his own Dictator; the Kings of Spain and of Italy are wiser in permitting Primo de Rivera and Mussolini to stand in their stead.

Although he is little more than forty years of age he has had a fairly long experience of rulership, for he was Regent for old Peter before he succeeded him nine years ago. He married one of the Rumanian princesses.

XII. BULGARIA'S AMBITION

WITH Bulgaria Yugo-Slavia exists on exceedingly bad terms. There are perpetual frontier incidents. As it now stands, Bulgaria has less than half the territory of its neighbours Rumania and Yugo-Slavia. Yet the Bulgarians, though still primitive, are in many respects the most promising of the Balkanic peoples. When they were liberated from Turkish rule, they spent money freely on education. Their Czar, Ferdinand, was easily the best of the Balkanic rulers; he gave the country roads and pavements, parks and handsome town buildings, public instruction and sound administration. He chose the German side in the war, and was defeated and driven into exile. But it remains true that he was the most capable public man—with the possible exception of Venizelos—in the Balkans.

The present King of Bulgaria is Boris, who happened to be making a trip through Europe at the same time as myself; and in each capital I was amused with the speculations as to the object of his travels. Here it was said that he was in search of a wife; there it was declared that he was suffering from an earache and was consulting specialists. It is true that in Vienna he saw an ear specialist; but it is also true that in Rome there were negotiations for the hand of an Italian Princess.

He neither courted publicity nor shrank from public rooms; a simple tourist, known as Count Stanislas Rilski, he was accompanied by his sister, the Princess Eudoxia; unpretentious, good-looking, and, so I judge, honest and intelligent, he is now in the thirties, and although Bulgaria is sadly diminished, Boris is what I believe is known as "an eligible bachelor."

Such is the tittle-tattle of travel; I hardly know whether I heard more about Boris' prospective marriage (and his earache) or about "Miss Hungary," who had just won a beauty contest and had received the new title of "Miss Europe," when I wandered about Central Europe this year. But while the attention given to King Boris was conversational, and nobody went out of his way to see him, the cafés to which "Miss Europe" consented to go on her triumphal progress were crowded by delirious throngs. . . .

The Bulgarians, after winning their own independence, twice tried to obtain hegemony in the Balkans. In 1913 they attacked their Allies, Greece and Serbia, over the partition of Macedonia; they saw in 1916 a chance of proving their superiority, and in fact they overran Serbia. Their ambition overleaped itself. . . . Now they are a little nation of five million people. Their capital, Sofia, has only 150,000 inhabitants.

The irredentist claims of Bulgaria are to the lower Dubrudja, which is now Rumanian; to Eastern and Western Thrace, now Greek; and to Macedonia, partly Greek, partly Serbian. Bulgaria wants outlets on the Black Sea and on the Ægean Sea. But above all Macedonia is coveted by Bulgaria. There are Bulgarians whose whole life is devoted to this cause; fierce passionate men who will sacrifice everything to the acquisition of this territory. It is for them the Promised Land. If Yugo-Slavia broke up, Bulgaria might realise its dream; but it is difficult to imagine the conditions in which the quest, which now seems hopeless, will become hopeful.

In the meantime the Bulgarian Comitadjis cross the Serbian frontier, for propagandist and terrorist purposes. That there can be good relations, that the Balkans will be safe, while these recurrent incidents disturb both Sofia and Belgrade, is impossible. Yet it is not altogether the fault of Sofia. The Macedonian bands are almost beyond the control of the Bulgarian Government. In the regions of the South-west, they make their centre, and the Liaptchef Cabinet is unable to suppress them, if it has the desire.

What is the remedy? There exists a neutral commission on the Greco-Bulgarian frontier; but on the Bulgaro-Yugo-Slavian frontier it would probably be useless. There is a perpetual danger of clashes which may, some day, arouse real anger; and the Balkans will again be ablaze. . . . The Balkans have seen war after war. They have brought Europe within an ace of war on many occasions. At last they brought the Great War. Grave problems remain; many perils persist. Maurice Pernot, who has written an authoritative work on the New Balkans, reports his conversations with experienced diplomatists who deem that the present situation is more dangerous than it was before 1914. The causes of friction have been multiplied, and, what is worse, it has become impossible to localise a Balkanic conflict.

Will the Balkans make an effort to break with the bad old traditions? Certainly treaties of friendship are being concluded which are truly different from those of former days; but then other treaties of friendship are, to all intents and purposes, similar to those which regulated the relations of the peoples fifteen years ago. Everything depends on the temper of the nations and not on the texts of treaties. There is an incessant upheaval. There is no certain authority. Governments change frequently. In Rumania, in Yugo-Slavia, in Albania, in Greece, in Bulgaria, I have counted two, three, and four ministries in the same year. And when the ministry changes, the officials change; industry, commerce, and banking are deeply affected; the State interferes with private affairs to a degree hardly imaginable in Western Europe. There is a narrow Nationalism, a xenophobia, which not only perpetuates hatreds between peoples, but prevents economic progress, inasmuch as foreign aid, which may become hegemony, is suspected and resented. Rancour and the thirst for revenge are still to be overcome. The best observers do not see any prospect of a "Balkan Locarno." Those who sincerely desire peace think everybody else is insincere.

XIII. VENIZELOS

THE maker of modern Greece is Eleutherios Venizelos who signalled his return to power in 1928 by visiting most of the European countries. This Odyssey of the new Ulysses had a practical purpose. Greece had mounted high, and had fallen low, and now the Prime Minister wished to win the goodwill of the world for his country.

I have known the Greek statesman for years. At the Peace Conference his was one of the dominant figures. His nation, once the glory of the world, the mother of our civilisation, once more took a proud position among the nations. Its spokesman was powerful in the counsels of the politicians who were the potentates of Europe.

He had a purpose. He had knowledge. He was persuasive. He was dignified in appearance. He had a legend. Even the enemies of Venizelos acknowledged that he was a giant among the pygmies. Even those who thought his policy was disastrous admitted that there was none who could bend his mighty bow.

The most surprising thing about Venizelos is that, after a tragic blunder, he should have regained the authority which he held for forty years in a land of perpetual political upheavals. If he looks like the placid scholar, his looks belie him. Crete, where he was born, was torn by civil wars, massacres, and revolutions—somebody indeed has calculated that there were thirty revolutions in the latter half of the Nineteenth Century. Venizelos was elected to the Assembly in 1887; he was constantly in peril; but he pursued steadily and clearly a definite aim—namely, to free Crete from the Turks who had held it from the Seventeenth Century, and to attach the island to Greece. He devoted more than a score of years to this task, and eventually succeeded. Then he had a second ambition. He determined to reform Greece, morally and materially, and make it the most notable nation of the East. From 1910 onwards, after the revolt of the Greek army which gave him his opportunity, Venizelos ruled Greece. He was nominally Prime Minister, but he possessed exceptional powers. The renaissance of Greece was amazing. The Balkan League—in which Greece, Bulgaria, Serbia and Montenegro stood together—was established. The League fought Turkey; and then Greece fought Bulgaria. Greek territory was doubled in extent. . . . Came the Great War, and the long struggle of Venizelos with King Constantine. The Prime Minister wished to join the Allies, hoping further to increase the size and prestige of his country. The King was neutral, and afterwards pro-German. The Allies landed forces in Salonika, and eventually deposed Constantine. Venizelos again took command. But at the Peace Conference

M. Venizelos

Venizelos, who had hitherto been right, made the mistake of asking for more territory than Greece could hold. The Turks were not subdued. The Allies were not prepared to fight them again. Venizelos, elated by his victory, made the extraordinary error of sending tired Greek armies against Turkey. The Turks rallied; to this ill-timed action of Venizelos, which aroused a new national spirit in Turkey, Turkey owes its present strength in the Near East. The Greeks were badly defeated and Greece for a time was ruined. Constantine returned, only however to be again displaced. For some years Venizelos was in eclipse. . . . Now he is back in power, and he has produced order from chaos.

He has gone far to abolish brigandage which has always existed in Greece; he has advanced the work for the settlement of refugees; he has compensated war victims in Greek Macedonia; he has put finances on a sounder basis; he has negotiated commercial treaties; he has reëstablished political stability. . . .

His pale face with soft grey beard, above which is a wild moustache, is again seen in European assemblies. Those keen eyes, which sparkle behind gold-rimmed glasses, seize every nuance of diplomatic meaning. When I last saw him he was merely an onlooker. He lived remote from the scene of action. Sometimes I encountered him in a certain hall where diplomatists gather to exchange their views; and he sat quietly, a black skull cap emphasising the height of his ivory forehead, an ironic smile on his lips, with closed eyes. He was working on a translation of Thucydides. He was writing history, not making it. But it was impossible for the old statesman to retire permanently; and realising his country's need for more energy, he asserted his active leadership of the Greek Liberal Party. At the elections which followed he swept the country, and so the man who was supposed by many to have given up politics, again played a prominent rôle.

After he had seen that all was well at home, he undertook his tour of Europe. He went to Rome and signed a Treaty of Friendship, Conciliation, and Juridical Settlement of Disputes between the Kingdom of Italy and the Hellenic Republic. That is a notable act. It shows that something has changed since those days when the Corfu incident set Italy and Greece in opposition. Italy had defied the League of Nations, and had insisted that it should conduct "police" operations as it pleased. Italy now wishes to be on good terms with Greece. Greece wishes to be on good terms with its neighbours. Between Italy and

Greece there had been outstanding subjects of silent contention, such as the ownership of the Dodecanese Islands, concerning which Venizelos signed an agreement with Italy at Paris in 1919. But though these former Turkish islands, with the exception of Rhodes, were to have gone to Greece, the Lausanne Conference of 1923 gave them to Italy.

And has this new relation not had the effect of disturbing other countries, such as Yugo-Slavia, for is it not a diplomatic maxim that a treaty is always made at the expense of a third party?

Not at all. Venizelos made it clear that his desire was to live in amity with all the Balkanic nations. He adopted conventions, already prepared, in respect of the Salonika port—the outlet to the Ægean Sea—and the Guevgueli railway, and so far as Greece and Yugo-Slavia are concerned the long dispute is settled. He likewise concluded a treaty of friendship with Yugo-Slavia.

With Bulgaria he has been, as I write, less successful; but with Turkey, Greece's old enemy, negotiations are making progress. Italy urged an Italo-Greco-Turkish accord; and Greece is clearing the tangled ground. There are financial problems and refugee problems. Perhaps Greece still thinks of Constantinople with regret. Perhaps Greece still has dreams of Smyrna. But Venizelos is practical, and there is no reason for delaying a settlement with the new Turkey.

Venizelos is not a cold, cunning, clever statesman; he is genuinely moved by warm human feelings. Hence his successes, and his failures. He inspired Greece; and he asked too much from Greece. I remember—and the incident is worth recording—that one day when I was walking in his company in the Champs-Elysées, he picked up a ball thrown against him by a child and returned it playfully. He has a love of little children; and his horror of the atrocities committed in the Balkans is profound. It is the mainspring of much of his policy. A righteous wrath is in him; he is moved by detestation of his enemies and by pity for the victims. His desire is not only to build up a Greater Greece but to make of it a Greece ordered and educated, with high ideals, a Greece which will turn its back upon the dark butcheries and squabblings of the Near East.

Although he is sceptical of the conception of a great Balkan Confederation, which will make the Balkan States independent of the Great Powers, and which will bind the peoples together in conditions making for peace instead of setting them against each other, he does at any rate approach the task of uniting the nations.

The Balkans have always been the dangerous plaything of bigger nations, and even to obtain their support he will not consent to be played with. The basis of the modern world is commerce. The Balkan countries have common economic interests. Trade may cause wars, but it may also have a pacifying influence. If the Balkans learn that they cannot be really prosperous at each other's expense, the problem of their union will be solved. Railways and roads and amicable Customs arrangements join up territories in much more than a material sense. The modern mind of M. Venizelos, striving to make not only Greece as well-ordered as England, but Greece's neighbours also, has been particularly impressed with the moral consequences of such matter-of-fact things. The Nationalist in him wants a big Greece—that is a Greece with boundaries: the Internationalist in him wants a still bigger Greece—that is a Greece without boundaries. But he does not believe in emergency measures or in wizardry. He will not hasten too quickly. The Confederation must evolve gradually, steadily; at every stage it must be tested. He had the daring idea of a common Foreign Office, but that is not an immediate possibility. International coöperation must be tried and found good in all its aspects: the nations must be saturated with a longing for brotherhood. The duty of statesmen, then, if M. Venizelos is right, is to preach this brotherhood and to demonstrate its advantages by results, until their peoples shall demand fullest copartnership. The Balkans have been the birthplace of wars; they may one day refuse to be the pawns of designing powers who take advantage of their feuds, and they may pledge themselves to peace.

PART VI
GERMANY

I. OUTWARD APPEARANCES

THE good qualities of the North Germans are so profound that they never come to the surface. So wrote a North German friend to me when I informed him that I was travelling through Germany and would stay in Berlin. Now it is possible to read that sentence as a piece of irony, and I can imagine its being repeated malevolently. It is not in this sense that I employ it. Germany has great virtues which unfortunately do not reveal themselves to the superficial observer. In this respect it is the antithesis of France. You may like or dislike France, but its vices and virtues appear on the surface. (I do not mean to deny their deep-rootedness but only to affirm their efflorescence.) Whereas, in Germany, it seems to me that all that is unpleasant is apparent, and all that is good is hidden. The French know how to express themselves gracefully; the Germans do not. I had not been in Berlin for ten minutes before I had my first annoying brush with a stupid and incredibly offensive Prussian officer. But at dinner that night I had for companion a political writer who displayed a universal culture and a philosophical outlook that I have rarely seen matched in either Anglo-Saxon or Latin countries.

The city itself offends my taste. Much the reader will care about my taste, but I record my impressions because they are typical, because the Germans have a knack of making themselves misunderstood. What a violent contrast with Paris! In Paris, too, the post-war uneasiness is seen in glaring eccentricities, but, if such a paradoxical observation will pass muster, even the glaring eccentricities of Paris keep within measure; they fit somehow into the framework of the beautiful capital, and only serve to emphasise the general sense of artistic order. In Berlin glaring eccentricities seem to strike the keynote. The Friedrichstrasse is blindingly lit and deafeningly uproarious. Unter den Linden is a magnified piece of provincial tawdriness. One is startled by a gigantic building which looks like a cubistic cathedral bathed in a purple light; and one discovers that it is a café. The immense façades are such as might have been invented for a film on the pattern of Doctor Caligari. It is the new architecture, which has the air of being crazy. And everywhere one is confronted with the enormity of masonry—

a pot-pourri of monstrous emporiums, colossal beer-halls, tri-umphal staircases and colonnades in every known style blended into some unknown style.

All this is the result of "experimentation," we are told. Doubtless it is good to experiment and to defy conventions; but ugliness is produced nine times out of ten. Of course many of these buildings are comparatively old, and have by no means been influenced by the new movement which challenges the simplest architectural axioms; yet somehow even the compara-tively old buildings take on an air of strangeness, probably by the proximity of strangeness. What is more puzzling is the question how these weird façades can be so prevalent along thoroughfares which have existed for many years. The thor-oughfares were not always like that; at what moment was the frontage thrown down and rebuilt by the experimenters? Has the process been gradual or sudden? I asked my companion, a Berliner, and he was extremely vague in his response. He as-serted that it was very new, but he could not remember when the streets had been metamorphosed. . . . It seemed to have happened without attracting anybody's attention; a normal avenue became abnormal overnight, and nobody noticed it. . . . This appears to indicate that normal minds became ab-normal overnight. . . .

"It is as if the change of régime has brought a new spirit; rigid rules have gone with the Empire; a go-as-you-please archi-tecture has come in with the Republic"—that was the nearest approach to an explanation I could obtain. In every town in the country—and even in the countryside—there are these manifestations of novelty in construction. When "die neue Sachlichkeit" (the new matter-of-factness) merely expresses itself in such ways as making offices of steel and glass in order that they may have light, there is nothing much to be urged against practicality—even though it is excessive. But, archi-tecturally at least, it is not true that the "new matter-of-fact-ness," which is born of our "machine-age," despises ornamenta-tion. There is more ornamentation than ever, but it is not pleas-ing; it is jazzy, it is startling, it consists in sharply contrasting planes, in unexpected angles, in geometric designs, in vivid colours and in weird lighting arrangements.

I went into a restaurant which struck me as a perfect Bedlam. It was planned as never a restaurant was planned before. There is a long corridor with steel mirrors which give one the sensa-

New German Architecture

tion of walking—dozens of one—upside down or sideways;
one moves amid the regiment of oneself. The floor space, where
it is usual to sit, is filled with artificial trees and flowers; there
are huge nightmare alembics from which water perpetually
flows; in the middle is a golden pillar; a circular staircase un-
winds itself in the air, apparently sustained by nothing. But
where then does one dine? One dines in tiers, one above the
other, in narrow square galleries which run round the hall; we
sit on each other's heads, as it were. . . . That would be quaint
enough, but what was worse were the gaudy parrots chained
to the artificial trees; they screeched incessantly and hideously;
they were the new orchestra; conversation was impossible; it
was barely possible to give one's orders; one's brain reeled, one
was giddy and blind and deaf, and it was a relief to get into the
street again. But the bulk of the diners seemed unperturbed;
they were hardly conscious of anything unusual; their faces
shone with the pleasure of eating; and their nerves were untroubled.

But were their nerves untroubled? I wondered whether this
indifference to noisy sights and to unsightly noises is not a proof
of some nervous commotion. Are these Berliners still suffering
from war strain?   Are they hysterical, and in some sense
détraqués? I wondered. . . .

"There is no reason," said an orthodox architect to me, "why
the new architecture should stop at anything. If it is simply
something inédit that is wanted, why it is easy to put the roof
in the cellar and the cellar where the roof ought to be."

In amusements there is the same disquieting search for something new. There was one place which summed up these tendencies; we entered a Wild West bar filled with cow-boys—
and cow-girls, picturesquely but insufficiently clad—and passed
into a Spanish cellar where matadors and gitanes were drinking
on barrels, walked through a Turkish café with gilded ceilings
and low divans, listened to Viennese folk songs under the vine-
covered arbours of Grinzing, lingered on a Rhine terrace, and
had samples of I do not know how many other countries under
the same roof of this popular establishment in which highly
respectable Fraus, staring dumbly, rubbed shoulders with their
less respectable sisters. . . . The night life of Berlin, as of Hamburg, is notorious; I cannot count the number of times my
arm was seized by touts for the most shameless resorts. In one
tiny street every building promised obscene spectacles. . . .

In the theatre perversity and eroticism are freely discussed; and this is defended on the ground that whatever is based on biology or philosophy is of interest to mankind. Unfortunately the general discussion of vice tends to create vice. But if vice, natural and (so-called) unnatural, flourishes, it is good to see that the Zoo is still crowded with stolid simple folk.

The side of Berlin that is the most conspicuous is, in short, the worst. My companion was perpetually apologising for it, and reminding me that below the surface is the most admirable domesticity, the most strenuous industry, the most earnest intellectual and artistic activity. I scarcely needed the reminder; I was aware of the serious side of Berlin, and I had some opportunities of renewing my acquaintance with the excellent German people. But if I have touched upon the side that is uppermost, it is to stress my point that Germany in general, morally as well as materially, has the habit of presenting itself in a poor light. I will not, to make out my case, go back to the origins of the War, though Germany has never contrived to put forward convincingly its strong arguments against exclusive war guilt; but everybody knows that since the War it has had arguments against the treatment it has been accorded that have never been heard at all. Germany always puts itself in the wrong even when it is in the right. We are all acquainted with people who are genuinely misunderstood; here is a people which is misunderstood, partly by its own fault, and partly by a sort of fatality. Is there some lachrymose love of martyrdom joined to a compensatory aggressiveness in the mental make-up of the German people?

II. BERLIN—OLD AND NEW

THERE are many German cities which are to be preferred to Berlin; I like, above all, Dresden, clean, well-kept, comfortable, and even elegant; Munich is amusing if one does not take its "artiness" too seriously; Cologne is delightful; Hamburg is richly and exotically picturesque; Leipzig, spacious, important, the town of books, has a character of its own; but for better or for worse Berlin is the capital, and it truly exercises an immense influence over the whole of Germany, despite occasional declarations that the Southern States do not intend to be merely "Prussian colonies." It does not exercise the irresistible attraction over Germans that Paris exercises over Frenchmen;

it is, for example, by no means the intellectual centre of Germany. But its development has been extraordinary, and it is destined to become still more important in the German economy. It is difficult to realise that Berlin is, in its present form, a very new city. The other day I read with exceptional interest a communication from an anonymous correspondent of The Times (I wish I knew his name!) who looked back on his fifty years' memories of Berlin. This is how he described its general appearance in his youth:

"A little town which seemed to stand among the spiky fir trees of a fairy tale still rises to many minds. On a winter morning children used to be taken for a special treat to a place far out in the woods to see the 'King's collection of wild beasts.' In those days the word 'Kaiser' sounded a little strange and was generally associated with a magnificent being in Vienna. One drove between the scattered houses and kitchen gardens of the Kurfürstendam (to-day a babel of cars, shops, and cafés) uninterrupted save by the shout of a coachman warning the leisurely geese which would not keep off the way. Little urchins in woolly caps or coloured and peaked forage caps with red mufflers pelted each other with snowballs, and an occasional St. Bernard dog sauntered along what to-day is the very centre of Berlin.

"The Baroness 'X,' an iron-grey upright lady of the old school, would tell her nursery-maid, a Wendish peasant-girl, who wore the stiff white headdress and red and black bodice of her people, how much freer one felt since the City Walls had been taken down about fifteen years before!"

What a picture! It is one which is doubtless vividly remembered by tens of thousands of Berliners to-day. And yet it seems incredible as one stands in the whirl of traffic, in these great thoroughfares, banked by huge buildings, with luxurious automobiles displayed behind huge plate-glass windows, and immense startling cinema announcements, and brilliantly lit skysigns. I cannot refrain from quoting yet another passage which evokes the old Berlin:

"In the middle of the Spree, north by east of what is now the Museum Island, there still arose the irregular fretwork of gables known as Old Kölln, the original Berlin, nestling in the shadow of the ancient castle of the Electors of Brandenburg. It has vanished completely now with all its world of winding alleyways covered by the projecting eaves of its long low houses.

Vanished, too, is that many-coloured scene that used to play all day there. The barges from the Spreewald, laden with vegetables and holly sprinkled with snow, the country girls, wide-eyed and flaxen pigtailed, with their baskets over one arm while with the other they held hands, rather frightened at the big foreign city, belong also to a forgotten past. So, too, the Jewish bagman in shuffling gabardine and wide-brimmed hat, the chimney-sweep in his top hat with his formidable array of brushes and ladders, the seller of gingerbread figures, and the carpenter in the old-fashioned livery of his guild, black velvet jacket, mother o' pearl buttons, and flapping trousers."

Berlin to-day looks like an upstart among cities. Its very cleanness seems a fault. When it strikes one as orderly, it strikes one as monotonous; and when it strikes one as fantastic, it strikes one as unrestrained. There is no good reason why Berlin should not be multiplied to infinity—the straight streets broken only by yawning caverns surmounted by a great U indicating the entrance to an underground station. Berlin is large but it is not grand; it is formidable but it is not splendid.

Berlin is what it is, not because it enjoys natural advantages which mark it out as the leading city of Germany, but because it happened to lie in the stronghold of the Hohenzollerns who imposed their authority on the straggling States of Germany. Certainly the Kaiser was proud of his capital and he encouraged all schemes for its enlargement and "beautification." The street-planning is formal but good; and open spaces and promenades are imposing enough. In historic buildings Berlin is, of course, deficient; it lacks those reminders of the Middle Ages which exist in many, if not most, German towns.

As for the Spree, it is, as it flows through Berlin itself, an undistinguished river; but outside the city it spreads out into a series of lakes which provide opportunities for boating and bathing. And out on the Wann-See is Potsdam, the former residence of the Emperor. . . . Few big agglomerations have such a fine playground so accessible. The athletic youth, and the out-of-doors-loving bourgeoisie, hurry away from the bricks and mortar of the metropolis. For me the memory of hours spent by these waters corrects the memory of hours spent in the city.

On the whole I thought the ordinary people whom one encounters in the streets, in public establishments, and by the lakes, looked in good condition and happy. They compared more than favourably with the ordinary people of other countries I had visited. Contradictory statistics are presented; and on them I will not pronounce. Whether Germany is rich or poor has been made a matter of political opinion. But there are now no signs of poverty. The workers may be poorly paid but they are for the most part neat and well nourished. The middle classes seem to have recovered from the terrible hardships which they in particular experienced; and they drink their beer and listen to the bands with a contented air. As for the classes who are bent on making money, they promote bigger enterprises than ever.

III. ARISTOCRACY

AND what of the aristocracy? I will give the views of one of them. He is a celebrated member of the old German aristocracy and an ardent Roman Catholic. Most of his money was lost in the period of inflation; and he then turned to journalism for a living. His opinions, extremely interesting, show something of the attitude of the intellectual nobility that has been financially ruined.

"We aristocrats," he said—and he called himself an aristocrat simply, naturally, without arrogance, without pride—"we aristocrats have a duty to perform. It does not, in the ultimate sense, in the least matter whether we are rich or poor. It does not in the least matter what opinions we hold. If we are faithful to our mission, if we are not degenerate, we must continue to be the leaders of Germany.

"That is the function of nobility—to supply leaders. We supplied leaders under the Empire, and we must supply leaders under the Republic. It is of no importance that the social world has been broken up, that there are no more petty courts, and no great court at Potsdam. In so far as the German nobility confined itself to social functions, or cared anything for social functions, it was wasting its time, and the time of the German people. It was betraying its essential duty."

He put down his knife and fork, leaned back in his chair, and thought a moment: "No, even as leaders of the social world, the German nobility was not false to itself. Aristocracy is leadership. Leadership of what?" He waved his hand. "Anything and everything. That is not the point. It may be an inferior form of leadership, perhaps, merely to lead the fashion, to lead in manners, but nevertheless leadership it is. And leadership for leadership's sake is worth while. . . .

"Those of us who take ourselves seriously, who consider our historic past, are quite undisturbed at the rise of democracy and at our own changed position. We must still lead. The circumstances are not the same, but our rôle is unaltered. I do not ask whether a member of the old nobility is now a Nationalist or a Socialist, or even a Communist. I shall myself fight the Communists and the Socialists; but I shall respect an aristocratic Communist who looks upon himself as a leader. . . . We must put ourselves at the head of democracy. If you examine the lists of leaders, in all domains, you will find that the German aristocracy worthily takes its place. It has not forgotten its traditions. On the contrary, it is now freer to fulfil them. It has never considered itself to be the prop of Monarchy, it has always represented the people, in opposition, when need arose, to the Monarchy. Indeed, as I think, we were becoming too subservient, we were forgetting to be leaders in the days of the Kaiser. Now we have our opportunity once more."

There was, I felt, something typical of the German mind in this claim—in the demonstration of earnestness, in the consciousness of duty, in the assertion of purpose; but I protested that though it were true that the most aristocratic names are to be found in the administrative and diplomatic services, in the press, in the professions, in politics, nevertheless it would appear that the Herr Professor dominates German life as he has always done. We scrutinised the names of the existing Government, and we discovered that Ministers, and Directors of Departments, who possessed the title of Doctor, numbered at least twenty.

He agreed that this, too, was characteristic: "The German people," he said, "have always had the highest regard for learning. They worship culture. In some respects this is bad, for learning in itself is apt to produce a stiff kind of mind, entirely unpractical, divorced from the realities of life. It is curious that we should have won a reputation for realism, when we are, and have always been, on the one hand romantic, and on the other hand doctor-ridden. But every country is full of such contradictions. Thus the United States is described as a nation of hard-headed businessmen, but it is perpetually swayed by sentimental considerations, it is moved by ideals. Thus Great Britain is at once commercial and poetical. Thus France is at the same

time logical and fantastic. There does exist a sense of realism in
the German people, but there also exists a veneration for
scholarship which is utterly remote from reality. The German
will work unstintedly, he will die heroically, for the sake of
some external thing which materially should not affect him,
for some external abstract idea in which he can have no selfish
interest. At heart every German is a pedagogue and a pedant:
this explains his stupidity and his intelligence, his gracelessness
and his courage.

"But if Germany is to be led by the scholars, it is incumbent
upon us aristocrats to be the leaders of the scholars."

Another observation which he made which struck me as
having much validity was this: "The Germans are interested in
every member of their own race. The French are interested only
in the soil of France. That is a vital distinction."

Certainly it is true that the French cannot bear to lose territorial acquisitions. If a parcel of land has belonged to them,
they will never rest until it comes back to them. It does not in
the least matter whether it is inhabited by Frenchmen or not.
Take the case of Alsace. In spite of the French demand for the
return of Alsace, and French enthusiasm on its return, the
majority of Frenchmen to-day, in confidential mood, will admit
that the Alsatians are not French in the same sense as the men
of the Midi, or the men of Normandy. But they *belong* to
France, and after 1870 the desire which burned in the breast
of every patriot was the reattachment of Alsace to France.

Were Strasburg to be peopled by a colony of Chinese, it
would still be French; for the French live under the old Roman
law of property. This explains the rapid assimilation of foreigners by France—a phenomenon that has been frequently
remarked upon. Poles and Italians, Spaniards and Czecho-Slovakians are welcomed. They are freely admitted into the French
family. They soon become more French than the French. They
never feel themselves to be a minority, because they are not
kept apart from the rest of the community. Such an attitude
facilitates their absorption. I have often seen in the Chamber
black deputies from France's oversea possessions arm-in-arm
with white deputies. The coloured men would be shocked at the
suggestion that they are not true Frenchmen, while the white
deputies would be equally shocked were it suggested that their
black brethren are different from themselves. The colour line
is not drawn in France because the only French test of nation-

ality is the occupation of French soil. That is why France is the most hospitable country in the world. A Frenchman could live all his life in England and never be recognised as English; but it is impossible to live long in France without acquiring something of the French spirit. For the French, the Frenchman abroad is an anomaly. He is queer and inexplicable. He is not French unless he is on French soil. The French expatriate, and even the French traveller, is looked at askance by his countrymen. Stress is laid by the French on the land.

Exactly the opposite sentiment prevails in Germany. Nobody can cease to be a German even though he becomes an American. Nobody can become a German by adoption. A few exceptions —such as Houston Stewart Chamberlain—may be cited; but they are so rare that they cannot invalidate the rule. Germany, for special reasons, may have proceeded to conquer other lands, but it has never succeeded in making Germans of alien populations. The Poles, for instance, under Germany, remained Poles. Partly this may have been by reason of the Polish temperament, but chiefly it was by reason of the inability of the German to accept the Pole as a compatriot. Frenchmen could accept the Pole as a compatriot, but Germans never. Racial feeling is greater than territorial feeling. It follows that the territorial losses of Germany in the peace-making would not in themselves trouble Germany overmuch. It could, if that were all, forget its humiliation. It could, from the economic viewpoint, be content with suitable contractual arrangements. Germany will never brood over Alsace as France brooded over Alsace. The soil may be necessary as a means, but it is not an end. The French peasant has a veritable passion for the soil; and the French nation has a veritable passion for territory. But the German is essentially interested only in his brother-Germans.

In his brother-Germans, however, he is irrevocably interested. Their sorrows are his sorrows, their joys are his joys. He yearns over them when they are forced under a foreign yoke. He will never be disinterested in their fate. If there is a German minority in Poland, Germany will always remember that minority. It will always champion the cause of that minority. The Fatherland is an expression that brings tears to the eyes of the sentimental German, but were he to analyse his sentiments he would discover that he is not thinking of the Fatherland at all, but of his fellow-Germans. His conception of Germany is more human than is the Frenchman's conception of France. The

Frenchman glorifies an imaginary personage whom he calls France. The German has a vision, not of an imaginary entity, but of individual Germans.

I remember Norman Angell's telling me of his travels in South America. Everybody spoke Spanish and Angell had difficulty in making himself understood. In a restaurant he exclaimed: "Can nobody here speak French or English?" Instantly a husky negro stepped forward and said: "Moi, je parle Français!"

Angell looked at him in some astonishment. "How do you come to speak French?" he asked.

And the negro drawing himself up proudly, beat himself upon the breast and declared: "Mais je suis Français—pur sang!" (I am a Frenchman of the purest blood.)

No Frenchman would see the point of this joke. Of course the negro, born in some far-off French island, would, despite his colour, be, for the French, of pure French blood. But no German—and probably no Englishman—would accept a negro born in a German or English colony as an equal, sharing in blood nationality. The claim would be preposterous and comical.

Germany, then, is concerned not with territorial possessions, but with spiritual affinities. In this respect the German is very like the Jew—and indeed Jewish blood has mingled freely with German blood. For the German, as for the Jew, it is not the country that counts but the race. Here is, I think, the key to Germany's relations with other peoples; and in this post-war period, the racial element of some of the gravest problems is the most important.

IV. MONARCHY

HERE is a conversation which I heard between a Monarchist and a Republican in Germany:

MONARCHIST: Germany has need of a supreme chief. That is why I am a Monarchist.

REPUBLICAN: But precisely by the reëstablishment of Monarchy will Germany be deprived of a supreme chief.

MONARCHIST: I do not understand. Everybody would look up to a King.

REPUBLICAN: Which King?

MONARCHIST: Why *the* King, of course.

REPUBLICAN: Then you want only one King?

MONARCHIST: Certainly.

REPUBLICAN: Why? There are a great many Kings who, according to the hereditary principle, have a right to reign over different parts of Germany. If you refuse any one of them his right, then you are unfairly discriminating. If you choose only one, then you are adopting the elective principle; and if you adopt the elective principle it is simpler to have a President. Do you want one King or a hundred Kings? Do you want German unity or petty provincialism? The defeat overturned the German thrones, but they were already crumbling. They were in contradiction to the modern evolution of Germany. Impossible to get rid of some of them, without getting rid of all of them! The war precipitated matters, but in any event Monarchism was doomed in Germany—doomed by the march of Germany towards political and economic unity.

To this speech the Monarchist had no answer ready, and I doubt whether he could have found a satisfactory reply. The Republic is probably stable because the Monarchical State had become unworkable. The failure of the Kapp Putsch was the last shot of the *ancien régime*.

There is neither an aggressive Royalist movement nor a Royalist press in Germany to-day. There are those who are in favour of changing the Constitution, but they would not over-throw the Republic. They point to the confusion of parties in the Reichstag, asserting with some apparent reason that Par-liamentarism produces chaos; they would therefore weaken the power of Parliament, but they would strengthen the power of the President. It is curious to note how history repeats itself: the history of the Third Republic in France strangely resembles the current history of Germany. Certainly the German, like the French Parliament, is defective; but the French Republic has lasted without substantial alteration. French attempts to increase Presidential powers have failed as German attempts will probably fail.

Howard Seipen, who is himself a German by birth though his mother is English, and who has lived long in the United States, is especially competent to judge German thought. He has been for some years the Berlin correspondent of the Chris-tian Science Monitor. To him I am greatly indebted in many ways. In substance he repeated to me in our long conversations this opinion: "The Germans are forgetting their former rulers. They hardly know what has become of the Kings and Princes.

They have no feeling either for or against the deposed Monarchs. Their indifference is absolutely damning.

"The German people fully understand that a restoration of the Monarchy at the present time would only complicate their foreign political problems. It is also quite obvious that the German people are enjoying self-government. To them it is a highly interesting experiment.

"Respect for the dynasty was greatly shaken by the behaviour of the Kaiser at the end of the war, by the continual exposure, in the press, in books, and on the stage, of the failings of the old royal families. In short, the glamour of the Monarchy has disappeared.

"The Kaiser's flight to Holland dealt confidence in the throne the first serious blow. The man for whom Germans had fought fled when the hour of trial came. Had he joined the soldiers in the trenches, his dynasty might have been saved; had he returned quietly to his country, no harm would have been done him."

Apart from these considerations, there could be no general agreement on a candidate for the throne. The ex-Kaiser and the Crown Prince cannot even be thought of. But what of the eldest son of the Crown Prince? There is nothing against him—except that he is a Hohenzollern; but there is no reason whatever why South Germany—particularly Bavaria—should consent again to come under the rule of a Hohenzollern. The House of Wittelsbach, which reigned over Bavaria, is equally impossible from the North German viewpoint. Moreover, some day Austria will probably join the Reich, and the Austrians could hardly accept a German Emperor.

The former rulers of Germany have wisely kept out of politics with the exception of Prince Rupprecht of Bavaria. Most of them live quietly, some of them in relative poverty, on their estates. The Crown Prince mingles with the fashionable society of Berlin, but he has no special privileges and comes and goes unnoticed.

Seipen told me—and this struck me as an admirable illustration of the complete change that has come over Germany—that on more than one occasion he has observed the Crown Prince driving his vivid crimson car in the West End of Berlin, stopping at a crossing in a cluster of automobiles, and waiting patiently for the traffic signal to give him passage.

Imagine how obsequiously the traffic controllers would have kept the road free for him ten years ago!

As for the younger princes, some of them travel in third-class carriages of suburban trains, unhonoured and uncheered. The Kaiser might have been a tragic figure. He has in fact become a figure of fun. Despite Allied threats to hang him, or at least to try him for his provocation and his conduct of the war (the elections in England were won by Mr. Lloyd George with the slogan of "Hang the Kaiser!") he was left unmolested to take up his residence at Doorn, in Holland, where he remarried, amused himself like Mr. Gladstone in chopping down trees, and received courtiers and delegations of Monarchists. When I was in Czecho-Slovakia, the Editor of a German newspaper showed me with loud chuckles a message of thanks from the Kaiser. "I sent him," he told me, "in the name of the Monarchists of Czecho-Slovakia, congratulations on his birthday, and an expression of our desire for his speedy restoration." The Editor continued to chuckle. I begged him to explain the joke.

"But it is really amusing," he assured me; and he repeated that, as secretary of the Czecho-Slovakian Monarchists, he had informed Wilhelm of his party's hope that the Kaiser would again mount the steps of his throne and reign at Potsdam.

"It is the best farce since the War," he asserted. "And that is the man who called himself an Emperor!"

A light began to break in. "Ah, it was a hoax? Who are the Czecho-Slovakian Monarchists?"

He condescended to explain between his chuckles: "Of course there is no such party. Yet the Kaiser took my communication seriously and sent me this solemn reply! Just imagine a man so ill-informed! Just imagine a man who aspires to the government of a people so light-headed as to make no inquiries about his correspondents! He had only to pick up a work of reference." I thought the Editor, who was chuckling himself into a condition of apoplexy, would have died of merriment. Certainly the joke is a poor one; but it does somehow illustrate the essential frivolousness of the old Kaiser.

I remember, too, the confidences of the people of Spa soon after the war ended. At Spa, in Belgium, the Kaiser had taken up his quarters with his chief officers. The little town had no complaints to make about his residence, the inhabitants were well treated, and the Kaiser's entourage spent money freely. But the impression Wilhelm produced was not that of a military commander; in perfect safety, he lived theatrically, surrounded by an atmosphere of fêtes, while his people starved and faced the guns of the Allies.

When Ludendorff's offensive failed in 1918, and peace proposals were made by Prince Max of Baden, President Wilson declared that it was indispensable for the Allies to know beyond a peradventure with whom they were dealing. Was it with the Kaiser and Ludendorff, or was it with the German people? Ludendorff resigned, and his subsequent behaviour proved him to be a scatter-brained man. Hindenburg, the German idol, whose wooden effigy the Germans had decorated with nails, stuck to his post in defeat as in triumph; and this steadfastness was afterwards remembered with gratitude by the German people. Prince Max asked Erzberger, who had drawn up a German scheme for a League of Nations, and General Winterfeld, formerly military attaché at Paris, to represent Germany at a rendezvous granted by Foch in the Forest of Compiègne; there the terms of Armistice were handed to them, to be accepted or rejected by eleven o'clock on the morning of November 11. The next day a Republic was proclaimed in Berlin, and seized by panic, the Kaiser abdicated, and took refuge in Holland. That cowardly flight will never be forgiven him. It would be difficult to discover in the whole of Germany, wholehearted partisans, except among princes and courtiers, of the once all-powerful chief. He is amply provided with money—indeed it is reckoned that he is richer than any other German—and he can be left without pity in his Dutch mansion amid the ruins of his Weltpolitik.

V. THE REVOLUTION

THERE was no general and deliberate intention of setting up a Republic. The Monarchy overthrew itself. The Germans were too well disciplined, too temperamentally placid, too wedded to tradition, to premeditate rebellion. But the situation had become impossible, and the reaction was automatic. Until the last months of the war public confidence was not shattered. Then came the Austrian collapse, the capitulation of Bulgaria, the Government's appeal to America, the inevitability of defeat —and the Kaiser's desertion. The nation was stunned, and it looked helplessly on. In the German fleet, at the end of October, there was a mutiny; the example of Russia was contagious;

the red flag was hoisted; workmen's and soldiers' councils were formed, and in the early days of November they spread from Hamburg to Frankfurt. All this was spontaneous and uninspired. It was the natural result of circumstances. There was absolutely no resistance.

In Bavaria, Kurt Eisner, a Jew of great learning and culture, holding pacifist and Socialist views, had, despite imprisonment and persecution, boldly proclaimed his abhorrence of war, and had organised the local democratic forces. Eisner has always appeared to me a true hero with lofty ideals; nobody in the Allied countries uttered with more earnestness the cry for peace, the affirmation of the confraternity of peoples. I place him in my gallery of noble figures beside President Wilson.

The moderate Socialists had for leaders Ebert and Scheidemann, who called on Prince Max to resign from the Chancellorship. Max gave way to Ebert, who, after the new Constitution was promulgated in 1919, became the first President of the German Republic.

Ebert was a working man—a harness-maker and the son of a tailor. He furnishes an example out of many in recent years of men who from the humblest origin have attained the topmost height of power. We are no longer expected to resign ourselves to the station to which it has pleased God to call us. As President he was a target for the caricaturists; for he was portly and plump, homely in his habits, shrinking from pomp and ceremony of any sort. He attracted little attention to himself after his election. Opinions differ as to the rôle played by the former harness-maker; for the revolutionary Socialist, in the teeth of his political philosophy, strained his energies to the establishment of law and order. During the War he had given his allegiance to the Government—as indeed did the Socialists in all countries. He publicly defended German militarism; he supported unrestricted submarine warfare. Patriotism triumphed over doctrine; and the successor of Bebel was first a German. When Communism threatened his country, Ebert, the Socialist President, was implacable. It is significant that all the rulers of Germany, since the Kaiser ran away, whether they belong to the Left or to the Right, have been chiefly concerned with the problem of redisciplining Germany. Ebert was just as authoritative, just as bent on the peaceful unity of Germany, as his successor Von Hindenburg.

Historically, a man like Ebert was needed. He stood between

the Communists and the Monarchists. Universal discontent might have produced a real social revolution, had there not been men like Ebert who had professed to be social revolutionaries. When he took office he made a characteristic declaration: "Fellow citizens: The Chancellor, with the assent of all his Ministers, has transferred to me the direction of affairs. I shall form a Government in association with the parties. The new Government will be a People's Government. Its aim must be to bring peace to the German people as quickly as possible, and to safeguard the freedom which it has won. Fellow citizens, I implore you to preserve tranquillity and order."

Karl Liebknecht (who had during the war circulated secret letters signed Spartacus) and Rosa Luxemburg stirred up discontent. They were sincere, and in their devotion to an ideal even admirable, but their violent opposition to the Government was unfortunately supported by all the ill-tempered elements of the great city—hot-heads and criminals who thought lightly of bloodshed. There were street clashes; there was a siege of the royal stables where armed sailors had taken refuge; the troops fired on the mob and many were killed.

The most distressing incident was the murder of Liebknecht and Rosa Luxemburg. They were captured; they underwent a preliminary examination; they were placed in a motor-car to be taken to prison. In the Tiergarten, the automobile came to a standstill. Liebknecht was dragged out and shot in cold blood. Rosa Luxemburg was likewise shot and her body thrown into a canal.

In spite of pushes from the Left and the Right, a bourgeois Republic was established by the Weimar Assembly. The Constitution was ably drawn up. Germany had existed on a federal basis, and the constituent States had enjoyed limited autonomy; they had kept their own sovereigns. Nevertheless it was Prussia who, chiefly by dynastic leadership, became the centre of power. With the abolition of the hereditary principle, Prussian predominance should have been diminished; but on the other hand, by the withdrawal of the individual rights of the Southern States, a more highly centralised government was formed with its seat in Berlin. Republicanism was imposed not only on the German Federation, but on each separate State. Federal law was proclaimed superior to State law. The Reich has the power of altering the boundaries of States. The Reich imposes direct taxation; it controls the railways, the posts, and the telegraph.

In short, the States are mere provinces; and never was Germany such a united country under the Empire as it is under the Republic. Foreign affairs and military organisation are of course the exclusive domain of the Federal authorities. In such matters as education and land laws, the Federation lays down a minimum standard for the States. Generally, this unification is welcomed, and should certainly improve the economic standing of Germany. Bavaria, it is true, talks of separatism, but not seriously.

The President, under the Weimar Constitution, is elected by the people for seven years; and although he has nominally large powers his decrees must be countersigned by a competent Minister. Presidents who are thus controlled may become mere irresponsible figure-heads as in France; but the popular method of election helps to make the German President, if he has a strong personality, an effective factor in political life. The Chancellor whom he appoints must have the confidence of the Reichstag—a body of deputies elected under a scheme of proportional representation by all men and women above the age of twenty. The Reichsrat is a small body representing the different States. Its function is chiefly consultative. There is, besides, a Federal Economic Council, such as Bismarck vainly tried to create. It is composed of groups of members representing every aspect of economic life. It has proved its worth in examining government proposals, initiating laws, drawing up reports, and bringing about a remarkable *rapprochement* of employers and workers.

VI. SOCIALISM

I HAVE, as an observer, always derived pleasure from the spectacle of the poacher turning policeman. The conversion is so thorough; the policeman hits so hard. When I was a boy, already interested in social questions, it was taken for granted that Socialism was revolutionary. This did not mean that Socialists would necessarily provoke a Revolution; but certainly they would not neglect the opportunity which might be offered by social upheavals. But when I became a man I found that all the Socialists whom I knew set themselves up as the guardians of the existing society. Since the war there are no anti-Communists, no anti-Revolutionaries, so fierce as the Socialists. They have become respectable and respected. They make the world safe for capitalism.

To Gustave Noske, therefore, I must devote a few paragraphs. No Monarchist or Militarist could have had a harder fist than his. He smote, without mercy, all who tried to make the Revolution social as well as political. He stood there with the guns he had captured from the flying Kaiser and the beaten Junkers; and, fearing the force of the popular movement, he turned them on the crowd. Republican Germany was only to be another edition of the old Germany. Nothing was to be changed except persons. The same forces which had carried Noske to power had now to be fought by Noske. Noske fought them without pity, and thus earned the gratitude of the Entente.

One must admire a "strong" man, a man who has the courage of his convictions, no matter what those convictions may be, no matter what methods he adopts. He is to be preferred to a man of infinitely finer character who is feeble and vacillating. Noske, rightly or wrongly, considered the wave of revolution and he decided that it should come no further. He bade it stop; and as political Canutes are often successful, the wave reddened and stopped. When you throw blood on troubled water it produces the same effect as oil. The blood of the Spartacists, of Karl Liebknecht, and of Rosa Luxemburg, of wise, gentle, old Kurt Eisner, tinged the roaring sea. Noske is the man who must bear the greatest share of responsibility for the stifling of the German Revolution. He was coldly ferocious in manner; he pronounced, with a placid air, the most deadly threats. He certainly was neither a blusterer nor a braggart: he adjusted his glasses quite calmly and announced that inexorable measures would be taken against revolutionaries. Once he was in power it was blasphemy to challenge him.

It must be admitted that had it not been for Noske, Germany would have gone to pieces. All institutions were collapsing with the collapse of the throne. The doctrine of defeatism had been preached in every country during the War, because in a country defeated and in distress any energetic section of the people armed with definite ideas may easily become the masters. Now Noske should have believed that the only war which matters is the class war. But he, like the majority of German Socialists, and of British and French Socialists, had merely adopted a convenient party designation, and had not found the strange fanatic faith which moved Liebknecht. Noske was another Kaiser. He might in other circumstances have been a more efficient and ruthless Wilhelm II.

There had been a profound change in the *moral* of the people. If a good face was put upon things, and troops returned with a certain pride in their port, everybody who was in Germany at that time will testify that the German people were thoroughly cured of militarism and its pomps and glories. They threw themselves on the mercy of the Allies who promised that their treatment of a democratic people would be very different from that reserved for a Kaiser-ridden people. Mr. Lloyd George declared again and again, often in my hearing, that the Germans were crushed in spirit and repentant. Yet the treaty-makers drew no distinction between the defeated people and their runaway rulers. The full weight of a repressive policy fell upon them; they were not helped and encouraged; everything was done to embitter them; for six months after the Armistice, without the smallest reason, the blockade of starving Germany was maintained.

Noske, having smashed the serious Socialists, having alienated the Left, was obliged to make a pact with the Right. The harder he struck, the more he was thrown towards the Monarchists and the Militarists. Having offended all the advanced elements in Germany he had to seek support in reactionary quarters. Gradually he found himself thrust into the arms of the men of the *ancien régime*.

Thus if Noske represents a necessary stage in the German Revolution and if the Allies owe him thanks for having saved Germany from complete chaos, the fatal course of events was that Noske, the Socialist who had fought the Socialists, should become the Nationalist upon whom the Military Party depended.

He it was who kept in being large armies which were not permitted by the Peace Treaty. He it was who obtained the consent of the Allies—always frightened by the Bolshevik scarecrow and forgetful of the peril of a counter-revolution—to this course. He it was who constituted all sorts of camouflaged forces. He it was who gave some sort of justification to the highest expectations of a glorious *revanche*. Germany was not disarmed; and many complications subsequently arose from the Allied complaisance at this moment.

Then the Right made its bid for power. He saw the blow coming, but it was useless to turn to the Left. He did indirectly appeal to the Allies. Some of the Allied representatives informed their Governments of the *coup d'état* that was preparing. But

what was to be done? It was too late. Noske in his turn fled.
But then happened what often happens: the blow from the
Right was the signal for a blow from the Left. The reaction
brought about a second uprising of the people, who had tolerated Noske and his cannons, but would have none of Von Kapp
and the nebulous figures which led him from behind.

All these alarums and excursions are ancient history; Germany has settled down. But it has not settled down to Socialism.
When the test came, the Socialists resisted Socialism (which,
as it was understood, is probably impracticable in any event)
and they rebuilt Germany on the old pattern. Nothing, in the
constitution of society, has profoundly changed; it is not the
substitution of one set of rulers for another that has much
importance. After this proof of the impotence of Socialism to
apply its teaching, how is it that Socialism has not been discredited in the new Europe? Why have the Socialist parties
made immense strides in every country? The answer is that
it is precisely because Socialism, as previously understood, is
dead, and Socialists dressed in silk stockings and knee-breeches
attend Court ceremonies in Monarchical countries, and arm
themselves in defence of the principle of property in other
countries, and never dream of going to prison as they did a few
years ago, and act when they are in office very much like Conservatives, and number titled persons and industrial magnates
in their ranks, that the old fear of orthodox persons has vanished; and a Socialist Government is a perfectly natural and
unexciting alternative to a Reactionary Government. In short,
Socialism, or Labourism, has lost any specific meaning. It is less
dangerous, from the point of view of the ordinary citizen
without ideas or ideals, than was the old Liberalism.

And if this transformation was not determined by Noske,
I hold that he best symbolises the transformation and helps us
to realise it. Therefore he is a key-figure in the new Europe.

VII. HERMANN MÜLLER

THE Peace Conference was proceeding in Paris. To those days
I devoted a little book; and I will not repeat my impressions
here. I will merely tell one story which illustrates how useless
are the precautions taken to exclude unauthorised persons from
the most important international gatherings.

The first plenary session was held at the Quai d'Orsay. There were gathered the chief political personages of all the belligerents. President Poincaré headed the Assembly; and Mr. Wilson, Mr. Lloyd George and equivalent representatives of each nation, together with Foch and other military men, were collected in one little crowded room. A single bombshell would have wiped out the leaders of the world. . . .

The gates were guarded by soldiers and policemen; and there were numerous international detectives. Every care was taken to admit only those who were strictly entitled to be present.

I had received my card of admission; but through some mischance as I approached the files of guardians at the Quai d'Orsay I found myself ticketless. It was too late to go home to search for it. What was to be done? I could not miss the ceremony. . . . It amused me to see whether I could enter without ticket. The afternoon was bitterly cold; snow was falling. I was wearing a heavy fur coat—and I have often noticed that a fur coat is taken as an external mark of the importance of its wearer. I boldly passed through the rows of guardians. At last a hand was stretched out to stop me. I brushed it aside and continued on my way. A second attempt to intercept me was more insistent; but I nevertheless pushed on. Finally I was informed that I could not proceed without producing my card.

"And do you ask me," I said sternly, "to unbutton my coat in this weather?"

I cannot account for the effect of this absurd speech; but certain it is that the guardian fell back nonplussed; he was not sure of himself; and I went ahead, before he could recover his presence of mind, sufficiently far to greet one of the organisers of the ceremony on the steps of the Foreign Office.

Doubtless it might not have happened like that had I not possessed an easy conscience as to the ultimate result, and had I not known the organiser on the Foreign Office steps. Yet I cannot help wondering how far brazenness will carry one. If I *had* been a bomb-thrower would it have carried me into the *Salle de l'Horloge?*

The most pathetic figure at the Peace Conference was that of Hermann Müller, then an obscure politician. He appeared on the scene only at Versailles. As he stepped forward to append his signature to the Treaty I examined him with curiosity. He was pale and agitated. There he was under the hostile gaze of the victorious Allied plenipotentiaries—who had drawn up

the Treaty without the smallest consultation of the principal
party—signing a document which registered the punishment
of the Fatherland. It was lamentable, but while feeling sorry
I had some admiration for him.

It was in this same hall—the *Galerie des Glaces*—that the
German Empire had been proclaimed nearly fifty years before.
Now the House of Hohenzollern, which had reached its peak,
was down in the dust. France, which had been defeated, was
victorious; and Germany, which had been victorious, was defeated. The whirligig of time had brought its revenges. The
wheel had turned full circle. How foolish seemed these fluctuations of military fortune! . . .

And how small and humble was the German plenipotentiary
who, hitherto almost unknown, volunteered to perform a necessary act from which older politicians shrank. His services were
to be rewarded, for thereafter he took his rank among German
statesmen. He has since been twice Chancellor, and as I write,
in 1929, he occupies that post.

I saw him afterwards in his hotel. He declared that Germany,
having been compelled to sign the Treaty, would honour its
signature. . . .

Müller has never shone as a remarkable statesman. He struck
me as honest but lacking in outstanding qualities. Do we sufficiently reflect that there is, after all, a high place in life for
mediocrity? The instincts of the ordinary man, which make
him look askance at the extraordinary man, are, perhaps, fairly
sound. Herr Müller saved Germany, after the conspicuous men
had made a sad mess of things.

The lesson may be a hard one for politicians who believe they
possess genius, but it is necessary that they should learn it:
exceptional cleverness and exceptional force, whether real or
imaginary, are dangerous attributes of a statesman, and may
be disastrous for the nation. One has only to cast one's eyes
around Europe to recognise what a nuisance are the Napoleons
who are always planning wonderful expeditions which ultimately fail, what a menace to the happiness of a country are its
Machiavellis who entangle it in all kinds of complications, what
doubtful blessings flow from Cæsarism! There are moments
when dazzling ability does not hurt overmuch, when it may
even be of value to a community. Generally, however, the plain
citizen is right to beware of brilliancy. If the brilliancy is false,

it is bad enough and may land us in trouble that stupidity would have avoided. If it is genuine—it may be fatal. The temptation is strong upon me to mention names and to give historical and contemporary instances of the incalculable harm wrought to the world by a little excess of grey matter. But that would involve me in all sorts of debatable judgments. . . .

Wilhelm and Noske successively plunged Germany into misery. On each occasion it was Müller, the quiet, ordinary, painstaking, honest politician who saved his country.

Is it not true, not only that the happiest nation is that which has no history, but also—and this is only expressing the same idea in other words—that the happiest nation is that which has no great men?

The great men who had been responsible for Germany's downfall all excused themselves in one way or another when the Treaty of Versailles had to be signed. The great man is one who will not perform the humble and humiliating tasks which his greatness has rendered necessary. Some of them had flown, others were sulking in their tents, and even Brockdorff-Rantzau guarded his greatness by making a *beau geste* of protestation and catching a train which would take him via Berlin into History. Then it was that Herr Müller, that is to say the average man, came forward to do the dirty work, to perform the thankless business for which neither his contemporaries nor posterity will give him glory.

At San Remo, I remember, Mr. Lloyd George did not cease to complain that the German statesmen in power were not wizards. According to his view, what Germany was suffering from was not so much lack of food, not so much lack of *moral,* not so much lack of raw materials and man-power, as lack of exceptional statesmen. "That is the trouble," he said over and over again, "that we have no really big man with whom to deal." Mr. Lloyd George did not like mediocrity in an opponent. Apparently he desired to be pitted against a Bismarck. You cannot expect a Jack Dempsey of the political prize-ring to meet the first-comer. Müller was not of the same calibre. Yet Müller returned, respected by the German people, when Lloyd George had long been in eclipse.

For the good governance of a nation it is not a champion, full of tricks, able to dodge uppercuts and slip under straight lefts, or stand doggedly exchanging blows, who is wanted. It

is simply a straightforward average man who can be trusted
to do his best. The German people, as represented by Müller,
were desirous only of getting to work, of obtaining enough
to eat, and of peacefully paying. The official reports from Germany indicated that the German people had not enough to eat.
While scientists tell us that 3,200 calories are required for the
sustenance of the human frame, the Germans were, after the
War, obtaining something like 1,400!

The primary business of a statesman is not to be agile, to be
dexterous, to be a wonderful orator, to be an unseizable diplomatist. His primary business is to be conscientious, industrious,
reliable—to possess, in short, those qualities of mediocrity which
nimbler spirits despise.

VIII. LUDENDORFF AND HINDENBURG

IF IT were the fashion to write parallel lives, those of Ludendorff and Hindenburg would furnish a rare theme. They
were the two outstanding military men on the German side;
and their talent was at least as great as any displayed on the
Allied side; but afterwards very different 'were their lots.
Ludendorff made himself ridiculous; Hindenburg became, in
spite of ill-fortune, the idol of the German people. . . .

General Erich Von Ludendorff comes from the Polish marshes
—from Posnania, which is now Polish soil again. When he was
only seventeen he began his army career, and he rapidly rose
in rank. The German plans for the mobilisation of the German
armies were in part his work. When Hindenburg became Chief
of the German General Staff he sent for Ludendorff, his old
associate, of whose ability he had the highest opinion, and appointed him First Quartermaster-General, second in authority
to himself. The brilliant strategy of Ludendorff will, I suppose,
be admitted by all impartial military students, though his im-
petuosity often placed him in perilous situations. It must be
remembered that Germany was fighting against time as well as
against the Allies, and the failures and successes of Ludendorff
are to be judged in accordance with this fact. In the end time
beat Ludendorff; and the "invincible" commander collapsed.
He took refuge in Bavaria. He meddled with politics. He was
involved in a farcical Monarchist "putsch," and was let off
lightly. He quarrelled with his fellow-generals, with the Cath-

olic clergy of Bavaria, with his oldest friends; and devising new and impossible parties he floundered more and more hopelessly. . . . In the end he was utterly discredited. He meant nothing to anybody—except to a few fanatics who believe with him that there is an international conspiracy of Jews, Jesuits, and Freemasons, (what a combination!) to obtain control of the world.

Let me give an example of the miserable imbecilities which Ludendorff finally uttered—for at least they are amusing.

"These super-national powers (Jews, Jesuits, and Freemasons) are organising a new world war against Russia, in which the fighting forces of the Germans, together with the Poles and the Rumanians, will be expected to intervene with the battle-cry of 'Down with Bolshevism!' Actually it is hoped that a further enslavement of Russians and Germans will be achieved through the spilling of their blood.

"A crusade is being conducted against unbelievers in Russia, but Jesuit orders still aim to establish the Roman Church's power over Russia. A murderous plot for the destruction of England is being hatched for the future, because the English have not yet submitted to the Pope.

"The Anglo-Saxon Powers will slaughter each other in a world war after the Russians and Germans have done likewise. Jewish-American billionaires, through a big American loan to the Soviet Union, intend to lend a new impetus to a world revolution, especially in England. These are fiendish plans." They are indeed!

Is it not lamentable? The Monarchist cause was irretrievably lost because it was represented by such men.

But the other outstanding warrior, Marshal Paul Von Hindenburg, after the débâcle displayed dignity and commonsense; and although he was approaching his eightieth birthday, the man into whose gigantic wooden effigy the Germans had driven nails, was drafted four years ago as President of the Republic. Those who feared the recrudescence of Monarchy thought his election an ominous sign. They were mistaken. The advent of Hindenburg was a proof that Monarchy is dead.

If Hindenburg could accept the Republic—Hindenburg, of noble family, of the most Conservative traditions, of unblemished character—then everybody could accept the Republic. It was foolish to suggest that he might be false to his oath, that he might prepare the return of his former master. As an old soldier, his loyalty is beyond reproach or suspicion. From his oath he was released by the abdication of the Kaiser. When he took the oath to the Republic he could not, if he would, be a traitor to the Republic.

Hindenburg, sturdy, erect in spite of his years, with his rough-hewn head, his deeply-lined face, his upstanding hair, his full-curved moustache, looks exactly what he is—an intellectually stolid, unimaginative, simple-hearted old man. He has a profound sense of duty, is intensely religious. Though he served the Monarchy for threescore years, he is now as stalwart a Republican as may be found.

I think his is one of the noblest personalities in the post-war Europe. Those who thought they could use him as their tool were sadly duped. "We calculated that his lifelong convictions would help us," they confessed, "but there is no room in his head for more than one idea at a time; he actually takes his oath of office seriously."

In the Reichstag he stood in May, 1926, under the flag of the Republic—black, red, and gold—and at the behest of Loebe, the Socialist President of the Reichstag, swore fidelity to the Constitution. He meant it, and his official act was to appoint as his secretary the Socialist Meisner, who had served Ebert.

A day of dupes! It was not easy for the plotters to realise that this huge man, whose honest eyes shine under shaggy brows, was incapable of playing a double game. With Hindenburg as President the Republic was consolidated. The masses were persuaded that they could not be more Royalist than the supreme Royalist; while the classes could not boycott his receptions as they had boycotted those of Ebert.

In spite of his age he stood immobile for five hours at the review of the veterans of Tannenberg; he marched stiffly but steadily down the steps of the Reichstag building on Constitution Day; at a dozen other great ceremonies he aroused the enthusiasm of the people by his simple nobility—a stalwart old man, obviously moved by a sense of duty, obviously longing for privacy, clad in an old-fashioned coat and an outmoded tall hat.

His nephew—Herbert Von Hindenburg—drew an excellent pen-picture of the old man which I summarise: "One of his most striking traits is his imperturbable calm; it is not the apathy of age, for he has always possessed it; it is a quality of deliberation in his whole person; it shows in his utterance; in the gravity of his voice, the most profound bass voice I have ever heard; never does he speak loudly. He is far from being severe; his countenance is marked by sweetness and goodness; children have no fear of him—on the contrary they come to him with instinctive trust; then his wrinkled face lights up with a smile full of tenderness. . . . Literature, art, science, interest him only in so far as they serve the people; he appreciates sport, not in its record-breaking aspect, but as a means of fortifying the youth of the nation; in painting he likes battle-scenes provided the uniforms are correctly depicted; in music he prefers military marches and religious hymns; he goes to the theatre only on official occasions; laxity in modern manners and psychoanalytical teachings are disagreeable to him; but he never expresses censorious opinions, and he respects convictions which shock him. . . ." This is a good portrait of a man whose very limitations make him lovable.

From his autobiography I select these few self-revelatory sentences: "Both my parents endeavoured by suggestion and the development of the tenderer sides of human feeling to give us the best thing that parents can ever give—a confident belief in our Lord God and a boundless love for our Fatherland."

*   *   *   *   *

"Although I am little inclined to cosmopolitanism, I have always been free from prejudice towards other nations. . . ."

*   *   *   *   *

"In our new headquarters at Allenstein (after the battle of Tannenberg) I entered the church, close by the old castle of the Teutonic Knights, while divine service was being held. As the clergyman uttered his closing words, all those present, young soldiers as well as elderly Landsturm, sank to their knees under the overwhelming impression of their experiences. It was a worthy curtain to their heroic achievements. . . ."

*   *   *   *   *

"In the great war ledger the page on which the Russian losses were written has been torn out. No one knows the figures. Five or eight millions? . . . All we know is that sometimes in our battles with the Russians we had to remove the mounds of enemy corpses from before our trenches in order to get a clear field of fire against fresh assaulting waves. . . ."

*   *   *   *   *

"War does not stimulate, it demoralizes. And this war had a more demoralizing influence than any previous war. It destroyed not only bodies but souls."

IX. THE FALL OF THE MARK

GERMANY was moving towards a more democratic system before the war; and in particular it demanded Parliamentarism as it is understood in England and America. The war may have destroyed many moral values, but those who fought gained a clearer conception of political freedom. Germany was momentarily drawn towards Soviet principles (which are not necessarily practised in Russia) but Germany was too well organised, too well educated, and the middle classes were too strong, to permit the installation of Bolshevism. Naturally the Germans, long deprived of self-government, lacking in new leaders, had many lessons to learn. Their experiences were bitter, but in the school of disillusionment they are quickly attaining political maturity.

Among their bitter experiences was the catastrophic fall of the currency. It will continue to be the subject of debate whether this collapse was deliberately provoked. Doubtless more could have been done to discourage the flight from the mark. Doubtless there was, consciously or unconsciously, a desperate attempt to escape reparations at any price—even at the price of national bankruptcy. Psychological factors of this kind cannot be ignored; yet the Germans were indeed in wretched plight. They had no heart to struggle against the threatened ruin. It all seemed so hopeless. At Paris and at Versailles, and at a dozen casinos and holiday resorts in Europe, lounging in hotels, sitting in cafés, gossiping in salons, going through the whole ritual of what is called conferences, I had accompanied the statesmen and had seen injustice after injustice imposed on Germany. Germany lost the whole of its colonies. It was obliged to cede Alsace-Lorraine to France, and Eupen and Malmédy to Belgium. The Saar coal mines were given to France, though the Saar, on no possible ground, could be regarded as French; it is true that the actual territory, as distinct from the mines, was to be administered by the League of Nations for fifteen years, at the end of which a plebiscite was to determine its fate, and that Germany was then to have the option of repurchasing the mines. Luxemburg was with-

drawn from the Zollverein. The Left and the Right Banks of
the Rhine were demilitarised. Northern Sleswig was to vote
whether it should become Danish or German. Posen, West
Prussia, and Upper Silesia went to the Poles; Danzig was made
a free city within the Polish Customs Union; East Prussia was
cut off from Germany by the so-called Polish Corridor. Altogether Germany lost an eighth part of its territorial area—in
addition to its overseas Empire. Its army was cut down to 100,-
000 men; its navy was surrendered, its fortresses dismantled;
military aeroplanes and dirigibles were forbidden. Its economic
position was rendered precarious by the loss of the best coal
and iron lands, while France still claimed deliveries of coal on
account of reparations. The greater part of its mercantile
marine was taken over. The Rhineland was to be occupied by
alien troops for fifteen years. In addition, an enormous though
undefined indemnity was demanded. When, after many conferences, it was seen that Germany could not pay, the Ruhr
itself, the industrial centre of Germany, was invaded by French
troops.

No wonder, then, that the mark fell; and once panic set in,
it was impossible to stop its downward course until it became
utterly worthless. While it was falling it was impossible to keep
prices at the level of the mark, and one could spend a week
in the best hotels for the equivalent of a pound or a few dollars.
Men and women of wealth found themselves reduced to beg-
gary. An acquaintance of mine bought a fine historic castle
for less money than would be needed to buy a cheap motor-car;
and the bargain was hardly concluded when even this price was
insufficient to purchase a postage stamp. A few people were
wise enough to get out before the crash came. Among them
was Hermann Sudermann, whose earnings were placed in Prussian real estate; and Gerhart Hauptmann, who, immensely
rich, for his plays were sometimes running in as many as ten
theatres, was, as early as 1915, advised to put his money in a
Swiss bank. These were exceptions among the artists, who, for
the most part, were left penniless. I remember the case of a
famous actress who had retired with a comfortable little fortune of three hundred thousand marks. Anticipating an old
age of leisured ease, she could scarcely believe that her entire fortune was not enough to buy an evening newspaper. She had to
come out of her retirement, and, as her vogue had passed,
only by hard work could she contrive to make a mediocre

living. The middle classes generally were the hardest hit. They
were inexperienced in money matters; they had not foreseen
the catastrophe. There was, for example, a distinguished scholar
who was visited by a friend of mine at Christmas; the household
bestirred itself, and by dint of various shifts, served a little
cooked ham as a special treat for the Christmas meal.

It was impossible for my friend to refrain from remarking
on the circumstance when he was alone with the scholar. The
scholar shook his head. "That was the best we could do. It is
the first meat we have eaten for months. But we must not complain. There are others in far worse case. It is something to
have had a little Christmas feast."

And this was once a well-to-do German family, living large-
handedly! There were, as said the scholar, plenty of others
who were far worse off. Let it be remembered that, during the
war years, food was scarcer in Germany than in any other
belligerent country, that fats were particularly lacking, that
the nation was in a state of semi-starvation, that the Allies un-
accountably and unpardonably maintained the blockade after
the capitulation, with the result that hundreds of thousands
of non-combatants died and many others were permanently
weakened. Now once more hundreds of thousands of Germans could hardly obtain enough to eat. It is possible to imagine
that a few persons found it in their interest to accelerate the
fall of the mark. It is possible to imagine that some Machiavel-
lian mind saw in the ruin of Germany the possibility of Germany's resurrection—its private and public debts obliterated,
its financial past wiped out. But it is impossible to imagine that
the German people deliberately invited this tragic situation.
The lot of the worker was bad enough, for wages could not
keep pace with the vertiginous descent of the mark. Those,
however, who actually had work, were, of course, paid; and
though their earnings were small they could live from hand to
mouth. When Germany began to recover and the new mark,
thanks to the Dawes report, was created, still more difficult
times loomed ahead, for as wages and prices found their level,
unemployment increased.

I briefly touch upon this chapter in recent German history,
because it indicates that the German Republic has come
through a fiery furnace. It has been tested as the Empire was
never tested. If the Republic did not succumb to these trials,

either in the Communistic or the Monarchical sense, it is surely solidly built.

X. WAR LITERATURE

I AM convinced that Germany sincerely desires to take a leading place among the peace-loving nations. There may be difficulties with Poland, though the Locarno accords, which are popularly supposed to ensure peace only between France and Belgium, on the one hand, and Germany on the other, provide that there should be arbitration of any disputes that may arise on the Eastern frontiers. It is true that Germany has not definitely pledged itself—except of course by the Versailles Treaty, which was imposed upon it against its will—to regard the Eastern frontiers as permanently settled; but in several ways it has committed itself to peaceful methods of adjusting quarrels. The Locarno accords are not negligible, even as they apply to Poland. Germany's membership in the League of Nations, which implies the renunciation of aggressive warfare, is important, however much one may doubt the ultimate efficacy of the League. Germany was the first of all nations to subscribe unreservedly to the Kellogg Pact, which outlaws war as an instrument of national policy. Let those who will look upon these things as scraps of paper; it is almost unthinkable that Germany will tear up so many of them in defiance of the opinion of the world.

The truth is that Germany does everything thoroughly. War was one of its weapons, and it prepared and sharpened this weapon thoroughly. Peace is now one of its weapons, and it will prepare and sharpen this weapon thoroughly. The Germans love ideas, and they will make as great sacrifices for the peace idea as for the war idea.

Of course there are bellicose persons in Germany. There are in every country. What is absurd is to take the bellicose utterances of an irresponsible minority as the voice of the German people. If a handful of chauvinists are to be regarded as representative, then every country in the world must be pictured as foaming at the mouth and straining madly on the leash. There are in Germany men like Von Seeckt and Wilhelm Groener, whose business it is to furnish Germany with the strongest possible army and navy. They are quite right to fulfil their functions. To every man his rôle. When I read in British or French or Polish publications sensational reports of the activities of Von Seeckt and Wilhelm Groener, I can only deplore the mischievous tendencies of the modern press. These men were given a job to do, and they did it to the best of their ability. Even if in their zeal they exceeded their instructions, they may have laid themselves open to personal blame, but they have not supplied evidence of Germany's evil intentions.

The other day a French captain presented himself at my country house in Normandy, and asked to be allowed to inspect the property to see how many soldiers could be accommodated in case of need in the outhouses. I asked why he should make such an inquiry.

"It is to have a record for use in the event of mobilisation," he answered.

"Mobilisation?" I cried. "Do you mean war? Have we not had enough of war?"

"Oh," he replied laughingly, "it will probably not be for tomorrow; it may be for ten years hence or for fifty; but it is our business to foresee all possibilities and be ready for any emergency."

And he proceeded to mark down in his note book that fifteen men could sleep in my stables and garage.

Am I therefore to assume that France is getting ready for war?

Certainly not. The captain and his superior officers are properly carrying out their duties. It would be crazy to draw any deductions as to the policy of France.

Most of the activities of the German military authorities of which, from time to time, we hear so much, are of this character. Military men exist in virtue of a hypothesis. But from hypothesis to reality is a far cry. Fortunately the German people, like the French people, while admitting the military hypothesis on sufferance, prefer the hypothesis of peace.

The German masses suffered far too much in the war period and in the after-war period to regard war with anything but horror. They do not want any more "turnip winters" as they call them. They do not cheer military parades; gone are the bright uniforms, the shining helmets, the coloured tassels. . . .

And when I say that coloured uniforms and shining helmets have gone, I mean it both literally and figuratively. Read, if you please, the war stories that have become so popular in

Germany. They are grim and drab. There is, for example, Fritz Von Unruh's "Way of Sacrifice"—a terrible description of the waste and the wretchedness of war. Or take "The Case of Sergeant Grischa," by Arnold Zweig, which depicts a Russian prisoner of war crushed by the Juggernaut of militarism. Or, once more, remark the success of Leonhard Frank's "Karl und Anna," produced as a play, as a film, as a book—and which, recently played in Paris, caused something of a scandal. Another anti-war story of which everybody was talking when I travelled through Central Europe told the adventures of the Good Soldier Schwejk. Ludwig Renn, the author of "War," was an officer, but he has managed to identify himself with the common soldier, and the lance-corporal in his book is generally taken to be a portrait of himself. . . . These are only a few of the volumes which, containing scathing criticisms of the imbecility, the ruthlessness, the dismal tragedy of war, find favour in German eyes.

The Germans do not want romantic accounts of war. They want the plain truth. They want to be reminded of their dreadful sufferings, of their fears, of their cowardice, of their bewilderment, of their stupidity. So-called expressionism, which was a literary revolt, has developed into a social revolt. Men like Heindrich Mann and Hasenclever mercilessly satirise the conventions which are best symbolised by the goose-step. The younger writers are definitely pacifist, and their descriptions of war are meant to sicken the reader of the very notion of war.

The best-known war-book of this kind is, of course, "All Quiet on the Western Front" (Im Westen Nichts Neues) by Erich Maria Remarque. It has been translated into every language, and has been read by millions of people. Ludwig Lewisohn first brought it to my attention. It had just been published in German, when Lewisohn, who was sick in bed, sent out for a batch of German novels. Among them was Remarque's book. Here was an unexpected discovery! There is always a thrill in finding an exceptional piece of writing; but the thrill was intensified by the theme. Remarque is no professed pacifist, but his plain narrative of the trenches should do more to make war impossible than all the bleatings of ideologues. He tells the unvarnished truth, which is much more impressive than economic reasoning, moral pleading, or sentimental effusiveness.

Lewisohn, after his manner, was enthusiastic. We discussed whether the book was the work of a supreme artist or of an exceptionally unsophisticated man with the rare gift of setting down precisely what he has seen without the smallest "literary" research. The question is, in its way, important. If Remarque is a conscious artist he will doubtless do other work; if he is the unexceptional man who narrates an exceptional experience, it is unlikely that any event in his life will be big enough to impress him as did the war. "You have never written anything so good as ——" said one writer to another. "Thank God!" was the reply; "I hope never to write anything so good; for it is good only because I lived through unspeakable sufferings." Is it so with Remarque? Is he a one-book man? That will be because he cannot go through another experience as tremendous as the war. In any case, whether "All Quiet" is unique or not, its author is sure of a permanent place in world literature. Here is a book which ought to prevent war; its sobriety, its recital of simple memories in naked words, its resignation, its air of detachment, make it more poignant than "Les Croix de Bois" of Roland Dorgélès; though for sheer realism "Le Feu" of Henri Barbusse, written during the war itself, remains supreme.

When I asked about Remarque I was told that he is a journalist—a young man in the early thirties. His family, of French origin, settled in Osnabrück, Westphalia, at the beginning of the Nineteenth Century. Erich was a student when the war broke out; after the war he taught, became a bookkeeper, was a clerk in the Civil Service, and then wrote for the newspapers —poor little things about accidents and cocktails. Educated men who went through the war were not only or chiefly afraid of death; they were afraid of life. What had life to offer after the holocaust, after the moral as well as physical horrors of the front? They would go back, if they escaped alive, weary, broken, burnt out, rootless. . . . On Remarque settled a deep depression; he was obsessed by the war. One day by a process of psychoanalysis he realised that he was haunted by all he had seen and felt in the trenches. It was to free his soul that he sat down to write. . . . In six weeks the book was finished.

That is the authentic way in which masterpieces are produced; not by slow patient work, but by the sudden release of something in the soul.

But no publisher saw that a masterpiece had been written.

Refusal followed refusal. At last the "Vossiche Zeitung" printed instalments; and there was a flood of letters.

In grimly painting the desolation of war, in penning the most powerful indictment of military folly, Remarque has struck a chord in the German spirit. "Defeatism," as it was called, was a crime during the war; it is now a virtue. Let us hope that chauvinism will be regarded as a crime in days of peace.

XI. CLOTHES AND THE MAN

WHEN I was in Berlin there was great agitation against the threat of a censorship. Trouble had arisen because the authorities had prevented the public presentation of a pacifist drama of Communistic tendencies. This restriction of liberty was strongly resented, and no fewer than seventeen German cultural organisations—including the Prussian Academy of Arts—held a meeting of protest. Herr Severing, Minister of the Interior, expressed himself in agreement with Heindrich Mann and Fritz Von Unruh, who declared that censorship of any sort was an obstacle to intellectual development; whatever is unworthy or harmful must quickly disappear. Hauptmann sent a letter denouncing censorship as a survival of the dark ages. . . .

The new Germany is indeed extraordinarily outspoken, not only in regard to military matters but in regard to sexual matters. Writers do not try decently to cover up their meaning.

Germany long ago earned an undesirable reputation on account of the alleged prevalence of unusual sexual practices. Doubtless it is largely undeserved, for I have seen many more evidences of these practices in other European countries. There has been no appreciable increase of abnormality since the war —but abnormality has come to be regarded as a form of normality.

There is a good deal to be said for serious discussion of these problems and of sexual problems in general. But I would not pretend that the German interest in these matters is always detached and serious. The night life of Berlin—though not as crapulous as that of Hamburg—is disgusting enough, as indeed it is in other European capitals.

It would not be fair, however, to refer to these things without putting in strong contrast with this morbidity the healthy German love of out-of-doors. On the lakes with little beaches from Berlin to Potsdam men and women joyously foregather. They do not always observe the discretion to which we are accustomed in and around cities—though we, too, have decided that discretion is unnecessary in fashionable seaside resorts. What is called "false shame" is particularly scoffed at in Germany.

There are fanatics who carry matters to extremes and who found societies in which clothes are considered superfluous. This Adamite movement has grown considerably. The apostles of nudity make an interesting theoretical case; but one shivers at the notion of nakedness in our treacherous climate. . . . There can never be many adherents of the new cult; and I refrain from the foolish temptation of poking fun at a sincere and courageous attempt to escape from the conventions of civilisation.

Doctor Zimmermann is one of the leaders in this revolt against clothes. He founded a camp at Klinberg, near Lübeck, and to it come professional men and women for holidays. They get up at sunrise, take "air baths," eat fruit, walk in the woods, swim in the pond, do gymnastics, listen to lectures and to music. . . . I observe that at meal times light clothing is worn. Why? There seems to me some inconsistency in going about naked all day and putting on pants for a salad dinner.

Young men and women are bent on bodily perfection. The Youth Movement means many things, but perhaps it most means a return to simple outdoor life. The educational system has been renovated from top to bottom; but what I find especially significant is the effort to get away from the stuffy atmosphere of the class-room. Perhaps the best expression of the new freedom is to be found in the growth of the Wandervogel. It started before the war, when Karl Fischer gathered round him the pupils of a gymnasium in Steglitz, a suburb of Berlin, and led them away from formalism. They wandered into the countryside, they camped out, they made friends with the peasants, they learned folk songs and folk dances. Such "hiking" was not simply recreation; it was part of a true educational effort. It became a revolt against a social system, a philosophy, a religion. . . . The young men wore short trousers and open-neck shirts. The young women wore one-piece dresses and dispensed with stockings. New theories about the relations of the sexes were formed: men and women were to be comrades. It was impossible that there should not be abuses, and indeed the admission of women into these societies was perhaps disintegrating. Be this as it may, here was a reaction against materialism and artificiality.

Alcohol and tobacco were banned. The ideals of the Wandervogel were clean-living, physical fitness, spontaneity, abolition of rules. The war came, and the Wandervogel, which had eschewed politics, could not by its nature help giving an impetus to the revolutionary spirit. Youth in Germany is opposed to all that has characterised the bourgeoisie. To show how rapidly the movement had developed, I will quote the official figures of the number of shelters which have been provided and equipped all over Germany for the reception of these sophisticated challengers of sophistication:

(Year)	(Shelters)	(Guests)
1911	17	3,000
1912	65	11,000
1913	83	21,000
1914	200	17,000
1920	700	186,000
1921	1,200	506,000
1922	1,400	1,074,000
1923	1,700	935,932
1924	2,100	1,100,000
1925	2,100	1,423,181
1926	2,283	2,159,204
1927	2,318	2,655,292

It was inevitable that religious and political bodies should endeavour to capture the movement, though it began by expressing its indifference to religious creeds and political doctrines. There are now Protestant groups and Catholic groups. There are Student groups and Industrial groups. There are Wealthy groups and Working-Class groups. There are Socialist groups. There are International groups which insist on youth's need of union in all countries.

Akin to this movement, which is intellectually anti-intellectual, is the general revival of interest in athletics of all kinds. Germany has always excelled in sports, but the physique of the nation was dreadfully undermined by anxiety and actual hunger. Long privation told its tale, and even the children of to-day inherit something of the unnatural solemnity broken by hysterical passions of their parents who were tried by the war years. Yet the nation is being built up again. Everywhere you

THE WANDERVOGEL

will see athletic fields and swimming pools. Everywhere are
colleges of physical culture. Everywhere are sports, such as
football, boxing, tennis, hockey. Girls go scantily clad and
bare-footed, in the snow, to shoot arrows in the forest. There
are Doctors of Sport—High-Schools of Exercise. The contrast
between the men and girls, with their tents and canoes, on the
rivers and in the woods of Germany, and the men and girls
along the reaches of the Thames, is striking. Along the Thames
the men wear neat sweaters and the girls wear pretty hats.
Along the Spree the men look like Boy Scouts, while the girls
don a convenient costume with trouser-legs to the ankles.
There is nothing coquettish in this attire—youth is in deadly
earnest.

These girls and boys believe that while they are making
themselves into ideal men and women, they are incidentally forwarding the cause of peace. The old athletic spirit in Germany
had a military purpose. The new generation thinks (perhaps
wrongly) that competitive instincts between nations can be
worked out on the athletic grounds and there is exceptional
keenness shown in the result of Olympic games and other international contests.

XII. A TRIO OF THINKERS

ONE of the most curious evidences of the spiritual unrest in
Germany is the success of Count Hermann Keyserling.
He has set himself up as a dealer in wisdom; and to his booth
rush all sorts and conditions of men and women. There are
many penetrating flashes of thought in the writings of Keyserling; and his generalisations about Europe are illuminating.
Doubtless there are also pretentious phrases that scarcely bear
analysis. It is not surprising that their author has been described as partly a philosopher and partly a *farceur*. It would
be false to suggest that there is conscious charlatanism in his
teaching; but he escapes criticism rather too easily by laying
stress on the personality of the teacher, instead of on the truth
of the teaching.

He was born of a distinguished family in Esthonia nearly
fifty years ago. Although his origins are German, by geographical and diplomatic accidents he is Russian by nationality, and
indeed Russian blood mingled with his German blood. He
studied at Dorpat, and later at Geneva. Chemistry, geology, and

biology, in succession attracted him. Meeting Houston Stewart Chamberlain, the strange Englishman who became more German than the Germans, and who extolled the virtues of the Nordic race, he was led to devote himself to the philosophical study of peoples. For some years he lived in Vienna and in Paris. He travelled in England, Italy, and Greece. The East called to him; he was influenced by the doctrines of Buddha and Confucius. Tagore expressed admiration for the Western philosopher. When the War broke out, his greatest work, "The Travel Diary of a Philosopher," was already written, and was in the hands of the printer. During the War he revised it, and in 1919 it appeared, making a great impression in Germany, in Great Britain, and in the United States.

"The shortest way to one's self is a voyage round the world." That is the keynote of this essay in spiritual topography.

In the confusion of the post-war period, when men's minds were troubled, when the foundations of Europe appeared to have been shattered, there were many who looked wistfully to the East. Would salvation come from the East? It was the mode to speak of the superior qualities of Oriental civilisation, which, unlike Occidental civilisation, is not mechanical. Poets and thinkers studied eagerly Eastern metaphysics. That phase is passing. It is good that the East should remind us of the needs of the soul, but the material triumphs of the West have also their importance and may extend the spiritual domain. To be sure, Keyserling realises the lack of virility of the East; he admires the pugnacity and courage of the West. The East is passive and without ambition. The West is active and believes in progress. There are static qualities; here are dynamic qualities; but we must beware lest life be dominated by the machine, and the tool become the master of the man. Europe is already largely impregnated with Eastern mysticism, which came to it, not through Latinised Christianity, but across the steppes of Russia. It is America which best represents Westernism. The true antithesis to Asia is the United States.

The travels of Keyserling confirmed him in his view that, despite upheavals, despite hostility, we are each of us indebted to the whole world for our culture. There must be introspection, but there must also be self-expression. We must look inward, but we must also look outward. Quietism must be balanced by vigour.

The chief effect of Keyserling's book was to give a new con-

sciousness of the inadequacy of the new materialism. It was on
materialism that the German Empire had been founded. Material might is, in the end, without avail. The weary nation,
turning towards new ideals, hailed Keyserling as scholar, artist,
prophet and priest.

He founded the school of wisdom at Darmstadt, and there
taught the need of meditation as in the East, and the need of
personality as in the West. This reconciliation of the two traditional attitudes towards life is alluring. The East is profoundly
right in insisting on the value of seclusion, but it is wrong in
urging a permanent escape from the world. We can be braced
by contacts, as we may be fortified by privacy. Even mechanisation can be spiritualised. The cultivation of the soul should
be with a view to service. Knowledge must be subordinated
to wisdom; being is greater than doing.

Doubtless there is much that is pontifical in all this. Keyserling proclaims his mission cocksurely. In his school, as I understand, he lays down that the personal relation of master and
pupil is chiefly important; and he exhorts the pupil to learn
for himself. Fruitless discussion is forbidden. The master's business is to say the magic word which will help the pupil, but
he does not disguise the fact that in saying the magic word he
is concerned with the development of his own wisdom.

Rudolf Steiner, who directed the Waldorf school at Stuttgart, and founded the Anthroposophical Society whose headquarters are the School of Spiritual Science at Dornach, has
attracted thousands of disciples who feel the need of mystic
leadership. The Anthroposophical Society has branches in various countries of Europe and in America. It would reconcile
thought and sensation, and spiritual intuition. Steiner allies
occultism with physical exercises; he seeks to produce a better
body by the practice of eurhythmy, and a better soul by the
practice of a sort of theosophy. Steiner's speculations on many
subjects, philosophical, political, educational, sociological, and
even economic, are interesting.

The history of this man who has been called the Emperor of
Mysticism is curious. Born in 1862 on the Austro-Hungarian
border, he appeared, after a fantastic and marvellous youth,
in Germany. From 1890 onwards he was known as an indefatigable writer, but he was, in his outlook, materialistic.
Haeckel he admired; at Weimar he occupied himself with the

cult of Goethe. In 1902 he was suddenly converted, and at once became the chief theosophist in Germany. His activity was amazing. His Geisteswissenschaft—the Science of the Spirit —appealed to innumerable seekers who were torn between the call of the soul and the call of science, and who welcomed the apparent removal of the antinomy. Steiner broke with Annie Besant, the High Priestess of Theosophy, when the young Hindu, Krishnamurti was brought forward as the possible incarnation of the Messiah. Since then Steiner has grown greater than ever; he has become the centre of a whole world of mystically-material and materially-mystical activities housed with architectural ingenuity. . . . Steiner, too, answers some longing of the German spirit.

As for Oswald Spengler, opinions necessarily differ on the value of his book—"The Decline of Western Civilisation." Sometimes the verdict is that it is the most important contribution to philosophical history of our time. Sometimes a critic like Charles A. Beard calls it "majestic nonsense." It cannot be taken literally; it must be taken for whatever is illuminating in its thought. Can the course of history be determined in advance? Is there an ascertainable cycle of changes? Is destiny immanent, with civilisation following civilisation to the tomb? Will Western civilisation pass, as other civilisations have passed —as the Indian cycles, the Antique cycles, and the Arabian cycles have already passed? Can we discern in every age its spring, its summer, its autumn and its winter? Has the world proceeded from the intuitive and the creative, to the conscious and critical, thence to the rational and reflective, and finally to a practical mechanical phase which spells the doom of spirituality? These are questions which are doubtless answered arbitrarily; but Spengler's erudition and suggestiveness are unquestionable.

His great work was written under the shadow of the War. He projected it in 1911, completed it in 1914, and reworked it in the war years. But even in 1911 the shadows of the War fell darkly athwart Europe. The second volume definitely belongs to the post-war period. . . . To the German people, "Untergang des Abendlandes" seemed to bring some consolation; the doom of Germany was only part of the doom of the West; it was a cosmic necessity; it was not produced by any particular guilt but by universal and ineluctable forces.

The rule of the machine—powerfully does Spengler depict it. "The intoxicated soul wills to fly above space and time. An ineffable longing tempts him to indefinable horizons. Man would free himself from earth, rise into the infinite, leave the bonds of the body, and circle in the universe of space amongst the stars. That which the glowing and soaring inwardness of St. Bernard sought at the beginning, that which Grünewald and Rembrandt conceived in their backgrounds, and Beethoven in the trans-earthly tone of his last quartets, comes back now in the intellectual intoxication of the inventions that crowd one upon another. Hence the fantastic traffic that crosses the continents in a few days, that puts itself across oceans in floating cities, that bores through mountains, rushes about in subterranean labyrinths, uses the steam-engine till its last possibilities have been exhausted, and then passes on to the gas-engine, and finally raises itself above the roads and railways and flies in the air; hence it is that the spoken word is sent in one moment over all the oceans; hence comes the ambition to break all records and beat all dimensions, to build giant halls for giant machines, vast ships and bridge-spans, buildings that deliriously scrape the clouds, fabulous forces pressed together to a focus to obey the hand of a child, stamping and quivering and droning works of steel and glass in which tiny man moves as unlimited monarch and, at the last, feels nature as beneath him.

"And these machines become in their forms less and ever less human, more ascetic, mystic, esoteric. They weave the earth over with an infinite web of subtle forces, currents, and tensions. Their bodies become ever more and more immaterial, ever less noisy. The wheels, rollers, and levers are vocal no more. All that matters withdraws itself into the interior. Man has felt the machine to be devilish, and rightly. It signifies in the eyes of the believer the deposition of God."

And even the rule of the machine is subordinated to the bidding of international high finance; and even international high finance will give way to some mysterious Cæsarism. . . .

These are, of course, only the men who by the boldness of their theme, or the vividness of their presentation, or their correspondence to our present mood, have particularly caught the public eye. More quietly, great German scholars are at work; I could not, if I would, summarise their labours; but, in a word,

German thought and research are to-day more widely and more influentially felt in England and America than ever before.

XIII. THOMAS MANN AND OTHERS

AMONG the German novelists there is none of greater significance than Thomas Mann. His range is immense; for him the novel is a vehicle which may contain anything—philosophical speculation and social criticism have as much right of city in the pages of a novel as the depiction of human characters and their miseries, joys, comedies, tragedies. His influence is great; and if the younger men go off in different directions, if they do not try to be as erudite, as universal, as profound as Thomas Mann, they look up to him, to his dignified conception of his art, to his careful craftsmanship, with unfailing respect.

My own relations with him are threefold; first, he has related something of his own life in his writings, holding that it is about the familiar landscape of one's own experiences the author should be most concerned; second, we have had a common friend; and, more directly, I have been given rare opportunities of seeing him and hearing him at close quarters. He is not voluble; of himself and his work he does not like to talk; but of the novel in general, as a medium of thoughts and sentiments, he spoke; and he spoke, too, of the need of closer understandings among the intelligentsia of the countries of the world.

For him, if I do not distort his ideas, the novel is not an airy and aimless piece of fiction, fashioned for entertainment. Nor is it meant for our æsthetic delight. Again, it is not a photographic essay in naturalism. It should be epic in its range; it should, while being faithful to fact, concern itself with the whole scene of mankind—his problems, ethical, religious, political, scientific, philosophical. . . . As for the men of letters of various nationalities, it is their business to form themselves into a family, to admit no frontiers of the spirit. . . .

He is now in the early fifties, simple and serious in appearance, by no means giving himself artistic airs. He might easily be taken for a prosperous industrialist; and he looks upon himself as a good citizen. He does not glow, he shows no outward restlessness, and he is not, in the glib sense, imaginative. He takes the matter of his life, of the life about him, he examines it, he broods over it, he narrates it carefully with an abundance

HEINRICH AND THOMAS MANN

of observations. One of the most penetrating commentators of his generation, he notes laboriously, with infinite patience, the thoughts and actions of his contemporaries—real people whom he has watched with detachment and sympathy.

He is conscientious and feels his responsibility as a writer. He will give only of his best, and when one reads his work, one has an extraordinary impression of its maturity. Externals interest him, but also, and chiefly, that which is internal.

The follies, the falsities, perhaps the decadence of society are not omitted from his pages; he records morbidity as well as sanity. There is sometimes a subdued mockery in his tone; but he is not aggressively satirical; seldom does he betray his emotion. In his most dialectical works there is an austere beauty. The "Magic Mountain," for example, is filled with long conversations on countless subjects, yet it is, with all its severity, moving. It took Mann seven years to write this book; there is in it a plethora of controversy; there seems to be no advance; but, at the end, when, in the sanatorium of Davos, his personages have talked interminably on every topic that presents itself, there is a consciousness of quiet progress throughout his thousand pages.

Here are collected the anxieties and longings of our modern world. The men and women on the icy mountain, consumptives who are living their last days, remote from the turmoil of town, the multifarious occupations of the country, are keenly aware of life's problems. But they are imperturbable. They are in a timeless world, far from realities. They see the earth on which they formerly existed from afar. They are surveying the scene of which they used to be part from a corner of Sirius. But in this clear atmosphere of Davos, all the details are plain. In the physical condition of each other they are acutely interested. Nothing escapes their attention. They see things at which we should shudder, without pain. They are almost disembodied, suffering no mental distress. The long days come and go; there seems no reason why they should ever end. Those who arrive for a short stay linger on for years. They are content to let life flow past—and to discuss it curiously, unemotionally, colourlessly. . . . Each has his point of view, the outcome of old experiences and passions. So from the Magic Mountain we watch the world. . . .

In his much earlier "Buddenbrooks," which belongs, of

course, to the pre-war period, Mann has traced the decline of the house of Buddenbrooks over four generations; the middle-class merchant family flourished in the purely material manner; spirituality, crushed and thwarted, eventually breaks from the prison-house of commerce; it is inevitable that the conflict between business traditions and suppressed instincts should shatter the bourgeois contentment. Thomas Mann shows us a whole society with its flaws and dooms.

Mann himself has led a quiet, almost a secluded life. He came on his father's side of merchant stock, of solid honest burghers; but his mother brought a wayward strain of Brazilian blood. His first efforts to write were praised; and he was appointed to the staff of "Simplicissimus" in Munich. After the success of "Buddenbrooks" he devoted himself to authorship, writing as honestly as his fathers traded.

It is in drama that the more revolutionary expression of German thought is to be found. My friend, Pierre Loving, in his admirable little book, "Revolt in German Drama," declares that, since the War, youth in Germany has ranged itself pitilessly against the older generation. Ernst Toller stands out "like a mountain peak above a level plain," the most arresting figure produced by the German political revolution. Toller spent five years in a Bavarian jail for his Communistic activities. But he wrote his plays in prison. The first, "Wandlung," (Transformation) shows us War Death, helmeted, and Civilian Death, top-hatted, greeting each other among graves. His thirteen scenes are a bitter protest against War and Nationalism. Then followed "Masse Mensch" (Man and the Masses). The proletariat is engaged in a struggle with capitalism. The characters are types rather than persons, though Sonia, the heroine, symbolising humanity's aspirations and love, is a moving figure. In her dreams she sees shares being sold in the poison gas industry, she sees mankind in chains, she sees the revolutionary victims. She has ranged herself on the side of rebellion, but she discovers that all violence is wrong. If the State is Moloch, so is the Mass; and she yearns for a united humanity. It is the same gospel which is the theme of the "Machine Wreckers," which deals with the Luddite riots in Nottingham. It is a sad business, this introduction of machinery, which enslaves men; but it is a sadder business, this shattering of machinery, which should liberate men. Kindness and helpfulness is Toller's counsel. Pity speaks out of every line; and doubtless some of his plays will live far beyond the period which gave them birth.

Georg Kaiser is best known abroad for "Gas." Again the theme is that of Man and the Machine—the machine which is ill-directed, and brings destruction instead of happiness. Many years ago the symbol of Frankenstein and his monster was given to the world; there is nothing new in this fear of the machine, but the modern German dramatists have imparted to it a fresh horror. Nothing is more characteristic of the changed German mind than this repeated protest against mechanisation. They bring upon the stage not single figures but surging crowds —the whole world of toilers—and they call imperiously for more equitable conditions if mankind is to escape destruction.

Kaiser has written much besides, and much of his work bears no resemblance to "Gas." He was "discovered" during the War and his plays were produced higgledy-piggledy without regard to the chronology of their writings.

Representing something of the same spirit, Georg Grosz with implacable pencil, has attacked the ugliness and shame of conventional life. He depicts the bourgeois in all his hideousness, his obscenity, his selfishness, his abominable complacency. His cartoons are terrible. Recently he was placed on trial for blasphemy. He had drawn a priest from whose mouth issued cannons and rifles. He had likewise drawn a picture of Jesus Christ on the battlefield, wearing a gas mask and military boots.

"We live in the most troubled times, and the foundations of society are shaken," said Grosz to his judges; "and the artist cannot, if he would, keep out of politics."

He was condemned, but the case was carried to a higher court, where he was acquitted. The judge, somewhat surprisingly, uttered wise and memorable words: his name, Siegert, should be remembered. "The artist," said Judge Siegert, "has made himself a spokesman for millions who disavow war. In his cartoons, the artist has shown that the Christian Church has served a cause which it should not have supported, that it has preached love of one's neighbour, and yet gloried in the death of the enemy.

"Art must be free. It cannot be put in a strait-jacket. The cultural value of art is more important than the misunderstanding and pain given to certain persons. What is permissible, and what should be forbidden, is not easily determined."

XIV. MAXIMILIAN HARDEN

MAXIMILIAN HARDEN was the greatest of German journalists, and he had a considerable influence over world opinion. I was particularly struck by his outspokenness on his visit to Paris in the summer of 1924, when, the Ruhr being still occupied, he declared for a Franco-German *rapprochement*. "France and Germany," he said, "have common interests. If they unite their forces, the future is safe for peace. We must adapt ourselves to economic necessities, and as Germany must, if it is to pay reparations, expand enormously, it must come to an economic and political understanding with France. . . ."

The idea has since been taken up by the Briands and the Stresemanns, but at that time it was daring. Harden's boldness had already brought upon him the wrath of the Nationalists. The dauntless polemist had, under the Empire, attacked the Kaiser himself; he had denounced the singular morals of the camarilla round the throne, and for his temerity had been imprisoned. At the Armistice he proclaimed the responsibility of the Kaiser for the War; and he recommended the Locarno policy long before the politicians.

In July, 1922, just after the assassination of Rathenau, an apostle of industrial rationalisation, who negotiated with Louis Loucheur accords for the payment of reparations in kind, Harden in his turn was assailed. He was beaten on the head with bars of iron. Perhaps these blows were ultimately responsible for his death. On the anniversary of this incident he would say "To-day is the anniversary of my death."

For thirty years he produced his review "Die Zukunft." Afterwards he wrote a good deal for a friend of mine, who enjoyed oddly confidential relations with him; and my friend now sends me this intimate picture:

"Harden was a master of *mise-en-scène*. Once I went to Berlin to see him—it was in 1921, after we had been corresponding for many months—and was informed over the telephone, by his wife, that he could not possibly receive me until two days later. When I did finally see him he explained with many expressions of regret that he invariably spent Wednesday and

Thursday correcting proofs and seeing his 'Zukunft' through the press. It was, however, clear to me that he merely wished to impress me that one does not 'drop in' on the great. . . .

"His study was lined with bookshelves, into which, pitched pell-mell, were paper-backed volumes in every European language. It seemed that another tome could not have been squeezed in anywhere, upright or sidewise. The maid lifted a pile of newspapers and reviews from a chair to make room for me to sit down. She placed the papers on the floor, where there were already many similar stacks. Every other chair in the room, except his desk chair, was laden with papers. The desk itself was piled high with periodicals and documents.

"When the 'cher Maître' appeared (I decided from the beginning to give him that appellation and he seemed to agree that it was correct) he seized my hand and shook it long and warmly, sighing and smiling so eloquently that he could only have meant: 'How fortunate I am that I should have lived to see this day!' He regretted that he had only that very moment learned I was waiting. 'Alas! One is not served as one would like! Poor Germany!'

"I told him I found his lovely cottage very charming. He sighed. 'Could I only have known you were coming, I should have offered you hospitality. But such poor hospitality, surely you would have begged off! Tell me, are you comfortably lodged in Berlin?'

" 'Very,' said I. I was at the Adlon.

" 'Ah, the Adlon! But only foreigners can afford it! (My room and bath were costing me about 5s. a day.) We Germans . . .' and he spread out his hands with a weary smile.

"Of course what ruined Harden's life and career was the exile of William. Say what he would against Noske, Ebert, *et al.*, he could never get *them* to jail him for *lèse-majesté*. After he was beaten up by a gang of hot-headed young monarchists, he was invited to make a lecture tour in America. It was said he received a large number of threatening letters from Germans in the U. S. That ought not to have deterred him. But there was the fact that he could not speak English, and so would have had to make his principal appeal in German-speaking communities where he was not popular.

"About that time I asked him—since he had a reading knowledge of English and was something of a Shakespearean scholar—why he did not study English pronunciation and read his lectures in English. He shook his head sadly. '*Non. Ce n'est pas mon genre.*' Upon inquiry in Berlin, I learned that on the platform he was inclined to work himself up into a frenzy, shouting, moaning, yelling and weeping.

"We always spoke French. His French was rather Eighteenth Century, full of polite formulas and courtly phrases.

"Each time I went to Berlin I called on him, taking care to make an appointment well in advance. The first time, as I was taking my leave, he said: 'But do you know your way back?'

"I was a little nonplussed at the question, as it was quite obvious that my taxi was still before the door. I pointed to it. '*Ah! Vous avez une voiture! Mais dans ce cas, peut-être. . . .*'

"He turned to Frau Harden. '*Monsieur Bird a une voiture, alors, comme il me fait la politesse. . . .*'

"Little dumpy, white-haired Frau Harden ran to get his muffler and overcoat and bundled him up with motherly care. We drove down the Kurfurstendamm. At a certain point he tapped on the window. The taxi halted and he said an affectionate—and elaborate—farewell.

"Thereafter it was always the same. Each time he rode back with me, and always alighted at the same place.

"About 1925 he spent a winter in Holland, on the bleak North Sea coast. (Noordwyk was the place.) It was a summer resort where he had obtained a cottage out of season for a small rental. He seemed to delight in walking on the beach while the wintry gales blew fine snow in our faces.

"He came over to the Hague to lunch with me. We strolled to the Peace Palace—that monument of architectural bad taste and diplomatic futility. Harden wagged his head. He had never been inside, nor had I, so we went in together. The first room we entered—right at the top of the grand—very grand!—staircase, was the Japanese room, all decorated in the Japanese-Dufayel of the day.

" '*Quel symbole!*' Harden breathed, or gasped—he was already feeling the asthma that carried him off. (He had a favourite theme—the ultimate antagonism between Orient and Occident.)

" '*On appelle cela le Palais de la Paix . . . je dirais plutôt son tombeau!*' he epigrammatised as we left.

"I took him to a jazz-tea. He told me it was the first time he had ever heard modern dance music. He found it 'extraordi-

naire.' All the society of the Hague was there. Many diplomatists came up to speak to him.

"The last time I saw him, a few months before his death,
was in Switzerland, at a mountain resort (Montana-Vermala,
summer, 1927). As usual when travelling, Madame Harden was
not with him. I had taken Bob McAlmon along. We had noti-
fied him of our arrival and he had invited us to lunch. Before
lunch we strolled in the woods, and he complained bitterly
about his health. I asked him with some anxiety if he were living
entirely alone.

" 'No, a very kind German lady is looking after me, but as
she speaks only German she will not join us at lunch.'

"The cottage was small and ill-constructed for a French
farce in which people are supposed to enter by one door while
others depart by another. It was difficult to avoid the lady. . . .
The various dishes had been disposed on chairs and tables about
the dining room, and as each course was finished Harden himself got up, removed the plates, and changed the service. Then
we went back to the study for coffee, which had been brought
by an unseen hand. When we left the house, I glanced back
towards the kitchen window, and glimpsed for a moment the
smiling face of a very charming Gretchen, who, however,
quickly bobbed back out of sight. The purpose of that comedy
I have never been able to fathom.

"In November of the same year, and in the same place, he
died, rather suddenly.

"I had always been told that Harden was a Polish Jew who
had been converted to Christianity. Once we were talking about
Poland, and to my surprise he said: 'The Poles are the only
people whom I never had any hope for.' I replied: 'Yet you are
yourself a Pole, are you not?' He expressed perfect amazement,
and declared, 'Why, not at all! I haven't the slightest drop of
Polish blood!'

"On a visit to Paris his first remark was that he didn't see
any signs of the famous French militarism that was so much
talked about in Germany. There were plenty of troops about
in those days, too, but he said they didn't look very ferocious—
just boys in uniform. The only really military looking troops
he could see were the Gardes Républicains in front of the public
offices.

"One night I suggested a taxi-ride in the Bois. When we got
to the Arc de Triomphe, where the flame was blazing up over

the Tomb of the Unknown Soldier, he asked the driver to stop. We sat there for several minutes while he gazed at the flame. He found it very impressive. He said: 'Do you know that in all Germany there is not a single monument to the men that died in the War?' I didn't know it, but he assured me it was so. He may have been wrong. Certainly some have been erected since."

XV. HUGO STINNES

HUGO STINNES, who for a time played a great part in German politics, seemed to me a portent. I met him first at Spa. Black-bearded, authoritative, he produced a sinister impression. This man, as black and gritty as the coal which he owned in enormous quantities, was Germany's richest industrialist; he controlled about fifteen groups of coal mines; he had immense metallurgical interests; he bought up everything, a celluloid concern, hotels, textile factories, a motor-car business, dockyards, a big printing-works, paper and pulp mills, timber forests, scores of newspapers, and I know not what besides. Such a man may be a danger to modern society, especially if he begins to meddle with politics which he subordinates to business. Private interests become more important than public interests. . . .

With Hugenberg, he became the greatest newspaper owner in Germany and was therefore to be feared. He purchased any journal which was for sale without hesitation.

"What do you do in life?" said one character in a cartoon. And the other replied: "I found Independent Socialist organs— to sell them to Stinnes."

Stinnes has passed on, but Dr. Alfred Hugenberg remains. Nobody who realises the power of the press can ignore Hugenberg, who has adopted a sort of Fascist policy. He would institute a Dictatorship in Germany. He opposed the Dawes Plan, the Treaty of Locarno, Germany's admission to the League of Nations. Keeping himself in the background, he not only owns a string of newspapers, but he controls a news agency to which subscribe most of the German newspapers, Socialist as well as Nationalist. Further, he supplies a large percentage of the German press with stereotyped articles and pictures. The Telegraph Union was founded at the end of the War. The inflation period favoured its growth. Stinnes placed Hugenberg in charge, and when Stinnes died Hugenberg assumed full command.

At Spa was the aged and pathetic Chancellor, Fehrenbach, who assured me tearfully that Germany was anxious to restore the ruined regions. "Those devastated provinces," he said, "are an open wound which should be healed. They make peace between France and Germany impossible, yet peace we must have. Let us then, since we have many men unemployed, send workers into Northern France to build and repair. It would be cheaper for us, but it would be equally effective for France— and without delay we will restore this territory which constitutes a standing reproach to Germany."

He argued that Germany could easily find the material as well as the men. He produced a scheme by which Germany offered to pay several times as much as anybody expects now. But the Allies would not listen to him, and the scheme was scarcely noticed in the newspapers.

The newspapers were more interested in Stinnes. It was necessary, at that moment, that there should be a dark devil who could be abused mercilessly. Hugo Stinnes looked the part, and so he was made the villain of the piece. International politics are like transpontine melodrama. Whether we deal with persons or with countries, they must be either absolutely bad or absolutely good. They are all either very very good, like the little girl who had a little curl right in the middle of her forehead, or else, like her, they are horrid.

By common consent, Herr Hugo Stinnes was horrid. He dared to speak to the Allied ministers of the "disease of victory." He claimed to state the German case as a right and not as a privilege. I found it good fun that he should bully and boss the Allied bigwigs as he bullied and bossed workmen and servants.

Lloyd George and Millerand were then in power; and I find, in looking up my notes, that I then wrote, long before the occupation of the Ruhr, of "the disastrous failure of Spa, which has committed England to the French plan for the occupation of the Ruhr Valley. When the time arrives, as arrive it will, for the advance to be made, difficulties will present themselves, interallied troubles will arise. There is nothing so dangerous as coercion, not only for the party who is coerced but for the party who is coercing. Spa is the greatest calamity that has fallen on Europe since the armistice. It placed a sword on the conference table. Let us take Stinnes as a symbolic figure, after the manner of the transpontine politicians, but let him stand for intransigence in general, and not merely for German intransigence, which has brought a new menace into international relations."

XVI. DR. STRESEMANN

CONFERENCE succeeded conference, and I attended most of them in my capacity of political commentator. The German ministers were certainly not first-class men. There was Wirth, whom M. Briand always referred to as *le bon Monsieur Wirth*, well-intentioned, but ineffectual; there was Cuno, openly favouring the Right; there was Wilhelm Marx, a lawyer, an official, the head of the Catholic Centre party; there was Hans Luther, once Burgomaster of Essen, a good administrator, not an inspiring figure. They did not strike me as big enough; they came and went without adding to or subtracting from their mediocre reputation.

There is, however, one statesman who has prominently occupied the international stage—Dr. Gustav Stresemann. He has managed to earn for himself a position not dissimilar from that of Briand in France. Briand in France is regarded as the great peace-maker, the apostle of European reconciliation, and it is generally forgotten that he is chiefly responsible for the policy of alliances which has been steadily pursued behind the façade of the League of Nations; that he is the man who first began the occupation of the Ruhr, when he seized the key-towns of Ruhrort, Duisbourg, and Dusseldorff, and that he was Prime Minister when the unfair partition of Upper Silesia was effected, and when Germany's debt was fixed at the impossible sum of 132 milliard gold marks. Briand is the self-appointed President of the proposed Pan-European Federation. Stresemann in Germany, a clever politician, is in the same way regarded as the German man of peace, though his actions have by no means been consistent. He was Chancellor for a short time at the end of 1923, but generally he has been content to serve as Minister of Foreign Affairs. When the current was against conciliation, he was defiant enough, and took care not to compromise his political future. When the tide turned, he showed the same opportunism; and a better partner to Briand could not have been found.

Dr. Stresemann

Albert Einstein

He has been successful in spite of his physical appearance and his manners, neither of which are prepossessing. If you travel through Germany you will see everywhere a multitude of Dr. Stresemanns. Henri Béraud has amusingly recounted his search for Dr. Stresemann. He pursued him to Carlsbad, to Berlin, to Baden-Baden, to Paris, and failed to catch up with him. In a German town he thought he had overtaken the Foreign Minister. "Whom did I suddenly see under the thick foliage of an alley of lime trees? Dr. Stresemann in person! It was certainly Stresemann—his rosy cranium, round and close cropped . . . his heavy shoulders . . . his fresh complexion . . . I continued on my way, and a little further, under another lime tree, there was a second Stresemann, who resembled the first like a twin brother. Then a third, then a fourth, and then other Stresemanns—all alike, flourishing, cropped, and corpulent."

Not always is Stresemann tactful. He is late for his appointments, he loses his temper over trifles, he brings his fist down on the table with unnecessary noise; in the Reichstag he turns feeling against him by his rude replies.

It is, however, his achievements that we should remember. Stresemann's initial achievement was the Locarno Pact which changed the whole current of European political thought. It was drawn up in the little Swiss town of Locarno, where Stresemann and Briand and Chamberlain unbent, where they went on friendly little excursions, indulging in junketings on penny steamers like jocular *citadins* in holiday mood. It would be easy to poke fun at these trivial diversions. On a former occasion, similar behaviour had wrecked an important conference.

It was at Cannes. An arrangement was almost reached by which Germany would have been treated less harshly, but unfortunately at this moment Mr. Lloyd George began to teach M. Briand how to play golf. . . .

The French, who are serious in serious affairs, were shocked. Newspapers contained long accounts of Briand's golfing exploits. I remember reading, for example, that he was making such progress as to produce a score of ten for one hole, whereas Mr. Lloyd George could only manage to obtain six. Again, we were informed that he could hit the ball on the rebound. This was funny enough, but the French grew indignant at the frivolity of their representative, and he was called to Paris. From that moment the occupation of the Ruhr was inevitable. . . .

Therefore it was with some misgiving that we witnessed what the common people, according to the late Lord Curzon, call "be-anos." On this occasion, however, everything passed off well. Germany accepted its frontiers with France and Belgium as permanently settled by the Treaty of Versailles, and agreed to the demilitarisation of Rhineland in perpetuity. Great Britain pledged itself to uphold the status quo in the West, and to range itself with France should France again be a victim of German aggression, and to range itself with Germany should Germany be a victim of French aggression. Quarrels of any kind would be referred to arbitration. In pursuance of this end, Germany was given a seat on the Council of the League of Nations.

There remained perplexing issues. Thus the French were pledged to support Poland, Czecho-Slovakia, and other nations, if the existing territorial arrangements were challenged. Now everybody felt that Germany would demand a revision of the frontiers on the Polish side, and although it was willing to enter into arbitration treaties with its Eastern neighbour, it was not prepared to renounce its claims as it had renounced its claims to Alsace. Nor would England fight for the preservation of the Eastern frontier.

Nevertheless, Locarno was a great contribution to European peace. It is easy to criticise the agreements, but the moral gesture marked the turning-point in European reconciliation. The documents are ambiguous and inadequate, but they have validity as part of the effective public law of the Continent. The Pact implied a fundamental change in Britain's diplomatic relations with France. No longer were the two countries allies in any special sense. England, in certain contingencies, would stand with Germany against France. France, at the best, could expect England to be arbiter. France could not hope that its influence in the League would be predominant when it was confronted by Germany.

As I wrote at the time, "the worth of the Pact is in rigorous relation with the spirit that may prevail on either side of the Rhine. In so far as it is the embodiment of a will-to-peace it is valuable; but if it is not the expression of a will-to-peace it is a scrap of paper. . . . The essential thing to be said about the Locarno Pact is that we must not sleep upon it as upon a

pillow. It may be an instrument of peace, but it is not an assurance of peace. It is a beginning, and not the end."

I think Stresemann genuinely earned the gratitude of good
Europeans by his dexterity in inducing Germany to accept
the Pact. His performance is the more creditable in that his
health has always been poor. When I saw him on the signing
of the Kellogg Pact for the renunciation of war as an instrument of national policy, he looked extremely ill. He was the
first to accept unreservedly the American proposal; and he
came to Paris to be present at the ceremony in spite of advice
that he should undergo no fatigue. Certainly he has now demonstrated that his thoughts are turned to pacific solutions. Bismarck or Wilson? The choice was not easy for him, nor for
Germany. At one moment he aspired to play the rôle of Bismarck in the German Republic. Traditions and training pointed
in that direction. But he made the right choice at the right
moment, and it is almost impossible to suppose that, having
made it, having created a reputation as a peace-maker, he will
lightly sacrifice that reputation.

In my book, "Those Europeans," written in 1924, when
Stresemann's attitude was still doubtful, I could only ask: "On
which side will Stresemann be found? On the side of war, or
on the side of peace?" The question can now, I think, be safely
answered.

XVII. DR. SCHACHT

DR. HJALMAR SCHACHT, President of the Reichsbank,
was appointed to his present post at the most critical
period of the fall of the mark. It is generally agreed that his
performance in restoring German finances, even with foreign
aid, was remarkable. The task would have been impossible had
it not been for the Dawes report, but the Dawes report could
not have been successfully applied had not Schacht been a man
of exceptional ability.

Of the Dawes Committee, with which I was brought into
daily contact, I will only tell one story; General Dawes himself, if my memory serves, related it. Members of the Committee had gone to Berlin to make some investigations on the
spot. General Dawes, installed in a leading Berlin hotel, was
waited upon assiduously by a waiter who spoke perfect English.
The manners of this waiter, though respectful, were particularly

polished; and Dawes, pleased by his attendant, began to converse with him. The waiter, little by little, began to impart information; encouraged by Dawes, he expressed views which revealed a profound knowledge of finances. Finally Dawes invited him to explain in detail the whole situation. The waiter acquitted himself with distinction. He was persuasive, he was convincing. . . .

The waiter was a financial expert, who had donned the uniform of a humble calling, in order to come into close contact with the President of the Committee, and judiciously influence his opinions!

Dr. Hjalmar Horace Greeley Schacht well illustrates the accidental character of nationality. He might have served Denmark; he might have served the United States of America. It happens that he has served Germany; but he is not, in the complete sense, a German. Until 1866 his father was a Danish subject, speaking Danish, and so Danish in sentiment that when Holstein and Schleswig were taken from Denmark by Germany, he emigrated to the United States. It was in Brooklyn that the elder Schacht married; the brother of Dr. Schacht was born in the American town. Then the emigrants, owing to the illness of the wife, returned to Northern Schleswig which was retroceded to Denmark in 1919.

Hjalmar Schacht has preserved his Danish associations; his children bear Danish names. He himself was educated in Hamburg which, although German, has Scandinavian traditions.

It would seem that he had few opportunities, as a member of an annexed minority race, to rise to an exalted position in Germany. But it was his father's American connections which gave him his start.

At the age of twenty-four he was the director of a commercial bank. At twenty-six he was placed on the Board of Directors of the Dresdner Bank. Then he served the Darmstadter Und National Bank. He was on the Reich Currency Commission in 1923 and finally became the head of the Reichsbank. His career has been rapid and brilliant, and the German currency has, under his direction, probably become the soundest in Europe.

He reëstablished German credit, and he organised Germany's economic and industrial recovery. Certainly he has no rival as an expert in Germany.

When it was decided, on the suggestion of Mr. Parker Gilbert,

the young American Agent-General for Reparations, that the
Dawes Plan needed revision, Dr. Schacht, who had conducted
Germany's affairs so admirably, was naturally asked to represent the Reich. He came to Paris. His appearance indicated
his character—shrewd but obstinate, intelligent but tenacious.
He has a high forehead from which his greyish hair, parted in
the middle, is brushed back. His eyes are deeply set under somewhat puckered brows, and behind his glasses they shine pierc-
ingly. His nose is peculiarly wrinkled in an expression of discontent. His short moustache, touched with grey, is set above
a disdainful mouth. His chin is squarely solid. . . .

He has political ambitions, but he is not a politician. His
manner is not that of a good negotiator. At Paris he was too
often lacking in tact. Whatever he is, he is not conciliatory. He
had already broken with the Democratic Party, because the
Party wanted to compromise on the question of the property
rights of members of the former reigning houses. And then
in Paris he showed a disposition to hold to minor points at the
risk of defeat. If he won through in the end it was because
Mr. Owen Young was determined to succeed at all costs.

Yet he made no protest against the proposal that Germany
should pay the Allied debts. Germany was, under the Treaty,
called upon to pay reparations. Now the reparations debt was
suddenly transformed into something else. It was no longer
"reparations proper" that the Allies demanded. Only one-third
of German payments were to pay for damages. The other two-
thirds were to supply France and England and the other
countries with the wherewithal to meet claims upon them.

Nowhere can I find legal justification for the demand that
Germany should pay the Allied debts. It was bound to pay
reparations, and this specific claim has dwindled to something
like thirteen milliard gold marks. The payment of the Allied
debts and certain charges roughly amount to twenty-six milliard gold marks. Let us assume that a great deal of generosity
has been shown by the Allies in reducing the amount for reparations proper, and that if the Allies had so chosen they could
have placed the total demand of about thirty-nine milliards
under the head of reparations. The fact remains that they did
not—that they deliberately agreed to alter the basis of their
claims in respect of two-thirds of the total. What would seem
to follow? It would seem to follow that Germany, taking advantage of Allied inconsistency, should have immediately of-

fered to pay the thirteen milliards, but should have declined
to pay the twenty-six milliards; should have protested that
you cannot substitute one demand for another—that the Allies
might have maintained their claims for full reparations, but
are out of court in reckoning how much they themselves owe
and calling upon Germany to foot the bill.

Precisely the opposite course was taken by Dr. Schacht. He
did not dispute the claim for the payment of Allied debts, but
he disputed the claim for reparations. He agreed to pay the
twenty-six milliards but he challenged the thirteen milliards.

It does not concern Germany whether the Allies repay their
borrowings from the United States with the money they receive
from Germany. But it does concern Germany that the Allies
should base their claims on the necessity of making these payments. It might, too, have been pointed out that each of the
Allies considers it a burden, which it can scarcely bear, to make
such payments (which come from Germany) to America, while
Germany is assumed to be in a position to pay easily not one
of these debts but all of them!

XVIII. EINSTEIN

EMIL LUDWIG, the celebrated German biographer of
Napoleon, Bismarck, William II, and I know not whom
besides, deplores the poverty of our day in the humanities, but
finds it especially rich in science and technical achievement.
He makes reservations about Bernard Shaw, about Hindenburg, about Clemenceau, about Mussolini, about Freud; Nan-
sen, Marconi, and others he mentions, but does not insist upon.
But when he deals with Edison and Einstein he is emphatic.
Of Edison he says that he swallows up all his pupils, and he
asks: "Has not the aged wizard created or perfected the
favourite technique of our century? No living man has so
diversified and adorned arts and sciences, social relations and
politics, as Edison." Then he puts beside the most practical
genius of our day, the greatest theorist—Einstein. Both, he
says, were born poor; both are self-made men; both are be-
holden solely to their own genius; both have shattered theories
held throughout the world.

This comparison of Edison and Einstein is, I think, particularly apt, and it would be difficult to refute Ludwig's contention that while we have no supreme musician, no supreme

painter, no supreme writer, our age will be remembered for its scientific and technical achievements.

The formulas of Einstein, expressed in a few pages, have shattered all our notions of time and space. Certainly it is difficult to state his discoveries in ordinary language; many attempts have been made, but unless one possesses a rare mathematical mind it is impossible to grasp Einstein's hypotheses. They run counter to our preconceived ideas; they are altogether outside the realm of experience; our senses do not aid us to comprehend, but on the contrary resist, the conception of relativity. The Pythagoreans gave divine attributes to figures, since by them we can raise ourselves above ordinary human understanding; and by mathematical symbols we can rise to a higher intellectual plane than we can reach by words. Einstein shows that time and space are not absolute, that they vary in accordance with the situation of the observer and the object observed, that time, as well as space, is modified by speed, that indeed time is a sort of fourth dimension of space. . . .

I saw Einstein in April 1922. He had then scarcely passed the landmark of the fortieth year and he appeared even younger. Yet he was world-famous and everybody was discussing him. A dark complexion, arched eyebrows, a brown moustache, shadowing a sensitive mouth, big sad eyes, clear and candid, flying shocks of black curly hair over a high broad forehead—this was the man who "opened a new door on eternity."

It was not in Berlin, it was in Paris that I had my glimpses of Einstein. His coming to the French capital was a notable event, for he was, I think, the first distinguished German to be invited by an official body to France after the War. The French, despite his greatness, were half ashamed of their welcome. One great newspaper tried to pass Einstein off as a Swiss, as though the German nationality of the illustrious mathematician were something to be concealed!

At the Collège de France he gave six lectures on the subject of relativity; the hall was packed. At the Académie des Sciences, Paul Painlevé, who has been an indifferent politician, but has memories of the days when he was considered a good mathematician, tried to refute some of the arguments of Einstein: he was not successful, and it was the general verdict that Painlevé's objections were based on mere misunderstandings.

Einstein certainly had no vulgar desire for self-advertisement, he did not provoke popular manifestations, or seek social triumphs. I find the following paragraphs among my 1922 notes:

Albert Einstein has, it is complained, played at hide and seek with the fashionable ladies of Paris. He has been the most elusive visitor. When the illustrious German arrived, he got out of the train on the wrong side, ran along the rails, and slipped away before he could be discovered. In his letter to the French savants who had asked him to explain his theories, he insisted that his visit should not be surrounded by publicity.

The prospect of being stared at by rich idlers, more concerned with his personality, more concerned to obtain the subject-matter of conversation at the dinner-table, than to understand him, seemed to shock Einstein.

Occasionally a professor at the Collège de France becomes a social lion, and during his course of lectures the rue des Écoles is filled with luxurious limousines. Einstein was anxious that only those persons who were already acquainted with his subject should be admitted. These were not popular lectures; they had a strictly technical character. In spite of pleas, admission was by special letter.

It was no false modesty which caused Einstein thus to show himself as little as possible. He simply considered that such interest as was excited should be purely scientific. Warmly did he express his delight at entering into contact with the French savants—at having helped to break down the barriers which would parcel out the kingdom of the intellect by geographical frontiers.

It is, of course, perfectly easy even for the most distinguished man—even with the most distinctive hat, such as Einstein wears—to hide himself in Paris. To hide oneself one has only to go among the crowds. Einstein did not reveal his address, but he wandered about the Paris streets with his friend, Professor Langevin, and when he went to see a French colleague he took the democratic auto-bus or the Metro.

Einstein was born in 1879 at Ulm. Afterwards his parents lived in Munich; then they went to Italy and later to Switzerland. His father was always poor, and as a boy Einstein suffered many hardships. Nor was he quick at learning—except at mathematics. But in those early Swiss days he acquired a large cosmopolitan vision, and his fundamental honesty and simplicity were soon to be tested. His talents brought him the offer of an important post; but he was asked to renounce the Jewish faith. He refused the condition and declined the post.

Yet, although he is a Jew, with all the traditions of his race, he has stated that he puts truth first; if Judaism were to interfere with his quest he would repudiate it.

He was unpopular in Germany during the War because he could not accept the views of his colleagues; he was a pacifist. The lot of the Jew during the War was pathetic in all countries, for all the best Jews, German or American, with whom I happen to be acquainted, were opposed to the conflict, and more than one of my friends was deprived of a University post.

Indeed when the German authorities themselves honoured Einstein on his fiftieth birthday by presenting him with a house, many difficulties arose. One of the Berlin newspapers launched an attack upon him; the word Jew was used as a term of opprobrium; Einstein's humanitarianism and pacifism were described as dangerous; his conclusions were said to be incomprehensible to everybody, including their author; and the award of the Nobel prize was held to be unjustified. . . .

The sound mathematician is not necessarily an artist; it is possible to have proficiency in this branch of learning without possessing imagination. But the great mathematician is always an artist, just as the great philosopher is always a poet. Mathematics calls for intuitive leaps, swift flashes of insight. It is not enough to plod precisely and methodically from one point to another. Henri Poincaré, the cousin of the French Prime Minister, rightly regarded in France as one of the foremost mathematicians of our time, made this assertion, and was himself a living proof of that which he advanced. It was not direct reasoning which made of Newton a genius; it was his capacity for sudden wild guesses which were afterwards tested by reason. One of my own friends—J. W. N. Sullivan—a well-known scientific writer, intimately acquainted with Einstein, expounding his theories with accuracy and clarity, has, in evenings which we have spent together, insisted on the relationship of mathematics and music, and bracketed together Einstein and Beethoven.

It is not, therefore, surprising to find that Einstein is no mean musician. He, like the French painter, has his *violon d'Ingres*—literally a violin, which he plays with skill and feeling. Music he studied as a boy, and it is his greatest pleasure still to play or to listen to musical performances. Music, like mathematics, is a universal language.

XIX. YOUTH

THE views of some young men at the University interested me. They are young men of good families, they are thoughtful, they are not radically inclined. Without the personal experience of war of their elders, they one and all reject the thesis that Germany's prestige depends on military glory. Yet they undoubtedly smart under a sense of grievance. They are keenly conscious that their country has been wronged.

Diplomatic mistakes by the Kaiser and his advisers in the pre-war days are acknowledged readily by the young men; but they believe that Germany was no more guilty of preparing and precipitating war than was Russia or France. It is well to understand that this conviction is not the result of ignorance influenced by propaganda. It is based on the evidence of documents and diplomatic confessions. For the young men whom I met have studied the facts, and they have formed their conclusions. As for the atrocities of war, they are not defended as such, nor denied, but it is emphatically asserted that they were inevitable in the heat of fighting, and that the Allies behaved quite as badly as the Germans. The senseless prolongation of the blockade by the Allies, which caused incalculable and unnecessary suffering, particularly rankles in the German soul.

It follows that the Treaty of Versailles is regarded as an unjustifiable burden, imposed by victorious countries on the countries which, in the hazard of war, were vanquished; and "reparations," without moral sanction, are a tribute extorted from the defeated.

Yet the young men in Germany appreciate the futility of war. What can be proved by this or that military success, which is bound to be balanced by this or that military rebuff? The problem which presents itself to them is difficult. They do not want revenge for the sake of revenge; but they do want a readjustment of an impossible situation. They would certainly prefer a peaceful settlement; but, among the most serious, educated, and intelligent young men, who spoke frankly and somewhat sorrowfully to me, there is an ominous determination to secure justice though the heavens fall. They are sad, because there seems to be no issue save the dreadful issue of force. They have no real faith, though they are willing to have hope, in the League of Nations. How can the League give them back German populations placed under alien rule? Those populations must come back to them whatever the cost. . . .

I was troubled when I heard these admirable young men talk; I realised their dilemma, the crisis of conscience and of reason. I was not reassured. I had a strong impression that the best German youth is in principle profoundly peace-loving, but that it is also moved by a stern sense of duty. What will come of this conflict? Will German youth, as it grows older, find its sad sense of duty dimmed, or will its sentiments of peace be blurred? Assuredly nothing should be neglected to keep the peace spirit alive, but it is useless to exalt peace as a substitute for justice. Peace without justice is a delusion and a snare; what we should blame is not a breach of peace but a breach of justice. Somehow we must reconcile peace and justice. That is what the foolish pacifists, the declamatory politicians, refuse to do. Peace as a negative thing favours the perpetuation of wrong; it is only worth while as a positive thing which assures the establishment of right among men.

We should not deceive ourselves. German youth thinks like this. . . .

As in other countries the young men have lost the taste for theological controversy that prevailed in my own youth. No longer do they care about doctrinal abstractions. There is widespread scepticism, and such religious sentiments as exist are rather a general conviction of the wisdom of righteousness than a precise persuasion of the truth of either revelation or authority.

Authority indeed is rejected. They deny the wisdom of their elders who have made such a sad mess of things. There is, I found, some melancholy in their attitude towards men of maturer years. They are not angry with us older folk—they turn upon us a pitying countenance. Why should they listen to us who have discredited ourselves so hopelessly?

Respect for our social, political, and moral standards has been lost. We have a poor record to place before the rising generation; we have made war angrily, idiotically, and perversely; we have encouraged racial prejudices; we have fallen into political corruption; we have constructed incomprehensible dogmas. In all my talks with young men I was aware that the gulf between two generations is wider than it has ever been before. This distrust is perfectly natural and is to the credit of the younger men.

PART VII
TEN YEARS AFTER

I. A GENERAL SURVEY

TEN years have elapsed, Lector, since the signing of the Versailles Treaty, and, looking back over that decade, an observer in Europe, like myself, while noting the progress towards a "liquidation" of the War, cannot but be disappointed at the lack of fundamental change. Have racial hatreds and suspicions diminished? Have they not rather increased? Is disarmament or any substantial reduction of armaments in sight? Is there less resort to the perilous method of partial alliances which tend to divide Europe into two or more camps? Has the League of Nations brought the peoples nearer together, has it smashed the "old diplomacy," or is it used as a screen by the diplomatists behind which they pursue their intrigues and combinations? Sincere answers to these questions are not soothing. There are minorities problems, economic problems, debt problems; foreign armies occupy the soil of friendly nations. . . .

Everything seemed so easy when, shortly after the Armistice, President Wilson came to Europe. In our enthusiasm we saw a new era opening. Since then we have been told of new eras opening many times, with the result that scepticism has been engendered.

What, then, is your impression, Scriptor, looking back over these ten years?

It is at once favourable and unfavourable. We have found no royal road to peace, as we thought was possible ten years ago, but when I think of the temper of the so-called Peace Conference, I realise that some advance has been made. I was an observer throughout those days of peace-making, and it was lamentable to see high expectations so quickly thwarted. In the retrospect, nearly everybody agrees that the Versailles Treaty was ill-conceived and badly shaped. The other treaties concluded at Paris had for effect the multiplication of frontiers and the placing of minorities under alien rule. It was good to give liberty to certain races, but it was done at the expense of other races. Generally the victors divided the spoils and the vanquished suffered many disabilities, some of them undeserved. It was a strange contrast with the hopes that prevailed soon after the Armistice.

Did nothing worth while come out of the peace-making? Were none of the aspirations fulfilled?

The peace-makers, Lector, drew up the Covenant of the League of Nations and though the League has shirked its real work, and has fallen into the hands of the Foreign Ministers who use it for their own ends, it still stands as witness to the popular demand for peace. Mr. Wilson was its chief protagonist on the American side and M. Léon Bourgeois on the French side. With M. Bourgeois it was an old idea. He had represented France at the two Peace Conferences of The Hague, and in his little book entitled "Solidarité" he had set forth the thesis of the interdependence of the world. I was myself permitted, as a personal friend, to discuss with him the precise form that the League should take. Yet it is fair to say that, had it not been for Mr. Wilson, the League would never have been founded. Thus it is not straining the facts to declare that the League of Nations is a legacy of the United States to Europe.

Nevertheless, Scriptor, the United States, afraid of entangling alliances, declined to ratify the treaty or to join the League.

That is so, but nothing can rob the United States of the honour of having given Europe an institution which, though it has not accomplished anything like the task which we set for it, and has indeed many defects in its constitution, and is in my opinion being improperly employed by those who profess to be its greatest friends, yet may, despite these restrictions, prove to be the means of Europe's political salvation.

It has not, Scriptor, reduced armaments and it has allowed European nations to conclude a series of pacts of alliance which are contrary to the mission of the League.

That is true, Lector, but it has facilitated the solution of a number of dangerous questions. Disarmament is perhaps a will-o'-the-wisp. If men are resolved on peace, it will not much matter whether they have large armies and navies, since these armies and navies will be without occupation. But obviously, these forces will automatically disappear if there is moral disarmament. Perhaps we are putting the cart before the horse in asking for disarmament first. Disarmament is a consequence of the will to peace. It will not, assuming that it is possible, necessarily produce the will to peace. As for the separate treaties which cover Europe like a net, they are a proof that Europe has not accepted the idea of the League. It is, as I think, unfortunate that the League should countenance alliances which recall the most dangerous features of the old system of diplomacy; but then the League is not strong enough to forbid them, and if ever it is strong enough, these alliances will become obsolete.

Then, after ten years, the condition of Europe is, to put it in a nutshell, a compromise between the old idea of security by alliances and security by the League.

Let us observe, Lector, that things are better than they were, inasmuch as there is the League idea to oppose to the alliance idea. Before the War there was nothing of the kind. Everybody openly sought allies and in the search admitted that it had enemies. Europe was engaged in ranging itself into two armies which were, humanly speaking, bound to come into conflict. Now, although it is true that the theory of alliances has not been dropped, yet there is a counter-theory which is undoubtedly making headway and will serve to neutralise these alliances.

Are there no other systems which might be adopted?

Yes, Lector, there is the system of a political federation. That may be called the construction of the United States of Europe. There are advocates of such United States based on the American model, but there are great objections and tremendous difficulties. In some respects, the noble ideal which was eloquently advocated by Victor Hugo sixty years ago might, even were it immediately attainable, be undesirable. We do not want to destroy national diversities. Above all, we do not want to do anything which might be interpreted as pitting continent against continent, as creating continental rivalries instead of national rivalries. Europe against America would be worse than Germany against France.

But is not the alternative a sort of European civil war?

Yes, Lector, if it is based on the old conception of a balance of power. That is dangerous. It prevailed before the War and prepared the way to war. Certain countries encouraged it, leaning first to one side and then to the other in order to keep the balance steady. It was a hopeless task. The scales were bound to tip over. But that is how the diplomatists worked. They gradually built up alliances. France and Russia were allies. England was drawn into the Triple Entente, as the association of France, Russia, and England was called; and Italy belonged to the Triple Alliance, that is to say, ranged itself with Germany and Austria-Hungary. Eventually Italy came in with the Triple Entente. The Balkanic countries were pawns in this game. Each side tried to become stronger than the other. War was the natural conclusion.

Is there any other method, Scriptor, besides that of the League of Nations?

There is another method of keeping peace—that of the preponderance, certain and indisputable, of one power or set of powers. That was the old Roman idea, and for hundreds of years it worked well. But it is practically impossible of realisation to-day, when no nation is sufficiently strong to exist by itself or to keep sufficient weaker nations, which have no conflicting interests, on its side. Yet many people think that France and its allies have temporarily obtained such control. There is much in French diplomacy which lends colour to this conclusion. At the beginning, French diplomacy aimed at the permanent suppression of Germany. But England and America would not permit the permanent crushing of Germany. The burden of reparations was made unduly heavy, but, though Germany suffered the loss of its colonies, and was compelled to yield territory to Poland, as well as to restore Alsace-Lorraine to France, one can roughly say that German unity was preserved. There have been many schemes which, if carried out, would have broken up Germany as Austria-Hungary was broken up. Nevertheless Germany grows daily in strength.

How then, Scriptor, can France be said to be predominant?

Temporarily, Lector, France is predominant because, with larger armies, it has managed to bring into its orbit the new nations and the new-old nations of Central Europe. France is allied with Poland, Czecho-Slovakia, Belgium, Yugo-Slavia, Rumania. Great Britain stands rather perplexed in the background. France has certainly done much in recent years to forward the League idea, but it uses the League on condition that the status quo is not disturbed and the treaties are not revised. The upsetting of the status quo would bring to an end whatever predominance France may possess.

Then this system, Scriptor, is as precarious as the system of the balance of power?

Unquestionably it is, and already we see, Lector, the attempt of Italy to obtain control in Central Europe. The members of the Little Entente, though they insist upon the preservation of the *status quo*, are making friends with Italy and Germany, as is Hungary. They are aware of the perils of tying themselves up too closely with France. Then there is Russia, which remains

GERMAN "MODERNISM"

OFFICES IN BERLIN

the great enigma of Europe. Whatever preponderance France
had, must soon go, and is already going.

What, then, are the prospects of the League of Nations,
Scriptor?

That is an immense question, Lector. Yet I will answer you
briefly and so conclude this dialogue. I believe that, unless the
League can be made to work and become the system to which
Europe unreservedly adheres, we shall be driven back to the old
struggle to establish a balance of power. But it is not lip-service
that is sufficient. The League should not be used as a mere façade
behind which the old diplomacy practises its operations. The
League above all must put in the forefront the notion of the
pacific solution of difficulties. It was never intended to preserve
the *status quo*. It was intended to destroy the *status quo* by
pacific means whenever readjustments should be necessary.

Those who try to build it on the *status quo* are its worst
enemies, whatever pleasant language they may use. We have to
renounce war, and that has already been done in words. Then
we have to strengthen the machinery for settling disputes, for
securing justice without regard to the pressure of this or that
power. The League has yet to be made a reality. Yet it is good
that, although Europe is still divided between two ideas, there
are in fact two ideas instead of one.

Alliances have not been renounced, the system of preponderance, the search for a balance of power, have not been abandoned, armaments have not been reduced, the *status quo* is still
held up as impregnable, but nevertheless it is clear that the
peoples of Europe are steadily forcing their governments to a
higher conception of the functions of the League of Nations.
Public opinion has done much to make possible a new Europe
founded on justice, which has no favourites and takes no heed
of relative strengths and alliances. More and more do we think
internationally—and that is the hope of Europe ten years afterwards.

II. MINORITIES

LET us look more carefully at the minorities question which
confronts us at every step we take in Europe. Nobody is
really anxious to thrash it out. It is, indeed, not at all simple.
If we set aside the Jews who belong to no nation and to every
nation, and who have been, and in some cases are still, persecuted

by nearly every Continental nation, the very term minorities is embarrassing. It implies that the peace-makers of 1919, with their eyes wide open, deliberately placed in subjection to a foreign power a racial group which resented such transference; and that the peace-makers, with a guilty conscience, then assured to the racial group, by special accords, privileges which are incompatible with the principle of national unity.

The existence of minorities is an anomaly. Either the diplomatists should have refused to include alien populations in the States they created, and so have rendered exceptional laws for their protection unnecessary; or they should have had the courage of their map-making ambitions, and have assumed that the citizens whom they gave to a certain State rightly belong to that State, and ask nothing better than to be assimilated.

It is unfair to the minority, and it is unfair to the nation, to include a minority in a nation, and compel the nation to treat the minority as a separate people which can never truly be absorbed. In practice it was of course impossible to draw boundaries in such fashion as to keep each nation pure. There were inevitably racial admixtures.

Yet it is unsatisfactory and illogical that there should be any need of international legislation for minorities. In strict justice Poland and Czecho-Slovakia, and the rest of the new States or newly-shaped States, should have been put under the obligation to treat all their citizens alike. That would have been to their interest. It is a terrible commentary not only on their sense of fairness, but on their political common sense, to assert that they first wished to construct the largest possible country, and then, having acquired an alien population, wished permanently to exclude it from national community. Poland, for example, is foolish if it schemed to obtain German territories for the purpose of self-aggrandisement, and having obtained these German territories, sought to exclude the inhabitants from Polish citizenship. Of two things, one: either it was wrong to give these territories to Poland; or the territories, being given, must be regarded as Polish.

There was much muddled thinking in 1919 and afterwards. Opposite principles were perpetually adopted. Wrongs were committed, and then, in remorse, the contrary wrongs were committed. Catch-phrases were employed without regard to their place in the general plan. For myself, I have the utmost sympathy for transplanted peoples. I think they should enjoy

the fullest liberty to maintain their cultural associations and
their racial traditions. Nevertheless it is surely nonsensical to
encourage them to differentiate themselves from the people
among whom their lot is cast. Such encouragement means that
we are fostering an irredentist spirit and therefore increasing
the possibilities of war.

Even in France there is a problem which bears some analogy
to a minority problem. The Alsatians have a different language,
and creeds and customs which are different from those of the
rest of the country. Nobody seriously disputes their French
nationality. Nobody would wish them to form a separate State
—except a few interested propagandists. The Radicals are undoubtedly right in declaring that Alsace should ultimately be
brought under French laws. But the Alsatians, who protest that
they cannot be forced to change their language and religion
and habits in a few years, are also right. Both sides in this
painful quarrel are, at the same time, wrong. The Radicals
are wrong in endeavouring unduly to hasten the process of absorption. The Alsatian agitators are wrong in endeavouring to
reinforce the barriers between France and Alsace. Time must be
allowed gradually to do its work. In the transition stage, the
greatest tolerance should be shown for Alsatian susceptibilities.

In similar manner Poland, and other countries which possess
minorities should, in their own interest, afford every facility
to those minorities to participate to the fullest degree in the
national life, while looking with indulgence upon manifestations of a regional character. At present it is to be remarked
that the tendency is to fall into a double fault. First, there is a
foolish inclination to deny complete participation in the national life. Second, there is resentment of regional manifestations. If the Governments knew their business they would not
require any prompting from the League of Nations, or from
any outside body, to strive for assimilation by the method of
kindliness.

Rome in its great days well knew the art of winning allegiance. In Gaul, for example, Rome did not attempt to destroy
the distinctive character of the people; it opened the Senate
to the Gauls, who represented not a revolting province or a
servile population, but an independent and self-respecting opposition. If Rome gradually substituted its own civilisation for
the Gallic civilisation, it did not do this by crushing the civilisation which it found. Obviously it is too much to ask that new

nations should pay heed to the lessons (mutatis mutandis) of history, but it is a sad reflexion on our post-war age that there should be any acute minorities problem produced by the folly of the victors and profiteers of the war.

On the other hand it is, in my opinion, equally to be deprecated that there should be an acute minorities problem produced by the political action of the minorities themselves and of their former compatriots. It is a pity that the map-making was not better done, but the chances are that it can only be undone (except perhaps in detail) by violence. However regrettable were many decisions, they must be accepted—at least until circumstances change—and we must assume their permanence. It follows that the true objective is assimilation and not differentiation. There is peril in laying continual stress on the rights of minorities, of urging them to live apart from the country to which they administratively belong, of countenancing their support by the country with which they have racial affinities. Minorities have duties as well as rights. They owe loyalty to their Government, and there is no Government which could permit political agitation in collusion with a rival nation. The problem, it will be seen, should therefore be considered in more than one aspect. It is a pertinent historic truth that wars have sprung from the patronage and protection of minorities by nations which have discovered in the existence of such minorities the excuse and the occasion of intervention.

Doubtless no serious use will be made of these pretexts for many years to come, but one discerns the desire to keep these pretexts alive. Before they can be used, it is to be trusted that the process of assimilation will be far advanced. There is no lack of inflammable material in Europe where it is calculated that the minorities number twenty millions. Nor does this figure include members of races which have more or less voluntarily allied themselves with members of other races. It does not, for instance, include the Croats and the Slovenes who, after the break-up of the Austro-Hungarian Empire, united with the Serbians in Yugo-Slavia. The Croats are not satisfied with the partnership, but it is now impossible to describe them as a minority. Similarly the Czechs and the Slovaks compose Czecho-Slovakia, but although the Slovaks are outnumbered, they are not technically a minority.

The Germans in Czecho-Slovakia are more numerous than the Slovaks, but they, unlike the Slovaks, are veritably a minority, for they were incorporated against their will. Happily, they appear to be receiving excellent treatment, and are taking part in the government of their country. The Magyars and the Ruthenians are other minorities in Czecho-Slovakia, as they are in Yugo-Slavia. Rumania has a serious minority question, and indeed most of the Central European and Balkanic countries have, in colloquial phraseology, bitten off more than they can conveniently chew. Greece and Turkey, to get rid of their minorities, adopted the expeditious though cruel solution of exchanging their minorities.

It is only fair to add that before the War there were a hundred million Europeans who complained that they were improperly attached to this or that State. Moreover, before the War, there were entire peoples under foreign domination—notably the Czechs, the Croats, and the Poles. Further, before the War, the minorities had no means of redress when they were oppressed, whereas to-day an institution has been established whose mission it is to protect them. But there are two dangers. One is that the League of Nations will shirk its responsibility —as it shows signs of doing. The other is that the minority question will become a diplomatic weapon.

It is comparatively easy to manipulate patriotic sentiments favourable to the country of racial origins and unfavourable to the country of administrative obligations. It is comparatively easy to create friction by intrigue and propaganda, and to pit two countries in racial rivalry against each other. While minorities are kept keenly conscious of themselves, and are egged on by countries with which they have natural sympathies, peace is in peril. Liberal opinion is properly aroused on behalf of minorities, but even liberal opinion can be mischievously directed. There must be unrest while one country feels that it contains unreliable citizens who are urged by another country into rebellion, and the other country feels that it has, outside its borders, nationals who are harshly treated. For the League, therefore, there is no more delicate problem. It cannot afford to neglect oppressed minorities, but neither can it afford to encourage minorities to consider themselves aggrieved. The prestige of the League will be diminished if it pigeon-holes petitions and is not active in the defence of minorities. Its prestige will be equally diminished if it interferes without clear cause, and, by impinging on the sovereignty of countries which contain minorities, invites rebuffs and stirs up ill-feeling. The distinction between domestic and international affairs is exceedingly fine. The League must fulfil its functions, but it must not become an instrument of political propaganda. It must insist on justice, but it must also hasten the fusion of races in each country.

III. WHO WON THE WAR?

REVISION is a dangerous word. It can be made a war weapon, but it can also be made an instrument of peace. Guglielmo Ferrero, whose comments on European affairs are always models of clear-sightedness and cool judgment, admirably points out, in one of his essays, that if the territorial clauses have not been touched, the treaties of 1919 have been modified so greatly in their application that they have already been revised. Particularly has the moral situation of the vanquished been alleviated, and irksome foreign controls are being removed.

The ignorance of the negotiators in Paris was colossal. They knew nothing of the old monarchical precepts which called for the strict limitation of demands. Every demand of the victors should be enforcible, and it should be recognised even by the victim as necessary, if not just. For the superiority of the victors is not a permanent state. It is, in its nature, transitory. As the vanquished nations recover their strength, they will denounce obligations which they have accepted under duress, unless those obligations are fair, and should, according to the code of honour, be kept.

The trouble with the Versailles Treaty is that it presupposed one set of European nations in a permanent condition of inferiority, and another set of nations in a condition of permanent superiority. The victors on this assumption could dictate whatever terms they pleased. They have indeed maintained their predominance longer than might properly have been expected, but they were driven by a consciousness that their own fate was bound up with the fate of the former enemy countries to save those countries from social confusion and financial bankruptcy. The irony of the treaties is that there was wrapped up in them a diabolical machine which must shatter them. By their excessive rigour they quickly became inapplicable. They were so destructive that the Allies had presently to help to construct. The Allies had to assist Austria, Hungary, and Bulgaria. They had to relieve these countries from their debts, and actually advance money to them. As for Germany, the Allies began by dictating their financial demands, but after a few years they had to beg Germany to come to a round-table conference and coöperate in the establishment of figures which might be freely accepted. It would have been better to have begun in that fashion.

The Allies foolishly imagined that they could be plaintiff and judge and executioner. They discovered that Germany would not consent to be the eternal victim, and they were impotent as executioners. The rubbish that was talked about the triumph of right was quickly shown to be the meaningless vapourings of romantic rhetoric; for either side might have won, and victory proved nothing. Nobody who has studied the available evidence—marshalled skilfully and impartially by Professor Sidney Bradshaw Fay in his "Origins of the World War"—can believe the lie of the Versailles Treaty that the exclusive guilt of the War falls upon Germany.

The statesmen who made a European settlement after the Napoleonic wars were realists. They admitted France into their counsels and they spared France. They were anxious to construct a lasting peace. They were careful not to leave unnecessary causes for war. But the statesmen of 1919, under the iniquitous cover of justice, were chiefly bent on punishing the nations that they denounced as wrongdoers, and they created more causes of future wars. Their petulance, their passion, their hypocrisy, surpassed anything that men who live by reason could have imagined. The result has been that since 1919 we have been engaged, reluctantly but compulsorily, in undoing the work of 1919.

The victory itself was exceedingly relative. The public is still inclined to believe that, as in a football match, one side won and the other side lost. That is, of course, not the truth. France and England may be said to have beaten Germany, but Germany completely crushed Russia and Rumania. The disappearance of Russia as a European power is not merely a moral compensation for Germany's defeat in the West. It changes the whole fabric of Europe. It frees Germany of its most implacable enemy. It enables Germany to reconstitute itself without hindrance from the East. Certainly the Allies created Poland to be a thorn in the flesh of Germany, but the Polish pressure, in years to come, will be comparatively light, and will indeed be negligible if there is a Germano-Russian alliance—as was adumbrated at Rapallo—against the Slav country which has come to birth at the expense of both Russia and Germany.

As for the Central European powers, while it is true that the little lands which now bear the name of Austria and Hungary were hopelessly defeated, there emerged from the Austro-Hungarian Empire a number of new nations or largely augmented nations, which, momentarily on the side of the Allies, may hereafter change their allegiance. It is not straining matters to say that the component parts of Austria-Hungary are on the side both of the vanquished and of the victors.

Again, take the case of Italy, which was allied to Germany and Austria. It happened to come in on the winning side—so far as there was a winning side—but it was itself badly beaten, it was denied the territorial gains for which it fought, and it by no means remains with its new allies. There are good observers who suggest that the next war—if there is to be a next war—will rage round the pretensions of Italy, which are inconsistent with the pretensions of other European countries, now proudly boasting of their victory.

And although France and England undoubtedly gained territory at the expense of Germany, and obtained many other advantages, it is impossible, for anyone who has followed events since 1919, to dub them victors without sardonically remembering their immense losses, financial and social. England no longer enjoys the undisputed control of the money markets or of the seas, and industrially it is in poor plight. France wrestles with huge debts and socialistic menaces. Alsace-Lorraine (or rather Alsace, for it is wrong to use the hyphenated word) is as violently opposed to the French administration as it was to the German administration.

Norman Angell is right in his contention that war cannot be made to pay.

Yet there is one nation which, coming in at the end, truly won the War. It is the United States of America. Amid European disillusionment there is some bitterness at the realisation that the United States of America is the only indisputable victor. Its rise to a position of predominance has been accelerated, if not determined, by the War. It is impossible to consider any European problem, without taking into consideration the United States, which, immensely wealthy, has invested enormously in Europe. I, for one, do not rail against America's good fortune. It may prove to be of great service to Europe; but it is a reality.

IV. EUROPE AND AMERICA

GEORGES CLEMENCEAU, when he bluntly declared in a letter to the United States that France is not for sale, expressed a European sentiment that is growing sharper and sharper. There is a fear of American domination of Europe. That is why such formidable opposition was raised against the ratification of the debt settlements. "It is merely a secret of comedy," wrote Clemenceau, "that fictitious payments are demanded, in order to lead to a loan, with a good mortgage on our territorial possessions, as was done in Turkey." When the reparations controversy was at its height, those of us who advocated reasonable treatment of Germany, in accordance with economic possibilities, usually protested against schemes which would Turkify Germany. Some of those schemes were French. The same Frenchmen who would complacently have Turkified Germany are now alarmed at the bogy of the Turkification of France and of Europe generally.

An influential American, who has always advocated the cancellation of Europe's debts by America, came to me the other day with carefully worked-out figures, showing that if Europe really endeavoured to pay its immense debt to America, it could only do so by further huge borrowings from the same source on definite pledges, and that in the course of fifty or sixty years America, by this process, would have bought up almost the whole of industrial Europe. It sounds absurd, and, as a practical proposition, is absurd. But theoretically the possibility exists. Since it is neither by a transference of gold nor of goods that Europe can pay, it is not difficult to demonstrate that in one way or another there must be effected a change of control and of possession of property inside Europe.

Take the case of Germany.

According to Arnold Rechberg, German steel manufacturers, finding themselves short of working capital after the period of inflation had ceased and stabilisation of the mark had been accomplished, were obliged to turn to American banks, backed by American steel interests, and obtained loans on condition of American participation. The ultimate object of America is to

secure a predominant holding. Now the German heavy industries, through the Hugenberg organisation, control the majority
of German newspapers and direct various patriotic associations
and parties; and if they are in their turn directed by America,
we shall have the paradoxical situation of American political
as well as financial control of Germany. In a single quarter of
an hour a loan of thirty million dollars was subscribed in New
York for Germany; and the rhythm of American investments
in Germany is such that, were it to remain unaltered, Germany's
national riches would in a few years pass into American hands.
One estimate puts American interests in Germany already at
35 per cent of the total.

Ludovic Naudeau, considering the present state of Italy,
observes that the sequel to the Rome-Washington debt accord
was a further loan to Italy. "While France, feeling itself fundamentally richer, energetically resisted, Fascist Italy submitted
to American pretensions. Italy has engaged itself to pay the
United States even though it is not paid by Germany and re-
gardless of the influence of payments on the rate of exchange. . . . In virtue of the Dawes Plan the transference of
marks for reparations will be suspended whenever such transference may depreciate the mark. Italy, on the contrary, must continue to pay the United States, despite prejudice caused to the
lira." Sixty-two State bonds corresponding to annual payments
are held by the United States, which may demand their exchange against bonds that the Italian Government must either
repurchase or admit on the Stock Exchange designated by
America. "So the United States may at any moment throw into
the market for sale two milliard dollars' worth of Italian bonds.
America holds the credit of Italy at its discretion. It may sub-
merge the market of public funds under an avalanche of obligations, and can determine the course of the lira. It dominates
the productive power of Italy, having the means of conquering
its essential elements by the sale of these bonds in Italy. The
total credits of the Anglo-Saxons, after the settlement of the
British debt, will cover half the total riches of Italy, and the
realisation of these credits will permit an Anglo-Saxon control
of the principal industrial, commercial, and financial affairs
of Italy."

The same phenomena are recorded in Belgium. In Poland an
American Syndicate holds the majority of shares in the greatest
zinc-producing company of Europe. Polish industry, like

Belgian industry, suffers from the need of credits, and those credits are being extended to Warsaw in dollars. There is an elaborate economic and financial programme which will go far in the direction of the Americanisation of Poland.

Many milliards of dollars have been sunk in European enterprises, and the current is swelling at the rate of a quarter of a milliard annually.

In *La Revue Économique Internationale,* a Belgian publication, M. Antonelli tries to show that the social and economic hegemony which Europe enjoyed in the nineteenth century is abolished. "At the beginning of the nineteenth century," writes M. Antonelli, "the production of coal in the whole world was twelve and a half million tons, of which England alone furnished ten millions. But in 1923 the United States produced an average of fifty million tons a month, while England did not produce more than twenty-five millions. The United States produced in 1923 three-quarters of the cast-iron and more than two-thirds of the raw steel of the whole world. For the five leading metals other than iron and steel, the part of Europe in their production, which was twenty-eight per cent in 1913, was only twenty per cent in 1923. Europe's part in their consumption, which was sixty-two per cent, is only forty-three per cent."

The economic decadence of Europe, as compared with the extraordinary development of the United States, is a constant theme. England, it may be, has arrived at a critical moment of its existence, with its permanent unemployment, far more serious than France's devastated regions which were quickly repaired; while the Continental countries are suffering from a profound disequilibrium.

V. "COLONISATION"?

UNDOUBTEDLY Europe and America are dependent one on the other. The debt of Europe to America can never be repaid, for it is not merely financial. America has long discovered that its interests are inseparable from the interests of Europe, and after a brief period in which it was customary to say that the United States would never allow itself to be mixed up with European concerns, everybody recognises that in practice the relations of Europe and America have become unprecedentedly close.

We can dismiss once and for all those theorists who would

have America keep to itself, for they have been overtaken by the facts. Those Europeans who find American intervention in their affairs irksome, forget that financially they called for such intervention, which saved them from ruin, and that politically American assistance has been wholesome.

There are problems which transcend continents. One of them is the problem of peace; and the signing of the Kellogg Pact in Paris demonstrates that the two continents are equally concerned about the maintenance of peace, however much they may differ about details and about methods.

Europe and America are moved by the same thoughts, have a common purpose; are, on a higher plane, united, and seek each other's collaboration. It may turn out that this sign of their solidarity, of the increasing consciousness of their wider interests, is the best thing about the Kellogg Pact.

There is not an activity of the League of Nations—from which the United States at first ostentatiously stood apart—that is not shared in some manner by the United States. The United States unreservedly brings its help to the solution of what may be called (though the term is perhaps inaccurate) non-controversial matters.

Officially or unofficially, America was all-important in preserving Hungary and Austria from complete collapse. America played a notable part in the relief and consolidation of the Near East. Americans broke the deadlock between France and Germany by sitting on the Dawes Commission and framing the Dawes Plan, and again it is to America that Europe owes the Young Plan.

Before 1914 it may properly be said that Europe brought to America greater support than America brought to Europe. The United States grew and became prosperous by the assistance of Europe. Europe furnished emigrants and capital. Possibly, America is right in restricting immigration now, but without immigration it could not have attained its present position.

After 1914, the United States, in its turn, supplied Europe with raw materials and foodstuffs. Europe needed money; Europe ceased to lend to America; Europe withdrew a good deal of its capital invested in America. It was the United States which lent money to Europe. Europe bought enormously in America, and to pay for these goods borrowed larger sums. It would be foolish to deny that America benefited, but it

would be equally foolish to deny that America rendered the
greatest services to Europe.

But what of the future? It would be impossible for America,
if it had the desire, to withdraw from Europe, for it has found
in Europe a favourable field for investment. It has lent tremendous sums to every country. To the Allied countries it lent
during the War, and to the enemy countries (as we may conveniently call them) it lent after the War.

Europe needs money to pay for its current purchases and to
reimburse its past borrowings. How is such money to be obtained? There are (speaking roundly) two ways. One is by the
continued borrowing of money. The other is by the greater
selling of goods.

Increased production is one of the keys to this problem, but
that is not the only necessity. If Europe continues to borrow
from America, it is not for the purpose of augmenting its production, which is large enough to pay for everything of which
Europe has need. It is useless to manufacture merely to glut the
market, though Europe could doubtless consume more of its
own products by raising the general standard of living.

Sir George Paish has well expressed the position. By means
of loans contracted in America, Europe to-day actually buys
American products double the value of those which the United
States buys from Europe. But there must ultimately come a
reckoning-day. Europe is getting deeper and deeper into debt.
How can Europe buy and America sell, unless America goes
on lending more and more to Europe, and Europe goes on consenting to borrow?

Surely that cannot last for ever. What is the alternative? It
is that America should purchase from Europe, directly or indirectly, the equivalent of that which it sells. Nay, more. That
would only keep the actual trade balance even. But the United
States looks to Europe for payments in respect of interest and
amortisation on the debts which Europe has contracted. Logically, therefore, since payments are in goods and services, the
United States should make sufficient purchases from Europe
to enable Europe to repay the debts.

That is precisely what the United States is resolved not to do.
It builds its tariff walls higher and higher; and is making it im-
possible, while continuing to dump its goods on Europe, for
Europe either to pay for them or to repay old debts. Sooner or

later we shall have to work out all the implications of the
situation resulting from the steady stream of American loans to
Europe for the past fourteen years, together with the increasing stream of American goods, making even the adjustment of
the ordinary commercial balance difficult.

It is held that the European debts hold out a menace to the
United States as well as to Europe. There is something farcical
in the system of a creditor supplying funds to a debtor to pay
his debts—and that farcical element must become more and
more evident. Besides, the tendency of American bankers is to
make lending more onerous and even to recuperate. If Europe,
by the drying up of American loans, is forced to economise, to
lower its level of existence, then it is obvious that American
products will not be received so readily in Europe.

But economists find a partial solution. It is that instead of
transferring to America European currencies, America should
apply those European currencies, as it is indeed doing, in
Europe. That means the Americanisation of Europe; and it is
certain that Europe will not permit itself to be "colonised"
without protest.

VI. EUROPE'S TWO DOCTRINES

BUT let us return to purely European problems. To understand the essential character of the European conflict, one
must be penetrated with the philosophy of history and apply
the teaching of time to the conditions of to-day. The real clash
is between two doctrines, and the future of Europe depends on
whether it is possible to reconcile, not the two doctrines, but
the devotees of the two doctrines. Put in naked form, stripped
of all embellishments, there confront each other the desire for
stabilisation and the desire for development. It is France which
takes the lead in the demand for the *status quo,* and it is Germany (followed by Italy) which takes the lead in the demand
for change.

Not by chance does one nation and its followers seek crystallisation, and the other nation and its followers seek freedom of
expansion. Their attitudes are dictated by a variety of motives,
many of which originate in the remote past, though they are
fortified by the events of recent years. France is a country
which centuries ago reached its greatest heights. It has main-

tained itself more or less successfully on those heights. Its very
shape was for the most part fashioned by inexorable geographical laws. The Pyrenees, the Alps, the Rhine, the Vosges, the
Mediterranean, the Atlantic and the North Sea set its limits.
True, in the North there are no natural boundaries, but this
defect has been remedied by the creation of buffer states. True,
also, that France has sometimes forgotten that its true strength
lies inside its natural frontiers, and under Louis XIV and under
the Revolution and the Empire, it foolishly tried to expand.
But always these lapses from unity have been shortlived and
have been punished, and France has recoiled to consolidate itself
on what is unquestionably French soil. On that soil, which has
been marked out for the French, the French are invincible. Like
Antæus, they acquire indomitable vigour when their foot
touches their mother earth. Territorially, France is a fixed
entity, and in spite of the fluctuations of military victory and
defeat, has been fundamentally a fixed entity for centuries.
France therefore looks upon changes in Europe as dangerous.
The dynamic factors which operate beyond the Rhine are regarded as a menace. To the transformation that the Continent
has undergone and which it appears still to be undergoing,
France opposes its conception of tranquillity. It would have
everything stereotyped. France is a nation which has achieved
itself. It is complete and coherent. What France aims at is immobility; what France fights against is the disturbance of the
status quo.

The conservatism of France is reinforced by a hundred different considerations, and it would be taking a narrow view of
somewhat accidental facts to insist on the political upheavals
in France itself which distinguished the nineteenth century.
Royalty was outworn, and great democratic currents swept
over France in 1789 and onwards, but whether the political
institutions were those of plebiscitary dictatorship, monarchy,
or republicanism, there is at bottom a strange resemblance between the successive epochs, and generally speaking, France
is governed to-day by the administrative machinery built by
Napoleon on the foundations laid down by the Bourbons. The
structure and the resources of the country which make it self-
contained and strong, cause it to wrap itself up, as it were, in
the mantle of its insularity. Its laws, its language and its social
instincts come from Rome, and it has a rigidity which is en-

tirely Roman. Once France was made, it was finished. Its civilisation was a settled thing. Its diplomacy, as a great historian,
Albert Sorel, has ably expounded, found a traditional basis
from which it has scarcely departed.

Now, against this desire for stability, this yearning for
"security," must be placed in sharp contrast the more fluid Germanic sentiment. The German Empire is of recent construction.
The Germanic peoples sprawled throughout Central Europe
and into the West. They were divided into hundreds of States.
There were no natural limits for them. In their long history
they have never had natural clear-cut frontiers. They may take
on the map whatever shape they please, and diplomatically may
be known by a variety of names. They have striven for a sort
of spiritual domination, an ethnical superiority, and have endeavoured to impose their hegemony, whether from Vienna or
from Berlin, over the Continent. When they gain or lose territory they are not fatally injured. To lop off a member of
France is to cripple France: but Germany resembles an amœba,
is an amorphous mass. France is static, while Germany is
dynamic. This is the hereditary quarrel between France and
Germany. It is as old as Charlemagne. What has happened in
the last few decades, and particularly during the last decade,
confirms the resolution of France to stick to the established
order, and inspires Germany to modify that established order.

At first the French did not realise what an admirable organ
from their point of view was the League of Nations; and
Clemenceau openly scoffed at the Geneva association; but
Briand has seen that the League of Nations may be utilised for
crystallisation purposes. That was not its original purpose, and
the Geneva organisation may, on the contrary, be employed for
the revision of the 1919 Treaties. Germany is not unaware of
the possibilities of change which reside in the League itself, and
it may be that England, and doubtless America, will assist Germany to employ that machinery. Yet for France and for the
new nations and the new-old nations which emerged from the
peace-making of Versailles, the main function of the League is
to oppose territorial and political change.

It is extremely difficult to be fair in one's judgment of nations: partisanship is almost inevitable: but in truth there is a
great deal to be said both for the French and the German mentality, and to blame one side or the other for actions which flow

The League of Nations Assembly at Geneva

from their respective mentalities is altogether unphilosophic. How difficult it is to decide what is bad or good in the political sphere, is admirably shown by M. Jules Cambon in a little book in which he refers to the League. "Let us reflect for a moment," he writes, "on what would have occurred if the League of Nations had existed when Cavour was trying to construct Italian unity. It is probable that the King of Naples, the Pontifical State, the Grand Duchy of Tuscany, would have appealed to the League of Nations. Their governments would have denounced at Geneva the aggressions with which they were menaced. The League of Nations would have intervened. Would it have succeeded in arresting Garibaldi and his Thousand on their march to Naples? . . ."

Thus, by a paradox, that association which appears to consecrate the transformation of Europe, would have been an obstacle to that very transformation. Many of those who look upon the League to-day with distrust, would then have applauded its rôle. Decidedly Voltaire was right, and "in everything there is contradiction."

If one considers the intensified production of pacts in Europe by diplomatists who are working overtime, one will perceive that they may be divided into two categories. In one category are the conventions which are meant to stereotype the decisions of 1919. In the other category are the agreements which are intended to aid in their overthrow. The Little Entente, for example, comprising Czecho-Slovakia, Rumania and Yugo-Slavia, is a defensive alliance to prevent any alteration. Poland, when it signs an accord with Rumania, guarantees the Bessarabian frontiers of Rumania in return for a Rumanian guarantee of the Danzig Corridor and the Eastern frontiers of Poland. France inspires the policy of Poland and the Little Entente.

On the other hand, the Russo-German pact points not to crystallisation but to renewal. It comes into the second category. Italy, under Mussolini is likewise dynamic, and its pacts are designed to bring about changes. On the one side is a consortium of nations with vested interests chiefly intent on defending their acquired possessions. On the other side there is a consortium of nations who labour under a sense of injustice and who consider the 1919 decisions as subject to appeal.

Movement or immobility? That is the question on the answer to which hinges the character of European diplomacy. Is the

1919 system eternal, or may it be modified without shock? It is thus that the European problem should be presented.

VII. DICTATORS AND DEMOCRACY

THE post-war problems, producing perturbations, political, financial, and social, have determined an anti-Parliamentary movement throughout Europe. Parliament, in most countries, mistook its mission. It should examine the proposals of the Government, but it should not endeavour to govern. If the executive authority is acting against the public interest—or even the public sentiment—it should be checked by Parliament. If public opinion calls for certain measures, Parliament should insist upon them. But it is obviously impossible for a mixed assembly of men without special knowledge, without special ability, men who are merely samples of the ordinary citizens of a country, to take the detailed task and responsibility of governing into its multiple hands.

Yet, despite the grave circumstances in which most countries found themselves, these heterogeneous bodies tried to handle technical matters such as currency questions. In some cases almost any solution would have been better than none; but Parliament wrangled interminably and nothing was done. "Bankruptcy, hideous bankruptcy, is at your door, and you deliberate!" thundered Mirabeau. Throughout Europe, Parliaments, which should have spoken only to good purpose, became more garrulous than before. They should have talked less as the danger grew greater; but the more difficult was the economic or the diplomatic position, the more numerous were the deputies who offered their advice, and as they differed from each other, they simply prevented action.

Parliaments were composed of men who, even in a national crisis, thought chiefly of obtaining oratorical effects, of upsetting the Ministry in sheer vanity, in the exercise of their faculties of intrigue, in the hope of securing posts for themselves and their friends. This kind of Parliamentary behaviour meant ruin. Thus there was a general demand for Strong Men—that is to say, Dictators. Sometimes the Dictators were careful to observe constitutional usages, and to humour Parliament, like Poincaré in France. At other times they brutally denounced Parliament and whipped the deputies from the Temple.

It is not therefore curious that when democratic feeling is

stronger than ever before—stronger than it was in the middle of the nineteenth century, when Liberalism reached its height in Europe—there should be more dictators, or demi-dictators, than European nations have known hitherto. Spain has celebrated the sixth anniversary of the dictatorship of General Primo de Rivera. Italy has tried to constitutionalise Fascism, though Signor Mussolini remains supreme. Poland comes under the intermittent dictatorship of Pilsudski. The Bolshevik chiefs in Russia exercise a collective dictatorship. Mustapha Kemal—if Turkey can still be considered a European country—is the Turkish Dictator. You will find, in French and Polish papers, the title of Dictator fastened upon Waldemaras, the Prime Minister of Lithuania. In Greece, Venizelos is not tender towards the opposition. In Hungary, Bethlen rules with iron hand in velvet glove. The little country of Albania has been kept under the sway of a politician, who has at last been proclaimed King. . . .

For the most part European dictators do not trouble to make themselves kings. Kingship, in the old sense, is discredited. The tsars and kaisers and emperors have been dethroned. There are few left, and such as there are do not govern their countries. The British King is a nominal sovereign, advised by his ministers. The Spanish and Italian Kings are more ornamental than powerful. A few northern countries have constitutional monarchs, but absolute monarchs have disappeared. Precisely at this moment the dictator, who has been a rare figure in history, makes his appearance in many places.

Then, Scriptor, democracy as we understand it, is declining? The peoples have discovered that it is impossible to be properly governed by the mob? Democracy has been found out?

We are living, Lector, in times of exceptional stress, when the old complacent methods are inadequate. Energetic action —not discourses—is needed. Somebody had to assume real responsibility. That is why kings were discredited. They, as mere successors of their fathers, were no longer the leaders that were wanted. They had lost their virtue. Precisely the same cause that overthrew kings or relegated kings to the background, bought forward the dictator. Paradoxical as it appears at first sight, the dictator may, at certain moments, be the true representative of democracy.

I understand, Scriptor, that the dictator may be diametrically opposed to the king, but I do not see how you reconcile dictatorship with democracy.

It is not very difficult, Lector. The king, as such—though there are kings who have whole-heartedly accepted democracy —is the negation of democracy. In France Louis XIV, in Germany Frederick the Great, in Russia the long line of Romanoffs, were Kings who governed according to their own pleasure. Their people may not have had cause for complaint, for dynastic interests are often identical with the interests of the nation. Yet the monarch primarily considered the aggrandisement of his house. To buttress his own power he surrounded himself with a class of hereditary nobles, who again were chiefly concerned with their own advancement.

Whether at a given moment of history this was good or bad —and generally it was good—the idea of hereditary kings was contrary to the idea of democracy. But the ideal dictator does not resemble in the smallest degree the hereditary monarch. He does not primarily consider his own interests, but the interests of the nation. He does not surround himself with hereditary nobles who have a class purpose. On the contrary, his power is based on broader foundations—namely, on the will of the people.

You have yet to show, Scriptor, that the dictator obeys the will of the people.

Please mark, Lector, that I do not say he obeys the will of the people. What I say is that, since he has no hereditary claims to office, no claims which arise out of his personal status, his will must in some way correspond to the will of the people, and the people must be convinced of his good intentions and of his skill, or he would never have succeeded in attaining power or in keeping power. It may be in a particular case you could prove that a dictator imposed himself on the people against their will. But if there be such a case, his dictatorship is doomed from the beginning. In the ideal sense, a dictator can only exist because the people call for his existence. He is their representative. After all, it does not much matter how a man is elected. Methods of election, in the constitutional countries, differ vastly.

What matters is that he should be truly accepted, and unless he is truly accepted he cannot last. Indeed, it is to be doubted whether in these days he could reach the pinnacle of power merely by the exercise of force. He could not collect sufficient partisans unless they saw in him a superior man. And afterwards, if he did not prove his superiority, how could he maintain his partisans? How would he be able to prevent the creation of a counter-organisation unless his partisans were a virtual majority—that is to say, the majority of active as distinct from passive citizens?

Possession, Scriptor, it is said, is nine parts of the law, and a dictator once installed can control all the forces of the country.

That assertion I cannot accept, Lector. He would have, for example, nominal control of the army, but the army would soon affirm its autonomy if it had not a genuine respect for the dictator. Unless the dictator in some manner suited not only partisans but the bulk of the nation, he would be deposed much more certainly, and much more easily, than, say, the Prime Minister of England, or the President of the United States. The Prime Minister of England and the President of the United States, and similar rulers, are elected persons, and once elected it would need a revolution—or at any rate great public clamour —to displace them before their term of office is fulfilled. They are elected for various periods—it may be four or five or seven years. The people having spoken cannot reverse their decision, unless the shortcomings of the elected person are exceptionally flagrant. The poorest President of the United States can properly count upon staying in the White House for four years. But the dictator, who is not elected, can count on nothing at all except repeated demonstrations of his efficiency.

Surely you are not suggesting that a dictator is to be preferred on democratic grounds to a duly elected president?

Not at all, Lector; it is necessary that the rules which a nation has laid down for its own guidance should be observed. Otherwise, there would be confusion, and with no certainty of tenure of office, neither president nor prime minister could accomplish anything. If it be not tacitly agreed that the ruler of a country has come to stay for an appointed time, there must be perpetual upheavals, successive conspiracies, and something like chaos. That is the main argument against the dictator—however excellent he may be, he is always liable to be upset. Normally, an ineffective president or prime minister is better than a superlative dictator, because in the one case the country knows where it is, and in the other case it does not know from month to month where it is likely to be.

Then what becomes of your contention, Scriptor, that the dictator must in a large degree represent the people?

It is surely simple, Lector. While a duly elected person has no need to keep in touch with the people, to retain the good-will of the people, in order to preserve his post (and there are plenty of instances of presidents and prime ministers who have gone on for years doing the exact contrary of that which the people demanded, as is subsequently shown by their overwhelming defeat at the polls) the dictator, on the other hand, must maintain himself precariously, if he does not correspond to a national demand, conscious or unconscious. However he came to power (and I admit that he might have come to power by a favourable combination of circumstances which we usually describe as accidental) he is hourly in peril unless the people wish him to remain.

Therefore my present point being that dictatorship may well be (though it is not invariably) compatible with democracy, I would submit that the existence of dictators in Europe does not necessarily imply a setback for democracy. Democracy has simply manifested itself in a relatively new form. The dictator is irregularly appointed, but it is quite possible that he is as effectively appointed—to say the least—as a regularly appointed person.

Then, in sum, the matter resolves itself into a question of elections or absence of elections, of rules or absence of rules.

That is so, though with the proviso that there should be elections and there should be rules. If there are not, we are in the realm of the arbitrary. Yet those rules have often little virtue in themselves, and only serve as a means of giving the electorate some consciousness of its rights and powers. The essential thing is that the person in power should not only interpret the will of the people, but guide the will of the people, and it is rare that an elected person does this.

The true dictator is the man who boldly indicates the course that national genius should take, and who is instantly recognised to be, from the standpoint of national genius, right. Although then I deprecate the circumstances which make possible a dictator, it is inaccurate, simply because of the existence of dictators, to speak of the decline of democracy in Europe.

VIII. REPARATIONS

REPARATIONS and security were the two principal demands of the victors which were both intended to maintain the vanquished—Germany in particular—in a permanent state of inferiority. While "security" furnished without difficulty the excuse for refusing to disarm after the enforced disarmament of Germany, "reparations," if they were to furnish an excuse for keeping economic and military pressure on Germany, had to be so enormous that they could never be paid.

So the Allies asked for reparations on a scale that had never hitherto been thought of. They wanted them a hundredfold greater than those of the Franco-Prussian war only fifty years before. Hence the resistance of Germany, the gradual collapse of Allied expectations, and an endless search for a compromise. At last a compromise is reached, but it cannot, despite General Dawes and Owen D. Young, be final; for it makes Germany responsible for Allied debts to America for a period of sixty years.

It would be closing one's eyes to obvious facts to suppose that the Young Commission of Experts has settled satisfactorily and definitely the perplexing question. No good can come of pretending that anything more than another temporary arrangement is reached.

I have, perhaps, been more intimately and continuously associated with the various conferences and committees which have dealt with the reparations problem than most of my colleagues. It began in 1919, and since that time I have had hundreds of discussions with statesmen and economists who have endeavoured to find practical solutions.

At the Versailles Conference the most extraordinary figures were mentioned. Nobody seemed to know what they meant. When we are told that the earth is so many millions of miles from the moon, we do not doubt the estimate, but we cannot realise what it means. It was so with the statesmen and economists at Versailles. That is why we invented the phrase, "astronomical figures."

There was one statesman-financier, I remember, who actually spoke of 400,000,000,000 gold marks, and somehow expected Germany to pay the amount without delay. Certainly warning voices were raised. Even then a few people—but they were very few—suggested that the Allies should deem themselves fortunate if they received as much as 40,000,000,000—that is to say, a tenth part of what was proposed. It may not be without interest to add that one of the American delegates on the Dawes Committee in private conversation fixed German payments at a maximum of 16,000,000,000.

This curious declension from four hundred to sixteen milliards will give the lay reader some idea of the temper of Versailles. It was useless to argue. It was useless to point out that no such sums of money could be obtained. Eventually it was decided to leave the amount and modalities of German payments to a later date. Thus there was no sudden disappointment, and for ten years Europe has been slowly awakening to realities.

I can hardly count the conferences which I subsequently attended in various parts of Europe. Always was this question of reparations the subject of earnest deliberations. At Spa, I recall, the Germans advanced a scheme under which they would have paid something like 100,000,000,000. Had the Allies been wise they would have jumped at such an offer. As it was, they thought it ridiculously low. To-day it would be regarded as preposterously high.

It sounded so ridiculously low that it was hardly mentioned in the newspapers. Yet I was convinced that Germany was quite sincere at that moment. There was another reason why it was not even taken into account. The scheme chiefly consisted in the provisions of reparations in kind. Germany could not pay the money, but Germany had the material and the men, and thought that it would be an excellent thing to send materials and men into the devastated regions. There was opposition on the French side to this method. French contractors did not wish to be deprived of the job of rebuilding. Later, it is true, M. Loucheur and Herr Rathenau worked out a plan of reparations in kind, but that plan was itself inadequate and was most inadequately carried out.

At Brussels a decision was reached on the percentages that each nation should have of the hypothetical reparations. France managed to obtain fifty-two per cent. "It is more important to decide," said one distinguished statesman to me, "how the cake shall be cut up, than to decide on the size of the cake." Perhaps: but in the meantime the cake was diminishing in size every day.

Balzac tells the story of a magical wild ass's skin—*La Peau de*

THE REPARATIONS CONFERENCE IN PARIS

Chagrin—which was to bring prosperity to its owner, but which, bit by bit, shrank away to nothing. That is reparations. In 1921, at London, a figure was actually fixed. That figure was 132,000,000,000.

M. Briand, who is now thoroughly convinced of the impossibility of receiving such sums, was then in power and he began the occupation of the Ruhr by seizing Ruhrort, Duisbourg, and Düsseldorf. M. Poincaré two years later occupied the whole of the Ruhr, but M. Poincaré, too, is now convinced that not a third of the amount can possibly be obtained.

Both these French statesmen were unable to grasp the meaning of these astronomical figures. They thought Germany was deliberately a defaulter. At Cannes M. Briand favoured a partial moratorium, but he was overthrown because France generally could not understand why Germany should escape its supposed liabilities. M. Poincaré, after the breakdown of the Paris Conference, at which Andrew Bonar Law represented England, though he felt compelled to occupy the Ruhr proper, tacitly admitted that France would be satisfied with 26,000,-000,000 marks.

Day after day I followed the struggle in the Reparations Commission. Germany, it was alleged, was not only recalcitrant, but was cheating the Allies by provoking the fall of the mark. Whatever may have been the causes of the fall of the mark—and doubtless not enough was done to prevent national bankruptcy—it became clear that Germany could not pay; hence at the end of 1923, M. Poincaré consented to the appointment of the Dawes Committee, and before he left office in 1924, agreed to the adoption of its findings.

Those findings were interesting and helpful, but by no means conclusive. They gave Europe a breathing space. But the task that was set the Dawes Committee was narrowly circumscribed. It was not asked to solve the reparations problem. It was merely asked to ascertain Germany's capacity of payment as expressed in annuities. The Dawes Committee was not empowered to change the total of the German debt, which therefore remained at 132,000,000,000. It was not even asked to state the number of annuities which should be paid.

If one now examines its conclusions coldly, one must pass the following verdict: that the temporary arrangement brought some peace to Europe and made possible a Franco-German *rapprochement* whence have sprung the Locarno Pact, the reëstablishment of the League of Nations, the restoration of Germany, and at last the Kellogg Pact; but that the Dawes Committee did not solve the reparations problem because, even had it been able to do so, it would not have been allowed to do so, and its figures bear no relation to the supposed German debt.

Any banker's clerk can see the absurdity of the Dawes Plan, examined from the viewpoint of the German debt of 132,000,-000,000. The normal payments annually under the Dawes Plan are 2,500,000,000. This means (to stick to round and approximate figures) that the German annuities do not represent much more than one and a half per cent on the capital sum. Now, no lender would dream of accepting such a rate of interest. There is no provision for amortisation. We will leave out of consideration questions of present and future value, of compound interest, and so forth. We will keep the sum as simple as possible. It is surely clear beyond all contention that if Germany paid 2,500,000,000 annually for 1,000 years, it would, nevertheless, owe more at the end of that time than it owes now.

That was the weakness of the Dawes Plan. There was neither a revision of the capital sum nor a time limit to the annuities. The Dawes Plan served its purpose, but its makers were well aware that, when Europe saw the situation more clearly, the Plan would have to be radically changed.

It follows that reparations were a pure fiction. If the total were taken seriously, then the Allies were cheating themselves. If it were not taken seriously, then the Allies were cheating Germany. Germany was either paying too little or too much.

Hence the appointment of the Young Commission of which Sir Josiah Stamp, the British delegate, was the most talented member, to find, ten years after the signing of the Versailles Treaty, how much Germany owes the Allies! By a strange coincidence it was discovered by the Governments, before the experts met, that Germany owes the Allies the amount that the Allies owe the United States—plus as much more as the Allies can get. This preliminary rule for the guidance of the Experts entirely vitiates their findings. They have no scientific basis; they are purely arbitrary, and are conditioned by Allied needs. Of course Germany does not owe anything in the same sense as the Allies owe money to America. The Allies borrowed and, normally, unless there is a general cancellation of debts, should repay. Germany borrowed nothing; and all the sums extorted from it, together with the colonies taken, the mines, the public works and the land acquired by the Allies in Europe, already constitute a formidable war indemnity.

It is, however, still believed by the Allies that for sixty years more Germany can be made to pay an annual tribute. For thirty-seven years Germany is called upon to pay, in round figures, an annuity of 2,000,000,000 marks, which corresponds to British and French and other payments to the United States, with an additional sum for "reparations proper." There is not even a pretence now that the bulk of Germany's payments are for "reparations proper"! Afterwards, for twenty-two years more, Germany is called upon to pay the rest of the Allied debt to America. There is no disguise about it. Frankness could not further go. Reparations have practically disappeared from the picture; and Germany is substituted by the Allies for themselves as the debtor of America on account of Allied borrowings.

This reversal of rôles is staggering. I confess that, watching in Paris the work of the Experts, I was breathless at the extraordinary audacity of the theory that what Germany owes are not reparations but Allied borrowings; but I waited in vain for a German protest. Dr. Schacht seemed to think it good tactics to join with the Allies in representing that the United States was the sole cause of European financial troubles; if the United States cancels the Allied debt, then Germany will have its debt cancelled, too; if the United States does not, then it is Germany which is the single sufferer.

In the meantime the Allies, rather than Germany, complain of the burden of their debts to America. Why? They have not to pay them, since Germany pays on their behalf. Yet France in particular groans loudly under a weight which Germany bears, and raises the most pathetic pleas, the most noble protests, the most bitter vituperations, against the obligation of repaying debts—which it is not repaying but simply forcing Germany to pay. France, then, and the rest of the victorious countries, are pressed down by debts which they do not carry; while Germany, the vanquished country, which does carry them, is angrily denounced as a defaulter if it ventures to suggest that, as the defeated country, it is hardly in a position to pay out for everybody. It is proper for the others to lament their single load which they have transferred, but for Germany to lament the several loads thus transferred is rank treason.

Of course this incredible condition of affairs cannot last. It is not "final and definitive."

I have no personal connections of any kind with Germany. I have no great liking for Germany, but it is impossible, if one thinks at all, to accept this topsy-turvy state of things as rational. If it were frankly admitted that the object is to hold Germany to ransom, at the highest price, then there would be nothing to say. But to argue that: (1) Germany owes reparations (2) the Allies have debts (3) therefore Germany must pay the Allied debts—is the craziest syllogism I have ever heard.

IX. OCCUPATION

OF COURSE the imposition of so-called reparations was intended as a method of holding Germany down. It provided the French with an excellent excuse, in 1923, for invading the Ruhr, from which they were with difficulty dislodged —the occupation of the Ruhr being described as a "pledge" of "reparations." It gave them an excellent excuse for exploiting the coal mines of the Saar, which is purely German territory, placed until 1935 under international control—the coal being regarded as "compensation" for the temporarily ruined mines of Northern France. Above all it gave them an excuse for occupying the Rhineland, where with the British and the Belgians they have been for ten years, and for fomenting separatist movements; though the occupation of the Rhineland has really nothing to do with "reparations."

Imagine the southern counties of England occupied by a foreign army for ten years! Imagine New York State and Massachusetts occupied by a foreign army for ten years! Civilised nations, which profess to be at peace, do not occupy each other's countries.

Once I declared that history will rank the occupation of Germany for ten years with the six months' blockade of starving Germany after the Armistice. There was some indignant dissent; but I repeat my declaration. This continued use of force, without valid purpose, is a proof that, despite more peace talk than has ever before been heard in the world, we permit the military spirit to manifest itself more mischievously and meaninglessly than in any earlier period.

At last, with the so-called settlement of the so-called reparations problem, Germany seriously demanded that the Allied troops should be withdrawn. It was generally felt that it had become impossible to maintain alien troops on German soil any longer. The Allied "watch on the Rhine" could not be indefinitely prolonged. The Young Report contemplated an early withdrawal since it failed to make provision for the payment by Germany of the upkeep of occupying armies beyond September of 1929.*

The actual number of Allied effectives in the Rhineland was variously estimated. Herr Müller, the German Chancellor, put them at sixty-seven thousand men; but according to my figures (obtained from official sources) the Allied forces were somewhat smaller. The French troops numbered forty-eight thousand, the Belgian troops over five thousand, and the British troops about the same.

If there were, roughly, sixty thousand men in the Rhineland, this was a considerable reduction in the forces of the earlier years when American soldiers were also in occupation. Then in round numbers Germany had to support a hundred thousand French soldiers, fifteen thousand Belgian soldiers and over eight thousand British soldiers. The American army, originally about seventeen thousand, dropped in 1922 to seven thousand, and was withdrawn in January 1923. The French curiously point out that, before the War, the Germans kept nearly the same number of soldiers in these districts which are now, so far as the Germans are concerned, demilitarised. But this argument misses the point; it is not the number of troops, but their nationality to which the Germans object.

Strictly, the Allies could argue that they were entitled to stay on the Rhine until 1935. Germany signed the Versailles Treaty which contains articles—from 428 to 432—permitting the Allies to occupy the west bank of the Rhine for a period of fifteen years. The fifteen years were to count from the coming into force of the Versailles Treaty—namely January 10, 1920.

At one time it was urged in France that the fifteen years should not begin to count until Germany was fulfilling all the conditions of the Treaty, and should not come to an end until every possible guarantee had been given. There is no doubt that, availing themselves of ambiguous clauses, certain Frenchmen would have endeavoured to occupy the Rhineland in perpetuity.

Indeed that was the idea which animated the French military

* At the Hague Conference it was agreed to withdraw the troops by July 1930.

men who called for the detachment of Rhineland from Germany. Marshal Foch asserted in his famous memorandum—as recorded by André Tardieu in the most authoritative book on the peace-making—that the frontiers of Germany should not extend beyond the Rhine. That has been the traditional diplomacy of France from the days of Richelieu. But nobody could pretend that the Rhineland was non-German, and Wilson and Lloyd George could not agree to any proposal which would tend to separate the Rhineland from the rest of Germany.

The period of fifteen years which was agreed to was a compromise. There was something to be said for retaining possession of the bridge-heads of the Rhine until such time as it was clearly seen that Germany could not resume the offensive and was prepared to execute the conditions of peace. But certainly the British and the American representatives regarded fifteen years as a maximum.

They made provision for evacuation in successive stages. At the end of five years the Cologne bridge-head and the territory attaching to it was to be evacuated. At the end of ten years the bridge-head of Coblentz, and the zone commanded by it was to be evacuated. Finally, at the end of fifteen years, the bridge-head of Mainz (Mayence) and the bridge-head of Kehl, and the rest of the German territories, should also be evacuated.

Owing to difficulties which arose in the execution of the Treaty, the evacuation of the Cologne zone was delayed for a year. Instead of leaving at the beginning of 1925, the Allies left at the beginning of 1926. The second zone—of Coblentz—should normally be evacuated by January, 1930. Thus there would remain only the third zone—that of Mainz—where the Allies might have stayed for another five years.

The occupation was defined by the Treaty as a guarantee of the execution by Germany of its obligations. The quinquennial evacuations were to be effected, if Germany faithfully observed the Treaty; and the withdrawal of the Cologne troops in 1926 indicated that, in the opinion of the Allies, Germany had faithfully observed the Treaty. But it was also laid down that if the guarantees against aggression were not considered sufficient by the Allies, the evacuation could be postponed even after 1935; it would be difficult to pretend that with the Locarno Pact and the Kellogg Pact, and the proper observance by Germany of the conditions of the Treaty, such reasonable guarantees have not been furnished.

Article 431 says that, if before the expiration of the fifteen years Germany satisfies its engagements, the occupational troops will be immediately withdrawn. Evacuation is specifically promised.

Nevertheless it was said that Germany had not satisfied its engagements, for it must go on paying reparations for nearly sixty years. This contention is not sound. It could never have been contemplated by the Allies that the occupation should last as long as the payment of reparations. Otherwise it would have been sheer mockery to limit the occupation ostensibly to fifteen years. There was no question of Germany's completion of payments in fifteen years. In the nature of the case this was an obligation which would extend over a much longer period; and the period of occupation therefore bears no relation to the completion of German payments.

Any ordinary reading of the Treaty would show that what was intended was the fulfilment of such engagements as could be fulfilled, and the continuing execution of such engagements as were spread over a long period of time. In support of this view—which, however, is a matter of common sense—we have only to refer to article 430. It states that, if after the withdrawal of Allied troops Germany refuses to carry out its reparation obligations, then the Rhineland may be reoccupied. Obviously there cannot be reoccupation until after evacuation, and equally obvious if reoccupation is the result of Germany's refusal to fulfil its reparation obligations, then the previous evacuation must have taken place before the completion of reparation obligations!

The French, nevertheless, demanded a price for "premature" evacuation. They asked for a supervisory commission "of conciliation" which would still keep Germany in subjection. With the League of Nations in existence, with a whole series of international agreements for the preservation of peace, why, ten years after the War, should it be assumed that Germany any more than another country, stands in need of special supervision? *

The legal aspect of this question is uninteresting. The peacemakers said fifteen years as they might have said five or fifty or five hundred. The period is purely arbitrary, and when the passions of 1919 disappeared, the situation should have been looked at with fresh eyes. When Germany was admitted on an equal footing with the rest of the great powers to the League

* It was eventually agreed to drop this demand for a special committee.

of Nations, it was generally agreed that the time-limit to exceptional treatment had been reached.

Military coercion raises a moral issue. Either we believe in
international friendships as the surest guarantee of peace, or we
believe that the unfriendly, and in modern times unprecedented,
course of maintaining troops on the territory of a great nation,
is the only way of preserving peace. In fact, military occupation of Germany, continued beyond a certain point, is a certain
path to war, for no nation with a sense of its dignity can fail
to resent the unjustifiable employment of force against it. The
War could not be over until the withdrawal of the last Allied
soldier. Only with the end of occupation would be closed the
period of enforced peace, and the period of genuine peace open.

X. DISARMAMENT

IT WAS stupidly thought that the disarmament of Germany
would in itself prevent another war. But the French soon
protested that the disarmament of Germany was illusory.
Nominally, Germany possesses an army of only 100,000 men,
but these men are volunteers who remain under arms for a long
period of years. They are professionals, who may at once become
officers, and lead large armies in the field. They constitute what
the French call an army of *cadres*—the framework of a very
much larger army. But where is the larger army to be found?
It is to be found, if necessary, in gymnastic societies and in other
associations which at least teach discipline and develop physical
strength and endurance. As for the material, the French assert
that it is comparatively easy to convert peace-time factories
into war-time factories. The French exaggerate for political
purposes, but there is, nevertheless, some truth in the contention
that civilian aeroplanes, for example, can be quickly turned into
military aeroplanes, that poison gases can be produced speedily
and in enormous quantities, that citizens can be transformed
into soldiers in a few months—as Great Britain and as the
United States made soldiers of citizens in a few months.

In short, Germany, with its larger population, is as strong as
France, despite the disarmament clauses of the Treaty. The
French, though they cling to their conception of conscription,
which gives them half a million men in garrisons, are not persuaded that their half-million men would be as effective as the
hundred thousand men of Germany. Here again France exag-

gerates, for while it is probable that the conscripts learn very little of soldiering and soon forget all they have learned, yet France has, in addition to its conscripts, a volunteer army as great as the German volunteer army, and, moreover, has reservoirs of black troops on which to draw.

The chief task of the League of Nations is to disarm France and Poland and Czecho-Slovakia and Yugo-Slavia and the rest of the nations which promised to reduce their armies in the same proportion as Germany. Unhappily it is a task that is beyond the power of the League of Nations. Disarmament conferences have become a byword. Nobody believes in them. At the best they might result in agreements to restrict expenditures on armies and navies to a point compatible with the various nations' conceptions of their needs, but no nation will voluntarily agree to the reduction of its relative strength. Mr. Hugh F. Spender, from his post of observation in Geneva, recently raised a cry of alarm. After ten years of peace, filled with efforts to find a basis for disarmament, it is seen that the tendency is to increase armaments; and the European countries, with the exception of Germany and other defeated nations, are spending as much to-day as they did in 1914, allowing for the difference in the value of money. France and Great Britain, he says, commenting on the statistics in the Armaments Year Book of the League for 1929, are now up to the 1913 standard of expenditure. Moreover, Germany, although limited by the Peace Treaty to a small standing army and navy, and forbidden to make big guns, tanks, or military aeroplanes, has largely increased its expenditure on armaments, while Hungary is known to be spending large sums in various inconspicuous ways.

"The military expenditure of the new States—Poland, Czecho-Slovakia and Yugo-Slavia—involves a heavy strain on the resources of their peoples, while Rumania has a larger standing army than it had in 1911, during the Balkanic wars. Other countries like Finland, Estonia and Latvia, are piling up their military expenditure as a protection against Russia, although anything that they can do would be of little use in a war with that colossus.

"Russia which might have been expected to show a reduction in armaments since its appeal for total disarmament, has, during the past three years, doubled its military expenditure. Italy is also rapidly adding to its armaments, and has a large militia of 'Black Shirts,' who are not included in the military establishment."

This statement is conclusive. Disarmament is merely a theme for politicians at Geneva, while the military men, working with the responsible Governments, are busily strengthening their fortifications, developing their armaments, and training their armies.

Over £500,000,000 a year is spent by an impoverished Europe on armaments.

When Germany or Russia presses for genuine disarmament, an embarrassed clamour is sent up. We are deafened with cries that these countries are only indulging in political manœuvres, that they are not sincere, that they are seeking to draw an admission of failure from the League in order that they can go ahead with their own armaments. It was interesting to observe the curious reaction to the proposed experiment of the Danish Government, to abolish the Ministries of War and Marine, to abandon conscription, to demolish existing fortifications, to reduce the army to a mere constabulary force and the navy to a few police vessels in territorial water. Instead of being welcomed as a practical beginning, as a bold example which smaller nations could better afford to set than greater nations, this Danish initiative aroused alarm.

For once, even the militarists made use of the unquestionable fact of interdependence among nations. It was argued that interdependence implies definite responsibilities, and that it is the duty of the whole world to rally to the support of any country which is the victim of injustice. But if the potential victim of injustice expects help in time of trouble, then it follows that it should be prepared in its turn to help other nations in their need. Thus no nation, big or little, should step outside the general understanding and reduce itself to entire helplessness.

This contention was set forth clearly in the leading European newspapers. It was suggested that Denmark would forfeit the right to assistance if it renounced the possibility of lending assistance. Disarmament should not, in present conditions, be carried below "the point compatible with national safety." Otherwise, by disarming, any particular nation throws itself as a burden on the rest of the world. It presents itself as a temptation to a strong neighbour, and increases rather than decreases the chances of conflict. As applied to Denmark, these arguments are absurd though specious. Nobody ever expected or could possibly demand effective assistance from a little country which will be neither more nor less safe with or without arms. The truth is that all the Great Powers are afraid lest the disarmament blather should be taken seriously. It is an excellent diversion for the peoples, and especially for the credulous pacifists, but there is a danger that some country will really start to disarm.

At present the world military forces approximate 5,500,000 soldiers. While sea power is decreasing, the navies of the world still have 5,047,300 tonnage of warships afloat. There may certainly be a halt if the race becomes too fierce, and even reductions, but such an arrangement will be in the nature of a truce, leaving things relatively as they are, and it will have nothing but an outward resemblance to the operation which the common people, and the pacifists, originally understood by disarmament.

Paradoxical as it may appear, it does not indeed much matter whether disarmament conferences result in disarmament or not. I hasten to explain that the mere mechanical reduction of armaments will not prevent war if the war-like spirit is still abroad. A battle between *apaches* armed with knives is no less bloody than a battle between *apaches* armed with revolvers. It is necessary to persuade the *apache* that personal combats are foolish, unnecessary, and dishonourable. So it is with nations. The debates about the employment of poison gas have always seemed to me beside the point. To rule out the Zeppelin and to admit the aeroplane cannot make for peace. The consecration of the dreadnought and the denunciation of the submarine may affect the conditions of naval warfare, may assure victory to one side or the other, but will not, in themselves, prevent naval warfare.

The old adage, "If you want peace, prepare for war," has been discredited; and we know that the piling up of weapons is perilous. If one collects explosives, they are likely to explode, and guns kept at full cock have a habit of going off by themselves. Yet, to assure peace it is not sufficient that the explosives should be cut by half, or even by nine-tenths. If that reduction does not represent a change of heart it will always be inadequate. The United States of America had, in 1917, no army and no munitions (I speak relatively), but army and munitions sprang from the ground at the tapping of a heel; and America's lack of army and munitions did not keep America out of the

War. Nor had England, in 1914, army or munitions; nevertheless, England entered the fray first, and found army and munitions afterwards. If troops were abolished and navies scrapped
tomorrow, conflicts would not thereby be rendered impossible.

This is, of course, reasoning in the abstract. In practice, disarmament presupposes a will to peace. It is the will to peace
that is vital. Theoretically, nations might agree to surrender
this or that instrument of warfare, without thereby expressing
a determination to outlaw war. They might, indeed, see a
belligerent advantage in the agreement. Disarmament, if it is
worth while, must be the consequence of peace, and of the
sincere desire for the perpetuation of peace. It is not, as such,
a preparation for peace, nor a guarantee of peace.

These remarks are commonplace, but they are to be repeated,
because commonplaces are too often forgotten nowadays. If
everybody had a sense of security, disarmament would follow
automatically. Without a sense of security, it is possible to conceive partial disarmament, but partial disarmament will not
affect events any more than the disbanding of the police
forces will affect crime—or, rather, the effect may be contrary
to our wishes.

Then you are arguing against disarmament, Scriptor? You
think that disarmament conferences are useless? You are asserting that the problem is being tackled at the wrong end?

Not at all, Lector. I believe in disarmament. I believe in
disarmament conferences. I am glad that the League holds its
deliberations on disarmament, even though most of the delegates are insincere or have their hands tied. I am glad when
naval conferences are convoked, even though they are, in the
upshot, abortive.

Why? Not because it greatly matters whether disarmament
is specifically and immediately advanced by an accord at the
disarmament conferences. What is valuable is the discussion itself, and the insistence on the need of international arrangements which will be, in some degree, an insurance against war.
The League has failed—if by failure one means that nothing is
accomplished on which one can put one's finger—but it has
succeeded in the only way it can succeed at present; namely,
in keeping the subject before the public, in arousing a popular
demand for disarmament, in proclaiming and reinforcing the
universal desire for perpetual peace.

The League has, of course, accomplished nothing after ten

years. The Powers ask for a "comprehensive" settlement, though if we wait until a comprehensive settlement is possible we shall have to wait for hundreds of years. The French, indeed, not only refuse to separate the problem of land forces from the problem of sea forces, but they pretend that all decisions must be postponed until we know everything about the potentialities of war—geographical situations, demographic figures, economic possibilities; they would have us ascertain whether automobile factories can make munitions, and if so, in what quantities; they would have us poring over railroad maps; they would, in a word, regard the entire resources of a nation from the military viewpoint. This theory is, philosophically, quite correct. Doubtless there is a link between the number of earthworms, determining the character of the soil, and the number of cannons in a country. Doubtless flora and fauna are not unrelated to flying men and field-marshals. But this is absurdly academic. It is reducing a sound intellectual concept to the ridiculous. It has been called scornfully the hogs-bogs-and-fogs theory; for hogs and bogs and fogs affect the maintenance of an army and the manœuvres of an army. Sensible men, however, are impatient when such a thesis, which would paralyse action, is put forward. We cannot remake the world completely, but we can make a beginning.

It must be admitted that there is disagreement all along the line; and, in Europe, Germany urges that the non-fulfilment of the Treaty promise, releases it from the unilateral disarmament clauses of the Treaty. It is certain that before long— if the process has not already begun—the European countries which were defeated and consented to the Allied limitations of their navies, armies, and aeroplanes, will ignore these stipulations and place themselves on an equality with the victors. Europe will be more heavily armed than it was before 1914.

If this pessimistic prognostication is to be routed, the subject must, at all costs, be kept before the public. It is important, too, that illusions should not be fostered. Many good people think it is good to profess gratification at the outcome of the Geneva discussions. They are surely wrong. The outcome should be denounced. One set of nations relies on conscripted armies, and in defiance of its own reasoning declines to count the hundreds of thousands, even millions, of trained reserves, in its estimates of its armies. France, the apostle of comprehensiveness, which would mobilise women and children as well as men, capital as well as labour, will not consider its reserves as part of its army.

XI. "THE NEXT WAR"

YET, while everybody is talking peace and thinking war, the most terrible warnings are given by some of the most distinguished savants against the chemical and bacteriological war which they declare is a possibility of the future. It would be difficult to exaggerate the importance of the document in which they make known their views.

Strangely enough, it is through the Commission of the League that this revelation of the inadequacy of international conventions is made. Whether we like it or not, we are bound to realise that, while it will be good to take every conceivable step to prevent war, to obtain as many promises as can be extracted, to form a solid front against aggressors, it would be folly not to bear in mind the chances of some particular country ignoring its engagements and beginning a destructive campaign with a swiftness and completeness that would render abortive the best laid scheme of the League.

That is where the danger lies, and it would be well to have no illusions. We should accept gratefully any safeguards that can be found, but we should not be lulled into a false sense of security. Perhaps the best thing the League has yet done is to issue a warning against excessive confidence in the speech-making of Geneva and the arrangements that may be subsequently concluded.

For the Commission, after pointing to the numerous and varied methods by which science can be pressed into the service of war, observes gravely that there is a veritable danger—a danger of death—for a nation to sleep upon international conventions. It may suddenly be awakened and find itself without protection against a new weapon. These are not my words. They are the words of the Commission, which believes it is necessary that the peoples should know what menace hangs over them.

The problem of disarmament is far more complicated than those who regard the matter superficially suspect. This remarkable report is intended to persuade the public that some means must be found of averting another war, but in exposing the evils of a fresh conflict, the Commission and its Experts make it clear that we should be mad to trust in mere words and measures which may prove to be belated and useless.

We have, says the American Professor W. B. Cannon, seen nothing in the course of the last war which can be compared with the probable destruction of industrial centres and massacres of the civil population in the event of another serious conflict: and the French Professor André Mayer rightly remarks that the peoples are not aware of the perils to which they are exposed. Here is an objective statement which cannot be refuted, which should, properly understood, make war unthinkable, but which should also make us more vigilant than ever, while a single nation animated by the war spirit and capable of contemplating revenge exists.

It is authoritatively asserted that it will be technically possible to attack the great cities with toxic gas from the air. Bombs of huge dimensions may be thrown upon vital centres—centres indispensable to the political and economic life of an enemy country. The effects will not be temporary. Gases will render whole districts uninhabitable for a long time. Defence will be difficult.

Typhus and cholera germs can be introduced into the water supply of great towns, and plague can be spread by means of rats. It is true that the experts consider the bacteriological arm less dangerous at present than the chemical arm, for there are means of counteracting the attempts to propagate disease. Filtration of waters and other preventive measures may be effective. But this assumes that the population will not be taken by surprise. It assumes that each country which may be attacked will not consider itself safe, will not suppose that war has been abolished for ever. In so far as the belief prevails that there will in future be no aggression, the country entertaining such belief will be open to the most terrible attacks.

Chemical warfare was indeed ruled out by earlier conventions, but all the belligerents, after the first violation of these conventions, resorted to the employment of gas in the last war. So far the use of this weapon has been confined to the various fronts, but unquestionably the non-combatants will suffer even more than the combatants if there is again fighting on a grand scale. Perhaps the safest place in the next war will be at the front!

The air raids of the Great War will be as nothing compared with the air raids which are foreseen by the Commission. The irritant, the asphyxiant, and the poison gases which may be used will be far more deadly than the explosives which, however powerful, have a limited area of destruction. The report enumerates the various chemical substances which can even now be brought into action. Temporary blindness can be produced by one gas, and fits of sneezing by another.

The lungs can be fatally affected by yet another chemical combination. Or paralysis of the whole nervous system can be produced. Even though some of these gases are unpleasant rather than deadly, they are all capable of putting large sections of the population *hors de combat*.

The gas mask becomes useless if the gas is of a certain density, and, moreover, it requires some practice to employ it efficaciously. We are told plainly that a crowd taken by surprise and untrained will be altogether helpless. During the War the soldiers, trusting in the conventions of The Hague, did not foresee the use of gas. A catastrophe may overtake an unprepared civilian population which trusts in conventions.

The noxious substances required for chemical warfare are currently used in time of peace. Therefore, the chemical arm, says the report, is at the disposition of any great industrial power which possesses chemical factories. The American Professor Zanetti declares that the extreme facility with which commercial factories can be transformed almost in a night into factories in which material intended for a chemical war can be manufactured, must give rise to a sentiment of fear and distrust of neighbouring nations which possess powerful chemical organisations.

Such nations with evil designs have an immense superiority. Secret chemical research may be undertaken almost anywhere. A dangerous chemical may be produced in immense quantities. Thrown upon an unprepared population, all possibility of resistance may be broken at the outset.

Such is the alarming prospect which is described, not by imaginative novelists or scaremongering publicists, but by the Commission of the League which has investigated the possibilities with the assistance of a number of well-known scientists.

These pages cannot be too widely read. They bring home to us the necessity of striving with all our might to prevent a new war with all its horrors. But they also bring home to us the necessity of facing up to realities, of not accepting mere verbal assurances, of not attaching undue importance even to the reduction of armies, of not proclaiming that there is peace when perhaps there is no peace.

XII. THE PEACE PACT

BUT it is not on that note that I would end this general survey of European conditions. One may properly be sceptical about the League of Nations. One may say that it is only half a league—half a league onward! One may say that "it touches nothing that it does not adjourn." One may dismiss as fudge nine-tenths of the pacific declarations of amiable ladies and astute diplomatists. But it may, if it drops a good deal of its terminology, and gets down to realities, accomplish useful educative work. It may marshal public opinion on the side of peace. The League has become an established institution with an army of officials and hangers-on; it has made the mistake of allowing itself to be monopolised and controlled by the Foreign Offices; it has timidly endorsed explosive pacts of alliance; it has encouraged wishy-washy sentiment that is more perilous than downright bellicosity; but in spite of these things it has truly promulgated the idea of peace. The world is athirst for peace, and every nation is bound by covenants and pledges which cannot be broken without arousing protests—protests that in the offending country itself will not be anti-patriotic, but of humanitarian validity. The moral factors in human relations are universally recognised and stressed. Ten years ago I witnessed the arrival of President Wilson in the French capital. With what enthusiasm was he greeted! The United States had not only made the winning of the War possible but—and this was regarded as much more important—had made the winning of the peace possible.

Opinions differ about the part played by Mr. Wilson, and for some years a wave of disillusionment swept over Europe. But when Mr. Kellogg took the same path as his distinguished predecessor, memories of those days of high hope, of earnest endeavour, crowded in upon me.

There never was a more popular figure in Europe than President Wilson. His clean, smiling face, squarely chiselled, stirred the emotions of men from London to Athens, from Moscow to Rome. Out of the fiery furnace the common people came with strong determination that never again should war devastate the world. They rejoiced in the advent of Mr. Wilson. He represented for them their aspiration. He was the embodiment of a universal demand.

Then ten years later it was my function to describe the scene in the *Salle de l'Horloge* at the Quai d'Orsay, when the plenipotentiaries of fifteen countries stepped forward one by one to append their signatures to the Treaty for the Renunciation of War which had been elaborated by M. Aristide Briand and Mr. Frank B. Kellogg. It was later to be accepted by the whole world. The ceremony was simple, but it was truly significant of the change that has come over men's minds.

The *Salle de l'Horloge* is named after the splendid chimney at the far end, in which is encrusted a fine clock. The marble and ormolu mantelpiece is exquisitely ornamented with a statue; a female form depicting Wisdom stretching forth an arm over the statesmen. Great candelabra, reflecting light in thousands of facets, hang from the ornate ceiling, heavily charged with scrolls and figures. Mirrors and tapestries and fluted columns contribute to the admirable aspect of the handsome hall.

Into this room, with its gilded armchairs, open other rooms, to which were admitted carefully selected representatives of the countries concerned.

Everybody realised that he was present at a spectacle which (whatever the sequel) will always find place in the history of mankind. We were agog with curiosity. There was much straining of necks, much eagerness to see and identify the principal actors as they entered, each in characteristic manner, the *Salle de l'Horloge*.

There were flowers everywhere, flowers which were emblems of peace. They were set in Sèvres vases, roses, scarlet and white, and varicoloured dahlias. Through the windows one caught glimpses of the green lawns and flower beds of the French Foreign Office. But there were other objects that looked strange in this dignified room. There were microphones, more or less cunningly concealed behind the tapestries, by which each word spoken could be broadcast throughout the world, and one of them registered speeches for the talking cinema, so that when the film was shown, the statesmen would be heard as well as seen.

Those cinema machines could not be kept out of the picture. There were seven of them working with a will. It occurred to me how interested we should be in witnessing this or that momentous scene in our country's history, that took

Aristide Briand

place hundreds of years ago. We cannot but hope our children will be fortunate enough to watch ceremonies which are the modern equivalents of the signing of the Magna Charta or the promulgation of the Declaration of Independence. So, for the sake of posterity, we must forgive the cinema men's intrusion with machines and arc lights.

There in the centre was Briand, flushed, with arched back, drooping moustache, keen eyes which belie the general impression of indolence. By him was quiet Kellogg, in the chair of President Wilson, moved at the thought of the crowning of his life work.   There was Stresemann, round-headed, deep-chested, the first German Minister on an official mission in the French capital since the Franco-Prussian War of 1871. Lord Cushendun, typical country gentleman, enormous and erect, bore the weight not only of Great Britain but of Northern Ireland, India and those parts of the Empire which have no separate representation at the League. Again one observed the Roman features, clean-cut, of Count Manzoni of Italy.

These were the principal personages in the Clock Room. But there were others equally prominent in this setting. Mackenzie King, stalwart, hearty delegate from Canada; Hymans, slim, sharp-faced minister from Belgium; Uchida, tiny and grave, who came from far-off Japan to sign the pact; Bénès, active, little, from Czecho-Slovakia; Zaleski, dreamy-eyed spokesman of Poland; Smit, stolid South African; McLachland, jolly Australian; Parr, acting on behalf of New Zealand; and Cosgrave, from the Free State of Ireland.

I am by no means *blasé* about the Pact. I think it possesses a genuine importance. I also think that, as a document, it is utterly worthless. Rarely have both sides in a controversy been so right as those who belittle the Pact and those who magnify the Pact. The Pact means nothing, and it means much. Should we be sceptical? Yes and no. We should be poor diplomatic students, if we were not somewhat cynically amused at the loopholes which have been left in the text or which have been created by interpretative and explanatory statements. Anybody can go to war for anything at any time, and reconcile his behaviour by reference to the correspondence that accompanied the negotiations. Yet I do not think that, in fact, anybody will go to war before turning round upon himself as many times as a dog which seeks a suitable sleeping place.

No diplomatist wished to sign this Pact. It is, in my somewhat lengthy experience, the Unwanted Pact *par excellence*. M. Briand threw out his suggestion nearly eighteen months before in a thoughtless moment as a harmless and inconsequential oratorical flourish. When it was taken up seriously in the United States, the French Foreign Office was greatly troubled, and raised every possible argument against the translation of a peroration into a Treaty. Mr. Kellogg for six months resisted the pressure that was put upon him to begin negotiations. Sir Austen Chamberlain and the British Foreign Office were suspicious. Signor Mussolini was contemptuous. Even Herr Stresemann, with special reasons for subscribing to any pacific declaration, only accepted the Pact because it was put forward by the United States.

Therein lies its essential virtue. The force of public opinion convinced the diplomatists that this Pact was necessary. The force of public opinion will hereafter convince them that it must be observed in its spirit and not in its letter.

From the narrow diplomatic standpoint we may say that nothing is changed. We may properly admit the axiom that vague phrases are without significance. But as observers, who believe in the imponderables, who believe in democracy, who believe in human progress, we shall be right in asserting that the signing of the Pact is a remarkable moral event. There are two ways of looking at the proceedings at the Quai d'Orsay. One way is diplomatic, the other way is moral.

Here is an act of faith. Here is a solemn announcement that war is ruled out. If in one year or in ten years this or that nation were to break the pledge, the public would be amazed. It would resent the deception. It would, presumably, rise against those who attempt to rely on subtle diplomatic phraseology. It disregards the annexes. It sees only the broad effect of the Pact. The reservations are, so far as the public is concerned, uttered *sotto voce*. They are not heard. They will be ignored. Governments are no longer free. They have, in raising public expectations, tied their own hands. If they have logically contrived a possible exit from the Pact, they will, at the first sign of a movement to escape, be driven back by an indignant public into the safe precincts of the Pact. For that matter, I believe the Governments will be voluntary prisoners. There is probably no Power which is willing again to run the risk of war. The reservations are merely the expression of the old traditional diplomacy which has been trained to conduct affairs with circumspection; it is a ghostly diplomacy which does not realise that it is dead and that its methods are futile.

Let me say what can be said about the defects of the Pact. The old Roundheads trusted in God, but they kept their powder dry. The old diplomatists may trust in the Pact, but they are not going to relinquish, if they can help it, their doctrines, their alliances, and their weapons. The Pact must not be understood to interfere with the Monroe Doctrine. It must not touch the vital interests of Great Britain in special areas. It must not prohibit defensive wars—and all wars can be regarded as, in some sense, defensive. If it is broken by one nation, it falls to the ground; and, precisely at the moment when there is genuine need of it, it becomes non-existent. Further, it does not abrogate existing arrangements such as the arrangements of Locarno, such as the arrangements of the League, such as the arrangements of the network of treaties, all of which conceivably imply war; and though it is pretended that there is no incompatibility between these arrangements and the Pact, everybody knows that they are in contradiction with the professed purpose of the Pact. No matter. If it comes to a clash, public opinion may well insist on the triumph of the Pact.

When we regard the actual military and diplomatic happenings, as distinct from the theoretical arguments, we shall see that there is much which can scarcely be squared with the acceptance of the Pact. One or two instances will suffice. Recently, the British authorities organised a mock air raid on London. They imagined the possibility of an attack by an aerial force which, in present circumstances, could only be that of the country with whom England enjoys the friendliest relations. The test was watched with interest in France. I do not think it had any significance. Nor was it supposed in France to have any significance. There is, on the part of the authorities, a curious lack of a sense of humour. It would be giving them too much credit to accuse them of irony in fixing the date of a sham air fight so near to the date of the signing of the Peace Pact. I am irresistibly reminded of M. Herriot's visit to London in 1924. He came to usher in a new era of peace. Mr. Ramsay MacDonald, who was also ushering in a new era of peace, thought proper to provide some innocent entertainment for him; and accordingly he took him down to Spithead, to gaze upon the most formidable naval demonstrations that had been held since the War!

A satirical commentary may be quoted in this connection: "A Pact is to be signed in Paris solemnly renouncing war as an instrument of national policy, except against China, Russia, Spain, the three Republics of the West Indies, the seven Central American Republics, the ten countries in South America, and a district known as 'certain regions of the globe.' This leaves a reasonable latitude."

The remark is fair enough as a warning that the Governments must now put their policy into consonance with their professions. The act of faith must not be made to look foolish. Either the Pact will soon be exposed as a hollow farce, or it will be shown as a reality.

I was particularly struck by a remark of the *Osservatore Romano*, in an article which semi-officially gave the views of the Vatican. "Nobody can deny," said the Roman writer, "that the War has completely failed to achieve its pretended ideals, and that the peace, born of blood, is not a just and durable peace, but a peace which possesses the spirit of the War which engendered it. That is why political efforts, noble in themselves, are bankrupt. That is why pacts, such as that of Mr. Kellogg, are discredited before they are signed."

In other words, one can only build on solid foundations. If the foundations of Europe are to-day rotten, no structure of peace built upon them will endure. The upheaval will come and the edifice will topple. Perhaps some of these feverish attempts to build the palace of peace are inspired by an uneasy feeling of the menace. The proper course was surely to put the foundations right first. It may be that we have set to work in the wrong order. It may be that we should have repaired and consolidated the substructure before we began to build with the idle hope of placing a weight on Europe to maintain the *status quo*.

It is now too late to begin again. But it is possible, if we are wise, even after the erection of the building, to repair and consolidate the foundations. If we will do that, then the palace of peace will stand. If we will not, then it will be always in danger of collapse. These are truths which seem to me worth enunciating—nay, which must be enunciated, if the act of faith is to be rendered foursquare and impregnable against all the assaults of perilous circumstance which will certainly beat upon it.

INDEX